MW00583020

SACRED STORIES, SPIRITUAL TRIBES

SACRED STORIES, SPIRITUAL TRIBES

Finding Religion in Everyday Life

Nancy Tatom Ammerman

OXFORD
UNIVERSITY PRESS

OXFORD
UNIVERSITY PRESS

Oxford University Press is a department of the University of Oxford.
It furthers the University's objective of excellence in research, scholarship,
and education by publishing worldwide.

Oxford   New York
Auckland   Cape Town   Dar es Salaam   Hong Kong   Karachi
Kuala Lumpur   Madrid   Melbourne   Mexico City   Nairobi
New Delhi   Shanghai   Taipei   Toronto

With offices in
Argentina   Austria   Brazil   Chile   Czech Republic   France   Greece
Guatemala   Hungary   Italy   Japan   Poland   Portugal   Singapore
South Korea   Switzerland   Thailand   Turkey   Ukraine   Vietnam

Oxford is a registered trademark of Oxford University Press
in the UK and certain other countries.

Published in the United States of America by
Oxford University Press
198 Madison Avenue, New York, NY 10016

© Oxford University Press 2014

All rights reserved. No part of this publication may be reproduced, stored in a
retrieval system, or transmitted, in any form or by any means, without the prior
permission in writing of Oxford University Press, or as expressly permitted by law,
by license, or under terms agreed with the appropriate reproduction rights organization.
Inquiries concerning reproduction outside the scope of the above should be sent to the
Rights Department, Oxford University Press, at the address above.

You must not circulate this work in any other form
and you must impose this same condition on any acquirer.

Ammerman, Nancy Tatom, 1950–Sacred stories, spiritual tribes:
finding religion in everyday life/Nancy Tatom Ammerman.
pages cm
Includes bibliographical references and index.
ISBN 978-0-19-991736-5 (pbk.: alk. paper)—ISBN 978-0-19-989644-8
(alk. paper)—ISBN 978-0-19-989645-5 (ebook)   1. Spirituality—United States.
2. Religion—United States.   3. United States—Religious life and customs.
I. Title. BL2525.A5635 2013 306.60973—dc23 2013006545

9 8 7 6 5 4 3 2 1
Printed in the United States of America
on acid-free paper

CONTENTS

List of Figures — *vii*

List of Tables — *xi*

Preface and Acknowledgments — *xiii*

1. In Search of Religion in Everyday Life — 1

2. "Spirituality" and "Religion": What Are We Talking About? — 23

3. Spiritual Practices in Everyday Life — 56

4. Religious Communities and Spiritual Conversations — 91

5. Everyday Life at Home — 128

6. Nine to Five: Spiritual Presence at Work — 171

7. Everyday Public Life: Circles of Spiritual Presence and Absence — 212

8. Bodies and Spirits: Health, Illness, and Mortality — 250

9. Spiritual Tribes: Toward a Sociology of Religion in Everyday Life — 288

Appendix 1. Participants and Their Religious Communities — *305*

Appendix 2. Coding and Analyzing Stories — *309*

Appendix 3. Research Protocols — *313*

Notes — *323*

Bibliography — *341*

Index of Participants (By Pseudonym) — *367*

General Index — *369*

LIST OF FIGURES

3.1   "It's a part of my office that I think of as where
I keep my religious life."—Sam Levitt   60

3.2   "I'm really grateful for these scriptures."
—Catherine Young   66

3.3   "This is the yoga studio. It's a bad feng shui place cause
it faces a cemetery, [but] it's not something that scares
me."—Ericka Lombardi   72

3.4   "This is the library.... Study and literature are important
to me personally and professionally and spiritually."
—Emma Cooper   79

3.5   "You're just happy to be alive and just totally living on
the edge."—Bill Hamilton   84

4.1   "I often go to confession here and we have Eucharistic
Adoration."—Jessica Kingman   95

4.2   "This is a typical ... altar layout where you have things in
the directions."—Anna Cook   97

4.3   "This is my Thursday morning scripture study."
—Mary Hage   103

4.4   "I run a support group, it's called Mastering
Motherhood, it's for moms that have young children."
—Jen Jackson   103

4.5 "Thanksgiving dinner for...whoever didn't have a
place to go."—Andrew Hsu   108

4.6 "That's just the typical Sunday morning scene."
—Francine Worthington   111

5.1 "God put us here."—Grace Shoemaker   131

5.2 "The heart of my home."—Laura Henderson   132

5.3 "We are often stuck at this traffic light, and this is
the courthouse building...I just like the way it
lights up. "—Nora Cole   141

5.4 "We always grew up, like, eating dinner together."—
Jessica Wilson   148

5.5 "I thank the Lord every morning, every day, every
time I take this walk."—Theresa Collins   153

5.6 "Lots of family came. This is when he started
praying for the baby."—Jen Jackson   162

5.7 "This was for Passover...I love our dining room
and I love entertaining."—Rachel Halpern   167

6.1 "My job, I guess, is to take the people through
when they come in."—Jim Childs   181

6.2 "There's been a lot of reorganization at work."
—Daphne LaCompte   185

6.3 "Every morning the in-patient team talks [here] about
how we can help these people."—Mark Fuller, M.D. 189

6.4 "This is where I write...I've got a lot of things
on my bulletin board, a lot of goddess images for
inspiration."—Emma Cooper   192

6.5 "Men that I work with, we get together, have lunch,
and...pray together."—Charles Curlew   205

7.1   "I went particularly looking for a church that
      gave back to the community."
      —Jennifer Hammond   222

7.2   "It was very beautiful and very peaceful."
      —Lily Mattison   226

7.3   "We sit there and we really, really have wonderful
      conversations."—Ann Rosa   232

7.4   "This is a group in the Church to which I belong.
      We are an arm of Georgia Right to
      Life."—Mary Hage   240

7.5   "This is where Colleen and I got married."
      —Robin Mitchell   247

8.1   "Where you go for your checkups and stuff."
      —Mary Poulsen   252

8.2   "This is not too far from my house where I went
      riding."—Alex Polani   259

8.3   "Any room that you go in for the Twelve-step
      program they always have on the wall the Twelve
      steps and the Twelve traditions."—Greg Collins 264

8.4   "I will feel a sense of His presence, a sense of sort of a
      soothing and a reassurance."—Bethany Armstrong 271

8.5   A prayer request being recorded for inclusion in
      Sunday worship.—Nancy Ammerman   279

LIST OF TABLES

2.1 Use of Theistic Discourse 32

2.2 Use of Extra-theistic Discourse 41

2.3 Dominant Spiritual Discourse by Religious Tradition and Attendance 43

2.4 Comparing U.S. and Italian Definitions of Spirituality 53

3.1 Effects of Spiritual Salience on Routine Scripture Study among Active Participants by Religious Tradition 67

4.1 Religious Participation by Spiritual Salience 92

4.2 Adult Participation by Childhood Traditions 119

5.1 Household Composition 129

6.1 Occupations of Study Participants 174

7.1 Political Stories and Spiritual Engagement 243

7.2 Political Engagement and Spiritual Engagement 243

Table A.1 Religious Distribution of the Sample Compared to National Population 306

PREFACE AND ACKNOWLEDGEMENTS

Since the 1990s, a growing number of sociologists have carved out new empirical and analytical territory in the study of religion. This book is an effort to further enlarge that territory by listening in new places and in new ways.

The two theoretical traditions that have dominated scholarly thinking about religion have become increasingly inadequate to the task at hand. One emphasized the impossibility of religious survival in the face of modern ideas, modern institutional complexity, and modern pluralism. The other pictured religion as a universal human effort to bargain for goods not otherwise available in this world, a bargain that could be enhanced by the competition and pluralism of that same modern world. For an increasing number of scholars, neither of these ways of understanding religion was sufficient. The first flew in the face of the continued prevalence of vigorous religious movements across an increasingly interconnected globe. The second offered us such a narrow and impoverished view of what religion encompassed that it could hardly do more than produce correlations among survey items. The failure of secularization theories has been a matter of discussion for some time, but rational choice theories are no more satisfactory as an alternative. It is against that backdrop that this book emerged. It builds on and contributes to a growing literature that documents and critically analyzes the social dynamics of religion in ordinary everyday life, dynamics often described as "lived religion."

This book not only builds on the growing intellectual base of research on lived religion. It is also built on the support and creative work of a wide array of partners. Generous financial support for data gathering and analysis came from the John Templeton Foundation. In spite of the ways in which this project diverges from the orientation of many of their key priorities, Kimon Sargeant saw the value in working with us to craft a Templeton proposal, and Christopher Stawski shepherded our relationship with the Foundation through to completion. Carving out space to write this book was made possible by a Sabbatical Grant from the Louisville Institute and by the support of

Boston University for that time away. For financial support from each of these institutions, I am very grateful; and the lively intellectual interchange of the Louisville Institute Winter Seminar was an invaluable contribution as well.

The research for this book took place in partnership between Boston University and Emory University. At Emory, Bradd Shore welcomed me to an affiliation with the Center for Myth and Ritual in American Life and provided, on multiple occasions, a forum for presenting emerging ideas. At Boston, our administrative and intellectual home was in the Institute on Culture, Religion, and World Affairs (CURA). Director and founder Peter Berger was there from the beginning, helping to form the ideas, patiently assisting the proposal through to approval, and cheering as the results have emerged. The Institute's administrator, Laurel Whalen, was an invaluable guide in navigating the financial terrain that accompanies any funded project, and behind the scenes were two very able day-to-day research administrators, Julian Gotobed and Kevin Taylor. Tracking and organizing data files and participant payments is no easy task, but without it, no project is possible.

The research team is described in more detail in Chapter One, but their remarkably creative and committed work runs through every page of this book. This project, for instance, employed a variety of methods for which we had scant existing models. Roman Williams dug into the existing research on photo elicitation methods and helped us hone our strategies and interpret our results. He, Amy Moff Hudec, Tracy Scott, and Melissa Scardaville proved amazingly adept interviewers at each stage of the process. They are the unseen conversation partners with whom the people you will meet here are talking. They recruited tenaciously, stayed persistently in touch, and established strong and empathetic relationships out of which those conversations—and thereby this book—have come.

On the other side of those conversations were the ninety-five people who agreed to be part of this study. They spent multiple hours with their researcher, more hours recording daily stories on a digital recorder, and still more photographing places in their everyday worlds. While we provided them with small monetary thank you gifts, we cannot fully repay their deep engagement with us and their willingness to share their stories. That is fundamentally what this book is about.

As the book has gestated over several years, my thinking has benefited from opportunities to present nascent analyses to groups and colleagues whose engagement has been invaluable. The cultural mapping outlined in Chapter Two was first presented in very preliminary form to the Culture and Social Analysis Workshop in Harvard's Sociology Department, an intellectual exchange presided over by Michele Lamont. Those ideas also appeared in equally preliminary form in my keynote address to the International Society for the Sociology of Religion and subsequently were published as "The Challenges of Pluralism: Locating Religion in a World of Diversity" in *Social Compass* (volume 57, no. 2 (2010): 154–67). Portions of Chapter Two were subsequently developed into an article, "Spiritual but Not Religious?: Beyond Binary Choices in the Study of Religion," published in *Journal for the Scientific Study of Religion* (volume 52, no. 2 (2013): 258–278). That effort at establishing some of the key definitional parameters benefited from multiple critical readings and conversations, especially from Stephen Warner but also from members of the research team itself. Stefania Palmisano and Anne Brigitte Pessi, each of whom spent time as visiting scholars in the Sociology Department at Boston University, were enormously helpful in thinking about the comparisons to Europe. Special thanks go to Stefania for providing statistics on Italian religion and spirituality from her survey.

Chapter Three's discussion of religious practices is better for the generous feedback provided by James Nieman as well as for Emily Ronald's extensive bibliographic assistance. Both attempted to help me be clear in how my use of "practice" is related to what others mean by that term. Chapter Four received the critical assessment of my colleagues on the Congregational Studies Project Team, and Christopher James provided bibliographic assistance for that chapter. Chris has also made sure that the entire manuscript and bibliography have been prepared properly for publication. Thanks to Amy Moff Hudec for attention to my discussion of households in Chapter Five and especially for insisting that my discussion of pets was an important part of the story. Justin Stoll's coding of the data on friendship was especially helpful, as was his reading of Chapter Six and navigation of the literature on the nature of work. My colleague Claire Wolfteich, in turn, read that chapter as a practical theologian and helped me to think more about the meaning of work.

Portions of Chapter Seven were presented to the conference on "Morality: The Role of Religion and Religious Communities" at the University of Helsinki. Special thanks to Anne Brigitte Pessi for her invitation to that conference and to the participants for their comments. A revised version of my presentation will be published as "Learning and Living the Golden Rule: Religious Communities and Morality" in *Christianity and the Roots of Morality*, edited by Petri Luomanen, Anne Birgitta Pessi, and Ilkka Pyysiäinen (Brill). Chapter Seven would not have been possible without the work done by Boston University student Kyle Bozentko. I draw extensively on his careful coding of the stories about political and civic engagement and his thinking about questions of agency and alienation.

My exploration of everyday health took me into new terrain, and I am indebted to Elyas Bahktiari for his stellar job in providing guidance to the burgeoning literature on spirituality and health and his surefooted sense of the larger questions in the sociology of health. Jenny Trinitapoli provided a careful and encouraging reading of that chapter, as did Wendy Cadge. Finally, my husband Jack Ammerman and my daughter Abbey Ammerman each provided helpful suggestions for making the introduction more readable. That is, of course, the least of the contributions they made to this project.

Almost from the beginning of the research and writing on this project I have been privileged to serve as chair of a growing and increasingly exciting group of scholars in the Sociology Department at Boston University. That work has admittedly made time for writing a precious commodity, but it has also given me a community whose collective contributions to our discipline have inspired me to do my best work. Their invitation to present my work in our Sociology Seminar Series provided just the right opportunity to draw together what I had learned and try out the conclusions to which I had come. Their challenging and enthusiastic questions did not disappoint me.

All of these intellectual communities are the conversation partners who have been my "tribe" over the years in which this project came to completion. The story I tell here is one overheard in the conversations of project participants and given shape in conversation with many colleagues. It is a story about everyday religion that will, I hope, help both participants and scholars tune their ears to voices and themes too long silent.

SACRED STORIES, SPIRITUAL TRIBES

1 IN SEARCH OF RELIGION IN EVERYDAY LIFE

Pam Jones[1] is a forty-six-year-old successful businesswoman, living with her husband and daughter in the suburbs of Boston. She and her family attend Cornerstone Baptist Church, whenever they can, but they also lead busy lives full of work and their daughter's extracurricular activities. This middle-class African American congregation is important to them, and Pam describes herself as a person of faith, even if they sometimes miss church more than they should. When asked to talk about what she means by being a person of faith, she told this story.

> I think it's my faith that can ground me when things seem to be spinning out of control. I can say, "I'm buying t-shirts, this is not life or death, this is—you know, it's not the most important—there are bigger things that are more important." I think it also helps me in managing people. You always want to treat others the way you want to be treated, which is something that I learned growing up in the church....I would say at work, people seem to think I'm a good example....I have an associate who reports directly to me, and she was having a difficult time learning how to work with my/our immediate boss. Our immediate boss probably tends to be gruffer around the edges and just doesn't always treat people well, and doesn't know often the—what's appropriate and what's not appropriate in terms of managing someone else's personal style. At my point in my career, if she said something that was offensive to me, I can easily push back with her and say, "It's not going to fly, you know; let's start again and talk some more." However, she was bullying my associate. And in bullying the associate—a woman who's very, very capable and going to be a great buyer someday—she was regressing in her career. So, literally, after being up at night worrying about it, praying about it, and talking to other people that I respect—you know, what do

I do with this situation?...eventually I confronted my boss with—you know, this is what I see is happening, and your mom always raised you to treat others the way you want to be treated.

This story from the very heart of the secular economic world is also a sacred story. Pam's faith provides a way to keep things in perspective and a basic guideline for how to treat people—"the way you want to be treated." We might call her a "Golden Rule Christian." She learned her faith at church and at home, it gets reinforced through prayer and conversations with trusted friends, and she practices it at work. It is her "everyday religion," and she is one of the people who will be our guides to the ordinary world in which religion today finds its expression.

I first stumbled across "Golden Rule Christians" in the early 1990s while studying some of America's changing communities.[2] These people were members of churches (and synagogues—there's a Jewish version too) in the communities I was studying, and my researchers and I had been asking them the kinds of questions about their beliefs and their religious affiliation that sociologists are supposed to ask: How long have you been a member? What do you believe about God and salvation? But we also asked them what it *means* for them to be a Christian or a Jew. It was often hard for people to articulate beliefs about God, but a remarkable number of them were quite sure about what faith means.[3] It means living by the Golden Rule, they said. The proof is in the pudding. No matter what you say you believe or how often you attend religious services, what matters is how you live your life. They were, in effect, putting sociologists on notice that measuring "religion" needed to take a new turn. If a sizable segment of Americans are connected to religious institutions but are *not* loyal, dedicated, orthodox believers, then perhaps something else is going on here. These were not exotic religious wildflowers that researchers so love to study. Nor were they the true believers that scholars and religious professionals alike usually agreed constitute the truly religious. The very ordinariness of their answers was intriguing.

Sociologists who study religion had answers, of course. Perhaps they are "free riders," people who are not really religious because they do not measure up to strict standards of belief and belonging.[4] Or perhaps this is creeping secularization.[5] If religious plausibility structures have weakened, perhaps they have left the people I was interviewing with a pale reflection of an earlier, more theologically robust faith. Or perhaps this is just evidence of the failure of churches and synagogues to pass along compelling reasons to attend and relevant versions of the faith. Perhaps. But the people themselves did not think they were without faith. Nor did they seem to think that religion was simply something to be kept within the four walls of religious institutions. Whatever it was that they were pointing to, it *was* religion and it was *not* solely private.

This book had its genesis in my evolving attempts to take Golden Rule religion seriously. Across American society, ordinary people were making everyday decisions about how to live, decisions that included a healthy dose of both sacred and secular sensibilities. What does that kind of everyday religion look like, I wondered? There are also other people for whom spiritual life is deeper and more complex than it is for these typical folk as well as people for whom spiritual life is completely alien. If we are to understand American religion, all of these people have to be taken into account. But it was the typical folk who first made me start asking questions about everyday religion.

My own earlier work occurred alongside books like Hoge, Johnson, and Luidens' *Vanishing Boundaries: The Religion of Mainline Protestant Baby Boomers* (1994) and other books about boomers and "seekers."[6] We were all describing religious lives that involved some core belief in a power beyond oneself as well as participation in communal rituals to mark the high holy moments in life—baptisms, weddings, and the big events of the shared religious calendar. These were people who wanted communities that could provide personal support, moral guidance, and a sense of belonging, but who also wanted to choose which communities those would be. Theirs was both an individual, custom-designed religious practice and one that weaves in and out of religious communities. Whatever spiritual tribe they belonged to, it was not one into which they were born or one to which they pledged undying and exclusive allegiance. They did not score very high on the typical sociological religiosity scales, nor did they make their pastors very happy.

They and the scholars who study religion in contemporary America often describe at least some of these not-orthodox and not-loyal people as "spiritual but not religious."[7] That way of describing them implicitly sees "spirituality" as the replacement or residue left behind by "religion." At least since the 1960s, various "spiritualities," running the gamut from LSD to Zen, have been seen as harbingers of things to come (Albanese 2001, Wuthnow 1976). With the growth of an unaffiliated population in the United States (Religion and Public Life 2008), it was not hard to tell a story of declining religious institutions and rising religious individualism.[8] In Europe, where the declines in religious belief and participation are far more dramatic than in the United States (Davie 2000), sociologists of religion have increasingly turned their attention to the new and revived spiritualities that are present in the wake of Christianity's apparent demise (Flanagan and Jupp 2007). There are still identifiable traditional religious institutions to be studied, but many scholars have turned their attention to what they see as a larger spiritual milieu that overlaps those institutions but may be developing its own organizational field (Heelas and Woodhead 2004). From yoga classes to Reiki practitioners, authors speculate that spiritual loyalties are being transferred from old institutions (churches) to new ones.

Both in Europe and in the United States, a perception of declining "religion" and growing "spirituality" implies that as there is less of one, there will be more of the other. It also implies the commonsense wisdom that "religion" is organized, traditional, and communal, while "spirituality" is improvised and individual. But are they really two ends of the same continuum—individual and spiritual versus organized and religious? Those who have tried to pay attention to both "religion" and "spirituality" have discovered that there is actually a good deal of overlap between the two domains, at least in the American population. Marler and Hadaway (2002) used survey data to show that the people who consider themselves most strongly spiritual are also the most religious, and Roof has provided an in-depth exploration of the overlap. But both studies still frame the analysis as a two-by-two table in which one may be spiritual, religious, both, or neither (Roof 2003). Examinations that take both religion and spirituality into account typically ask survey respondents whether (or how strongly) they consider themselves to be spiritual and whether (or how strongly) they consider themselves to be religious. What the surveys fail to tell us is what the respondents mean by either of those terms.[9] Nor do they tell us much about how people who claim to be one or the other or both actually live their lives. If we are to understand the role of religion in everyday life, we will need to leave open the question of how spirituality and religion are related to each other and what roles are played by individual improvisation and organized traditions. Finding and understanding everyday religion—a religion that includes spirituality—is the goal that drives this book.

Reframing the Questions

The question of "religion" in "society" can be pursued in many ways. Many assessments assume that religion is best measured in terms of the power of official religious organizations and their leaders over the population in which they are located. Can churches enforce their norms, either formally or informally? Other ways of studying religion look for the influence of religious ideas in the culture or the economy. Do Protestants really work hard and reinvest? Finding and understanding everyday lived religion is no less about studying religion in society, but it means paying attention to the nonexperts.[10] It means looking for the ad hoc religious beliefs, practices, and communities that also constitute the presence of religion in society, and that means that definitions and categories have to be expanded. We have to put away the biases about "real religion" that have often characterized scientific attempts at explanation.[11] Like religious professionals (the experts), scholars often look for coherent arguments about the nature of God and salvation and scripture, membership in a recognized religious body, attendance at officially recognized ritual events. All are perfectly useful indicators, but they do not exhaust the range of ideas, memberships, and practices that bring the spiritual and the mundane world into conversation with each other. If we want to understand that intersection, we will need to do better than surveys that correlate beliefs with other social behaviors and traits. "Religion and" studies can only get us so far.

A variety of new developments in the social sciences make this an opportune moment to rethink the relationship between religion and society. Research over the past two decades has already begun to undermine many of the old assumptions about the social processes that were thought to erode religion's social power. As Peter Berger has written, "To say the least, the relation between religion and modernity is rather complicated" (1999, 3). The notion that religion is bound to disappear has become increasingly untenable. There are far too many spiritually serious, well-educated, economically sophisticated, civically engaged religious people in the world. There is no doubt that the nature and role of religion has changed, but these founding myths of social science have run their course. Rather than assuming that spiritual beliefs are irrational and religious participation is regressive, researchers are now asking *whether and under what conditions* different sorts of beliefs and spiritual practices have what kinds of effects.

Telling a more complicated story about modern religious lives was a task for which a very creative group of colleagues laid the groundwork in November 2003 in a consultation that resulted in the essays I collected in my book *Everyday Religion: Observing Modern Religious Lives* (Ammerman 2006). We all recognized the extreme theoretical poverty of the "rational choice" ideas that had begun to dominate the sociology of religion. By attempting to reduce the complexity of human behavior to calculations of costs and benefits, these theories, we were convinced, were distorting the religious phenomena they purported to explain.[12] Working from the widely disparate research projects our group brought to the table, we arrived at a variety of useful new insights. By working from what we had observed in the places where religion was being lived and created, we began to challenge some of our field's received wisdom and suggest new ways forward.

One of those insights was the recognition that all institutional boundaries—including religious ones—are porous. While it is certainly the case that modern societies are complex, with relatively specialized and distinct spheres of activity, individuals carry frameworks and expectations and practices from one part of life to another, and organizations often learn from each other. Even the notion of "public" as distinct from "private" life has been widely challenged. Work and politics are given meaning and direction by conversations over the dinner table, while family caregiving is interlaced over time and space with obligations to jobs and communities. What we do and why and how we do it are questions that cannot be answered with the "institutional logic" of the single place we happen to be at any given moment. The study of modern social life now recognizes the influences that flow back and forth across institutional lines.[13] The simple recognition that all boundaries are porous forces us to ask why we assume that religion is a special case, incapable of escaping the one institution to which it has been consigned.

Our work in a variety of social locations also made clear just how diverse human spiritual life is, prompting us to explore expanded definitions of what counts as "religious" in the first place. As much as traditional religious institutions and their doctrines remain an important factor in many individual lives, contemporary spiritual realities encompass a much broader range of practices, experiences, beliefs, and affiliations. Indeed, people have probably always been religious in many ways that would have made their official religious leaders uncomfortable (Douglas 1983; McGuire 2007). As researchers have given attention to diverse spiritual lives, we have discovered that religiosity in practice does not neatly conform to the survey questions with which we have tried to explain religion's presence or absence, rise or decline.[14] Understanding everyday religion requires a more open stance but without throwing out the institutions and the orthodoxies. Just as institutional religion is not the whole story, so attention to spirituality without institutions skews the picture.

There are, in other words, interesting things still to learn about religion, but in a time of significant change, we cannot assume we will find religion in the predictable places or in the predictable forms. And if we do not find as much of it in those predictable places as we did before, we cannot assume that it is disappearing. Religion is not an insignificant force in the social world today, but discovering its presence and impact may require asking our questions in new ways. If Golden Rule religion—and all the other ways faith finds its way into a life—count as religion, what does it look like in the workplace or in the home? What characterizes the spiritual life of typical Americans? How are typical lives different from the lives of those who expend considerable time and concentration on spirituality? And how are both different from the seemingly growing population of people for whom religious and spiritual life is of no interest at all? By opening up the definitions and the boundaries, this book explores religious life across that full spectrum.

A Life in Stories

As important as it is to open up the definitions and boundaries, it is also essential to note that what people carry with them across those boundaries are practices and narratives more than tightly argued philosophical systems. For the experts, cognitive coherence is critical, but for the nonexperts, ideas about the nature of God and of the world are most often carried in stories and rituals. We don't tell stories about God intervening in the world if we do not believe that God exists, but what we know about divine character and divine interaction with humanity is carried by the stories that play out across the domains of our lives. Recent research has shown, for instance, that religiously ingrained practices of charity, nurtured in communities of faith, shape habits of community volunteering (Ammerman 2005b; Wuthnow 1995).[15] Likewise, narratives about "good Samaritans" are remarkably robust in shaping behavior across the many institutional contexts of modern life (Allahyari 2001; Bender 2003). By looking for religion in practices and narratives, we gain a new perspective that allows us to see how spiritual resources are generated, nurtured, and deployed across the many religious and secular contexts in which people live their lives.

Across a number of disciplines, in the past three decades, we have seen a "narrative turn," but what that means varies enormously. Within sociology, it has been most visible in the study of social movements, where theorists have discovered the power of stories as tools of mobilization,[16] explaining how leaders do their work and why participants become involved (Ganz 2009). More broadly, however, sociologists (like psychologists) have increasingly realized that human beings give order to their world through stories.[17] We do not think primarily in concepts or causal chains but in stories that carry those ideas and imply the causes. As sociologist Margaret Somers declares, "All of us come to be who we are (however ephemeral, multiple, and changing) by being located or locating ourselves (usually unconsciously) in social narratives" (Somers 1994, 606).

A few sociologists have also noted the importance of narratives in the understanding of religion (Ammerman 2003; Roof 1993a). Some have pointed to conversion as a particular kind of narrative genre (Manglos 2010) along with healing stories (Singleton 2001) and testimony (Nelson 2005). Smilde (2005), for example, carefully analyzes how Pentecostal men tell their conversion stories, noting the way those stories construct an understanding of divine authority that has implications for their personal identity and action. Davidman and Greil (2007) understand the nature of deconversion through the notion of an "exit narrative" that must be composed when one wishes to leave an Orthodox Jewish community. Still others have talked about narratives as constitutive of congregational identity (Ammerman 1997b; Collins 2004; Hopewell 1987). Whether personal or collective, religious stories are increasingly recognized as important sites for analysis.[18]

Stories are important, in part, because they are not merely personal. They exist at the intersection of personal and public. Some narratives become elaborate public myths, such as the founding stories of a religious tradition, and others function as "metanarratives" that implicitly shape the way we think about history and the future (Smith 2003). But the more modest stories of a single life or even of a single episode contain within themselves elements of these larger narrative frames. Social institutions and categories provide recognized "accounts" one can give of one's behavior, accounts that identify where one belongs, what one is doing and why.[19] People develop individual life stories that are guiding internal scripts but are intertwined with public shared stories. They contain memories of "how I always behave" but also provide shared situational narratives of "how people like us behave." Our implicit narrative sense structures the everyday meaning-making that forms what Bourdieu might call a "habitus."[20] We live inside a range of socially constructed stories that are not always of our own making or even fully conscious to us.

Narratives give meaning to an event by implying what has come before and what ought to come after, identifying the relevant characters and their relation to each other as well as pointing to the bundle of practices that constitute possible "strategies of action" (Swidler 1986). The implicit causal structure in a narrative is not, however, inflexible. There may be an overarching plot, but actors can always use their imaginations to improvise (Emirbayer and Mische 1998). As Smilde (2003, 320) notes, "The act of narrating consists precisely of taking canonical storylines and accommodating them to particular circumstances and actors." Listening to stories of everyday religious life means listening both for the canonical storylines that come from shared religious traditions and for the way they are improvised in new circumstances.

What can we learn about a religious tradition from the way its practitioners narrate their lives? What can we learn about beliefs by listening to accounts that may or may not include divine actors? And what can we learn by probing for stories about times of unsettling and change? As both Bruner (1993) and Swidler (1986) argue, the most fertile location for observing the construction of new narratives is at the points where habitual action has become unsettled. The ordinary and habitual, says Bruner, do not provoke us to ask why; but when something does provoke us to ask why, we will likely tell a story. Both in crisis and in the ordinary and habitual, the structures of everyday life can be reconstructed through narratives.

Like all stories, narratives of everyday religion are complicated. They are multilayered, with characters and plots interwoven across and within situations. Stories from one social arena are often transposed into another, so religious narratives may appear in settings outside officially religious bounds (and vice versa). More importantly, the stories we are looking for are neither purely spiritual and sacred and otherworldly, nor simply this-worldly and mundane. To be "really religious" does not imply existing in an utterly separate "sacred" domain where only spiritual things happen. To call a story a "spiritual narrative" is simply to recognize that something about it concerns the life of the spirit and the communities of discourse in which spiritual traditions are made real. The spirituality we are listening for is neither a quest for a sacred center that will orient all of life (as Pargament [2011] suggests) nor a supernatural force that will provide assistance or salvation (as Riesebrodt [2010] theorizes). It is a more modest, but nonetheless profound recognition that the world is not wholly a story that can be empirically told. There is another layer of consciousness that can weave, more or less pervasively, in and out of ordinary events. As philosopher Charles Taylor (2007) would put it, not everything can fit within the "immanent frame" of objective science. Or, to use Bellah's (2011) notion, both ordinary and nonordinary reality can exist together.

This book sets out, then, to listen for spiritual narratives among the stories people tell about their everyday lives. If stories, large and small, are the mechanism through which the world is socially constructed, we can learn a great deal about the social shape of religion by listening for how everyday stories are told. In what ways do people experience and invoke transcendence and how does that occur in the many different social spheres of their lives? What kinds of situations call forth spiritual accounts, and what effect do those perceived spiritual realities have? By systematically exploring the stories people tell about their everyday lives, we will trace the patterns of religious presence and absence in the social world. Where and how do spiritual characters, relationships, activities, moral imperatives, and emotions find their way into everyday stories?

Sacred stories also imply audiences—what I will call "spiritual tribes"— who listen and cocreate the tale. Each story is situated in a context, with circles of listeners who play a role, sacred or otherwise. It is important, then, to pay attention to the role of religious communities themselves. To what extent do those religious settings provide relationships, practices, and ways of thinking that show up in the stories people tell? How is that different for people who are highly involved, compared to those who are only minimally so? But are there other places where "spiritual tribes" gather, as well? Are there mediated communities on the internet or in circles of readers, viewers, and fans? French social theorist Michel Maffesoli suggests that societies are held together by a new kind of tribe that is "characterized by fluidity, occasional gatherings and dispersal" (1995, 76). As we listen for the sacred stories, we will also be looking for the spiritual tribes in which they are heard, learned, and told.

Looking for Storytellers

Theoretically, the domain we wish to describe here includes all the stories everyone tells about everyday life. Given the impossibility of that task, a number of practical strategies enabled us to gather stories that would tap into the lives of a broad sample of American adults. We set out to recruit a group of participants that would, as closely as possible, mirror the religious demography of the United States A detailed description of the sample, with comparisons to the U.S. population, can be found in Appendix 1.[21] We put together a set of sampling targets based on religious tradition, age cohort, gender, and frequency of attendance at religious services. That is, we knew how many older female frequent-attender liberal Protestants we wanted to recruit as well as how many young male nonaffiliates—and everything in-between. We also knew that our funding, while generous, would be invested in depth rather than breadth. We would recruit participants with whom we would work in multiple forms of data gathering over several months, and that meant that we could work with no more than one hundred participants in all. The final group recruited totaled ninety-five.[22]

How to find the nonaffiliates and liberal Protestant and all the rest remained, of course, a challenge. The logistics of doing the research demanded that this not be a national study, but to preserve the possibility of cultural comparisons across religiously different places, we selected two contrasting cities—Boston and Atlanta. Boston, Massachusetts, is a city of vast religious diversity—from the Enlightenment-informed Unitarians to new and old Catholic immigrants whose origins span continents, from venerable Congregationalists who bear the Puritan legacy to Muslims and Hindus just building their first permanent gathering places. It is at once a place where religion is routinely on the front page of the newspaper and a place where Yankee reticence keeps personal religious displays to a minimum. Atlanta, Georgia, has at least as much religious diversity as Boston, but it remains shaped by its southern evangelical heritage. There are still far more Baptists than Buddhists, and it is not uncommon to ask a person's religious affiliation as easily as one inquires about occupation and neighborhood. These differing regional religious cultures, then, provided us with contrasting settings in which to listen to everyday stories.

Within each city, we found religious affiliates using a "stratified quota." That is, we started by selecting specific congregations proportionate to the various traditions we wanted to include and then selected participants from within them to fill the demographic and participation target numbers. We attempted to tap diversity in social class by selecting parishes from neighborhoods that varied from typically working class to typically more affluent. Because we wanted to have some sense of the interaction between individual stories and the collective public narratives of religious communities, we selected a cluster of five respondents from each of the congregations that agreed to participate. Seventeen parishes, congregations, temples, a ward, and a sacred circle signed on. Fifteen were from the traditional organized religious mainstream—Catholic, liberal Protestant, conservative Protestant, African American Protestant, and Jewish—accounting for 77 percent of American adults and seventy-four of our participants. While these seventy-four came into the study by way of their congregational affiliation, not nearly all of them were active participants, and some had dropped out altogether.

We also wanted to include participants who are part of a more "sectarian" tradition that has been less accepted in the American mainstream, and for that we chose a Mormon ward. The final organized group from which we selected was a group with a more innovative spiritual tradition drawing from Wicca and Neopaganism. Making sure we had enough participants in the smaller groups to see any common patterns meant that we oversampled each of them and (as a result) slightly undersampled the white Protestant and Catholic populations.

We also wanted to find some people who were "congregating" in cyberspace, and for that we selected an internet religious chat room. This "group" turned out not to be much of a cohesive unit, however, and they are counted throughout the book with the tradition they otherwise identify with. The nonaffiliates, finally, were recruited through advertisements in coffee shops and other public places, seeking people who consider themselves "not religious and not spiritual." Just as some of the people recruited through congregations turned out to be essentially unaffiliated, so some of these recruits turned out to be more spiritually active than it first appeared. Here, too, initial categories had to be recalibrated as analysis progressed.

While our participants provide a remarkably good mirror for American religious demography, there are some significant limitations that should be noted here at the outset. First, we were only able to field English-speaking researchers, so the increasingly important Latino Catholic and Protestant presence is not included here. One of our Catholic parishes included a significant Hispanic membership, but we were unable to recruit any of them for our study. Second, the design of the sample means that rural populations are not present, and third, the size of our sample made it impossible to include meaningful representation of the many non-Judeo-Christian traditions. Hindu, Muslim, Sikh, Buddhist, and other traditions would have greatly enriched these findings, but those voices will have to wait for another day and other studies. Our oversample of the Jewish population is not really a substitute, but it provides a sufficient group of voices from outside Christianity to make clear some of the points where a different religious tradition provides different ways of telling spiritual stories.

Finally, quite unintentionally, the group of people who ended up participating in the study was disproportionately well educated and well off. Our selection of diverse parishes was supposed to avoid this, and it was not until we began to analyze the demographic data we collected on each participant that it became clear that this social status skew had happened. Finding and persuading less educated and more economically marginal people is less easy than convincing a college-educated professional to talk with a university graduate student as part of a research project. It is a challenge researchers often face, but it again means that a valuable set of voices is less present (although not entirely absent). The unintended benefit to this limitation is that we have overrepresented precisely the population that theorists might have expected to be the most secularized and privatized. They are, in other words, disproportionately "modern." If we find them telling spiritual stories about their everyday lives it will not be because we talked to people who have been sheltered from the influences of higher education and public participation.

The voices in this book—like the American population—are mostly Christian and Jewish. They are—like the American population—mostly connected in some way to a religious tradition and a local congregation. And they include—like the American population—a substantial number of people who are either religiously inactive or would be counted as "nones" (nonaffiliated). This is a book not about spiritual adventurers but about the broad mainstream of ordinary, more and less spiritually engaged Americans. It is a book primarily about what happens in everyday life, but the reach of religious participation is not absent. For a significant portion of the American population, that too is part of everyday spiritual life.

Methods for Studying Religious Narratives

Data gathering for this project began in the late summer of 2006. Roman Williams and Amy Moff Hudec, graduate students in the Sociology Department at Boston University were the lead researchers for the Boston cases, while Professor Tracy Scott and graduate student Melissa Scardaville from Emory University's Sociology Department handled the Atlanta data gathering. We began our work with a team-training event in Boston. At various points, I accompanied them on interviews, and all of us stayed in close touch via e-mail, discussing recruitment issues, strategies for interviewing, and other logistics.

To elicit the widest and deepest possible range of stories from our participants, we devised a range of methods that extended well beyond the usual survey (see Appendix 3).[23] We began with one of the most common tools—the interview. Psychologist Jerome Bruner notes that as researchers seek to understand selves "in practice," following people around to ask them what they are doing and why is obviously impractical, but we can "do the inquiry retrospectively, through autobiography...an account of what one thinks one did in what settings in what ways for what felt reasons" (Bruner 1993, 119). Often, however, interviews are quite unlike normal conversations and not conducive to storytelling. Like many other social science tools, interviews are typically shaped by the researcher's determination of the relevant lines of inquiry and the academy's definitions of the relevant categories of response. Eliot Mishler (1986) has been among the most vocal critics of the way the standardized interview frames the subject's knowledge in precategorized boxes, preventing us from discovering new patterns in the social world. If we are to have stories to analyze, the way we conduct interviews must go beyond questions that presume an existing range of responses and questions that ask for conceptual and categorical answers—all the more so when religious and spiritual categories are being culturally redefined.

Our first meeting with our participants was a conversation that usually lasted about an hour and a half and included both comprehensive life history kinds of questions and smaller event- and episode-focused narratives.[24] We began with an invitation to tell "the story of your life," organized into whatever chapters the teller chose. As many observers have noted, the telling of one's life story to a researcher is not random. It is tailored to the perceived audience (the interviewer and whatever culture and institutions that person is perceived to represent), but it is also a moment in which the storyteller is likely to see and organize the events of a life in a new way (Atkinson 1998; Linde 1993). The story that emerges is cocreated in the socially contingent event of an interview (Maynes, Pierce, and Laslett 2008; Mishler 1986). Our participants were clearly alerted to our interest in the subjects of religion and spirituality, and that influenced their selection of events for inclusion in their life story. But they were not utterly constrained by our interests. People for whom these were relatively alien or antagonistic domains often fumbled, experimented, and resisted, highlighting the degree to which they were altering the story for our ears. Others told a polished religious tale that reflected their experience in religious communities where testimony is common. This opening question, in other words, was an initial opportunity to approach the narrative territory, with interviewers suggesting events and kinds of experiences to talk about but participants beginning the process of claiming, rejecting, or reframing those suggestions in their own terms—beginning, in other words, to exercise agency in the telling of their stories.

Beyond the initial big story, interviews were punctuated throughout by invitations to "tell me about a time when…." Rather than asking them how much their faith influences their lives, we asked them to tell us about a time when they made an important decision, and we simply listened for whether and how faith was invoked. Rather than asking about hypothetical ethical or moral issues, we asked them to talk about the things they see and hear every day that strike them as disturbing and wrong. By consistently framing questions in ways that asked about actions and events and decisions, people fell easily into telling stories rather than providing checklist answers.

Establishing trust is always an important issue in interviewing but especially so when we hope to get past cultural assumptions about "proper" responses. Writing about illness narratives, communication scholar Arthur Bochner suggests that the act of telling a story is an agentic and political act. So long as the hearer is a stranger, only the dominant ways of telling the story may be used, but when the listener becomes a friend, it is possible for the storyteller to do more radical narrative work. "Inevitably, the ill person must negotiate the spaces between the domination of cultural scripts of bodily dysfunction out of which one's meanings are constructed and defined, and the situated understanding of one's experience that seeks a unique and personal meaning for suffering" (Bochner 2001, 147). Similarly, in many cases there are hegemonic cultural scripts for how one speaks of religion, and our challenge was to develop sufficient intimacy to enable other narratives to emerge.

That intimacy and trust was enhanced by the manner in which interviews took place, but it was also enhanced because the initial interview was not the last interaction (Merrill and West 2009). Over the ensuing months, researchers were also visiting the religious communities to which the affiliates among our participants belonged. These were not in-depth ethnographic case studies but a modest firsthand window on places where our participants hear other people talking about religion and spirituality. Researchers attended several services and study groups, getting to know the ideas and people and practices and adding field notes to the growing body of data being amassed. As participants and researchers saw each other at church or temple or in a sacred circle, the sense of a trusted common conversation was enlarged.

We also saw participants on multiple additional research occasions. At the conclusion of the initial meeting, our researchers left a disposable camera with the participant with the invitation to take pictures of the "important places in your life." Just as we were convinced that meaning comes in story form, we were also convinced that everyday lives are structured around material places and objects, a physical environment that is often arranged as a meaningful setting for life. As Sarah Pink (2012) has argued, practices of everyday life are situated in the sensual environments through which we pass and that are, in turn, constituted by the practices that take place in them. One cannot study the practices of everyday life without paying attention to the places in which those practices are entangled. We have ample evidence, in fact, that religion is itself visual and material. Houses of worship (of all kinds) are part of everyone's landscape (Vergara 2005), and the materiality of everyday religious faith and practice is evident in everything from religious clothing to garden statues (McDannell 1995).[25]

Inviting participants to photograph whatever settings they deemed important provided another way to elicit everyday stories. Known as photo elicitation interviewing (PEI), this technique is "based on the simple idea of inserting a photograph into a research interview" (Harper 2002, 13). Sometimes photographs are made by the researcher (Vassenden and Andersson 2010), sometimes by the participant (Clark-Ibáñez 2004), and sometimes by a third party (e.g., a professional photographer or found images). Here the photos were participant generated (also known as "autodriven"; Clark [1999]; Heisley and Levy [1991]). Participants were assured that the photos did not need to be professional quality; we were simply interested in snapshots from at least five or six different locations. After two to four weeks, researchers retrieved the disposable camera, prepared print and digital images, and scheduled a follow-up interview.

At the time of the photo interview, participants were given the opportunity to shuffle through their pictures and to organize them in a way that made sense to them (topically, chronologically, geographically, relationally, and so forth), often laying them out on the kitchen table, coffee table, or desk where the interview was conducted. They were then invited to describe what happens in the places they photographed and talk about why they think of that place as important, always encouraging specific stories more than generalizations. After the final photograph was discussed, interviewers invited participants to talk about what photographs they would have taken but for whatever reason did not. As we listen to the stories they told in the pages that follow, we will often be able to see the places that elicited those stories, allowing the action to come off the page in a new way.

Taking the visual turn not only introduced a new set of stories, it also added depth to some of the ones we had already heard. It also began to transform the research process. The seemingly simple act of putting a camera in the hands of participants can redefine participants' relationship to the research (cf. Clark and Dierberg 2012). They are no longer passive subjects responding to a researcher's queries; they become fieldworkers who reveal answers to questions researchers might never have asked. The data are produced by participants: *they* are in the driver's seat, *they* make decisions about what is important (or not). A picture can also sometimes bridge cultural differences between interviewer and participant, as images and places are allowed to explain a social world. As a result, researchers see the social world in new ways and understand better how to ask questions, but the exercise is also a reflective one for the photographer. As participants stepped back from their taken for granted social lives to reflect on their own visual images, the stories they told introduced insights that might not have been anticipated by interviews alone.

While interviews provide excellent access to individual autobiographical narratives, and photo elicitation provides access that allows place and practice to intertwine, the mundane happenings of everyday life are harder to capture. Research questions that address lived religion, that expect religion to exist "outside the box," require ways of gaining access to those unexpected places. How can we bring to the participant's mind the routine and habitual activities that are sometimes obscured by more reflective exercises and conversations? Just as taking photographs can take the participant into everyday places, keeping a diary or journal—recorded in any of a variety of formats—can evoke the daily patterns of activity.

Diaries have rarely been used in the study of religion, but they are fairly common in other research in the social sciences and beyond.[26] "Time diaries" have become familiar tools for people studying household labor, health behaviors, and the like (Bianchi et al. 2006; Juster and Stafford 1985), and some researchers have used naturalistic recording of household activity, as well (Thomas-Lepore et al. 2004). The technique we chose was a self-directed daily oral recording, for which we provided some open-ended guidance. We provided the participant with a digital recorder, taught them how to use it, and asked them to record five to fifteen minutes of stories each day for a week. They were given a document that included a set of suggestions for what kinds of stories they might tell, but they were left free to choose when to record and exactly what to record. We suggested that they think of the exercise "as if you were keeping a diary, or perhaps as if you were talking to a friend or family member and telling them stories about what's going on in your life." We asked them to start each day's recording by musing about what might be most memorable about the day when they later looked back on it. But we also told them, "Even if nothing special seemed to happen, what were the ordinary things that happened?" and suggested that they think about family, work, leisure, friends. But we also said, "Feel free to talk about other things that you think are important for understanding your everyday life."

A few participants found this sort of routine recording of thoughts and events to be very awkward, but the vast majority completed either two or three separate weeklong rounds of recording, spread over the next several months. As we analyzed the resulting data, we learned more about the work, household, and leisure lives of these participants than interviews had revealed, seeing more clearly how and where spiritual dimensions of life were enacted (or not). Comparing the stories told in the oral diaries to stories told in photo elicitation and initial interviews, spiritual talk was no more nor less present. Oral diaries were not, in other words, peculiarly likely to evoke introspection or religious insight. Rather, participants used this method of communicating with us in ways that reflected their overall propensity to see life as spiritual (or not). As medical researcher Barbara Gibson has noted, diaries (in her case, video diaries) are not best understood as more "direct" measures of actual activity. Like all other accounts, they are part of the identity work being done by participants and are inevitably oriented to a specific research context (Gibson 2005).

How participants used their diaries was likely shaped by the particular genres and modes of communication and storytelling familiar to them (Maynes et al. 2008). Daily entries, for instance, sometimes resembled one end of a phone conversation between friends—"Hello Ellen, this is Sally...." Checking in with a friend, talking about what is happening at the moment, even ranting about particular frustrations is a familiar genre of speech in which the conversation partner (like the imagined researcher) is not physically present. Other participants slipped more comfortably into a devotional mode, even occasionally speaking as if to God. Just as they might speak a prayer to a divine conversation partner who is not physically present, a few people adopted this genre in talking about their lives to their digital recorder. In each case, what diaries made possible was a much more on-the-ground look at the "everyday" that amplified and nuanced stories gained through other sources, further making clear how, where, and with whom religious interaction takes place. They also built on the increasing trust between researcher and participant that was fostered by an extended period of multimethod interaction. Stories told in general, vague, or overly positive terms in an initial interview were elaborated, specified, and sometimes contradicted by the stories recorded in the oral diaries.

At each stage of our research, data collection techniques informed and shaped the relationship between participants and researchers in productive ways. As the formality of semistructured interviews gave way to the familiarity of snapshots of everyday life, and as coffee table conversations over these images prompted intimacy in daily oral diaries, subjects became coinvestigators, and expert researchers became confidants. While we may have anticipated the purchase of these methods in generating data, we underestimated the dramatic ways in which this progression of techniques produced intimacy, trust, and agency.

Sacred Stories and Spiritual Tribes: The Path

Listening for "spiritual" narratives requires that we begin with the difficult task of definition. Rather than starting with a preconceived set of categories, we invited participants to use these terms—religious, spiritual, sacred—in their own ways. Whenever they told a story in a way that included some element that they flagged in these terms, that story is one we included among the "sacred stories." That designation is not just for grand mythic tales or official scriptural accounts. It is a broadly expansive category that includes all sorts of allusions to realities beyond the mundane. (More detail on coding categories and strategies is included in Appendix 2.)

From stories about religion and spirituality, a range of meanings emerged, and those definitions will be explored in depth in Chapter Two. What I will describe there are three dominant discursive terrains and one contested territory. The contested territory is what we might call religious spirituality and is tied specifically to belief and belonging, to adherence to traditional religious organizations. For those inside those traditions, this is a good thing. Belief and belonging are part of how they understand their own spirituality. For those outside religious traditions, belief and belonging are what they have rejected. The other common discourses about spirituality are not so contested, although they are used more and less by people in different cultural locations. A Theistic cultural package ties spirituality to the divine; an Extra-theistic package locates spirituality in various naturalistic forms of transcendence, and an Ethical spirituality focuses on everyday compassion. These meanings are distinct but overlapping and are present both inside and outside religious communities. What we will listen for in the remainder of the book, then, is the presence of any of these spiritual discourses in the stories being told as well as when the kind of spirituality being referenced makes a difference.

Having identified spiritual ways of talking and thinking about the world, we can ask what activities may cultivate and concentrate attention on that spiritual dimension of life. What activities are directed toward a connection to something beyond ourselves? We asked our participants to talk about any activity they considered spiritual, whether or not they thought other people would think so. Chapter Three begins with the most pervasive practice they described—the practice of prayer, but we will also note the wide variation in what people mean when they talk about praying and the wide net prayer casts over the domains of everyday life. Beyond prayer, we will also examine the range of other practices people described to us, from reading sacred texts to exercise, from meditating to listening to music and reading fiction. We will note the way these practices cluster around different religious traditions and different notions about what spirituality is. We will also pay attention to how practices are embodied and material as well as invisible and spiritual.

Spirituality is not simply a solitary pursuit, however, nor is it untouched by religious tradition. In Chapter Four, we will focus on the ways religious communities offer times and places where people experience a connection to the divine; but we will also see the importance of the social spaces within congregations where people have conversations about the intersection of spirituality and everyday life. What happens in religious communities is not an otherworldly sacred retreat but a place where mundane concerns mix freely with spiritual realities. Throughout the book, we will see that active religious participants are different from those with only loose ties to any religious community, and people in different religious traditions have distinctive patterns for incorporating spirituality in their everyday lives. Organized religion matters, even when the subject is individual spirituality.

With Chapter Five, we turn from the language, practices, and communities specifically focused on spirituality to the places modern society has often described as "secular." By many accountings, households sit at that intersection between private and public and between sacred and secular. While we do not necessarily expect household life to be spiritual, we are not surprised (or offended) when it is. As our participants told stories about their households, nearly half the stories included some reference to the religious and spiritual dimensions of what was happening. This chapter tells those stories by beginning with the space itself and how people mark their home territory as significant. It continues with attention to relationships to partners, children, and extended circles of kin that define the human contours of the household. And the final section looks at how household stories are shaped by clocks and calendars. Routine religious practices are present, as are spiritual accounts of the joys and crises of the household. The differences we find among our participants are much more a matter of the religious traditions they have adopted than of their social and demographic status. Most bring religion to the household rather than finding it there, but sharing spiritual conversations at home can mark this as territory inhabited by a spiritual tribe, as well.

Are there sacred stories to be told about work? Our participants talked a great deal about what they do for a living and the people with whom they work. Language about vocation was not especially common, however; an overarching sacred narrative about work is not where we find the primary resistance to the secular economic "iron cage" Weber described (Weber 1958). Chapter Six examines the themes and variations in stories about work, looking especially for how people in different occupations tell their stories differently. Where the workplace is deemed a spiritual site, it is sometimes a matter of individual attitude ("Lord, give me patience"), but it is more often a matter of the nature of relationships and interactions ("Help me to be kind and honest"). But what about the work itself? A musician describes his creative work as spiritual, and a pediatrician sees everything he does as a calling, but how are they different from the salesman for whom stories about work are shaped by a secular narrative of education, advancement, and relocation? Again, the answers are largely in the religious traditions and relationships that provide support for spiritual interpretations. More than we might imagine, people find spiritual compatriots even in the workplace.

The public world of strangers is not only seldom present in everyday stories but also seldom given a sacred telling. In Chapter Seven, I will note how relatively rarely people talked about social and political issues, even when prompted, and how difficult it was for them to describe either everyday injustices or larger visions of what they hoped for in a "better world." Where strangers have a face, however, that is less so. This chapter will chart out the ways in which neighborhood, community, and charitable activity are the everyday face of public engagement for most of our participants. The "Ethical spirituality" mode is especially important here, allowing some people to imagine these engagements in spiritual terms.

If economic and political life are sometimes (but not nearly always) sacralized, what about health and medicine? Interpreters immersed in a secular "immanent" view of the world often look at the human body as merely a site for rational medical interventions and health as an individual pursuit. Our participants were indeed perfectly happy to have scientists explaining things and doctors treating them, but they were also extremely likely to see health as a spiritual practice and illness as something to be shared in community. Whether talking about their regular exercise routine or their parents' declining health, their own chronic illness or the death of a friend, these people were fully engaged with modern medicine and modern science. That was a constant. What varied was the degree to which they *also* understood their physical existence to have a spiritual dimension. Physical bodies, in all their complications, are neither solely profane nor solely sacred but a complex mix of the two. Nor is health solely a matter of individual concern. One of the most striking aspects of the stories we heard is the degree to which caring for each other is not only a matter of mutual family responsibility but also a matter of religious virtue and community connection. People who participate in religious communities extend the circle of "brothers and sisters" not only to others in their congregations but also to the neighbors and friends they are taught to include in their attentions.

In the end, we will draw together what we have learned about the presence and absence of a spiritual sensibility in the domains of everyday life. As different kinds of people narrate their work and family lives, where and how do events take on a more-than-mundane dimension? Are public life and the world of medicine the ultimate secular frontier? And if sacred stories enter these domains by way of spiritual conversations, where do those conversations happen? Should we understand what we have seen as organized religious communities producing spiritual worldviews and dispensing them into the public? Are there other spiritual tribes gathering and dispersing? What should we make of the spiritual conversations we have uncovered and the pervasive degree to which they engender sacred stories about everyday life? If the chapters to follow allow some new answers to those questions, we will have a substantial step forward in understanding the nature of religion in society.

2 "SPIRITUALITY" AND "RELIGION": WHAT ARE WE TALKING ABOUT?

Talk about spirituality seems to be everywhere these days. Spirituality is touted as a boon to business as well as to health, books on spirituality occupy their own section in airport bookstores, and both spirituality.org and spirituality.com occupy space on the internet. Eckhart Tolle, the Dalai Lama, Deepak Chopra, and Dan Millman have become household names as their books, CDs, and appearances draw the attention of millions in the United States and beyond.[1] At a time when talking about "religion" can be considered contentious, talk about spirituality can be heard from sources as diverse as Oprah Winfrey and Madonna. Spirituality talk has clearly entered the national vocabulary, but attempts at definition are often greeted with the assertion that spirituality means something different to each person. It is an intensely personal experience, we are told, something that is beyond the reach of prodding scientists or potentially constraining institutions and traditions.

That does not mean, of course, that sociologists have avoided attention to spirituality. In the wake of the 1960s, scholars turned attention to Eastern and "New Age" spiritualities as a growing part of the American religious landscape (Albanese 2001; Wuthnow 1976). Since that time, studies of seekers (e.g., Roof 1993b; Wuthnow 1998) and the "spiritual marketplace" (Roof 1999) have become part of the sociological canon. In Europe, sociologists of religion have turned their attention to new and revived spiritualities and the "holistic milieu" of new spiritual organizations (Flanagan and Jupp 2007; Heelas and Woodhead 2004; Hervieu-Leger 1993). Noticing that such a milieu exists has become commonplace; identifying its defining characteristics or internal variation has been more difficult. Spirituality is out there in the culture, and it is being studied, but the boundaries and contours are ill defined.

Understanding the social contours of spirituality has often been hampered by the temptation to follow conventional wisdom in defining "spirituality" as improvised and individual. Because "religion" is understood as organized, traditional, and communal, it is easily measurable with widely applicable questions about beliefs and memberships. Because spirituality is unique to each person, it is treated as sociologically unmeasurable. This methodological dividing line echoes the culture's common wisdom: religion is about institutions that assert external authority, while spirituality is about internal individual pursuits. In his study of the spirituality of artists, for instance, Robert Wuthnow notes that his subjects see spirituality as "more authentic" than organized religion because they themselves have created it (Wuthnow 2001, 7). The problem with taking them at their word, as Courtney Bender (2010) points out, is that when we define a phenomenon as an interior "experience," we place it beyond the reach of sociological explanation. Even sociological examinations that take both religion and spirituality into account—making clear that one may be spiritual and religious at the same time—do not challenge the implicitly individual and interior nature of spirituality. Perhaps it is best to leave the fuzzy world of spirituality for pop culture commentators and psychologists after all.

Whether in interviews or surveys, sociological or psychological, responses about spirituality often remain something of an unexamined black box—simply whatever religion isn't.[2] What might happen if we opened up "spirituality" for examination on its own terms? Is spirituality so individual that no cultural footprints can be seen? Is religion so thoroughly institutional that it is divorced from spiritual experience? Most studies of spirituality start with a definition,[3] but we chose instead to look for the way definitions show up in conversations about everyday life. Our participants knew that the project they were part of was called "spiritual narratives in everyday life," so the question of definition often came up early in our first interview. When it did, we always turned that question back to them: "What do you think spirituality is?" In our own questions, we inquired about a broad range of activities, interpretations, and experiences, asking whether they thought of those things as spiritual. They often ruminated aloud about what might count, pointing to the ambiguities that exist surrounding this term. Theresa Collins, a sixty-six-year-old active Episcopalian reflected in her diary that "Spirituality is certainly something that, first of all it's hard to define in a way, but um, it's important to me and I still do believe that it's, you know, the focus of my life really. It should be the focus of everybody's life. I mean we all have spirits and our spirits are going to live forever."

Like others, her attempts at an explicit definition were less helpful than the ways she *used* the category to describe life. When all the conversations had been transcribed, there were over 1,100 places where spirituality was referenced by our participants, and these were the starting point for identifying whatever cultural patterns might be present. In the stories people told us, what were they talking about when they referenced spirituality or described something as spiritual?

An Initial Mapping

The journey through all that talk about spirituality revealed the beginnings of ways to map the terrain.[4] It was possible to identify the prairies and canyons, the wetlands and coastlines. There were, that is, identifiable themes and experiences for which our participants used the designation "spiritual." They might or might not claim to *be* spiritual in this way, but they *use* the category to point toward specific things they have observed.

- Seventy-nine percent clearly associated spirituality with *religious tradition*. They talked about participating in or identifying with a religious institution or tradition as spiritual. As Pam Jones, a Black Baptist in Boston said in one of her oral diary entries, "You go to church to get the sustenance that you need spiritually."
- Seventy-three percent spoke of spirituality in terms of *Morality*, living a life of caring and service, being a good person who lives by the Golden Rule. Phyllis Carrigan, a Boston Catholic said, "To be there for people... as I grow spiritually, and it's a long journey, that's what it is about."
- Perhaps not surprisingly, 72 percent made a link between spirituality and *God (or goddesses)*. Andrew Hsu, a young Evangelical in Boston talked about this divine presence and relationship in one of his diary entries. "As a Christian man I'm aware of my spirituality, i.e., my relationship with God and that I have a friendship with him and I try to walk with him." From a quite different theological perspective, Anna Cook, a participant in the north Georgia women's spirituality circle, told our interviewer about the labrys she wears, describing it as "a sacred spiritual symbol to me from the aspect of the Goddess."
- Sixty percent identified spirituality with particular *practices* in which people engage, disciplines, and activities such as study and prayer that people see as links to the spiritual domain.[5] Marjorie Buckley referred in one of her diary entries to reading a Latter-day Saints magazine as part of her spiritual practice. "I'm going back this evening to finish reading the *Ensign* because I do need to be spiritually fed," she said. "I'm so grateful for this church magazine and the wonderful articles there are in it."

- Roughly half (53 percent) specifically linked spirituality with *mystery*, with miraculous or unexplained happenings that they saw as signaling something more than everyday reality. As Hank Matthews, a Boston Episcopalian, put it, "You know, there are so many things that can't be explained scientifically.... There are things out there that can't be explained and, uh, let's recognize it for what it is."

- Almost equally common (51 percent) was a use of spirituality to indicate a sense of *meaning*. Where people find life to have a kind of wholeness or purpose, they sometimes place that sense of meaning in the category of spirituality. Sam Levitt, a Jew from Boston's North Shore talked in one of his diary entries about the work he does and the spiritual reasons behind why he does it. He says it is about "being part of the order of the universe, part of God's order of the universe."

- Linking spirituality to *belief* was present in about half (49 percent) of our participants, as well. In one of her diary entries, Barbara Robinson, an African American Protestant in Atlanta, asserted, "I'm spiritual. I don't go to church. Um, but I am very spiritual. I believe in God." Robin Mitchell made a similar definitional move, even though she was not herself convinced. She described a religious studies class she took in college: "None of this ever made me feel like I believed in God, but it did give me a window into a whole world of spirituality that I never knew existed."

- Durkheim might be surprised that only 49 percent of our participants talked about spirituality in terms of a transcendent sense of *connection* to others and to the world. Mary Margaret Perkins, a parishioner at St. Michael's Catholic Church in Atlanta described serving Communion: "Some people when they come up to me at Communion, I look at them and they look at me, and it just gives me shivers. And the weird thing is, I'll ask them later, and they'll look at me and go, 'Yeah, me too.' And it's kind of a cool thing that, for some reason, we've touched each other spiritually."

- The Catholic Mass was but one of the many kinds of *ritual* cited by 47 percent of our participants as indicative of things spiritual. The members of the Georgia women's spirituality circle talked extensively about their experiences in their group rituals, but several, like Shirley Knight, talked about their own inventions, as well:

  I just knew that before I would move in, I would walk the house, and I had my own little ritual that I did. I wouldn't call it a ritual, I just did it. I would just walk through every room in the house and I would say, 'If there's anything bad here, you have to leave. If there's a spirit here, that's good or neutral or whatever, you are welcome to stay. But if you

intend to harm anybody or anything that comes into this house, you
must leave now.'

- Popular treatments of "spirituality" often mention experiences of *awe* in
the face of the natural world or things of beauty. Forty-one percent of our
participants turned to similar ideas. Secular Bostonian Alicia Waters confessed at one point in a diary entry, "Although I'm not spiritual, it was quite
a spiritual experience." She was describing snowmobiling in the backcoun-
try near Telluride, Colorado, in what she described as "pristine wilderness,
and the closest I can come to serene, calm, and beauty."
- Those same popular treatments often point to cultivating the *self* as a common modern form of spirituality. That is a phenomenon 31 percent of our
participants identified, as well. Alex Polani's only religious participation
is in an internet chat room, but he sees spirituality as located in each person. "Everyone has something that is a gift that they can offer that is really
distinctive of their personality, and those people I think are in a zone. It's
almost like spiritual alignment with that purpose."

Some of these descriptions are easy to link with traditional measures of
religiosity, such as belief or participation in ritual. Others, such as a sense of
connection, would typically be missed by surveys. Some, such as awe and self-
cultivation, are often linked in popular treatments with a presumably larger
and growing spiritual domain that exists outside religious institutions. This
initial mapping still leaves a good deal of messiness. The numbers attached to
these distinct points on the spiritual map also make clear that all our participants—affiliates and nonaffiliates alike—employed multiple definitional tacks
over the course of their contributions in the interview, diaries, and descriptions
of their photos. They do not dwell in a single spiritual location. Indeed, the
vast majority of their references to spirituality moved across multiple meanings—awe and God, ritual and mystery, meaning and morality—often within
the same story. The cultural world in which they live supplies them with multiple ways to indicate the things that belong in the spiritual realm, and they
often seem fairly indiscriminate in drawing from that cultural repertoire. Does
this mean, then, that there is no coherence in this cultural field? Is "spirituality" a signifier that can mean whatever each person wants it to mean?

Cultural Landscapes

Looking more closely at how this array of Americans described their lives, I am
convinced that we can see some larger cultural and institutional patterning

that is at work. We can begin to see those patterns by asking how and by whom these various definitions are used. While they are widely employed across the population we studied, this long list clusters around an underlying structure of cultural meanings. Discovering that underlying pattern began by using a statistical technique to tease out which definitions were most likely to be used by the same person. That is, from among all the possible uses to which the notion of spirituality is put, which tend to be used together? If a person talks about spirituality in one sense, which other ways of describing it are likely to be present, as well? If a person speaks of spirituality as inherent in meaning, are they also likely to speak of spirituality in terms of awe? The results of the statistical sorting then have to be assessed on their own terms. Does it make sense that this cluster of meanings would occur together?

What emerged from all that sorting were two distinct cultural packages, what I will call Theistic and Extra-theistic, two domains of cultural discourse within which these Americans approach the notion of spirituality. A third discursive path runs through the entire landscape, as well, defined by the single definitional signpost of an Ethical spirituality of moral goodness. A fourth discourse marks a contested terrain in which the politics of being "spiritual but not religious" can be seen. Exploring these cultural landscapes and identifying their particular social locations is a necessary beginning for understanding how stories of everyday life may or may not be marked by religious and spiritual themes.

The Theistic Landscape

The first and most robust cluster of meanings is the Theistic cluster. Those who employ this spiritual genre move easily among three ways of talking about spiritual life—it is about God, it is about practices intended to develop one's relationship with God, and it is about the mysterious encounters and happenings that come to those who are open to them.[6] Whatever else spirituality may indicate, its most dominant function is to mark a territory in which there are divine actors. When our subjects were talking about things they deemed to be spiritual, they were very likely to be talking about God. Theresa Collins showed us the picture she took of the family's boat and said, "I love to be out on that boat on the ocean for the same reason I like to be in my garden, 'cause I feel close to the Lord and the beauty of the world." And in her diary, she recounted one evening, "We looked up at all the stars and we thought about God and, um, how he created the world and the universe, and said a prayer of thanksgiving for everything." For her these were described as spiritual experiences. Marjorie Buckley, the Mormon woman we met above, described the connection as more personal but no less specifically Theistic: "I have a 24 hour a day connection with my friend upstairs. I call him my friend, so when I refer to my friend you know I'm referring to Jesus Christ, because he is my friend." Charles Curlew, a statistician and an Atlanta Baptist, also talked about spirituality in terms of God's presence and activity: "I have this idea about sensitivity and obedience; that sometimes God prompts us with certain ideas and that if we're sensitive to God we will be aware of this prompting and if we obey, obviously we've done a good thing." What we hear in these references is more than *just* a link to the divine, but it is that.

Those same people were also likely to talk about spirituality as something to be pursued. One of the ways our subjects talked about being spiritual was to identify specific activities—activities that would evoke the spirit, discipline the spirit, and help the spirit to grow stronger. "It is really important that I am preparing and practicing in physical and spiritual things, so that I have confidence in myself and confidence not to fear the future," said Catherine Young, a twenty-nine-year-old Latter-day Saint. Most commonly these were activities such as prayer and Bible reading that have long been encouraged in the Christian tradition (especially among Evangelicals), but as we will see in the next chapter, the range of practices was much broader than that. Ann Rosa, a sixty-four-year-old active Catholic in Boston noted the combined effect of church attendance and other practices: "When you are close at all to the parish, to the Bible reading, to sermons, to examples of lives of faith and so forth…, that focus on God should become more and more consuming." For both of these women, religious institutions have helped them establish habits, routines, and intentional practices that reinforce a spiritual view of the world.

The result of this focus on one's spiritual life is, at least for many of our participants, openness to seeing a miraculous dimension in life. Sociologists and other modern philosophers have long posited that religion is what provides explanations for what is otherwise not unexplainable.[7] Indeed a dose of magic and mystery have been seen as essential to the power of religious authorities (Weber 1922 [1963]). Things operating in the spiritual realm, by this reading, are mysterious forces causing outcomes that cannot be explained by ordinary means. For our participants, mystery could be both explanation for what has happened and a desire for intervention in what might happen. But it was not always so active or interventionist. More often it was simply a way of perceiving the everyday world. This kind of spirituality involves the ability to see the openness of the world, to see events as both ordinary and extraordinary, both material and spiritual. Philosopher Charles Taylor (2007) would contrast this to the closed "immanent frame" in which modern life exists in a single horizontal plane where everything is merely natural and empirically explainable. Spirituality means being able to see a layer of mystery alongside the mundane empirical scene.

Many of those who spoke of unexplained events were talking about the limits of human understanding, about their sense that no matter how much we come to understand the natural world, there will always be some part of it that is beyond us.[8] A forty-four-year-old doctor, Stephen James, member of Cornerstone Baptist in suburban Boston, said, "I can't explain half—I can't explain a tenth of what occurs in here [the body] just based on what I read…in medicine. There's…something more going on here." Because he recognizes an unexplained transcendent order alongside the natural world, he describes himself and his way of thinking as spiritual. He does not cease taking the physical explanations seriously, but he recognizes other realities at work alongside them. Similarly, others saw spiritual dimensions to the little coincidences of everyday life. They spoke of an order and plan in the world that is only glimpsed occasionally or seen "through eyes of faith." "But that wasn't a coincidence," said Vicki Johnson, a sixty-one-year-old retired nurse who is an active member in her Catholic parish in Atlanta. "That was a God thing. That's an expression I use. That was a God thing." Ordinary events come together in unexpected ways that are seen as meaningful when interpreted through a spiritual lens. Ordinary realities have multiple layers of meaning beyond the flatness of a material and historical accounting.

Some spiritual stories were not ordinary at all. Jessica Kingman, a young and devout Boston Catholic, talked extensively about things that were clearly beyond routine everyday occurrences. In one of her diary entries, she told us a story she had heard from a friend she met on a pilgrimage to Lourdes (a shrine in France).

> He said he was driving…very fast. He said he was coming round a corner and he heard a voice say, "Slow down, slow down." And he said he looked up and on the side of the curb he said he saw a white figure, and it wasn't like a human—like how I would see him or he would see me—but he said he saw her in, like, a white spirit form. He said it looked like Our Lady, and he said, "I believe it was." He said he turned the corner and there was a huge accident.

Having been warned to slow down, he avoided becoming part of the crash. The appearance of a "white figure" was accepted by Jessica and her friend as a mysterious spiritual message. Similarly, Alexis Nouvian, a thirty-year-old Atlanta Presbyterian, spoke of having "experiences of being visited by God…experiences of God coming in my room and rocking me." Rather than an unexplained spiritual domain running parallel to everyday life, these mysterious happenings were intrusions into everyday life, breaking into the mundane.

In both cases, the religious culture in which these women live provided ways to tell the story. The actor is God or Our Lady, not an unnamed ghost or a natural aberration of the mind. They speak in ways they share with the religious communities of which they are a part, using symbols developed in the long history of religious efforts to organize, categorize, and encourage human experiences of transcendence. As Peter Berger notes in *The Sacred Canopy*, experiences of "the nightside of consciousness" are extraordinarily common in human life, and religions have "served to integrate these realities with the reality of everyday life, sometimes (in contrast to our modern approach) by ascribing to them a *higher* cognitive status" (Berger 1969, 43, emphasis in original). Not all of our participants made the link between spirituality and these alternative realities, but a few did; and they are clearly within the domain of what humanity has long identified with religious and spiritual life.

What we hear in these uses of spirituality is a seamless adoption of the term as an adjunct to religious talk about God. Far from standing in opposition to traditional religious understandings of the world, gods and goddesses adopted from religious traditions define this spiritual genre. The boundaries between talk about spirituality and talk about deities beyond oneself are completely permeable. In discursive practice, a large portion of our American sample is spiritually religious and religiously spiritual.

One does not have to be an active religious participant to have access to this Theistic spiritual terrain, however. These Theistic images of a god who intervenes and gives meaning to life are widely available in American media culture beyond the churches and synagogues. Movies, television shows, and websites employ images and stories that originate in religious traditions, and these stories are then appropriated with few authoritative strings attached. As Lynn Schofield Clark (2003) discovered in studying American teenagers, the world of angels and demons is of endless fascination. Stories that began as biblical tales are adopted into media tropes and then find their way second- and third-hand into the life narratives of youth (Clark 2007). Like those youth, our participants could also draw from that cultural store, from the remnants of theological traditions that have simply been dispersed into the culture and are available to anyone.

The pattern of use we see among our participants, however, makes clear that they were not simply drawing their Theistic spirituality from the culture at large. Organizational participation matters in the production and maintenance of this Theistic mode of discourse. It is more likely among those who are in Christian traditions than among Jews and nonaffiliates and more likely among those who attend services regularly than among those who seldom darken a church door (see Table 2.1). Not only do we see differences among

Table 2.1 Use of Theistic Discourse

Category (number in category)	Percentage with "Broad" Use of Theistic Meanings[a]
***Religious Traditions	
Mainline Protestant (14)	86%
Conservative Protestant (20)	95%
African American Protestant (10)	90%
Catholic (20)	60%
Jewish (10)	30%
Mormon (5)	100%
Neopagan (5)	80%
Nonaffiliates (11)	27%
***Attendance	
Rare or never (34)	50%
Average or more (61)	82%
*Education	
Less than college (12)	92%
College or more (83)	67%
*Age	
65 or less (81)	67%
Over 65 (14)	93%
*Ethnicity	
African American (12)	92%
All others (83)	67%
Gender	
Men (35)	69%
Women (65)	72%
OVERALL AVERAGE	*71%*

[a] Broad use is defined here as telling stories that draw on at least two separate Theistic meanings. Differences among categories assessed by comparisons of means, with a one-way analysis of variance. *p < .10; **p < .05; ***p < .001.

the Christian and Jewish traditions, but we also see that the Neopagans we interviewed were nearly as likely to link spirituality to deities and miracles and practices as were the Protestants. Their discourse about spirituality has very similar contours, that is, to that of active Christians. The content of what they believe and practice is obviously quite different, but their community provides a rich array of symbols, deities, rituals, and ways of interpreting the world.[9] The nature and meaning of spirituality is no less institutionally shaped just because the community is a minority one. As we will see in much more detail in Chapter Four, all religious communities create a discursive arena, a community of conversation in which the presence of a spiritual layer of reality can be perceived.

It is worth pausing here to note that such minority religious groups cannot simply be lumped together as "alternative spiritualties." Heelas and Woodhead's (2004) study of the "holistic milieu" in the small English town of Kendal is a case in point. They included both groups and practitioners offering various alternative healing, mind-body, and other spiritual practices. Heelas argues that these disparate holistic practitioners are socially connected with each other and have transcendent beliefs and rules of life (Heelas 2006), constituting something that approaches a coherent institutional context. But the fluidity of this holistic milieu and its tiny size (perhaps 1 percent of the population spread over many different kinds of activities and groups),[10] make alternative spiritual *groups* difficult to include, en masse, in a comprehensive picture of religious and spiritual life in a society. Their specific beliefs and practices are so varied that we cannot draw conclusions about a single "alternative spirituality."[11] Because the sacred circle we studied was specifically Neopagan, the participants in it had developed a distinctive discourse about the nature of spirituality. It was parallel in structure to the Theistic spirituality of liturgical Christians, but the spiritual territory being described had its own deities, practices, mysteries, and rituals. In this case, the "alternative" spirituality being described has more in common with the theism of "organized religion" than with the various discourses about spirituality that did not presume a god as a defining feature.

Theistic spiritual discourse is, then, produced and sustained through participation in religious communities. Beyond that, there are distinct corners of the larger culture where this is the primary way people talk about what spirituality is. African Americans, for instance, were more likely than others to tell stories drawing on a broad range of Theistic meanings (see Table 2.1), even comparing attenders (and nonattenders) to each other across ethnicity. Survey studies, as well, have often indicated that African American culture remains more pervasively Theistic than any other segment of the American population (Chatters et al. 2008; Putnam and Campbell 2010). Other cultural differences that might have been expected were simply not present or were relatively weak. There were no differences between our Atlanta and Boston participants or between men and women, and the patterns across age groups were very mixed. Those over sixty-five were slightly more conversant in Theistic spirituality than everyone else, but younger people vary in unpredictable ways, not in a straight line of decline with age. Those with a college degree were somewhat less likely to speak of spirituality with a broadly Theistic vocabulary, suggesting perhaps that the college experience attenuates the range of Theistic discourse. We will return to the effects of educational experiences later to note, however, that this is not a straightforward indicator that less educated people are more religious. As Schwadel (2011) has shown, higher education has very mixed effects on different aspects of religious belief and practice.

Theistic spirituality is not a cultural territory equally inhabited by all, but it is also not one subject to straightforward demographic predictors. Rather, it is primarily a product of the specific interactions and cultural activity sustained in religious institutions and in particular ethnic cultures. Christians who are actively engaged in their congregations, across the various denominations we included, are very likely to talk seamlessly about the spiritual life in religious terms centered on God. To whatever degree nonaffiliates and nonattenders talk about spirituality at all, they are much less likely to have a broadly Theistic vocabulary.

The Extra-theistic Landscape

If, in everyday usage, many Americans use a Theistic spiritual discourse that is anchored in participation in religious organizations, what about the "spirituality" that is not centered on Theistic images? Here, too, the cultural patterns are not random. A second cluster of definitions emerges from the stories we heard, different themes in the talk about spirituality that cluster together into the same territory. People who reference one are also likely to reference others. They speak of a world of experiences that do not depend on the Christian (or any other) God but that nevertheless signal transcendence, a reaching beyond the ordinary. This genre of spiritual discourse encompasses attention to transcendent connections to others, the sense of awe engendered by the natural world and moments of beauty, life philosophies crafted by an individual seeking meaning, and the inner core of individual self-worth.[12] These ways of thinking about spirituality are often described in the literature as "immanent," flowing from the person, the community, and the natural world and needing no authority beyond the person's own experience.[13] That may be so, but when our participants talked about this kind of spirituality, they spoke of rising beyond the mundane and the everyday, beyond simple pleasure or rational calculation, beyond self-interest or explanation. The way spirituality was invoked seemed akin to what philosopher Charles Taylor has called "fullness," places where ordinary life is touched by an affectively charged perception that things have meaning, where the "immanent frame" of explainability and calculation is opened to something beyond (Taylor 2007). What they are describing may not come from a transcendent deity, but it is nevertheless transcendent.

Works of art, music, nature, and other objects of beauty, for instance, were "spiritual" when they evoked awe, when they asked a person to stop, step out of the ordinary business of life, stretching the mind and imagination toward what might be. Experiencing a sense of awe is not unrelated to what some people described when they talked about unexplained and mysterious happenings; but if a Theistic spirituality of mystery is about the cognitive domain—what cannot otherwise be explained—a spirituality of awe is about affect, what one feels. Neuroscientists have spent a good deal of time in recent years dissecting the brainwaves of such experiences. Princeton neuroscientist Michael Graziano confesses, "When I am listening to certain pieces of music I feel a reverence creeping over me, an awe that has a spiritual quality," and despite being an atheist, he wants to understand this experience. His explanation has to do with imputations of complexity and intentionality that our brains attribute to a soul-like personality behind the music. He experiences an emotional resonance with the music that he claims is similar to the emotional resonance others have to a deity (Graziano 2011). His is but one of dozens of explorations into the neurological structures that may account for this common human experience.[14]

Despite differences in how they are explained, experiences of awe are real, and they point to a reality that is greater than the sum of the parts that can be seen. Jonathan Snow, one of our secular participants in Atlanta said, "I think there are huge things in the universe that we don't understand. And experiencing things that are calming and healing in what might almost be a spiritual way. I've had that from lots of things. Music, movies that I love, and books. Even poetry, although I'm not a big poetry person." We heard similar thoughts earlier about the ocean and the stars from Episcopalian Theresa Collins. Lawyer Thomas Miller, a Jew living on Boston's North Shore, was another person whose description of the places he photographed included this connection between nature and spirituality. And one of his fellow members from Congregation Sinai, Rebecca Klein, told us,

> Sam and I often will ride our bikes on Sunday morning, and I feel really lucky to live where I live because it's the most beautiful place. And, like, the birds are right outside my window all the time. I don't take it for granted. I live right by the beach and it's amazing. Every night we hear the ocean and it puts us to sleep and it's quite something. It is spiritual.

Encountering beauty in all its forms seems to evoke for many of our respondents "rumors of angels" (Berger 1970), hints of "something beyond."

If our secular participants have any spiritual sensibility at all, this is it. Note Jonathan's "might almost be spiritual" way of describing his experiences. Robin Mitchell, a financial planner with no religious affiliation, showed us one of the pictures she took and said,

> This painting is very nice, it's got a ladder going up to the sky. It's got a sort of spiritual feel to it. I think it's supposed to be like Hopi Indian dwellings with a sense of possibility and upward looking. There's a sun or a glow in the sky, something positive. Just the colors themselves are really very enriching and vibrant.

That fairly tenuous connection to a bit of hopeful, vibrant beauty in a painting was as close as she was likely to get to using a discourse of spirituality. But she and other secular participants recognized beauty as calling out a connection to something they have learned can be called spiritual. While others may link awe and spirituality in a more surefooted way, they are all inhabiting the same discursive world.

If spirituality is sometimes signaled by the beauty of the natural world, it is also sometimes experienced in the transcendence of the social world. Finding (or losing) oneself in the ocean of a common human spirit is another of the things people mean when they say something is spiritual. Durkheim would, of course, not be surprised (Durkheim 1964). In the "collective effervescence" of rituals and the sense of solidarity engendered by group symbols, people experience themselves as part of something beyond themselves, something they identify as a god but that is actually, he claimed, the transcendent reality of society itself. Indeed, some of our participants spoke of spirituality in terms of the interconnectedness of all of life, the importance of "community," or of experiencing a deep sense of compassion. That sense of interconnection was especially strong in the stories told by the Neopagans. Emma Cooper said,

> If you really believe that deity is immanent, you're going to walk dif-ferently on the earth. Just like practical things, you're going to do your recycling. You know, you're not going to throw cigarette butts out the car window, because everything around you is a manifestation of the divine, and we're all part of it. We're all pieces. It's all really, really interconnected.

After our interview with Carolyn Horton, a forty-seven-year-old artist and scientific researcher in Atlanta, she sent an email note about something that had occurred to her:

> I think joy is an essential part of spiritual well-being—it's what drives that sense of connectedness. And for me there is no joy like making love. I have often thought of this as spiritual but for some reason it didn't occur to me today in a conversation about religion and spiritual-ity to bring it up. But it's right at the heart of my experience of…what-ever that is…god? love anyway. oneness.

Carolyn is one of our unaffiliated participants, and she plays here with what to name the experience of connection she feels. She claims it as real and impor-tant and spiritual, but she does not have a shared language that allows her to communicate easily what it is about.

Cynthia Gardener, from All Saints Episcopal on Boston's North Shore, had less hesitation in naming the spirituality of human connection. She recounted in one of her diary entries that she has a song from *Les Miserables* as her phone's ring tone, "one of the lines from *Les Miz*, which is one of my favorite lines from any poetry or songs or anything, and that line is 'to love another person is to see the face of God,' and I just love that. I think it's very true. To love another person is to see the face of God." A Theistic spirituality, in other words, often included paths linking it to a spirituality of human con-nection. Some of our more religiously conservative subjects talked about God sending people their way. Andrew Hsu said, for instance, "I'm happy to have Amy as my new friend. I should tell you that meeting Amy and her husband reminded me of how God works in mysterious ways, how we get to know people and get to know their spiritual side, and it helps." Jessica Kingman recalled some recent premarital advice her priest had given her: "The couples that had higher levels of common spirituality, they're the ones that, sexually, things were better. Their conflict resolution was better. Their marriage was healthier." For each of these highly involved religious participants, human connection was seen as spiritual in a way that bridged Theistic and Extra-theistic ways of talking. As we will see, they were not alone in being equally conversant in both languages of spirituality.

Transcendent moments in nature or in community were ways of describing spirituality that often appeared alongside a third mode of spiritual talk—seeing a meaningful pattern in one's own life. Much of sociological theorizing about religion has, in fact, taken "meaning-making" as a starting point. Human beings, Peter Berger taught us, are animals who must construct a meaningful world for themselves (Berger 1969). Not all meanings are spiritual, but an individual life of meaning and a meaningful cosmos are often connected. For many of our respondents, having one's life directed in a meaningful way is the essence of spirituality. The seekers among our participants often talked about what they were seeking in terms of a "path" or "truth" that would guide their lives. This is how Anna Cook, a forty-seven-year-old Atlanta nurse described her discovery of Wicca.

> That just felt right to me. It just did. It was like a truth. It was like hear-ing something that you just innately know the moment you hear it, "Ah, there is the truth, that's the truth." And that's what this spiritual-ity, this path—it rang true to me from the very beginning.

Alex Polani, an active seeker, spoke of sometimes getting "a strong hunch about a certain area regarding my path." He recounted in his diary how he had "been influenced by metaphysics a lot recently and a lot of movies that are out, and a lot of books I've been reading and paralleling each other." Taken together with his passions and hunches, these sources of spirituality contrib-ute to his sense of life direction.

Spirituality in this sense is described as a philosophy of life that allows the person to make decisions and get beyond the moment and beyond the self. Sometimes meaning was about living a life that matters, that has an impact. More often, it was about finding a path through the chaos. Wuthnow asserts, in his study of artists, "Creating some semblance of wholeness in our lives becomes a prevailing spiritual problem" (Wuthnow 2001, 75). The degree to which seeking meaning is a spiritual pursuit can be seen, as well, in its mirror opposite, namely the determined rejection of meaning by those who reject spirituality. Atheist Richard Dawkins observes that humans seem programmed to seek meaning and impute intention, but it is a delusion, he thinks. His reading of the evolutionary evidence leads him to conclude, "The universe that we observe has precisely the properties we should expect if there is, at bottom, no design, no purpose, no evil and no good, nothing but pitiless indifference" (Dawkins 1995, 85). To seek and assert such a design is the sort of spiritual pursuit Dawkins rejects.

Nonbelievers in our study, however, sometimes talked about just such a pursuit of meaning. Greg Collins (a lapsed Catholic) said, "There is a bigger purpose and you have to set aside time to—I don't know that you ever figure out that purpose, but you have to set aside time to at least open yourself up to thinking about that purpose, to being open to some purpose that doesn't come from inside of you." Others were not so sure that meaning had to come from outside, but they were sure that spirituality involves being attuned to an overarching narrative of life that links each action to some measure of coherence and moral order. The "mystics" Courtney Bender (2010, 83–85) studied built meaning-making into their practice, engaging in forms of reflection that allowed them to see how any given event was connected to others in the past or future.

The final of these interrelated Extra-theistic discourses on spirituality was the turn to the inward self. Here was talk about finding one's own "spark of the divine." John Lehman is a member of St. Felix parish in Boston but has not attended in years. He described spirituality this way:

> To me, although I don't believe in soul, that there is survival after death of personality, that I—for me, spirit is the psyche, the spiritual fulfillment, emotional fulfillment of feeling the gusto for life, enjoyment, in the senses, a thoughtful pursuit of your life…to think about who I am as a person.

As we heard Alex Polani say above, "Everyone has something that is a gift that they can offer that is really distinctive of their personality." Sylvia Carter is a young Jewish woman in Atlanta, puzzling over what to do next in life. She concluded, "I have a faith that things will work out for me. They're going to work out for me because I'm working on it and not because of my faith in God but because of my faith in myself. So I do have faith in myself."

Having "faith in myself" is a discourse that dominates American culture and modern life more generally. It often signals insistence on spiritual autonomy, and it can sometimes mask the human interconnections and institutions that are actually present and essential to human flourishing (Heclo

2008). Bellah and his co-authors enshrined in Sheila Larson and her pro-
fessed "Sheilaism" a worry about what they saw as an utterly individualized
"habit of the heart," where one's own inner voice is taken as the ultimate life
guide.[15] Wade Clark Roof's study of the "spiritual marketplace" described
spirituality in similar individual and inward terms, as "inner awareness and
personal integration" (Roof 1999, 35). Americans' spiritual heroes include
people such as Henry David Thoreau at Walden Pond, someone who could
retreat from worldly distractions to tap a mystical universal truth about life.
Historian Leigh Eric Schmidt traces out this romantic elevation of solitude
in the nineteenth century and shows how it comes to define the way scholars
(and many religious people) identified the core of true religion. He quotes
William James's working definition of religion: "the feelings, acts, and experiences of individual men in their solitude, so far as they apprehend themselves
to stand in relation to whatever they may consider the divine" (quoted in
Schmidt 2005, 98). The solitary, contemplating person has become the icon
of American spirituality, and this sort of spiritual experience the essence of
authentic religiosity.

By the last third of the twentieth century, it had become a commonplace
in American culture to claim spiritual privilege for the individual. Seekers
were expected to shed institutional strictures but also to borrow freely from
them to fit individual needs. Historian Catherine Albanese provides a helpful reminder of the particular strands that came together in the 1960s to
make this especially so (Albanese 2001). Roman Catholic monastics such as
Thomas Merton had led the way in transforming ancient practices of mysti-
cism into something that began to be called "spirituality" (rather than piety
or spiritual exercises) and began to spread more broadly in American culture.
That openness paved the way for the sixties fascination with Eastern religions
and the "New Age" (largely borrowed from nineteenth-century Theosophical
and New Thought sources). She reminds us, as well, that Protestant (and
especially evangelical) piety is no stranger to this language of individual spirit
and soul. As Bender (2010) argues, these wildly disparate historical strands,
the wellsprings of today's spiritualities, are often hidden from view, as inhabitants of contemporary American culture simply assert their determination to
follow an individual spiritual path.

The Extra-theistic landscape then, echoes with talk about seeking—seeking transcendence in nature and beauty, seeking a sense of unity and connection, seeking meaning to guide life's journey, and seeking the mystical truth
that lies within. This is a language about spirituality that can be spoken by
people who do not claim religious affiliation. Among our participants, those

who rarely or never attend religious services were more likely than the average religious participant to use expansive Extra-theistic vocabularies to describe and talk about spirituality (see Table 2.2). As we have seen, people who think of themselves as nonreligious, if they have any spiritual vocabulary at all, are likely to speak of it as meaning, awe, connection, and inner wisdom.

Table 2.2 Use of Extra-theistic Discourse

Category (number in category)	Percentage with "Broad" Use of Extra-theistic Meanings[a]
***Religious Traditions	
Mainline Protestant (14)	57%
Conservative Protestant (20)	25%
African American Protestant (10)	50%
Catholic (20)	60%
Jewish (10)	70%
Mormon (5)	40%
Neopagan (5)	100%
Nonaffiliates (11)	91%
**Attendance	
Rare or never (34)	71%
Average or more (61)	49%
Education	
Less than college (12)	42%
College or more (83)	59%
*Age	
21–35 (22)	50%
36–65 (59)	64%
Over 65 (14)	36%
Ethnicity	
African American (12)	42%
All others (83)	59%
Gender	
Men (35)	60%
Women (65)	55%
OVERALL AVERAGE	*57%*

[a] Broad use is defined here as telling stories that draw on at least two Extra-theistic meanings. Differences among categories assessed by comparisons of means, with a one-way analysis of variance. *p < .10 (boomers compared to all others); **p < .05; ***p < .01.

This is a distinct landscape and one more comfortable for seekers, but not one that is alien to most of those whose primary home is in a Theistic landscape. Stories inflected with Extra-theistic notions of spirituality were told by both religiously indifferent and religiously active study participants. While Extra-theistic spirituality does occur most often among those who do not frequent the churches and synagogues, it is by no means absent from the discourse of those who do. Note, in fact, that many of those quoted above are among these very groups: mainline Protestants, Catholics, and African American Protestants who are active attenders. Having gauged the breadth of each person's use of both discourses, it was possible to look at the mix, at which mode was more common for them (see Table 2.3). What we discover is that some religious participants employ a robust set of Extra-theistic meanings *along with* their wide array of Theistic ones. They are perfectly conversant with the spiritual language of their traditions, but they also see spirituality in experiences beyond those traditions, even interpreting each in light of the other. The churches themselves sometimes promote just this sort of crossover, offering classes in meditation or yoga, for instance, that are framed in generic ways that obscure their religious roots outside Christianity and emphasize instead the development of one's interior self.[16] The permeable boundaries between some established Christian communities and the larger culture can be seen in this mixed discursive field.

The participants in some other Christian communities, however, seemed less drawn to describing spirituality in these broader terms. Conservative Protestants and Mormons are distinctive for the relative absence of spiritual language that moves beyond theism. Both groups inhabit a spiritual world saturated with symbols and experiences that focus on a clearly identified deity, and they have a long list of things one can do to be in relation to that deity. Theirs is a culture where the individual self is rarely invoked as a source of inspiration, absent a focus on God. What happens in the natural world as well as in their own souls has specific theological significance in these communities. It is more routinely described in Theistic terms rather than with broader, generic spiritual descriptors. We cannot tell from the stories we heard whether these conservative traditions actively discourage recognition of the sorts of spirituality beyond theism, but there are hints that they may. Active conservative Protestants, for instance, are far less likely to invoke Extra-theistic themes than are their nonattending conservative compatriots.

Who uses which discourse is far more a matter of religious affiliation, in fact, than a matter of the usual demographic and social divisions. The Extra-theistic landscape is inhabited about equally by men and women, college

Table 2.3 Dominant Spiritual Discourse by Religious Tradition and Attendance

Dominant[a] Spirituality Discourse	Attend Religious Services Rarely or Never (N = 34)	Jewish Attenders (N = 5)	Neopagan Attenders (N = 5)	Mainline Protestant Attenders (N = 12)	African American Protestant Attenders (N = 8)	Catholic Attenders (N = 12)	Conservative Protestant Attenders (N = 14)	Latter-day Saint Attenders (N = 5)
Theistic	18%	0	0	25%	38%	8%	71%	60%
Both equally	32%	20%	80%	58%	50%	67%	29%	40%
Extra-theistic	41%	80%	20%	8%	0	25%	0	0
Neither	9%	0	0	8%	13%	0%	0	0

[a] Taking into account the "broad" and "narrow" uses of each discourse, the dominant discourse is one in which the participant has a broader range.

educated and not. There are differences, but our sample was not large enough to determine whether those differences would be likely in a larger population. While African Americans were more active in using Theistic language for spirituality, as we have seen, they are likely to blend that Theistic discourse with Extra-theistic images, much as White mainline Protestant and Catholic people did. Our oldest participants were the most likely to use Theistic categories and the least likely to use Extra-theistic ones. However, this does not seem to represent a direct linear historical movement, since the most prolific users of Extra-theistic discourse are not the youngest cohort but the two middle ones (those born between 1942 and 1972; see Table 2.2). The experiences of our baby boomers still show up in their heightened openness to Extra-theistic spirituality.[17] There is slightly more reference to Extra-theistic spirituality among our Boston participants than in Atlanta, but this is a product of the differing mix of religious traditions in the two cities, not some other artifact of urban culture. That is, people within a given tradition were similar, whichever city they lived in, but the cities were different because of who lives there. Our sample followed the lines of religious demography to include more mainline Protestants and Catholics in Boston and more conservative Protestants in Atlanta. The two cities do have different discursive landscapes, then, because of the different mix of religious traditions.

When compared to the Theistic discourse, this Extra-theistic spirituality is decidedly less prevalent, on average. Given popular attention to the supposed displacement of religion by spirituality, this may seem odd. One key difference between this study and many others, however, is that we were listening for talk about spirituality not just among seekers or people disaffected from religious institutions. We included active religious participants, along with nonaffiliates, seekers, and seculars, people for whom a spiritual life was very important and people who were spiritually uninterested—the whole religious range of the population, in other words. We neither presented them with a fixed checklist of definitions nor collapsed everything into one undifferentiated "spiritual" category with which one could identify more or less. Our participants were left to their own discursive devices, and they talked about God more than sociologists might have thought and about inner enlightenment less.

Ethical Spirituality—The Common Denominator

Theistic and Extra-theistic discursive strategies involve a variety of ways of identifying the cultural territory occupied by spirituality, and those strategies have distinctive, if overlapping cultural locations. The one thing almost everyone agrees on, however, is that real spirituality is about living a virtuous life, one characterized by helping others, transcending one's own selfish interests to seek what is right. Roughly three-quarters identified spirituality in moral terms not unlike the people I first described as "Golden Rule Christians" (Ammerman 1997a). While mainline Protestants seem especially prone to this notion of spirituality, they are by no means alone. Olivia Howell, a thirty-six-year-old Southern Baptist in Atlanta, was explicit about what real spirituality means. "The whole point is though if you don't love your neighbor, anything that's accomplished, even in God's name, right, even if you say you're doing good in God's name it does not matter. Because God said and Jesus said, you know, that love was, was supreme. Love of God first, but then love of your neighbor."

Participants, across all religious and nonreligious categories, made the point that spiritual life must be linked to deeds. Joe Silverman, from Temple Beth Torah in Atlanta, reminds us, in fact, that the Golden Rule did not originate with Christians. He noted, "There's a lot of Reform Jews who do a lot of community work. They may not go to synagogue but they have shelters; they do different things around the city for people, which is a *mitzvah* in itself, a kindness itself." Engaging with the world is central to what Jews mean by spirituality. Similarly, for Joshua Roberts love of neighbor was very concrete. He recorded a long story in his diary about a social service program he participates in through his historic Black church.

So one of the ideas of the basic initiative was to bring about a plan for the youth to be involved in an environment where they can view positive images and be around people who are like minded who had the spiritual guidance to lead them in a productive manner. Not so much as to enforce our spirituality on them but to use those principles in spirituality to entice them to go forth in their life in education and in productivity...do something better with your life and then give back to the community which you come out of.

For him, principles of spiritual guidance entailed both hard productive work and humanitarian generosity—in the Jewish terminology, *mitzvot*. How life is lived is what counts. One of our Neopagan participants voiced her own version of the same idea as the "whole idea of karma, living a good life, you know, what you send out comes back, that sort of thing."

Church and synagogue members were not the only ones, then, to point in this ethical direction with their talk about spirituality. Some of those least connected to religious communities opined that this is what *should* count. If people are going to claim to be religious, nonbelievers want to see it in the way they live. Although Eric Patterson is a member of the Vineyard Community Church in Atlanta, he is an infrequent participant and said, "The God that I was taught about and sort of where I am at spiritually now is all about love." Laura Henderson described her spiritual connection to one of her friends this way: "One of the things that I like about him on a spiritual level is because he, even though he's not a day-to-day practitioner of what I would call spirituality, he's one of the best people I know. He's just a good person. He tries to live his life in a very moral way."

When our participants told stories about their everyday worlds, they sometimes recognized spirituality by the character of the actions they observed. Like the "Aunt Susan" invented by researchers Robert Putnam and David Campbell, caring lives are counted as evidence that this is a person who is headed for heaven, even if other religious doctrines in one's own tradition would say otherwise (Putnam and Campbell 2010). Our participants identified moments when people reached past rational self-interest to sacrifice on behalf of others as moments of spirituality. They saw hints of transcendence in "random acts of kindness."

The Spiritualities of Everyday Life

To listen for the presence of spirituality in everyday life is to listen for the variety of ways in which people may reach beyond the mundane surface of their existence. It is to listen for what Robert Bellah has called "nonordinary reality" (Bellah 2011).[18] Even those who have little if any interest in doing so themselves recognize that there is such a spiritual domain for others. It comes in many forms, but it is not utterly individual. There are cultural forces at work patterning the way spiritualities are identified. In one mode, spirituality takes personal shape around deities. Most often this is the God worshiped in one of the great monotheisms, but it can also be the gods and goddesses of other traditions. The beliefs surrounding what these gods are like and how they act in the world vary enormously, but Theistic spiritualities are distinctive in placing human action in relation to divine persons.

Extra-theistic spiritualities leave divine persons to the side but, nevertheless, retain marks of transcendence, aspects of life that are more than mundane. As events are woven together into meaning or people woven together into a community, a fullness of life is identified as spiritual. In the inner beauty of the self or in the natural beauty of the universe, the world is perceived as more than what it appears at first to be. And to name a moral life as a spiritual one is to recognize that acts of kindness seem to require something more than rational calculation.

The stories we will encounter throughout this book encompass all of these spiritualities. All of them represent a refusal to narrate life in "merely" mundane terms. We will listen for how they may shape everyday stories, where they are present and absent, and how different kinds of spiritual discourses may lend themselves to the telling of different kinds of stories.

Spiritualities and "Religion"

We noted earlier that statistical analysis of the initial list of meanings yielded a fourth factor, a tendency to equate spirituality with both religious beliefs and traditional religious communities.[19] Returning to the stories themselves, it became apparent that this cluster of meanings was quite unlike the others. It is certainly true that people who are talking about spirituality slip easily into the institutionally religious domain; and it perhaps reflects the particularly Protestant character of American culture that "belief" is so often assumed to be part of that domain, as well. For roughly half our U.S. participants, spirituality is understood to be about believing, and for more than three-quarters it is about being part of a religious tradition; and the use of those two definitions together is highly likely.

Our participants were very likely to link belief and belonging to spirituality, but they did so from two widely divergent positions. What it means to define spirituality in belief-and-belonging terms varies across the religious terrain. Some people who are conventionally religious included these typical dimensions of religiosity in their understanding of spiritual life. But so, in roughly equal numbers, do secular participants who have *rejected* religious institutions. A closer look at the stories themselves made clear that the meaning of this religiously defined spirituality is contested. Believing, for instance, could either be a way of talking about devout spirituality or a way of describing superstition.[20] One theme in the secular stories was an encounter with knowledge, usually during their college years, that challenged the beliefs they had been taught. Since belief was seen as central to what religion and spirituality are, the implausibility of religious beliefs was a critical factor in their exodus from both. Lily Mattison, an ex-Catholic in Atlanta, described the "annoying" religious people on her campus. "They had all these views that they didn't substantiate with any, like, factual reasoning, and we were in college, and I felt like you needed to at least have some kind of academic or intellectual reasoning behind things." Robin Mitchell's story about her college religious studies class (noted at the beginning of the chapter) was another example. Spirituality is about believing, but believing is not something they find plausible.

The link between spirituality and traditional religious identities and memberships is a similar mixed bag. Those who are actively engaged with a religious tradition were very likely to link their belonging positively with their sense of what spirituality is. Being part of the Jewish people, belonging to a local church, claiming one's Catholic identity, were interwoven with stories about spirituality. But so did those who have rejected religion. Greg Collins put it this way, "I started out like most good Catholic kids believing in the Catholic Church and believing the word of the pope; believing that it was the one true church. I don't believe that any more." Samantha Bailey contrasts what she sees in her southern community with the choice she has made to become part of a Neopagan community:

> I find that a lot of people, and I don't know if it's just around here or everywhere, they just go through the motions. Like you need to go to church on Sunday because that's what God likes and that's how you get into heaven. So you log in your time at church every Sunday to buy your ticket into heaven. Then the rest of the time you just live your own life or whatever. I'm truly trying to integrate spirituality into every second of my day.

The spirituality she affirms—something integrated into a moral life—stands in contrast to merely going through the motions of believing and belonging.

The link to believing and belonging, then, is a strong component in the cultural patterning of American religion. Most people place "spirituality" in the same cultural box with religious belonging and belief. Those inside religious communities tend to wrap belief and belonging together with the traditional Christian or Jewish discourses on spirituality that they embrace. Their ongoing experiences and relationships lend a positive valence to the spirituality they associate with religious traditions. By contrast, those who have rejected religious participation, separate out spirituality, contrasting it, as one person put it, with "a structured organized check all the boxes" regime. Throughout this chapter the imprint of organized religion on the shaping of discourse about spirituality has been clear. Here it is also clear that what is being shaped is not the content of the definition but its interpretation and evaluation.

This divide begins to provide clues for understanding the popular cultural rhetoric about being "spiritual but not religious." Even some social scientists have taken as a truism that there is a "growing division between organized religion and spirituality" (Ellingson 2001), but that division is anything but clear in how our participants talked. The world most of our participants inhabit is both spiritual and religious at the same time. For a large majority, spirituality is defined by and interchangeable with the experiences their religious communities have offered them and taught them how to interpret. When they think of spirituality, they think of God, their relationship with God, and what God does in the world. This is a discursive and experiential world shaped by organized religious communities, and for most of those who are actively involved in a congregation, there was more reference to the ways they find spirituality at church or synagogue than to any necessary conflict between them. They are quite comfortable being both religious and spiritual.

Talk that contrasted religion and spirituality was not absent, however. It appeared in two distinctly different cultural places. Nonaffiliates and nonattenders, not surprisingly, often used the language of "spiritual but not religious" to describe themselves. People who have little or no contact with a religious community are more than twice as likely, compared to attenders, to draw a distinction between religion and spirituality. Robin Mitchell was among the more eloquent. In one of her diary entries, she mused,

> If there's anything in the Bible that I would resonate with it would be the idea of Jesus. Not the idea of Jesus, excuse me, the teachings of Jesus. He seemed sort of like a John Lennon type, and I think it's just a shame that what has been layered onto Christianity obscures so thickly the basic message of loving thy neighbor and taking care of other people. I know this has been said a million times, but it is how I feel, especially as a lesbian in the face of all this religiously fueled bigotry and hatred. The ironies are so great.

Robin does not claim to be spiritual, but she is describing an Ethical spirituality here. She has seen the moral lapses of organized religion and decided that it is not the best way to live. Disaffected Catholic John Lehman was one of the people who found spirituality in exploring and deepening his own inner self and living a moral life, and church had become irrelevant for him.

> I had found—probably twenty years ago, I had found that religious practice had—there was no interest in the—for me—with prayer,

ceremony, sacraments....I had not really found a need or an urge to (pauses) involve myself in those activities. I had felt, really, felt guilt for not. I came to realize that, just by being a moral person or a law-abiding citizen, that that was probably sufficient, that I had found enough satisfaction in my daily living.

Robin and John represent a cultural rhetoric linking religiosity to hypocrisy and empty ritual while claiming that a good and caring life is the best form of spiritual connection.

The other cultural location where the religious versus spiritual contrast is alive is conservative Protestantism. Empty "religion" is rejected in favor of deep personal "spirituality." What is required is a personal spiritual relationship with Jesus.[21] Olivia Howell (the young Atlanta Baptist) reflected in one of her diary entries, "I have been wanting the *church* to be the center of how I serve and how I define myself and my Christian identity, and the truth of the matter is that that's just as fake as everything else." Similarly, Jessica Fletcher, a member of the Vineyard Community Church in Atlanta, recounted her life before her conversion, "I didn't have a relationship with God or with Jesus at that point anyway. It was just a relationship with the religious aspect of it." What is important, for both women, is a personal spiritual relationship with God. The evangelical heritage of personal salvation, born of the seventeenth-century Reformers' insistence that no priest or church could grant salvation, resonates in its own way with today's valorization of the individual and condemnation of organized religion.

The irony, of course, is that most of the unaffiliated or nonparticipating people who claim spirituality as a positive alternative to religion are themselves neither. So who really fits the "spiritual not religious" label? In one case it is used to describe people who are very pious and very active in their churches (conservative Protestants); and in another, it is used to describe a hypothetical distinction between two categories, neither of which apply to the person making the distinction. When we look at practices instead of rhetoric, in the vast majority of our participants, religious participation and spiritual engagement occur alongside talk that intermingles the two. Similarly, a combination of religious disengagement and spiritual disinterest was the most common characteristic of the participants who insisted on making the invidious distinction. Just one of our participants, Alex Polani, really fits the "spiritual not religious" label in practice. He has no religious affiliation and never participates in services in any traditional religious community. He is, however, very spiritually active, and we will look more closely in the next chapter at his wide range of spiritual practices. He exemplifies the "seeker" model, but he is only one among our ninety-five.

One additional small segment of our participant population seems on the surface to fit the "spiritual not religious" designation. They are at least moderately active in pursuing a spiritual life but rarely or never attend religious services. The profile fails to fit several of them, however, since their reasons for not attending are related to age and health and work schedules, not rejection of organized religion. Six others are religiously affiliated—two mainline Protestants, two Catholics, and two Jews—but have drifted to the margins of their religious communities. Grace Shoemaker, an occasional attender at All Saints Episcopal north of Boston, is one of them. She told us, "I think of myself as spiritual. Because it doesn't matter what church I'm in, I am who I am." She went on to say,

> When you're in church or in the service it's just their format, and it's lovely. I have nothing against it but that doesn't hold me on a day-to-day basis, that one church service. So, to me, that's the religion. The spiritual part of it is what I have every day, what carries me through the day.

We've already encountered Greg Collins's declaration of independence from Catholic doctrine, but he also told us, "Religion, per se, not sure…spirituality at least, is something that's been important to me, and it's part of my life. I tend to do a lot of reading and I read a lot of spiritual books. I love watching movies that are spiritual topics." These affiliated but not active people know the world described by the institutionally religious discourses, but they find the spiritual world available in the larger culture more compelling. They sit on the margins between inside and outside, drawing on both Theistic and Extra-theistic packages of discourse about spirituality.

It is perhaps more helpful, then, to hear talk about being "spiritual but not religious" as a boundary-maintaining device and source of legitimacy than as a description of the empirical situation. Sociologist Michele Lamont analyzes the way people use all kinds of cultural differences as "moral boundaries" that distinguish them from other classes of people (Lamont 1992). In this case, people are equating "religion" to the implausible beliefs and discredited institutions they have rejected.[22] They are claiming "spirituality" as a reasonably positive and generic category and one that each individual can fill with the content of her own choosing. As Cadge (2013) notes in her study of hospital chaplaincy, having a generic category can be very useful in settings that must deal with religious pluralism, but in hospitals as elsewhere it is a category with little content in practice. Among our participants, being "spiritual but not religious" is a way of describing the religious social world that fits prevailing secularization assumptions nicely, but reflects moral and political categories more than analytical ones.

Defining Spirituality Beyond U.S. Borders

Having outlined these emerging cultural discourses about spirituality, it was striking to discover the work of Stefania Palmisano. Her research in Italy reveals that spirituality there, as a culturally defined phenomenon, may not be different *in kind* from what we discovered among our U.S. participants. Unlike many European studies that simply start from the assumption that European spirituality (to the extent that it exists at all) has taken an inward turn away from church, Palmisano took a step back to ask what sorts of spiritualities do exist and how they are and are not related to traditional religious institutions and ideas (Palmisano 2010). She provided her representative sample of 3,160 Italians with a list of ten possible responses to the question "What does the word 'spirituality' mean to you?" The results of her survey are shown in Table 2.4, alongside roughly corresponding categories that emerged from our participants.

More striking even than the item comparison is the fact that a factor analysis of Palmisano's ten items yielded three factors that parallel very closely three of the clusters we identified: what she terms an "ethic spirituality," a "religious spirituality," and an "inner self spirituality." Her checklist did not contain any items that paralleled the Theistic spirituality our participants described. We do not know whether a similar factor might have emerged if similar items had been present. What we do know is that the cultural domain occupied by spirituality has quite similar dimensions on both sides of the Atlantic. Sometimes people are talking about belief and belonging, sometimes about living a moral life, and sometimes about more expansive experiences of transcendence.

There is also more similarity in frequency than might have been expected. In both countries, spirituality is strongly linked to "belief and belonging," and in both countries similarly large majorities say spirituality is about leading a good ethical life. "Seeking to be a good person," "to help others and give your time to others," and "to be able to distinguish between right and wrong" were the fourth, sixth, and seventh highest responses on the Italian survey. Discourse about cultivating the self, however, was far more prevalent in the Italian survey than among our participants. There "seeking the inner

Table 2.4 Comparing U.S. and Italian Definitions of Spirituality

U.S. Interviews—Discursive Themes			Italian Survey—Spirituality means...
"Morality"—Spirituality is being moral, living a life of caring and service	73%	77.9%	Seeking to be a good person, lead a good life
		73.9%	To help others and give your time to others
		71.9%	To be able to distinguish between right and wrong
"Religion"—Spirituality is "the church" or a traditional religious identity	79%	50.6%	Going to church and following its expectations
"Belief"—Spirituality is about believing, holding correct doctrines	49%	76.4%	Belief in God, following his teachings
		70.7%	Belief in higher, transcendent power, something beyond oneself
"God"—Spirituality is about the divine presence and relationship	72%		No parallel
"Practices"—Spirituality is something sought through disciplines/ activities such as study and prayer	60%		No parallel
"Mystery"—Spirituality is mysterious happenings, things not explainable	53%		No parallel
"Meaning"—Spirituality is a sense of meaning, wholeness, purpose	51%	84.6%	Seeking the meaning of life

(*Continued*)

Table 2.4 (*Continued*)

U.S. Interviews— Discursive Themes		Italian Survey— Spirituality means...	
"Connection"— Spirituality is a deep interpersonal connection, a sense of community	48%	87.8%	To strive for a state of harmony and inner peace in yourself and in others
"Awe"—Spirituality is a sense of wonder at things of beauty, especially in nature	41%		
"Self"—Spirituality is finding one's true inner self	31%	81.2%	Seeking the inner self, developing your spiritual qualities
		63.8%	To affirm sense of personal worth, to affirm one's capabilities in everyday life

self, developing your spiritual qualities" was the third-ranked response behind similar items about striving "for a state of harmony and inner peace" (number 1) and "seeking the meaning of life" (number 2), each garnering assent from over 80 percent of the respondents. Given Italy's religious demography, compared to our U.S. sample, this is perhaps not surprising. With almost no conservative Protestants or Mormons in the Italian population, and a far larger nonparticipating and functionally unaffiliated Catholic population, the prevalence of Extra-theistic discourse about spirituality is perhaps to be expected. This may or may not signal their participation in alternative spiritual communities, but it does suggest that an alternative discursive domain about spirituality has a strong foothold in Italian society and probably in a variety of other European locations. And as in the United States, the cultural lines are not neatly drawn at the church door.

Conclusion

The spirituality we will be listening for in the everyday stories of our participants will sometimes draw on the distancing rhetoric of being spiritual but not religious, but much more often we will hear stories that draw on the Theistic, Extra-theistic, and Ethical spiritualities I have mapped out here. Spirituality is neither the utterly personal creation of each individual nor a single cultural domain. There are patterns in how people imagine what they are seeing and doing when they are there. But no matter which sort of spiritual language is being invoked, stories that are spiritual in any way stand in contrast to the mundane stories that simply recount events as such. Mostly the ordinary events and the spiritual realities are interwoven in the activities of working and having a life. But sometimes the spirit is itself the focus of the activity. Understanding the everyday stories will begin with attention to the practices where spirituality is at the center of what people are doing.

3 SPIRITUAL PRACTICES IN EVERYDAY LIFE

The shape of everyday discourse about religion and spirituality tells us a great deal about the sacred and secular in American society, but discourse is not the whole of reality. Action in the world is shaped both by the words we use to describe and envision it and by the durable habits and improvisations that give form to everyday life. In this chapter we turn our attention to practices of spirituality. In sociology, "practice theory" has emerged as an important mode of analysis, while in theology a "theology of practice" has likewise emerged. The former tends to emphasize the habitual, everyday nature of practices and the structures of power in which that activity occurs, while the latter tends to emphasize the voluntary, intentional nature of activity and the ends toward which activity is directed. At the most basic level, a "practice" is simply a cluster of actions given meaning by the social structure in which it is lodged and the people who occupy that social field. Either the habits or the deliberate choices can be deemed "practices," depending on which theoretical lens one chooses.[1] Likewise, practices can be either sacred or secular in their content and orientation, but the ones that will concern us here are the meaningful actions that are deemed spiritual by the people who described them to us.

Social theorist Pierre Bourdieu's ideas about practice are among the most influential in sociology and beyond. He emphasizes the givenness of human actions that then shape our awareness of the world and reproduce the "natural" quality of the power relations in that world. Childhood, for example, inscribes certain things in our bodies as a "living memory pad." Sitting up straight or bowing can carry a whole cosmology (Bourdieu 1990). In later life, commuting, occupying a corporate cubicle, and even mowing the lawn can be seen as habits shaped by powerful economic and cultural forces. DeCerteau's *The Practice of Everyday Life* retains the emphasis on social forces at work but distinguishes the activities of the powerful from those of the powerless (DeCerteau 1984). The practices of power are *strategies*, while the powerless may engage in *tactics*, makeshift and temporary activities that claim small victories in the daily fight to survive. To speak of "practice" in this sense, then, is to emphasize the unconscious and natural feeling of certain activities and to examine how they demonstrate relationships of power or resistance to power. Spiritual practices, seen from this angle, are bound to the institutions and structures of power that make them seem "given."[2] When feminist religious leaders enact the Christian Eucharist with milk and honey, rather than bread and wine, the backlash is testimony to the givenness and institutional power of the bread and wine.[3] Michel Foucault's late work on the "technologies of the self" extends this argument further (Foucault 1999 [1980]). Examining classical techniques of self-improvement—from confession to psychotherapy—Foucault studied how these voluntary and intentional activities, often originating in Christian practice, were also enmeshed in power relations that disciplined and reshaped selves, sometimes in unintended ways.

The second stream of theorizing about "practice" turns that emphasis around and directs attention at the agency and intention of the actor. In *After Virtue*, Alasdair MacIntyre (1984) advocates "practices" that are coherent, complex activities aimed at achieving excellence, ways of living shaped by "goods" (goals) internal to the practice itself. Practice is about the pursuit of the good and the virtues that support that good. Theologians and ethicists draw on this sense of the word when they speak of rituals and activities that are aimed at deepening the believer's connection to the religious tradition and the deity (Volf and Bass 2001). Both the goods and the rituals are shaped by transcendent forces outside the person, but the person must make choices and exercise discipline in pursuit of those goals. Sociologist Robert Wuthnow, in this vein, describes spiritual practices as serious, deliberate, long lasting, requiring significant energy, and transforming. They require deep reflection and precipitate the development of a core biographical narrative that provides coherence (Wuthnow 1998, 16).

The spiritual practices we will describe here fall somewhere between this intentional transformative ideal and the unconscious enacting of structural prescriptions. The things named as spiritual practices by our participants are not merely habits and are not undertaken without some sense of agency, and they do often reflect the imprint of institutions that give them shape. They often lie at the creative tension between structuring patterns and individual agency.[4] As we did in discerning the meaning of spirituality itself, we relied on our participants to identify the things they do that they think of as practices that are spiritual. Like theorist Martin Riesebrodt, I am adopting an "inside view" that takes the content of the action seriously in defining a practice as spiritual. Unlike Riesebrodt, I am not limiting the category to the "relation to personal and impersonal superhuman powers" (Riesebrodt 2010, ch. 4) or to institutionalized actions (what he calls liturgies). Like the theologians and philosophers, we are looking for the patterns of action that are undertaken with intention and that are given spiritual meaning by the narrator. Unlike the theologians and philosophers (and Riesebrodt), our net is designed to catch patterns of varying degrees of seriousness and across a wide range of definitions of spirituality. The list of activities that emerged here goes far beyond the usual survey checklist. Prayer, Bible reading, and church attendance are the things most commonly measured on surveys (e.g., Iannaccone 1990), and those things are relevant for some of our participants. But the analysis I will undertake here allows the participants themselves to tell us what counts as a spiritual practice, even if they only engage that practice in an arm's-length or occasional fashion.

Many of the stories we will examine came in response to questions in our initial conversations. We asked participants about activities that were important enough to them to try to make sure to do them every day. After we got past the chuckles over making sure to brush their teeth and take a shower, they quickly moved into a list of practices that ranged from a daily workout to trying to maintain a kindly attitude. In the midst of those lists were explicitly religious and spiritual practices—things about which there is common cultural agreement. But we followed up by asking them whether they routinely do things that other people might not think of as spiritual, but they do. Throughout the interview, we asked them to give us examples and tell us stories, and those stories sometimes included references to the practices they had identified earlier. When they took pictures, we often heard much more detail, since many of those pictures turned out to be shots of the places where they engage in religious practices and of the spiritual objects with which they surround themselves. When they recorded their diaries, in turn, the daily rhythms they described often elaborated on the practice stories we had heard in the interviews.

This rich collection of everyday stories has provided us, then, with a broad window on how and where spiritual encounters are pursued in American life. A total of 778 stories about practices were identified and analyzed. For each of them, the elements of the story were recorded, as well. Who is involved in the story? Where does it take place? What material objects or bodily postures does it involve? Is it a regular routine or something that happens only at special occasions or crises? What definition of spirituality is operative? In addition to analyzing the stories themselves, we made an overall assessment of how important spirituality is to each of these people. From their own responses to our direct questions about just that to all the ways they talked about this aspect of their lives, a numeric "salience" score was established (from zero for those who truly exhibited no interest at all to five for those who seem to center much of their identity and activity on spiritual life). This is the subjective side of the activities I will describe, and having this assessment will allow us to see when this sense of spiritual identity plays a role in the practices we are trying to understand.

Praying through the Day

We begin—as many of our participants say they begin each day—with the single most common spiritual practice about which we heard. The surveys are not entirely misguided in asking about prayer. When our participants thought about doing something spiritual, their stories often turned to some form of communication with the divine. Marjorie Buckley, an elderly Mormon woman, told us,

> I like to always say my prayers as soon as I get out of bed because I think Heavenly Father should be thanked first for the comfort of the night and for the warmth of the bed and for the beginning of another day.

Camilla Hart, a middle-aged member of Cornerstone Baptist, had said in her interview that she was not really attached to any particular religious practices, but in her oral diary she reflected,

> I go to bed every night and I say, "Dear God, thank you for getting me through this day. Dear Lord, thank you for helping me to get through this day, for the strength." And—sometimes I go on and on. And I realize when I wake up in the morning—I say, "Lord, please help me to get through this day. Be there, hold my hand, lead me, whatever it is." It's not a routine but I realize that it is a routine.

Sam Levitt is very clear that what he does each morning is a routine and that it is very important for setting his day right. The first picture he took was of his study (see Figure 3.1). "That's where I pray in the mornings," he said. Jessica Kingman, a young Boston Catholic, photographed the window where her daily prayers begin at sunrise. Baptist Charles Curlew describes the morning time as "morning devotions," and he too took a picture of the place where

FIGURE 3.1 "It's a part of my office that I think of as where I keep my religious life."—Sam Levitt

that happens. "I took this picture because every morning I get up at 5:10 and spend a little time in devotions, and uh, I, after reading the scripture and praying a little bit, I go to my room and I get on my knees right here in front of the bed and pray."

Each of these people is a regular participant in a religious community, and each of them draws on the resources, language, and norms of those communities in shaping their daily routine. Jews and Catholics, like Sam and Jessica, have regular scripted rituals of prayer; Mormons, Black Protestants, and conservative Protestants, like Marjorie, Camilla, and Charles, are encouraged to be extemporaneous. For each of them, the norms of the community strongly encourage daily prayer, and their faithful routines stand in contrast to the relative absence of such practices among people who have no such religious community, whose communities do not emphasize prayer, or who attend so rarely that the community's expectations have little effect on them. Not everyone who attends services, in these or other traditions, also prays every day, but daily prayer is more common among those who attend the most frequently. Demographics matter almost not at all. Men and women, old and young, the most well off and the least, Atlanta and Boston, college educated or not—the likelihood of beginning the day with prayer was shaped by a person's religious tradition and the degree to which they are active in it.[5]

When national survey respondents are asked about how often they pray, roughly half claim to pray at least once a day.[6] By those standards, our sample is slightly less observant, with 41 percent describing some sort of daily prayer. Perhaps the survey numbers are higher, in part, because it is easier to check a box on a survey than to describe one's activities in detail in the sorts of conversations we had with our participants. Both the national surveys and our conversations tell us, however, that everyday prayer—not just the liturgical rituals of religious communities—is exceedingly common in American society.

Morning prayers by no means exhaust the forms of prayer our participants reported to us. Many also talked about ending the day with prayer, keeping a prayer journal, and even attempting to pray all day long, encouraged by traditions that imagine divine presence in personal, relational terms.[7] Olivia Howell, talked about "sort of prayer conversations, you know; just whenever I get a moment." Others simply stop before meals to say grace, although fewer than the national surveys might have led us to expect.[8] Perhaps it seemed too routine to mention for some, but African American Protestants and Mormons were especially likely to emphasize that prayer at mealtime is a must. Dr. Stephen James is a busy physician and member of Cornerstone Baptist. He and his wife pray "in the morning, every day. We do, of course, every meal—always say grace." All five of our LDS participants emphasized various daily routines of prayer, including before they eat.[9] Catherine Young, with her relatively new infant, voiced the aspirations: "Prayer is something that we try to do before every meal, and in the morning, and before we go to bed at night, like to have family prayer." As Putnam and Campbell (2010) have reported, saying grace is an excellent gauge of overall religiosity, and most of those who shared stories like this were indeed deeply committed to their religious traditions and to their own spirituality.

For a few, however, grace and other forms of daily prayer stand in contrast to lives that might not otherwise be described as especially devout. In some cases people maintain a routine of prayer in spite of being inactive in their religious communities. Grace Shoemaker currently finds her Episcopal parish less spiritually satisfying than the several other ways she is spiritually connected, but one bottom line is her nightly conversation with God.

Grace: Every night when I get in bed. That's when I do my praying.
[We asked: And what does that consist of?]
Grace: Mostly talking to God. Showing my gratitude, just being grateful for what I've had that day, whatever. If it was an ordinary day, just grateful for that. If it was a troubling day, sometimes I would say, "Thank you

God for the day, even though it was difficult, I'm sure something good will come of it."...Every night I thank God for my bed, that I have a place to sleep with blankets over me. I'm so grateful. You know, it could be the other way. I don't take anything for granted.

Charlotte McKenna, unlike Grace, has not been an active churchgoer for a very long time, nor does she describe herself as a spiritual person. Still, she was adamant that she has a personal relationship with God. "It is just in your mind, you are talking—just talking and just address God, you know it is like talking to God." When she is in the car and otherwise unbothered, she asks God to bless her work, and after praying she says she feels calm and in control. She wondered at length about the theology of prayer—how it works and just what sort of God she really believes in—but despite her doubts, this practice of carrying on a conversation with God is one she is likely to continue.

About as common as religiously inactive people who regularly pray, however, are the religiously active people who pray only sporadically. Some (especially the Evangelicals) expressed some guilt about not praying more often, but for many Catholics and Jews prayer is associated with the rhythms of the life-cycle and the ritual year, not with daily personal obligations—saying the rosary during Lent or the mourner's Kaddish prayers on the annual anniversary of a parent's death, perhaps. In addition, a few of our liberal Protestants were "social attenders" whose religious participation had little connection to any personal sense of spirituality. They were happy to participate in the songs and prayers of their churches but felt no need to extend the prayers into daily life.

Even those who pray infrequently may, of course, be prompted to petition God when life hits a crisis. As Hank Matthews's mother lay dying, he reached for sources he thought would comfort her (and himself) and drew on the prayers in his Episcopal *Book of Common Prayer*, especially the Psalms from the Bible. He concluded his oral diary one day, "I did pray with her....This time I'm pretty certain that she heard me." And the next day he recorded,

I did read to my mother again a few prayers and from the Psalter and just leafing through the Psalms, Psalm 100, and actually a portion of several others. And these writings, having been produced so long ago— the human condition I suppose doesn't change, because they spoke to the situation and are just as relevant now as when they were written.

Wendy Simmons is a fairly casual participant in Jewish life, but there have been times when she was sure she needed prayer. She told the story of facing uncertain surgery.

> This one priest used to come in all the time. He would always say hello
> to me. The night before my surgery, he came over to me, to wish me
> well. I asked him if he could pray for me. I said because it doesn't mat-
> ter. I believe there's only one God. I'm not saying he's a Christian God
> or he's a Jewish God. I believe in this force and I don't care if you're
> Muslim, if you're Jewish, if you're Christian. I don't care. If you could
> just pray to something up there!

Health crises often prompted spiritual practices that were not part of a
person's regular routine. Francis Parker, by contrast, already had an active
spiritual life when he was diagnosed with lung cancer, and his diaries during
those initial days were filled with talk about prayer.

> We do look to God, and we hope God will make this all go away, and
> one day we can look back and laugh about it. But right now we're
> not laughing, we're crying, and it hurts, you know it hurts; you know
> I don't want to be dead at fifty-five.... Every day I pray, and every day
> I hope that my prayers are answered.

Such "foxhole" prayers were common, but most of the people who told stories
about praying in a crisis also talked about praying at other times. Still, "Oh
Lord, get me through this" was perhaps the most common prayer we heard
about.[10]

In the chapters ahead, we will encounter prayer again and again. One does
not have to be a member of a specific spiritual tribe to have at least a rudimen-
tary acquaintance with the practice of prayer. Prayer seems to be a core element in the human experience of religion. Whatever form it takes, it expresses
the human action of reaching toward the divine—in gratitude, praise, or petition. It is also a primary way spirituality is carried from one place to another.
Hank prayed in his mother's hospital room, and Grace is grateful to God for
her warm bed. From the most private of spaces (a bed and blankets) to larger
family, work, leisure, health, and community spaces, people pray while they
are in those places, even if no one around them would be the wiser. They also
pray about what happens in those places even when they are somewhere else.
Asking whether their prayers are answered, whether bodies or communities
or jobs are materially changed, is beside the point. The point here is that the
narrative world in which these people live includes an ongoing conversation

with a divine Other. Just as we pay attention to the impact of human relationships across the domains of everyday life, we should attend to these conversations, as well.

What do people pray about? These spiritual conversations ranged across the many domains of everyday life, but they did not often include concerns for strangers or far-off troubles. The health, safety, and general well-being of one's immediate household, in fact, dominated the stories we heard about prayer. While some of our participants may hear a "prayer for the world" in their worship service, praying for the well-being of humanity and creation seems not to be a common individual spiritual practice. A couple of people mentioned praying that the world would become a "better place," and one woman mentioned praying for all the troubled children with whom she works, but these were rare exceptions to the larger pattern of intimate concern. As we will see, this does not mean that these people are unconcerned about the state of the world or that no one is involved in trying to make a difference—or even that they see activism as unconnected to their spiritual lives. What it does mean is that, for them, the spiritual practice of praying is more likely to concentrate the mind on the intimate world than on the global one.[11]

In all the situations we have seen so far, the prayers in question have been addressed to the Judeo-Christian deity, although Wendy Simmons was willing to stretch that to include the Muslim God or whatever other power might be out there to help her. Some of our Jewish participants, in fact, were not entirely sure they believe in the God to whom their prayers are addressed, but they pray anyway. People who have a more Extra-theistic sense of spirituality, by contrast, do not "pray" in the same way that these theist traditions have made common. They have no personified deity with whom to cultivate a personal relationship or of whom to ask favors. A few others did personalize the powers of the universe in nonmonotheistic ways, including multiple deities in their spiritual conversations. Such practices would, of course, be common in many parts of the world in many religious traditions. Shirley Knight, for instance, practices both daily prayer and occasional prayers of petition.

> Yeah, it's important to me every day to say "thank you" and "help me through this day." I feel an affinity for a lot of different—even the Eastern—deities, like Quan Yin and Ganesh. And I speak to them most every day on my way to work. And [Ganesh is] the god of everything beginning and ending, and he is the god of removing obstacles. So I ask him every day, especially since I've been trying to get this job,

just to help me to remove the obstacles that might keep me from getting the job.

She and her sister participants in the Neopagan group have names and images
for the divine powers they invoke, and they were as active in doing so as were
the Jews and Christians in our study. While Christian prayer dominates spiritual practice in the United States, those from other religious traditions are
adding their petitions to the mix.

Studying Scripture

Another very common survey measure of religious practice is the frequency
with which one reads the Bible. For most of our participants, however, that is
not a particularly good assessment of the spiritual things they do. Only conservative Protestants and Mormons are part of communities that expect them
to study scripture on a daily basis. It is part of being a member of these spiritual tribes. Even those who admit that they fall short know what the standard
is to which they are accountable. When Evangelicals are asked about religious
practices, their twin responses were often like Mary Margaret Sironi's: "I pray
every day. I read my Bible." Sometimes this is described as a conversation—
you speak to God in prayer, and God speaks to you through scripture. More
than two-thirds of the conservative Protestants in our study told stories about
their daily lives that included some sort of regular time with scripture, and a
couple of others said they read the Bible at least occasionally. The four who
did not talk about reading scripture were all among those who rarely attend
church. Going to an Evangelical church introduces and reinforces narratives
of piety that include daily Bible reading.

The same is true for the Latter-day Saints. Like conservative Protestants,
the religious community provides both encouragement and tools for individual scripture study. Catherine Young took a picture of her Book of Mormon
(see Figure 3.2) and explained to us that she gets guidance and inspiration
from a variety of authoritative Mormon sources:

> Daily scripture study also is really helpful, too.... There is the Book of
> Mormon, Doctrine and Covenants, and the Pearl of Great Price. So
> Doctrine and Covenants are a lot of the revelations that were given
> to Joseph Smith...so I do think the scriptures are really powerful and
> helping, they have been powerful in helping me understand.

FIGURE 3.2 "I'm really grateful for these scriptures."—Catherine Young

The stories of Mormon participants were laced throughout with references to routine scripture study as well as turning to scripture for guidance in making decisions. When Julia Oliva showed us the pictures she took, she included one in her bedroom.

> This is right next to my bed and the reason I took it is because the Book of Mormon is there and I really—I haven't been able to read it much this last few months, this last six months, but it feels so good to read that book. It gives me a different perspective. Regardless of if you're happy or sad, it is nice to be able to have some guidance, to be able to know that there is a God. And the way that the Book of Mormon is written is beautiful; it's very inspiring. And so I just wanted to show that is part of my life.

Like some of our evangelical participants, Julia had created a sacred space that centered on the physical presence of her book of scripture. Even when she fails to read as often as she thinks she should, that presence is a spiritual connection in itself.

No other traditions place scripture and individual study quite so centrally in their array of preferred practices. An Evangelical-style emphasis on the Bible was heard among some of the African American Protestant participants in our study, but mostly they tended to mirror the mainline Protestants and Catholics. Mainline Protestants have never left behind a theology that makes scripture central, but the advent of historical-critical interpretation and the legacy of defining themselves in opposition to literalist fundamentalists have considerably diminished the emphasis on Bible study in these churches.[12] The Catholic Church, of course, came late to the notion that lay people could or should read scripture on their own. Like mainline Protestants, our Catholic participants often voiced a sense of incompetence in the face of a book they know to be historically and theologically complicated. If mainline Protestants, Catholics, and Jews were involved in scripture study at all, it was as likely to be in a group as individually.

Among both the liberal Christians and the Jews in our study, individual reading of scripture was an expression of extraordinary individual spiritual commitment, rather than adherence to religious norms (see Table 3.1). The minority who placed spiritual engagement high on their personal agendas did spend time with scripture, while the typical members did not. Theresa Collins, for instance, has a daily routine that includes an evening reading from *Forward Day by Day*, an Episcopal publication that includes meditations on designated Bible verses for each day. She also reads "one or two Psalms, and I say my evening prayers and that completes my daily spiritual routine." During Lent, she noted in her diary that she had added to that evening routine.

I started reading the Gospels during Lent this year and I'm continuing. I don't always read the Bible every day. But I've decided to try and read

Table 3.1 Effects of Spiritual Salience on Routine Scripture Study among Active Participants by Religious Tradition

	Percentage Who Told at Least One Story about Their Routine Scripture Study (number of persons)	
	Moderately Spiritually Engaged	Highly Spiritually Engaged
Mainline and African American Protestant, Catholic, and Jewish	13% (23)	25% (12)
Conservative Protestant and Mormon	83% (6)	92% (13)

the Gospels again. I read Mark in Lent because it was shortest, and now I'm reading John, and then I'm going to read Matthew and Luke, and then after that I think I'd like to read a book about the apostles themselves who wrote those Gospels.

Her combination of devotional reading and reading for knowledge about her tradition was echoed in occasional stories we heard from Jewish participants, as well. As we have seen, Sam Levitt is one of those people for whom religious and spiritual pursuits are important, and he eagerly reported that Torah study was something he loved. During the time he was recording his oral diaries, his rabbi asked him to lead a study of the weekly Torah portion one Sabbath. He told us, "Whenever you teach you have to learn something ahead of time. So I did, not only read the Torah portion but read several commentaries on it." Like liberal Protestants and Catholics, Sam rejects literal readings of scripture and values knowledge about the historical context out of which the writings have come. Torah is a sacred object of devotion, but more than that, it is a source of insight into life.

The rare nonreligious or nonspiritual persons who mentioned reading holy texts said they did so to seek insight. Steve Sims is unaffiliated, and he had no use for the Bible at all. "When you speak of the Bible, especially the New Testament, that's been interpreted 200 some odd different ways. I can't believe in a book—and live my life by a book." He has, however, been exploring Buddhist teachings.[13] "I've taken up reading, um, verses from a book called *Everyday Mind*, which is 366 reflections on the Buddhist path." He finds them "amazingly true," he said, in their call to recognize "our need to be more compassionate towards humankind and towards nature and towards every other thing." Steve is unusual, however. For the most part people who are disconnected from religious traditions simply do not include attention to any sort of scripture in their everyday lives.

Beyond Prayer and Bible Study

This is roughly where the surveys stop. "Religious practices" are measured in terms of prayer—which is indeed a widespread practice that crosses many religious lines—and the study of scripture, which is far more circumscribed as a normative practice. When we opened the door for people to tell us their own stories, however, the range of activities they included was enormous. People told us, on average, eight stories about things they do, either occasionally or with some regularity, that are for them ways of connecting with a spiritual dimension in life.

Some of those practices are specific to a particular religious tradition and not shared outside that community. The best example of that might be the Latter-day Saints practice of wearing "garments," a piece of sacred clothing worn next to the skin in a way that reminds believers of their sacred commitments, especially the commitment to their marriage. Three of the five Mormons we interviewed talked about this practice, and the other two probably would have if we had initially realized that this is a subject that would require prompting. Similarly but more visibly, observant Jewish and Muslim men and women, like members of many other religious communities, wear distinctive clothing that signals their devotion—yarmulkes, hijab, turbans, and more. The Reform and Conservative Jews in our study wore special items only during prayer times or synagogue services, if at all, but for many religious people modes of dress are a constant reminder of their relationship to a community and to a spiritual power beyond themselves.[14]

Other practices we heard about had to do with what one does and does not eat. Mormons have strict dietary rules that prohibit caffeine and alcohol and encourage healthy eating. The Jews in our study did not keep strictly kosher diets, but all of them had wrestled with whether and how much of that regime they would follow. Even if they do not fully observe Sabbath rules, they were likely to plan a special meal for Friday night.[15] And a few of our Christian respondents (both Catholic and Protestant) mentioned various forms of fasting undertaken, especially during Lent. African American Baptist Stephen James told us,

> For the last few years we've fasted during Lent, so determining what you give up—And I remember big discussions about why do it, and what type of spirit you have to put into it. Is it really about giving something up, or is it about taking the time each day to spend thinking instead of eating? Using that time to pray.

Mary Hage, who is Catholic, noted in the diary she recorded during Holy Week, "I am trying to observe the Friday—not just Good Friday—but the Friday abstinence of not eating meat, and I've done perfectly well with that." As with clothing practices, food practices are widespread across the world's religions, and about a dozen of our participants noted at least some time in their lives when decisions about how to eat were spiritual decisions more than simply matters of budget, taste, and health.[16]

Clothing and food are among the most common sites for the practice of distinctive religious disciplines, but at least a few traditions also have something to say about money. The Muslim zakat, the Jewish and Christian tithe, and many forms of ritual offering mark the giving of money as a valued spiritual tradition. The Mormons in our study were the most likely to mention tithing as one of their spiritual practices, but it also showed up among a few conservative and African American Protestants. A few other participants also talked about how they spend their money as a spiritual discipline. Melissa Parker's historic Black church emphasizes both tithing and "good stewardship" of the rest of one's money.

> As far as raising children, my kids don't ask for crazy stuff like a hundred dollar tennis shoes, I mean that's just stupid. . . . I guess it's as we get older, going through some rough times, and we're learning how to be good stewards.

Tithing and being a good steward are among the religiously specific practices on the list. Where a religious community teaches these practices, at least some of its members incorporate them into their lives.

Meditation

Most of the practices we have described so far are predominantly Judeo-Christian, theist activities that typically assume some sort of personal deity. Meditation, on the other hand, requires no such divine conversation partner. Although practices of meditation may include focusing on the presence of a particular deity or saint, meditation is often an expression of Extra-theistic spirituality. Stories we heard told of spending a period of quiet contemplation, placing life in perspective, or tapping into the powers of the universe or of one's own inner being. Stories about meditation came from across the religious spectrum, even, occasionally, from otherwise nonspiritual participants.

Yoga classes were a common setting for these meditation stories. Debates rage over whether yoga is merely a form of exercise, a Hindu religious practice, or perhaps a spiritual hybrid of some sort. Some yoga classes are offered in sports clubs where the spiritual associations are downplayed or nonexistent, while at the other end of the spectrum Hindu advocates argue for "taking back" the tradition, and fundamentalist Christians warn their followers that the practice is inherently Hindu and can corrupt their Christian faith.[17] In the middle are hundreds of thousands of yoga devotees who appreciate the mixture of physical and spiritual, meditation and relaxation that they experience. Many classes are actually offered in Christian religious spaces, and even if the church thinks it is simply renting to a friendly tenant, the space itself often shapes the way the practice is taught.[18]

Whatever else it may be, then, yoga *can* be a spiritual practice, and a handful of our participants (two Catholics, two Jews, a liberal Protestant, and two who are unaffiliated)—none of whom claimed any other prayer practice—talked about yoga as part of their spiritual repertoire. They all appreciated the meditative side of their yoga classes, but it is also fair to say that exercise and stress relief were as much a part of the picture as spiritual engagement. Ericka Lombardi certainly embodied these multilayered meanings. She is deeply steeped in Catholic traditions and connections but is also resolute in claiming her own unbelief, lack of spirituality, and alienation from the Church. She is also a regular yoga practitioner.

> I do a meditative class that's once a week. So I use that kind of as a prayer time. Not in any formal way and not for very long, but I don't, I don't consider my yoga practice to be particularly spiritual but I would like to find a way to do that.

Yoga is important enough to her that she took pictures of the studio where she takes her class and of her yoga materials at home (see Figure 3.3). She talked about reading a yoga journal, recounted how she and her husband used to do "deep meditation" in the evenings before bed, and filled her diaries with stories about her various classes and instructors. The porous boundaries between her Catholic heritage and her yoga practice were especially apparent in a story she recorded in her diary:

> On New Year's weekend we, my husband and I, had gone to the Kripalu Center in the Berkshires, the yoga center. We spent a long New Year's weekend there doing a Thai for two, Thai yoga massage for couples retreat.... The Kripalu Center is an old Jesuit seminary, so it's kind of funny, 'cause it's this new AAG yoga Eastern retreat center, but there's a statue of St. Francis in the back...and just the way things are structured to be a sacred space—and the largest room, meeting room, which is where the Thai couple massage was, is where had clearly been the chapel at one point in time. So it felt...very spiritual and it was such a bonding time for us and the other couples.

No one else was quite that serious about their yoga practice, but for a few people yoga's physical poses and deep breathing were moments in which the link between body and spirit was experienced.

FIGURE 3.3 "This is the yoga studio. It's a bad feng shui place cause it faces a cemetery, [but] it's not something that scares me."—Ericka Lombardi

Other, less structured forms of meditation made appearances, as well. Otherwise nonspiritual people and the members of the Neopagan group recounted meditating more than members of traditional Christian and Jewish religious communities did. The numbers are, however, small. Despite popular press that might suggest everyone is meditating over the lunch hour, only about a third of our participants mentioned anything resembling meditation, and for about half of those it was much more a casual exercise than a habitual routine. Samantha Bailey, a member of the Neopagan group, was more serious than most. When asked how she makes important decisions, she said, "A lot of meditation. Again, it's that inner voice. If you're quiet enough and if you listen then it will guide you." She and others spoke about the group's sacred space as a site for meditation, as well. Nonreligious Steve Sims had adopted a secular meditation regimen.

> I found when I meditated and controlled my breathing and kind of trained my thought processes, and rethought things and got my energy focused in the right direction through meditation, then I found I could settle myself. Basically mind over matter. I could overcome the negative stuff.

Most nonreligious participants had *neither* prayer nor meditation routines; but for a few, the disciplines of meditation and yoga provided opportunities to explore an internal spirituality that promised insight, life meaning, and many of the positive effects often attributed to prayer.

Meditation, however, was not simply in the purview of people who have left (or never had) a religious tradition. Some of the most dedicated conventionally religious people talked about "meditation" as a way to describe the parts of their praying that involved "listening" rather than speaking. Pam Jones talked about commuting time as a site for her routine spiritual practices, where she can "talk to the Lord, say my prayers, think about things, meditate." Joshua Roberts, like Pam part of an African American religious community, talked about "that little small voice that's inside that you hear while you're meditating or while you're praying." The notion of meditating was simply incorporated into spiritual practices of praying.

For most people, in fact, meditation and praying were not mutually exclusive. The *most* committed churchgoers and people who think *only* in Theistic terms told relatively few stories that involved practices of meditation. What they practice is prayer, not meditation. People with understandings of spirituality that drew on both Theistic and Extra-theistic discourses, on the other hand, were the most likely to talk about meditation. Episcopal parishioner Grace Shoemaker, for example, has aspirations about meditating but continually falls short. "I always say every day, today I'm going to sit down and meditate, but I never do it," she confessed in our initial conversation. Later, in one of her diary entries, however, she told this story:

> I haven't been sleeping well. And after I did my little bit of praying last night, I went into a meditation and just let my mind flow, and I was able to fall asleep so much easier and I slept so much better last night.

The practice of meditating (or praying) is, for people like this, an occasional experiment. It is not something they have spent much time learning or perfecting, but it is seen as a positive activity to be adopted from time to time. Mainline Protestants and liberal Catholics and Jews experience few barriers within their traditions that would prevent adopting meditation, yoga, or other practices that are widely available in American culture. Those who do branch out largely add new practices rather than dropping old ones.

Music and the Spirit

When people talk about meditating, they often speak of it as "quiet time," or time to quiet the mind. It is almost always something they do alone and in a private space at home (unless they are taking a yoga class). It may involve a special place and special positioning of the body, and some people use candles or adjust the lighting to set the scene, as well. A number of people also mentioned the importance of music. Like meditation, listening to music is a practice that crosses theological and spiritual lines. Alexis Nouvian, an Atlanta Presbyterian with an eclectic range of practices said, "Music is a way really, that I've been using to get to God lately, and meditation; I'm working on it." James Dupree would certainly agree. His is a full spiritual life grounded in his participation at Grimsby Congregational but also including an Eckhart Tolle[19] CD he routinely listens to and his professional and personal musical activities. Speaking of one of his own favorite musicians, he said,

> He has the ability to take Gregorian chant now and make it modern. So he's like my role model for writing music. So every morning, I put his CD on. I look forward to it actually.... I light the candles, get out, maybe make a fire if it's cold, I look forward to it. Those are all I consider very important practices of the morning 'cause Gregory Norbert's stuff goes right to the heart of things.

Music plays a role during the day, as well. "If I'm driving, I keep on trying to come back to God in my heart. I sing little songs—'I've got peace within me,' or whatever little song in my head." Listening to music is both an accompaniment for other practices and a practice in itself. When individuals seek connection to something deeper, something beyond the ordinary, something they identify as spiritual, they sometimes find a quiet place and put on a CD.

The music that connects people to the divine is often in a more public setting. Some of our participants freely confessed that the best thing about going to church was the music, music that provides the spiritual uplift they seek. William Pullinger, now at Grimsby Congregational, was blunt: "Music is terribly important to us, and that's one of the reasons we changed churches." It is the music of an excellent choir and organ that he readily named as the most memorable thing about a typical service. When we asked Francine Worthington, from nearby All Saints Episcopal, what if anything reminds her of God, she said, "I hear and see God in beautiful music. That these incredible masses—the spiritual music at Christmas and Easter—are just unparalleled, and these composers are certainly gifted, given a gift and commissioned, often by the Church. So, I see the hand of God in that." Sacred music sometimes connects even a relatively alienated Jew, like Sylvia Carter to her tradition. "There are certain prayers I like, I guess just because I like the tune of them."

People with no special attachment to any religious tradition occasionally talked about playing or listening to music as something spiritual for them, as well. Steve Sims recorded a story in his diary about just such an experience:

> I went to a concert performance by Badly Drawn Boy…at a place called Center Stage in Atlanta last night, and it was a really phenomenally good show. I am a pretty big music fan. I love all types of music, and I think music is the universal language. I also think it brings us a level of joy that very few things bring to the table like it. I had that experience last night.

Alex Polani is more than a fan; he is himself a musician. His "day job" is teaching in schools, but it is performing that he loves. Describing his decision to major in music, he said, "Music was the only thing that literally sent a shiver down my spine. I felt like this is what I got to do with my life. And so I kind of went with it." When someone is doing what they are meant to do, he said, it is like they are "in a zone. It's almost like spiritual alignment with that purpose. And I think that when I am on a stage playing music with something that's inspiring, it's like what I am meant to do. Time stops; you know what I mean?"

Neither Steve nor Alex is religious in conventional terms, but each intentionally seeks out musical experiences they describe in transcendent language, experiences that connect them with the purposes of the universe and a sense of joy. The communities in which the experience happens are transient and not all focused on a common spiritual goal; they are only marginally "spiritual tribes." The spiritual meaning is individually imputed, even if it still requires a collective to produce.[20] Practices like these are largely described in Extratheistic terms of awe and meaning-making that allow the person to open up to something beyond the self. Arts of various sorts are widely interpreted in such spiritual terms. Bender (2010) writes about art as one of the spheres of cultural production in which the perceived link between spirituality and creativity is produced and maintained.[21] She describes a variety of occasions in which the "new metaphysicals" of Cambridge, who were her subject of study, intentionally blurred the line between performance and worship, where producing and experiencing artistic creations was governed both by the conventions of the art world and by expectations clearly religious in character. Unlike her participants but like the American public, our population includes many more theists than metaphysicals. The theists among our participants also talked about experiences of aesthetic transcendence, but they were much more likely to use the terms supplied by their traditions, chief among them discourses about God's creation and "gifts" of beauty and human creativity. What the extratheists have adopted is a language recognized beyond the churches and synagogues, a normative vocabulary about beauty and creativity that can describe practices and experiences they value and pursue.

The Spiritual Cornucopia

When invited to speak broadly about spiritual things they do, our participants told stories that went far beyond the usual checklist. Both theists and extratheists reached within and beyond whatever traditions they knew best to engage in practices they found meaningful. All kinds of everyday activities could be sacralized, and not-so-ordinary experiences and rituals from across the religious spectrum were sometimes adopted into people's repertoire of practices. Here is just a sampling.

- A few mentioned times when dead ancestors have served as spiritual guides for them.[22]
- Others have living spiritual counselors, a practice institutionalized in some traditions as "spiritual direction."[23]
- Jessica Kingman recalled her pilgrimage to Medadgorje and took her recorder to Lourdes to record diary entries for our project during her pilgrimage.[24] Others intentionally include visits to shrines when they travel.
- Some have set up sacred images in their homes to create a space for meditation or worship.[25]
- A few keep a journal that helps them focus their spiritual thoughts.[26]
- Some have participated in healing rituals for themselves and others.[27]
- Many wear a cross or other religious symbol as an intentional way to remind themselves of what is most important.
- Jessica Fletcher (a young conservative Protestant) has a tattoo depicting a stained glass window,[28] and Melissa Parker is growing dreadlocks, a process that she describes as a "spiritual journey."

These are practices that can be shaped to fit either a Theistic spirituality or an Extra-theistic one. They exist in a fertile boundary zone where spiritualities meet. Most tended to be mentioned by only two or three people in our study, although most are common enough in American society to have thousands of practitioners and ample visibility in scholarly and popular literature. They spread through networks of friends, mass communication, and religious communities themselves, allowing individuals to dip into this vast reservoir to adopt particular habits that allow them their own paths to spiritual connection. Institutions of all sorts are providing content and structure, but individuals are taking the initiative to choose the activities they will adopt, activities that may introduce them to new spiritual tribes.

Extra-theistic Spiritual Practices

Some practices appeared only in the stories of people whose orientation is predominantly Extra-theistic. Some were about the experience of awe, but more often what is sought is insight and a sense of meaning. People of virtually every spiritual persuasion sometimes linked spiritual practices to meaning, purpose, and direction in their lives, but pursuing wholeness and coherence was what religiously unaffiliated people often said they were doing. Practices of centering and meditation were often articulated as efforts to place life in perspective and find its meaning (or at least to figure out a way through a difficulty). Alicia Waters, who describes herself as not at all spiritual, reported one day in her diary, "I also spent an hour and a half at the health club swimming, which was relaxing and nurturing, and helped me think through how I was going to approach [a problem]." Equally irreligious Daphne LeCompte described her car as "sacred" and her commuting time as meditative. Mundane routines of swimming or commuting can become "set apart" ways to get beyond the stresses and problems of the moment to something deeper, to some insight about how to live.

Figuring out how to live and what life means is, of course, often done within the context of a religious community and its stories. The focus on individual life meaning is certainly not absent among those with a Theistic spirituality, but it is a much greater preoccupation among people who think of spirituality in other terms. Not only do they stretch the definition of spirituality in new directions, but they were also likely to include practices that might not at first seem spiritual. Rebecca Klein rarely attends religious services, but she also rarely misses her daily soak in the hot tub. "It's like my meditation...I get in that water and I feel like I'm reborn every day," she said. It is a time for interior insight, where she gets "fabulous ideas." Disaffected Catholic Larry Waugh recounted, "I do acupuncture, and when I'm doing that I kind of meditate, and I'm always thinking, and you know...feeling energy coming in, abundant and healthy and alive and prosperous and all these things."

Physical practices like these were not nearly so common as more cerebral approaches to a search for meaning. People who were not involved in any religious community could nevertheless seek religious and spiritual ideas through books, CDs, the internet, and occasionally television. Carolyn Horton's story of her religious journey was typical.

> I continued to really study Zen on my own and think about Zen as sort of my central organizing principle. Then, when I was closer to thirty I started thinking about—I read some feminist theology kind of books, revisionist history kind of—the "patriarchy is new, women used to run the world" kind of books. And I got real interested in paganism and old religions and what that stuff is about. And went to Charis Books a lot and poked around in the religion and philosophy section. And again, I never really joined a group, but I just dabbled in it for a little while and thought of that as my organizing central principle for a while. And now I don't know, I just don't really have—I don't really identify with any one religion. I've sort of picked and chosen from a lot of them.

Her picking and choosing has largely been from the bookshelves of her local bookstores.

Reading has been a spiritual practice for her, although she described it more as a continuing journey than a discipline.[29] Emma Cooper identified her local library as a source of spiritual resources (see Figure 3.4), and Lily Mattison was eloquent in describing her graduate studies as themselves a regular spiritual pursuit.

> Things that I think are spiritual, that I do every day? Like, I go to class, and I write papers, and I think out thoughts on how I see the world really working. And I think that's being very in touch with God. And I think reading books is such a spiritual act, because you're in the mind of somebody else. It's finding unity with something, and very meaningful for me.

Diving into a world of books and ideas, including ideas about the spiritual nature of the universe, is the way some otherwise nonreligious people find a sense of meaning in life.

The spiritual reading most people do is less intense than what either Lily or Carolyn are describing. The more typical pattern we observed was

FIGURE 3.4 "This is the library.... Study and literature are important to me personally and professionally and spiritually."—Emma Cooper

an occasional curiosity that drove some of our nonreligious participants to books about religion. Most could name several things they had read in recent years—*The Art of Happiness* by the Dalai Lama, Harold Kushner's *When Bad Things Happen to Good People*, Christopher Hitchens's *God Is Not Great*, among others. Some involved exploration of traditions other than the ones they grew up with. Steve Sims is reading Buddhist sayings every day, and Daphne LeCompte listens to CDs from Lama Surya Das. Rebecca Klein values the knowledge that comes from her Jewish tradition and reads Jewish sources fairly regularly on her own. Jonathan Snow is an eclectic collector of wise sayings and said, "I don't read a Bible or anything, but I really like looking through the quotations. It reminds me of the things that I do believe in."

Unlike people who are a regular part of a religious community and read scripture and other sources together, the vast majority of the spiritual reading reported by these people is done alone. But like the other eclectic practices engaged by unaffiliated people, that does not mean that these practices are utterly "individual." Recommendations may come through friendship networks or through other reading and media consumption, and there may be occasional conversations precipitated by the reading. The books they read are often in wide cultural circulation, and knowing about them allows readers to join that cultural conversation. Books on the *New York Times* bestseller list are culturally marked as acceptable reading, their spiritual content legitimated for readers who wish not to be thought of as religious. In the world of bookstores and popular literature, the boundaries between sacred and secular are blurred sufficiently to allow nonreligious persons to explore this terrain with some cultural safety.

Reading, of course, is not just something nonreligious people do. The most devout religious people named various forms of religious reading and other media consumption just as often as did the unaffiliated. Many of our religiously active participants read books as an important avenue for spiritual growth and challenge. Although we specifically asked about television, the internet, and other media, not many of our participants included these other media in the stories of their spiritual lives. No one claimed to be a regular consumer of religious TV shows. A couple of members of Boston's evangelical Centre Street Church talked about listening to early morning Christian radio, and Mary Hage, an Atlanta Catholic, said that she listens to Christian talk radio in her car when she is commuting. Although we recruited four of our participants through a religious internet chat room, Victoria Edwards was the only one of them who defined the web as part of her spiritual practice.[30] She told us the story about how she started her blog.

> There has got to be Catholic bloggers out there who actually talk about their real lives and actually get upset about stuff and don't hide behind this cloak of piousness or Republican politics. There's got to be other people out there like me, right? That was sort of my thought. And at some point I was like, there are none. How terrible. I'll have to start one. So I think part of it—like I started [this site] because—'cause I felt like I wanted to read something like that.

Clearly the internet is awash in religious and spiritual content, and a variety of recent research has begun to document and analyze just what spirituality looks like when mediated through the web (Brasher 2001; Lovheim 2004). Among most of our participants, however, an occasional Google search for religious information was the only spiritual connection being made.

Ethical Spirituality in Practice

Just as there are practices shaped by Theistic and Extra-theistic spiritualities, so too there are practices shaped by Ethical spirituality. As we noted in the previous chapter, a moral focus is common in talk about spirituality across the religious spectrum, and it is present in practices, as well. To reach beyond one's own interests and to act with compassion was a spiritual discipline for some of our participants. A quarter of them talked about a regular routine in their life that expressed Ethical spirituality, and another quarter told at least one story about some specific act of kindness that was described as a spiritual act. Phyllis Carrigan was one of the former. She is a middle-aged member of St. Sabina's Catholic parish in Boston, and she was struggling financially when we met her; but she mused, you "can't out-give God." Her spiritual discipline for the Lenten season was to turn her own anxiety about work into good deeds for others. John Tavisano told several stories about the people he visits as part of his parish's St. Vincent de Paul Society. "Spiritually," he said, "making these home visits.... It is something to be able to talk with these people at length and understand their problems and be of assistance and try to do God's work and help them."

The Catholic tradition has provided John and Phyllis with models of this sort of spirituality (think Mother Teresa). It teaches social principles to its children and sustains vast charitable organizations like the St. Vincent de Paul Society, which can channel the charitable impulses it encourages. The Jewish tradition is equally focused on doing good in the world. A theology of *tikkun* (repair of the world) is pervasive in American Judaism and encourages Jews to do deeds of kindness and justice as an expression of their devotion. Stories like this were not absent in what we heard from Protestants, but they were not quite so common.

Practices of love and charity were the most common of these moral spiritual practices, but there were also stories that involved more active efforts to attack the roots of the world's ills. We will explore the whole range of charitable and political action in more depth in Chapter Seven, but it is important here to note the degree to which such activities are, for some, spiritual practices, even for people not otherwise spiritually or religiously engaged. The clearest example is Robin Mitchell. She is involved in a number of political causes and active on the board of GLAD (Gay & Lesbian Advocates & Defenders), which won the marriage case in Massachusetts. Talking about that work, she said, "It's all about, for me, trying to capture some of the passion I feel about the world and activism and whatnot."

This work for her community is a passionate commitment for her and not unlike the practices others named as spiritual. Emma Cooper made the connection directly, saying, "But that, to me, is like a religious mission, and so it's like the stuff that I write to my representatives about, I would have to say, comes out of my spiritual convictions. Like, I'm always writing on women's issues and civil liberties and environmental stuff and all of that. These are spiritual values to me."

Similarly, several of the Catholics, mainline Protestants, and Jews who are disconnected from their religious communities and not especially interested in other spiritual pursuits nevertheless found Ethical spiritual practices to their liking. For Carlos Fernandez, the important thing about spirituality is

> how you live your life and the things that you do. Lately I felt I wanted to get more involved with what the Catholic Church is doing and one of things that found me more involved was the AIDS Ministry....I thought that if I could have sort of an active role in the community in doing something useful, as opposed to just going to church, that I would feel much better about, you know, going to church.

For him, a spirituality of activism actually served as a bridge to a more traditional practice of attending church. For others it was more a remnant of a tradition they no longer embraced. Practices of everyday compassion and justice are another of the places where sacred and secular blend and where actively religious and disaffected people often meet on common ethically spiritual ground.

The Places of Devotion

The public face of an activist spirituality stands apart from most of the other practices we have seen. Most stories about spiritual practice are framed primarily in terms of a private relationship between the person and a deity, a conversation that often takes place silently in the mind and spirit of the person. But even those conversations have material dimensions. They take place in physical spaces, are enacted by human bodies, involve material objects. Most of the stories we have noted have been situated at home, often in the most private spaces of the home—the bedroom and even the bed itself. Many also take place around the dining table. Spiritual practices situated in intimate places are not especially surprising, but the physical and material shape of spiritual practice does not end there.

One of the most surprising "sacred spaces" we heard about was the interior of an automobile. Recall Daphne LeCompte's declaration that her car is sacred space and Charlotte McKenna's assertion that her car is where she is otherwise unbothered and can carry on a conversation with God. When we asked Francis Parker if he had a special place where he liked to pray, he said, "It's in my car. That's because I have an extra forty-five minutes to work and forty-five minutes back from work. That gives me that time to reflect and start to talk to God." And Samantha Bailey actually took a picture for us of the CD player in her car, saying, "I'll go in my car and drive and listen to music. And, you know, begin this creative process that really kind of brings me back to, um, center, I think.... We listen to a lot of music at the house, but this kind of meditation doesn't happen unless I'm in the car." A good deal has been written about the attachments people have to their cars (Gardner and Abraham 2007) and about the sense of privacy and autonomy they engender (Siren and Hakamies-Blomqvist 2005). Ethicists have preached against the environmental and cultural harm cars can do.[31] What few have noted, however, is that the car might be a sacred space. It might almost be described as "liminal," an in-between space where one is transformed from family member to worker and back again, a place where other activities and relationships are suspended as the driver negotiates often-familiar terrain. It may be a space for anticipatory thinking (e.g., Charlotte's prayers over an upcoming job or Samantha's getting into a creative mode) or for consolidating insight (as in Francis's reflecting about his life). Even watching the changing seasons in the passing landscape can engender a larger spiritual perspective on life.

Watching the changing seasons and wondering at the beauty of the outdoors was integral to the spiritual practices of several of our participants. Jennifer Hammond is a busy mother and not very involved in her Congregationalist Church at the moment, but she looked back on her pre-mother days and said, "When I was walking it was meditation.... Walking indoors on a treadmill doesn't get me there.... I am always amazed when I take a walk at what's around us. What was created. And so that kind of helps center you, I think, and gives you some calm." Nature is so central for the Neopagan group that their ritual space is located outdoors. But perhaps the most interesting outdoor spiritual practice we heard about came from seeker Alex Polani, who combines meditation and mountain biking. "So it's interesting to note that I've found an enthusiastic mountain biker like myself who is also into Eastern philosophy, meditation, and all that other stuff. It's like synchronicity, but we've actually decided to mountain bike while meditating together and we're actually planning on doing silent rides."

Nature is both a location and an inspiration for the spiritual practices of more than a third of our participants. They enjoy outdoor activity, but they use that activity to turn their attention away from the mundane worries of life toward the beauty and complexity around them (see Figure 3.5). Whether a hike in nearby woods in the fall, a trip to a spectacular natural location, or working in their own gardens, our participants perceived that when they were "in nature," the barriers between them and the divine were lowered. When they wanted to get in touch with the spiritual dimensions of the world, they often went outside.[32]

As these stories suggest, both place and embodiment are part of the spiritual story. Spiritual practices often happened in the midst of exercise routines (including, as we already saw, yoga classes). Jessica Wilson is a student and a member of Deer Valley Church in Atlanta. She lamented, "I really try to exercise; I can't do that every day anymore, but as much as I can. And sometimes that is my quiet time. Every lap I swim I pray for somebody else, or something, you know." Her fellow evangelical church member, Debbie Rogers, is a walker and described Jesus as "right there walking with me."[33] John Travisano

FIGURE 3.5 "You're just happy to be alive and just totally living on the edge."—Bill Hamilton

is retired and likes to run five miles a day. He noted in one of his diary entries, "I've been finding out lately that when I run or jog I shut my radio off that I usually listen to while I run or jog. And, uh, I say prayers. I also have been doing the rosary that way. It seems to keep me in touch with God." Hiking, biking, swimming, and other physical exertions were on the list of spiritual practices, but so was belly dancing.[34] Emma Cooper described it as

> an improvisational form, so it's about being totally in the moment and opening up your spirit to receive the music which then expresses itself as movement through your body. So it's interaction of your body and your spirit with the music and with the energy around you, whether it's an audience or just your cats.

Exercise was not the only way spiritual practices were embodied, however. Sam Levitt spoke of "davening," his Jewish tradition of prayer that involves standing and swaying. A few Christians—primarily the most pious Evangelicals, Mormons, and Catholics—reported that their prayer included getting on their knees. In fact, four of the five Mormons we interviewed specifically described at least one prayer time each day that involved the whole family kneeling together. Undoubtedly many of our Catholic participants routinely make the sign of the cross and genuflect, but these nearly unconscious gestures did not make their way into the narratives they related to us.[35] Throughout the world and throughout history, people have gestured toward the heavens and bowed bodies to the earth in devotion to their gods. Only about one in six of the people in our sample told a story about these kinds of sacred postures, but prostration and physical praise are commonplace in American culture and beyond. Muslims bow deeply on a prayer rug in whatever spaces they can find (Smith and Bender 2004), and many formerly staid Evangelicals have learned to use uplifted hands as a visible sign of devotion. The notion that one might embody a prayer is not likely to disappear.

The materiality of spiritual practice extends beyond the body to encompass spaces, clothing, and a variety of other objects, as well. Sam Levitt keeps handy his traditional Jewish prayer shawls and the *tefillin* that he straps on for his davening. Amelia James talked excitedly about her new rosary. She is just learning the ways of her Catholic faith, and she reported in her diary that "a friend had given me a little package…with rosary beads and some other religious articles for me to use to get started on becoming more religious. I look forward to praying the rosary every night." Jessica Kingman is much further along in her Catholic faith journey and has a long list of spiritual practices, many of which take tangible as well as spiritual form. The story she recounted in one of her diary entries illustrates just how materially entangled prayer can be, even into cyberspace.

> I have been doing a novena, which is a prayer to a particular saint called Saint Rita…asking for her to intercede. And her name is Saint Rita of the Impossible. This morning I received two emails from co-workers that normally I don't really share any strong religious beliefs with, but both of them emailed me something, with a picture, about Saint Rita.… It prompted me to call a friend of mine who I've had on my list of asking Saint Rita to intercede for, and I told her that I'd been praying for her.… I told her about the picture.

They shared the image via the internet and marveled that the woman they saw reflected the very saint whose presence they felt with them. Computers, office mates, and illnesses intertwine here with the practice of praying a novena. Catholicism is certainly not the only religious tradition with such a visible and material sacred world, but it is among the most enthusiastically material of the traditions prevalent in the United States.[36]

Attending Religious Services

Everyday spiritual practices are shaped in myriad ways by the organized religious communities to which people are (or have been) attached, and for many of them "going to church" is a spiritual practice in itself. "Of course going to church," said Dr. Stephen James about his spiritual disciplines. "That's why I carve out my Sundays where I don't work on Sunday." Going to mass every day is just one of the many spiritual practices in Jessica Kingman's life, but it is an important one. Rachel Halpern was clear that the temple was part of her family's Sabbath and holiday observances. "We go to temple every Friday night, if not both of us, at least me definitely. If Josh can't go, that doesn't mean I don't go." Laura Henderson reflected in her diary that when Samhain (the Neopagan new year festival that falls on October 31) is in the middle of the week, they have to schedule their ritual observance on the weekend. "So we actually did our circle group and had our ritual on Sunday night, and it was probably one of the strongest, most wonderful Samhain rituals that I've ever been to." Emma Cooper was doing oral diaries then, too, and she agreed. "It was very magical. We had a very strong circle and really gave the wheel a good turning."

Unlike the daily practices of praying, studying scripture, meditating, and the like, attending services is often a family activity, done with spouse and/or children. And for religiously affiliated people with few other spiritual inclinations, this may be the primary spiritual practice in their lives. They make it to religious services with some regularity but expressed few if any other interests in spirituality. For most of our participants, service attendance is spiritual practice and religious obligation at the same time, with a good-sized dollop of social congregating, aesthetic pleasure, and family bonding thrown in for good measure. As we will see in the next chapter, whether the individual named service attendance as a spiritual practice is not the critical question. The amount and character of participation is far more important. Still, it is worth reminding ourselves that when asked about spiritual practices, participating in organized religion is a part of the picture.

Summing Up—Modes of Spiritual Practice

The everyday lives of the Americans who participated in this project were neither completely saturated by nor devoid of spiritual activity. The degree of their spiritual interest and engagement varied from nearly (but not quite) non-existent to intense levels of interest and activity. The group we might call "spiritually engaged" describe themselves as spiritual people and cultivate a long list of activities aimed at seeking spiritual connections. How spiritually active our participants were was not a product of age or gender or income or education, but it was strongly connected to how active they were in their religious communities. The more often they attend services and other activities, the more stories they told about individual practices beyond the religious community. But it was not just a matter of more and less. The particular religious communities of which people were a part provided a repertoire of practices and expectations—family prayer among Mormons, scripture study among conservative Protestants, and social activist forms of spirituality among Catholics, for instance. People in spiritual tribes with tightly defined Theistic spiritualities tended to be moderately active in the practices typical of their community. They stand in contrast to those who use only Extra-theistic images, who tended to live in more diffuse spiritual tribes, less often involved in an organized religious community and drawing more randomly on practices available in the culture. They are simply less active in any spiritual practices at all.

The most spiritually active, however, were people who speak in both Theistic and Extra-theistic spiritual images, drawing on what their particular tradition has provided for them, but also reaching beyond. Cynthia Gardner is just such a person. She is highly committed to a spiritual journey and has experimented with a fairly broad array of spiritual practices. She is also deeply involved in her Episcopal Church, so much so that she is participating in the Education for Ministry program (which trains lay leaders) and is thinking about exploring an ordained vocation as a deacon. Her involvement at All Saints has been an important part of her life for the time she has lived in Massachusetts, and it has connected her with a wide array of spiritual opportunities, including retreats, events at the nearby Episcopal seminary, and involvement in the Episcopal monastery of St. John the Evangelist in Cambridge. There she can "go and listen to the monks chant the Psalms. [That's] a time when I can just be, and God can fill me up." She has also enrolled in a class where she is learning to paint icons, which she describes as a deeply spiritual experience. In the midst of all that, she has also maintained a fairly regular practice of meditation she learned at a Buddhist meditation center.

> For years I used to go to a Buddhist meditation center on Monday night sits. There's a guy named Jack Kornfield who is one of the preeminent Buddhist monks and meditation teachers in the States. He started a meditation center in Barre, Massachusetts, and he started a meditation center in Marin County, California, called Spirit Rock; and he holds Monday night sits where you sit and meditate for forty-five minutes to an hour and then he gives a Dharma talk afterwards. Again, I don't do it every single day, but I do it several times a week.

Immersion in the spiritual traditions of the Episcopal Church does not erect insurmountable barriers against other spiritual practices. Rather it leaves open a door that has allowed this broad array of spiritual practices to shape Cynthia's life.

At the other end of the spectrum, a few participants truly seem to deserve the nonspiritual label they took for themselves in responding to our invitation to participate. The eleven nonaffiliates were joined in this "spiritually disengaged" category by three additional participants. These were people who were on the rolls of a religious community from which we recruited participants, but they no longer attended or found spirituality of much interest. None of them reported more than one or two practices that might be considered spiritual, mostly things they do only very occasionally and with some ambivalence. Two of the nonaffiliates, by contrast, turned out to be relatively open to the spiritual dimensions of life, even if they do not spend a great deal of time in spiritual pursuits. Lily Mattison and Steve Sims could hardly be called seekers, but they were open to experiences and activities that connected them to larger meanings in life. Being spiritually disengaged is a relative category, then, not an absolute one.

Musician Alex Polani is the one participant in our study who truly looks like a seeker. We recruited him via a spiritual chat room on the internet, and he told us, "You're talking to someone that is really passionate about spirituality." He immediately added, "I'm a health freak so I eat a lot of healthy foods, I do my juicing." He also meditates at least twenty minutes each morning, and he is the one who talked about meditative mountain biking. He describes his most important commitments as "personal growth and spirituality," adding, "I do a lot of reading." In the past, he said, he had gone "on a whole journey of Eastern philosophy, out-of-body experiences, a bunch of things." He also keeps his eyes open for interesting lectures and workshops. He especially likes the Theosophical Society in Arlington. "It's a great place because they have lectures there and classes there once in a while. And it's very open minded to Christianity, Buddhism, Jewish, anything, even stuff that is nonreligious.... There is actually a group that meets there, Lucid Dreaming, and I am interested in that type of phenomenon." A couple of months later, when he was doing his second round of oral diary entries for our project, he told a long story about a workshop he had attended that weekend on out-of-body experiences. Raised Roman Catholic, Alex describes the beliefs he heard at church as stuff other people told him and not, therefore, relevant to him. By the time he was a teenager, he was spiritually curious, and the people who stoked his curiosity were agnostics and explorers. He completely lost interest in Catholicism but not in spirituality. Today he will join his family for Easter dinner but not for the services. He pursues his many faceted spiritual life in the company of friends, teachers, and books. Like others whose accent is on Extra-theistic discourses, Alex's activities take him into a broad arena of books, workshops, and internet chat rooms that exist in what Heelas and Woodhead (2004) might call a "spiritual milieu."

In the large middle, not nearly so serious as either Cynthia or Alex, are the people for whom spiritual practices are present but do not dominate their lives. They are "typically engaged." Some are active in religious communities; others are not. They may pray with some regularity, explore yoga and meditation, take regular walks in the out-of-doors, search for life's meaning in books or other media, commit to disciplined practices of moral and ethical engagement, or any of dozens of other activities that provide opportunities to step back from the mundane and reach toward some larger reality. In the chapters ahead, we will return to ask whether and how these spiritual practices shape the stories people tell about home, work, leisure, and more. But first, we need to look more thoroughly at what happens in the religious communities themselves. If attendance is so often linked to individual spiritual practice, we need to understand what attendance means and how typical people are different from either the spiritually engaged or the spiritually disengaged.

4 RELIGIOUS COMMUNITIES AND SPIRITUAL CONVERSATIONS

In a "modern" culture presumably characterized by individualized religiosity, the importance of organized traditions is easy to overlook. With so many places to encounter spiritual traditions, why go to church or synagogue? With few social constraints keeping participants locked into family- and community-based loyalty (or legally compelling their membership), why do people still belong? But they do. In striking contrast to Europe, people in the United States both belong and *attend* at rates that confound attempts to make easy predictions about an inevitable slide toward secularization.[1] More than 80 percent of Americans are counted as "religious adherents" by virtue of being able to identify themselves with a specific religious tradition (Religion and Public Life 2008). The number who actually belong to a local religious body is likely about 50 percent, but membership numbers are notoriously difficult to estimate because religious groups count in so many different ways (Association of Statisticians of American Religious Bodies 2010). Also difficult to count is weekly attendance. Although the polls consistently place that number close to 40 percent of the adult U.S. population, estimates based on actual counts place the number at roughly half that (Hadaway et al. 1993). Not nearly everyone is in services on a given weekend, but a sizeable portion of the American population has more than a passing acquaintance with organized religion. Any institutional sector that claims that many participants has to be taken seriously as a potential producer and organizer of cultural patterns in the population.

Our participants, like the population as a whole, span the range from "nones" to active affiliates. Eleven were unaffiliated, but the five Neopagans would probably have been added to the unaffiliated category in a national survey. Twenty-three would have been counted by the surveys as "affiliated," but are not currently active in a religious community. Counting the Neopagans, sixty-one of our participants did have an active affiliation. While we did not ask the attendance question the same way the national surveys do ("Did you attend last week?"), based on all the information we have, roughly one-third would probably have been counted present. That is, our participants are slightly more affiliated and active than the U.S. population but not appreciably so.[2] The question to be addressed here, however, is not how many people are attending church or synagogue. What is most important for our purposes is that there are significant differences within our participant population that allow us to ask about how affiliation and attendance are related to individual spiritual lives within and beyond the four walls of places of worship. That is, *how* do they participate, and what difference does that make?

Not only are our participants diverse in their organizational participation, as we saw in the previous chapters, but they also are diverse in their spiritual orientations and level of spiritual engagement. Understanding how they participate in organized religious communities begins with the recognition that those two things are strongly correlated (see Table 4.1). Among those who are individually spiritually uninterested, only two attend religious services with any regularity. And among those who are highly spiritually engaged, all but one (our seeker) attend on a regular basis. In between, especially among the middle-range, typically spiritual people, there is a great deal of variation in organized participation. Attendance and individual spiritual practice are not, that is, simply two aspects of the same thing, even if they are strongly correlated.

We begin, then, with the observation that the participants in religious communities are not all equally engaged in spiritual life, and spiritually engaged people are not all regular attenders. Asking how each spiritual population participates differently will allow us to explore the ways individuals

Table 4.1 Religious Participation by Spiritual Salience

	Minimal Spiritual Interest	Typical Spiritual Interest	High Spiritual Interest
Attend rarely or never	14 *Spiritually disengaged*	19 *Marginal members*	1 *Seeker*
Attend 1–3 times per month	2 *Spiritually typical*	20 *Spiritually typical*	9 *Spiritually engaged*
Attend weekly or more	0	13 *Spiritually typical*	17 *Spiritually engaged*
Total	16	52	27

understand what they are doing and why. Our ninety-five participants told a total of 1,186 stories about religious communities, and for each of them, the elements of the story were analyzed alongside all the other things we know about the storytellers (see Appendix 2 for details). Who are the players in this story and how are they related? What specific kind of activity is being described, and is it something that is routine or only happens occasionally (or happened in the past)? Does the storyteller have a leadership role? And what are the emotions running through the story? These stories give us a window on what people are doing, learning, and experiencing in these explicitly religious sites, and how it is interwoven with what they do in the other spaces of their lives. To what extent are these social interactions the building blocks of spiritual lives? To begin to understand that process we turn first to those for whom spiritual life is a priority.

Religious Participation in the Lives of the Spiritually Engaged

Based on the picture of spiritual life that emerged in the previous chapter, twenty-seven people can be identified as "spiritually engaged."[3] They speak about their spiritual lives as highly salient, and they actively pursue individual spiritual practices. When we asked about spirituality, they had plenty to say. And as Table 4.1 demonstrates, they are very likely to be frequent participants in a local religious congregation.[4] Roughly two-thirds of this spiritually engaged contingent find their way to church or synagogue weekly or more, with the remainder keeping up attendance every couple of weeks. Only the one seeker among them avoids organized religious services entirely, and we will look at his experience separately. The other twenty-six rarely miss a weekly worship service, but they are also there for Bible or Torah study, for daily Mass, or to help with the food pantry. Far from standing in opposition to spirituality, the life of their congregations is intimately tied to their own spiritual nurture and growth.

This link between individual and collective spiritual engagement exists across religious traditions. The most spiritually engaged Catholics and Jews are just as likely to be active in their congregations as are the most spiritually engaged Evangelicals. But conservative Protestants and Mormons were disproportionately likely to be among the most spiritually engaged, which makes the picture complicated. Overall, about a quarter of all the participants are in the highly engaged spiritual category, but half of conservative Protestants and Mormons are. Mainline Protestants were more likely to be found in the middle ranges of spiritual involvement, while Catholics and Jews had more than their share of people who were relatively disengaged from spiritual life. As we look at the links between individual spiritual life and religious participation, then, the patterns may sometimes look like distinctively evangelical and Mormon patterns, but it is important to remember that while particular traditions put the accent in different places, the link between spiritual seriousness and organized participation is common to all of them. A closer look at what all the spiritually engaged participants are doing and why will fill in the picture, allowing us to see the contours of the connection between their organized religious communities and their spiritual lives.

Gathering for Worship

"My week is not the same if I have not been in church for worship," declared Bethany Armstrong, a forty-two-year-old home decorator who is a member of Centre Street Church in Boston. When we asked what was different when she missed church, she said, "I find that I'm not as well grounded.... [When I go] I always learn something new. I find that very encouraging and challenging and necessary, and so in the weeks without it it's easier to fall out of your disciplines of praying daily. It's easy to fall out of the discipline of reading scripture and trying to stay quiet and to try to stay focused." Jen Jackson is part of the Vineyard Church in Atlanta and took several pictures at her church. Pointing to one, she said, "My job is important to me but my church, this is what centers me, this is really what I—this is where everything I do kind of stems from (laughs)—this is it." The importance of regular worship attendance was not just something we heard about from Evangelicals like these. We heard similar affirmations from spiritually engaged Episcopalians, Jews, Catholics, and others. Whether they became worship participants because they are spiritually engaged or whether their worship participation elicited spiritual commitment, the relationship between individual spiritual life and collective assemblies for worship is undeniable. Virtually all of those who have active individual spiritual practices told multiple stories about experiences of corporate worship, past and present.

When the spiritually engaged mainline Protestants and Catholics talked about worship, their stories were often marked by talk about specific formal rituals. Theresa Collins, for instance, enjoys the 8:00 Sunday morning service when they use the more traditional "Rite One" Episcopal liturgy, but she also attends every Thursday morning "when they have a 9 o'clock Holy Communion, and it's a lovely little service. I mean I love music in the church and all, but this is one of those quiet little services; there are anywhere from eight to ten people there," plus, she noted, both the rector's black Labrador and her Collie attend, as well. Jessica Kingman attends Sunday Mass at St. Felix parish, but her real preference is for the daily services she also attends and the Eucharistic Adoration she does at the St. Francis Shrine in the Prudential Center (Figure 4.1). "It's a time that you pray, get reconnected, get away from the world to sit in silence and just meditate on whatever you want to." Even individual moments of meditation like this are shaped by the institutional settings and routines that have defined the ritual.

Among Latter-day Saints, the central ritual is the "sacrament meeting" held every Sunday. When asked what is most memorable about her weekly attendance at her ward's three hours of Sunday morning meetings, Catherine Young (like each of her fellow Mormons) named the sacrament itself as the most important. "So that sacrament meal is really, I think, powerful. It is neat to take the sacrament because you have the opportunity to reflect on that you are really trying to be like Jesus Christ and you've taken his name upon you." Here too, organized ritual provides a time of individual introspection,

FIGURE 4.1 "I often go to confession here and we have Eucharistic Adoration."
—Jessica Kingman

but introspection shaped by the scripts and actions of particular communities, a time when individual and communal spirituality meet. People could conceivably spend quiet time at home praying and centering on their relationship with God, but the structured times and places provided by the religious community organize a process of entering into focused attention, providing a lexicon of meanings for the actions undertaken together (Laidlow and Humphrey 2006).

All of the spiritually engaged people told stories about specific ritual events, the range of which was as wide as the range of religious traditions represented among our participants. The Neopagans we interviewed introduced us to their celebration of Samhain, which occurs on October 31. Laura Henderson was doing oral diaries for the project when Samhain came around, and she explained how she intentionally employs the symbols and rituals of her circle:

> I have always decorated my house for the Halloween season for the neighborhood with true harvest decorations. I wanted in my own small way to put forth to our neighbors what the season is about. I guess it's [laughs] in a strange analogy, I guess it's sort of like what the Christians think they're doing for Christmas. But instead of doing the, you know, the blood-dripping vampires and things like that in the front yard like some of my neighbors do, we decorate with a lot of pumpkins, a lot of gourds, cornstalks, nuts, twigs; and on the night of the Halloween or the trick-or-treating, we put a lot of candles out, and we make it to be as atmospheric as possible.... But after the kids go away that night and the lights start going off on all the porches, I put on my cloak, I take my staff, and normally I take my dog, and I walk. And I connect back with the Mother, and I try to feel the ancestors around me in the quiet, in the cold and on this incredibly special night.

Because Samhain rarely falls on a weekend, the day itself is often marked individually or in the household, as Laura's story indicates. The circle then gathers a few days after for a collective ceremony that Emma Cooper described as "alive and magical."

For the members of this circle, the outdoor space where they gather is part of what makes the ritual magical (Figure 4.2), but other spiritually engaged worshippers made note of their ritual spaces, as well. Margi Perkins is thrilled that her parish has an adoration chapel, and Joe Silverman enjoys a similar kind of space in his Reform Temple in Atlanta. Showing us his pictures, he

FIGURE 4.2 "This is a typical…altar layout where you have things in the directions."—Anna Cook

said, "This is inside, I believe, the small chapel in the synagogue, and that's the Torah right there. A lot of times I'll go there before regular service, and there's a small chapel, and nobody's in there, and I'll sit there and meditate—it's very, very quiet." Each is individually interacting with a space that has been collectively defined as sacred. Their religious community has set apart a place where outside noise and distraction can be excluded, allowing (indeed calling for) focused spiritual attention.

One of the mechanisms for filling a space with symbolic meaning is to introduce art and architecture that evoke the stories of the community (Wuthnow 2003). Joe went on to recount researching the art at Temple Beth Torah for an upcoming anniversary booklet. He explained, "There's a thing up here in the chapel called the *Ner Tamid* which is called the eternal light; it's always on. I found out that the guy that designed that is a world famous artist." The elaborate art and symbolism of many Jewish and Catholic worship spaces can be a stimulus to spiritual reflection, but so can the austerity of a New England meetinghouse. Andrew Hsu has enough formal theological education to know the reasoning behind the space in which he worships.

For us, you know, in terms of architecture, what this says is, like, you know, you see this high pulpit that is kind of elevated above everything

else, and there's actually a Bible on the pulpit, and this is very usual for
Reformation churches, for Protestant churches.... They have a strong
emphasis on the preaching of the word of God and also, you know,
respect for the word of God.

This theological excursus is not the only reason he took pictures of the sanctu-
ary at his church, however. It was clear in the telling that this is an important
space for him, one that reminds him of who he is, much as Joe has learned to
connect the art of the temple with his Jewish identity.

Andrew's evangelical faith, however, puts much more emphasis on learning
and belief than on emotion and aesthetics. Even when he talked about singing
hymns at Centre Street Church, he focused in on the words and the theology
they conveyed. Most other accounts of singing, by contrast, included a significant affective component. When spiritually engaged people talked about
music, the point was much less about the ideas than about the experience of
singing together. Joshua Roberts, Pam Jones, and Jen Jackson—all spiritually
engaged African Americans, but in different traditions—each talked about
loving the music at their churches. Others, across ethnic groups, talked about
learning hymns as a child and loving the familiarity of singing them "from the
heart" today.[5] And still others pointed to the experience of singing in a choir
or praise team as one of their most important commitments. Sylvia Jameson,
a member at Brookfield Baptist, said,

> I love singing on the Worship Team, and I'm with them probably
> about two to three times a week. And they are a strength to me, and
> we have so much fun doing it. So I was just so thankful when the Lord
> opened the door for me to start doing that.

As her account makes clear, singing in a choir is both relational and spiritual. When we met him, Joshua Roberts had only been in Atlanta about eighteen months, having moved from New Orleans after he lost everything to
Hurricane Katrina. He recounted, "The choir—that was a big religious help
if I may say. Their help, you know, gave me encouragement for some of the
certain things that were going on in my life at the time." Jen Jackson recalled
joining the choir that eventually formed the nucleus of the Vineyard Church,
where she became active:

> Spiritual things were happening kind of around me with this choir,
> because we were meeting every week and we were going out and

singing different places, at churches, at schools. It was just beautiful,
I just loved it.

She included pictures from a choir reunion in what she photographed for our
project.

These pictures are pictures of choir members, and ... these are very special.... we've kind of all sort of grown and changed together. But this
choir was really integral 'cause this was like how I really came to know
God and really—I made a lot of changes in my life as a result of being a
part of this choir. It really was a big thing for me to be in.

For conservative Protestants and African American Protestants, singing and
leading in song are important parts of what it means to participate in collective worship experiences.[6]

When spiritually engaged people of any tradition talked about worship,
preaching was a surprisingly rare part of the story, completely absent from
the stories of the most engaged Catholic participants. For Catholics, church
participation was about many things, but neither singing nor listening to
sermons prompted them to tell us stories. Sermons were important, on the
other hand, to at least a few of the spiritually engaged Protestants and Jews
we interviewed. Sam Levitt loves Jewish learning, so it is not surprising that
he says, "So when I'm in services on Saturday we always read the Bible. And
it's read in Hebrew, but the English is right there. And the rabbi leads a discussion and the rabbi's discussions are often really excellent." Stephen James
likes Cornerstone Baptist, where he is a member, but he also visits a nearby
Pentecostal church fairly often and especially likes the preacher there. "He is
so articulate about the Bible. And he is such an educated man that you can't
help but come out of that service with a new level of understanding of some
element of the Lord." Several mentioned at least one occasion when a sermon
made an impression on them.

This emphasis on learning and doctrine was not, however, the more common way preaching was remembered. More often what was remembered was
a moral or spiritual lesson, rather than a cognitive one. As Bethany Armstrong
put it, "It's not ultimately about head knowledge; it's about moving people
emotionally. And not necessarily having an emotional experience, but to
be able to get people to move interesting things that they learn about God,
to move that from their head to how do I live it." Miles Parker reflected on
what he hears from his Vineyard pastor: "You got a thirty-year-old pastor

that will still speak what's on his mind, but yet will also be honest." These two Evangelicals are highly attuned to the emotional and spiritual honesty of what they hear, and they want to hear a message that has a connection to everyday life. That emphasis on everyday connection was also there for Episcopalian Theresa Collins in a story she recorded in her diary:

> [The rector] gave a really wonderful sermon that will stay with me always. This week I will really enjoy thinking about it in depth as I do in my walk in the morning. It was based on this scripture from the gospel from John about Jesus appearing for the third time to the disciples. This time when he went down and they were fishing, and then he invited them to come and have some fish by the fire, and they recognized him. The point of the sermon was how Jesus—That was an ordinary situation, an ordinary spot as opposed to being on top of a mountain surrounded by angels or something, and that Jesus is everywhere. Wherever you look, Jesus is there. So that was a really memorable sermon.

In the interaction of these spiritually engaged listeners and these sermons, an interpretive space was present that allowed imaginative connections between religion and everyday life. It was not an if-then set of doctrinal deductions but an opportunity to hear stories that suggest new ways of narrating their own lives.[7]

Stories of morally inspiring sermons were present among all the kinds of Protestants in our study as well as among the Latter-day Saints. But overall, preaching appeared in the stories of only ten of the twenty-six people who constitute the most spiritually active members in our study. And people who are less spiritually engaged were just as likely to talk about sermons. Something more than sermons is going on here. Ritual, music, art, and sacred space carry layers of potential for meaning-making, and spiritually engaged participants seem especially attuned to the multiple dimensions of worship life. They have learned the rhythms of the rituals and the collective meanings they embody, but theirs is not simply routinized action. They seem to step out of the ordinary world and into a place where their religious sensibilities are focused and reinforced, allowing new meanings to emerge. When they step back into the world, there are new stories to be lived.[8]

Education and Spiritual Growth Groups

Worship is not, however, the whole story. More than stories about sermons, spiritually engaged people told us stories about adult education and growth groups as their sources of insight and inspiration. In this, spiritually engaged people were quite distinct from people with less interest in their spiritual lives. The more strongly a person claimed spirituality as salient and the more active they were in individual spiritual practices, the more they were also involved in organized educational and spiritual nurture activities in their congregations—no matter what their religious tradition. When we look for what makes the religious participation of the most spiritually engaged people distinctive, this is one of the key factors. Worship is something everyone does; classes and workshops and retreats are where the most spiritually engaged people are found.

On one level, they are there to gain knowledge. From the first time a Mormon missionary knocks on a potential convert's door until the day they die, Latter-day Saints are engaged in learning and teaching. Marjorie Buckley recalled that when she was a young married woman, just after World War II, missionaries visited her:

> The missionaries would visit, and we would discuss things....And like I tell the missionaries now, you know...the missionaries' job is to teach people....I've learned so many things since then.

One of the ways she and others learn is to have (or be) a "visiting teacher," who checks in personally at least once a month for a conversation about questions and issues members are facing. In addition, they are likely to attend Sunday school every Sunday (in addition to Sacrament meeting and either Relief Society for women or Priesthood meeting for men). Catherine Young described the well-planned programs presented each week in Relief Society:

> Relief Society lessons are taught about the gospel, and experiences are related that help us come closer to Christ....So it really is an opportunity to learn more attributes of Christ through the different sisters that you come into contact with.

Women learn from each other's examples and questions, but they are also guided by ample books and publications from the Church.

No other tradition has such an intense round of activities designed to educate and form its participants, but Evangelicals told many stories about the Bible study groups in which they participate, as well. Jews talked about Torah study and lectures hosted by the temple. Mainline Protestants have Lenten study series and programs such as Stephen Ministries and the Episcopal

Church's Education for Ministry (EFM). Both train lay leaders to be active in caring for others and provide regular opportunities for education and spiritual development. Cynthia Gardner has participated in EFM for a number of years, and that keeps her busy learning. "I'm in EFM, so I'm reading the Bible and my EFM books every week," she said. Learning for Neopagans tends to be more individualized, sometimes with a single mentor or perhaps in a local group. Laura Henderson reflected on the challenges:

> I do like to read a lot of Craft books that are out because now, especially with the internet, and you can find out about the Craft books, and more and more and more of them are being written. What I find, unfortunately, is that a lot of them, the vast majority of them, 80 percent at least, are written...are dumbed down. They're written for the charmed crowd or they're Wicca 101 or whatever. There's a lot of talk in the community about the fact that our elders are not coming forward with advanced books.... So, it's always exciting to see a new good book come out.

Each of these traditions provides ways for spiritually engaged people to deepen their ongoing commitments, but as a newer and more loosely organized tradition, Paganism has fewer resources. Catholicism's challenge, on the other hand, is that large parishes rarely have the resources to go around.[9]

The one Catholic exception was the story we heard from Mary Hage about her Thursday morning women's group, Women of Grace, connected to St. Agnes in Atlanta (Figure 4.3). Like many of the other opportunities for adult education, it is about much more than just learning about the Bible or about the history of one's religious tradition. Jen Jackson said of her "Mastering Motherhood" group, "We do a lot of things together. It's a really close-knit group. I think too, we've all kind of grown together" (Figure 4.4). Groups like this are often relatively small and structured with the explicit goal of making links between spirituality and everyday life. Talking with fellow members of a faith community allows even traumatic experiences to be integrated into a faith story, as Stephen James reflected about his wife's health crisis: "As we talk about these experiences with people...we start to realize how important it is to go through those experiences, and to go through them in a way that allows you to really exhibit the faith that you have."

Making the connections between faith and everyday life is explicit in most groups. Cynthia Gardner noted that her EFM group always starts with an "onboard question" that lets everyone share what is happening in their lives.

FIGURE 4.3 "This is my Thursday morning scripture study."—Mary Hage

FIGURE 4.4 "I run a support group. It's called Mastering Motherhood. It's for moms that have young children."—Jen Jackson

"It's always a question like, where have you noticed God in your life this week." As she herself was wrestling with a decision about a possible job move, she recounted this experience at EFM in her oral diary:

> There was a prayer brought in by one of the women, and I'm just going to read the prayer, because it's so perfect for this particular situation. And it just came up out of nowhere, which is how things happen. That's the way I see it. That's how God gives us guidance and talks to us in our lives, if we're quiet and pay attention and can listen. And so here's the prayer that we had tonight. The prayer is: "Oh, God, by whom the meek are guided in judgment and light rises up in darkness for the godly. Grant us in all our doubts and uncertainties the grace to ask what Thou wouldst have us to do, that the spirit of wisdom may save us from all false choices and by Thy light we may see light and in Thy straight path may not stumble. Through Jesus Christ, Our Lord. Amen." And then another prayer that was there tonight. I mean it's just amazing that these two prayers came tonight. "Lord, help me to unclutter my life, to lead me in the direction of simplicity, teach me to listen to my heart, teach me to welcome change instead of fearing it. Lord, I give you these stirrings inside of me. I give you my discontent, my restlessness, my doubt. I give you my despair. I give you all my longings I hold inside. Help me to listen to these signs of change, of growth. To listen seriously and follow wherever they lead through the breathtaking empty space of your open door. Amen." Like I said I don't believe in coincidence and to have these two prayers happen the same day that I hear about all these changes and the, and the possibility of me having a job all of a sudden in the Northwest and moving back to the West Coast.... It's not a coincidence.

In an explicitly spiritual setting, where participants are encouraged to make connections between religion and everyday life, it is possible to try out new ways of telling one's life story, ways that may have consequences for what one does next.

Adult confirmation programs and regular Sunday school classes appeared in stories, as well, but so did special events. Jessica Kingman recounted the visit of an Irish mystic to Boston:

> There were so many people there tonight, they actually had to turn away people because of the fire code.... There were people that came from Jersey and all over.... It was a beautiful talk.

Jessica was given the job of picking the speaker up at the airport and also enjoyed the opportunity to consult and pray with her before the event. In Sylvia Jameson's Southern Baptist Church, the celebrity teacher we heard about was Beth Moore, whose events are often attended by thousands of women. Sylvia regularly participates in a small Bible study group in her church but was excited that the ladies in her group would be seeing a live simulcast of an upcoming Beth Moore event. Sam Levitt talked about hearing a famous Jewish literary figure lecture, and Andrew Hsu and Bethany Armstrong both talked about being inspired by the international gathering of missionaries that happens at their church each fall. In each case, being surrounded by a large group of other spiritually serious people and listening to a noted "saint," gave affective and social reinforcement, but it also supplied new stories of faith and new opportunities to reflect on one's own spiritual life.

Other important congregational conversations were one-on-one, often with the person's pastor, rabbi, or priest. Jessica seeks advice from her priest about everything from work to her love life. Lawrence Urban named the bishop of his Mormon ward as one of his closest friends and an important example to him of how to live. From the stories we heard, the rabbi at Temple Beth Torah in Atlanta is evidently that sort of example and advisor, as well. Joe Silverman depends on her for both religious and emotional support and learning. "In fact I'm going to talk to her today," he said. "Probably once every five or six weeks, we chat for about thirty minutes about different things. She's my Dear Abby too." Humorist Garrison Keillor recounts his mythical Lake Wobegon Lutheran "Pastor Liz" being asked, "Is it okay to encourage my son to go into law enforcement, given the teachings in the Sermon on the Mount about turning the other cheek?" (Keillor 2011). Not every congregational leader is someone members turn to, but everything from theological quandaries to everyday life challenges can send some of the most spiritually engaged to their clergyperson's office. Victoria Edwards has a key lay leadership position in her Catholic parish and often sits on the other side of those conversations.

> I like how people let you into their lives. They invite you in—to experience their joys and experience their pains, and experience their lives with them. In that way it's a real privileged place to be, that people just invite you to share and be witness to their lives.

Pastoral care is a particular kind of spiritual conversation that allows explorations that are often affectively charged and oriented toward future action. As member and pastor or rabbi explore issues together, there is yet another opportunity to frame the stories of everyday life in spiritual terms.

Friends and Fellowship

Hinted at in all these stories is the importance of relationships, of being together and talking with others who share a similar religious and spiritual orientation. Among all the stories about religious participation, no matter how spiritually engaged the teller, stories about fellowship activities were second in number only to stories about worship. When people think about religious communities, they not only think about the rituals of religious services, but also about the people who make up the community that gathers. Putnam and Campbell (2010) found that theology and worship may be the deciding factors in choosing a congregation, but friendships are the deciding factor in keeping people there. As they admit, the mechanism at work is hard to discern—do people stay because they have friends or do they naturally accumulate friends as they stay? We found that the more often persons attend services, the more likely they were to include someone from the religious community among those they listed as their closest friends. Only 15 percent of those who rarely or never attend listed a congregation-related friend, but half of those who are regular attenders included a fellow attender when we asked about the people they are closest to.

This link between friendship and participation is present no matter how individually spiritual a person is. The most spiritually engaged, of course, also attend more frequently, but it is attendance itself that accounts for the number of friendship stories they told. Shared time and conversation with friends at church or synagogue spills over into shared lives the rest of the week. This is the core of the spiritual tribe, and these stories were among the most heartfelt tales we heard. Pam Jones admitted that she has missed more Sundays than she'd like, in part because they live a good distance from Cornerstone Baptist, but she said, "Nothing stands up to the church that I love, and I do love going to [Cornerstone]." "What is it that you love?" we asked. "I love the music. And the sense of family. The sense of people actually caring about each other." Sam Levitt said, "It would be very hard for me to retire to a distant place because I wouldn't have the synagogue there. It's an important reference point, and the people there are important to me." One of the reasons Cynthia Gardner was struggling so hard with whether to take her new job opportunity was that it would mean leaving a set of religious communities where she has established deep friendships that she would dearly miss.

Congregations are institutions with fellowship as part of their core functional mission (Ammerman 2005a). American culture expects them to provide opportunities to build social ties and to be, among other things, mutual aid societies. When Margi Perkins's husband unexpectedly had to have heart surgery, she felt completely surrounded by the care of St. Michael's parish and especially the mom's group she belongs to.

> All I had to do was say Richard's going in for surgery. I could have had meals for a month! I mean the outpouring of—"what do you need? I'll take care of this. I'll do this." I could have picked up the phone and had anything I needed at any hour of the day. You can't—it's an unbelievable blessing to know that you have that kind of backup and that kind of support from people.

Most congregations attempt to organize just such assistance for their members who are in need, and the infrastructure is especially robust in a Mormon ward. Relief Society was something Catherine Young talked often about. "There's a lot of service-oriented lessons and activities that go on there," she said, "and we really seek to serve one another and help one another." That might mean teaching and praying for one another, but it might also mean very tangible assistance, as well. She recorded in her diary a story she would be sharing with her sisters that night when she was to give a testimony of how service had affected her life.

> So I have been thinking about that a lot lately.... Since having my baby last year I have just been served by the sisters a ton, and I have just, I often don't like to let people serve me because I hate to be a burden on people.... Me and my husband had actually talked about that before, like, do we really want them to bring meals now? We can cook for ourselves.... So my visiting teacher ... arranged all these meals for me, and I just remember that first night coming home with a new baby, and my mom wasn't able to stay, and just having someone bring over a meal for me, it just meant the world to me actually. Because I had so many new worries on my mind, and just having someone care about me to do a simple thing ... just to have something comfortable and waiting for me when I got home that I didn't have to worry about, just meant so much to me ... because I didn't have any family coming to stay with me (sobbing). I was just so thankful for people's love.

The love of the community, expressed in a homecooked meal, was a physical, emotional, and spiritual boon, one of the key ingredients in tying her everyday stories to the stories of people with whom she shares a spiritual connection.

The friendship and support cultivated in these religious communities is not just about the hard times, of course. We also heard many stories about the sheer joy and fun of doing things together. Catherine, in fact, recorded stories about a ward beach day, about two separate youth parties she and her husband helped to chaperone, and about having friends from the ward over for dinner. Andrew Hsu talked about gathering other single people from church for holiday dinners (Figure 4.5), and Bethany Armstrong told about the fun of her church group's Christmas party. Sam Levitt enjoys the Sabbath dinner groups he and his wife participate in; and Rachael Halpern recalled that when she and her husband arrived at Temple Beth Torah, they decided that the younger couples needed a place to congregate, so they started a *havurah* group. "We started looking for couples, mid-twenties, thirties, without kids…and sure enough, from that, we got a few other couples that we've gotten to know. So we've got our *havurah* off the ground." Like Jen Jackson's Mastering Motherhood group and many of the other groups we heard about, Rachael's *havurah* group is friendship, mutual aid, and spiritual support rolled into one, a tribe where all kinds of stories can be told.

Many of the stories shared by spiritually engaged people highlighted the depth and openness that develops in these spiritual settings. Miles Parker, a member of the Vineyard Church, took a picture of the discipleship class he works with each Tuesday night.

FIGURE 4.5 "Thanksgiving dinner for…whoever didn't have a place to go."
—Andrew Hsu

We walked through each of our lives; we got to see the good and bad and ugly over two months. And we got to see men grow and change, you know—conflicts with their spouses, everything you can imagine, you know. Within that class you had ex-meth addicts; you had guys fighting drug addiction, pornographic addictions; one guy who lost his child no more than nine months previously.

Jessica Wilson had only been going to Deer Valley Church for a few months, but she likes it because there are people like her, with tattoos and piercings, and it isn't, as she put it, "fluffy and frilly." Places that are fluffy and frilly, she said, are places where people "don't let their real self come out. And they put on a different face and don't let their weaknesses show, and they don't share their pain with their fellow Christian brother or sister, and 'everything's perfect in my world.' And that's not real." Centre Street Church formalizes this in relationships they call "accountability partners," much as Catherine's ward has "visiting teachers." That sense of deep sharing and accountability was most often heard from conservative Protestants and Mormons, but it was also present among some of the most spiritually engaged in other traditions. It is certainly part of what Cynthia Gardner tries to foster in the women's spirituality group she started at All Saints. She was not the only one to talk about how these circles of spiritual friends are important sounding boards for life's decisions. These relationships are distinctive for the way they span the multiple social roles of their participants—parenting, health, leisure and entertainment, work, and more. The boundaries between the spiritual world and the everyday world are thoroughly permeable.

Taking all of this together, we can see why Lim and Putnam (2010) found that the oft-noted link between religious participation and life satisfaction is actually a product of the friendships people develop in their congregations. Being there more often makes relationships more likely, and those relationships, in turn, provide material, social, and spiritual support and satisfaction.

Given how important relationships are to these people, it is also unsurprising that not everything is rosy all the time. It sometimes takes a while to make new friends after a move, and more than one unmarried person lamented how difficult it is to be one of only a few singles (or the only one who does not seem to be having any luck finding a mate). In addition, feelings get hurt, and quarrels happen. Brookfield Baptist seemed to be going through an especially rocky time when our participants were recording their diaries. We heard about troublesome petty quarrels and more than a little angst about whether it might be better just to go somewhere else. Because these are very spiritually engaged people, the tensions are prayed over and discussed with trusted friends. For Charles Curlew, the question of staying at Brookfield came down to a sense of calling.

> I just looked at all the people that were there. I was sitting more toward the back and thought, boy, this is really some church. I guess I do have thoughts occasionally of would I leave the church, because I have reasons why I might like to. But I thought then, how could I leave these people? They were people from—Americans there, and Nicaraguans there, and Africans there, and everything—and just thinking it's a good group of Christian people together, and they have—they need— we need each other.

Summing Up—The Spirituality of Congregational Life

Congregations are human communities and socially sanctioned religious spaces all at once. As explicitly religious spaces, we would expect the majority of stories told about them to be inflected with spiritual significance, and that was the case. About two-thirds of all the stories about religious participation included explicit reference to the spiritual or religious character of the events, often speaking of the role of God in what happens. Among these most spiritually engaged participants, more than three-quarters of the stories about congregations had a spiritual component. No matter what their dominant spiritual discourse or religious tradition, people who have active spiritual lives narrate their religious participation as a spiritual story.

Religious communities create multiple opportunities for spiritual conversation that elaborates that story. They engage in rituals and singing that give participants embodied experiences of spiritual presence. They form small groups where people learn and share and assist each other through life. As a result, people gain close friends whose presence bridges religious and everyday life concerns. Religious communities are set apart sacred territory, but the boundaries between ordinary life and congregational activity are extremely permeable. Spiritually engaged people bring the everyday world with them into the congregation, talk about all of it with their spiritual friends, and take reframed life narratives with them back into the everyday world.

Organized Religion in the Middle of the Spiritual Road

What, then, about more spiritually typical people? Not everyone claims spirituality as so central in life or maintains the disciplined round of individual spiritual practice that is also so closely aligned with active participation in a religious community. Among those with less-salient spirituality, rates of participation in religious communities vary widely (see Table 4.1). A quarter of them attend services at least weekly. Just over a third (38 percent) attend regularly (once or twice a month), but an equal number attend rarely or never (Figure 4.6). Here in the middle of the spectrum it is not so much spirituality that drives participation but participation that shapes spirituality. For instance, no matter what the spiritual commitments of the individual person, people who *attend* more often tell more emotionally positive stories about participation, and those who attend infrequently tell more emotionally negative ones. In other ways, individual spiritual commitment and level of participation amplify each other. For instance, both individual spirituality and frequency of participation independently affect how likely it is that activities at church or synagogue will be talked about *as* spiritual activities. As we look at the people with typically modest spiritual engagements, then, the effects of the religious community itself are particularly apparent.

FIGURE 4.6 "That's just the typical Sunday morning scene."—Francine Worthington

Thirty-five of our participants stand in this middle ground, maintaining a moderately active attention to spirituality in their individual lives and attending services with some regularity. We might think of them as "typical members." Worship is the most common subject of participation stories for this group, just as it is for the more spiritually engaged. Whether Neopagans recounting the joys of seasonal festivals or Evangelical Mary Margaret Sironi talking about communing with God in the services at Centre Street Church, worship is described as an experience that centers life. Both Gwen Mothersbaugh and James Dupree talked about appreciating the times of silence that are built into the service at Grimsby Congregational, and the experience of the Eucharist was something that routinely drew both Mary Hage and Elizabeth Evans to their Atlanta Catholic parishes. As spiritually typical people made their way into religious communities, the sacred spaces of worship were opportunities for spiritual focus and intensity.

They were especially likely to talk about the music they hear in worship. Mike Howard was effusive in his praise for the music at New Beginnings, an AME church in Atlanta: "They have an awesome music department in here. It's awesome! I know one Sunday they did this 'Holy, Holy,' and it was so awesome! It looked like they just opened up heaven on me." This joined several other accounts of memorable music in African American churches,[10] but the congregation that produced by far the most music stories was Grimsby Congregational. Three of the five participants we interviewed from that church pointed to the music as a highlight of the services.[11] William Pullinger named music as the most important part: "Religious music is extremely important to us.... The choir is great; the organ is just fantastic." Jennifer Hammond agreed, although she put more emphasis on the congregation's own participation. "I love the music. Yeah, I do....It's one of the parts that I love the best....I like to sing. I like music and it's spiritual. It's just moving." Neither Jennifer nor William has an extensive individual spiritual practice, but they still come to church, and the music is largely responsible for keeping them there. Much as visual arts open up spaces for meaning-making, so artistic performances can be the vehicle for focusing ritual attention. Well-executed music can structure the emotional journey of worshipers from high-energy praise to deep introspection to resolute spiritual commitment. The rhythms and harmonies themselves tap deeply resonant structures of religious meaning.[12]

Francine Worthington, from nearby All Saints Episcopal, loves the music at her church, too. She recorded this in her diary about a Sunday service:

The choir did a wonderful job. I think they often do a wonderful job, and I was reminded of the fact that I remember being told that one doesn't go to church because they like the music; that that might be a pleasure that the choir brings, but you don't necessarily go to church just because you love the music. I've thought about that for years now, and if one believes that the beautiful hymns and the canticles are a gift from God, then why not? Why not go for the music? You pay attention to the poetry of the music and the poetry of the canticles. Maybe one gets more out of that than they do from the creeds or from the sermon. It's always a pleasure to look at that choir; disparate people coming together. Maybe the individuals don't have great voices, but collectively they're wonderful and, of course, we have a phenomenally gifted organist.

Not all kinds of religious communities place music at the heart of the worship experience, but where it is, it seems to provide an important spiritual link for some who are not themselves spiritual virtuosi.

These same people of ordinary spiritual commitments also notice the sermons at their churches more often than do the most spiritually engaged. For typical members, sermons were more noteworthy than adult education programs, which is the reverse of the pattern among the more spiritually engaged. For that group, talk about sermons faded in light of talk about all the other things they do at church or synagogue, but the typical members pointed to what they learned from sermons, to the inspiration and life wisdom their preachers provided. (They were also more likely to note when the sermons were not so good.) Jessica Fletcher is enjoying being part of the Vineyard Church in Atlanta, and she told us she especially likes the preacher. "He doesn't really blow the sermon up, you know, not a lot of fantastical things. He's just really, almost like he's just talking to you. It's like a real person....I really appreciate that truthfulness, that realness about it." Camilla Hart simply described the pastor at Cornerstone Baptist as "inspiring." While Protestants were much more likely to mention sermons than were members of any other groups, there were a few Catholic stories. John Travisano was approaching eighty when we interviewed him, so one particular homily on mortality caused him to reflect on his own life and to tell us about it in his diary. In fact, we heard about nearly a dozen different specific sermons in the daily recordings these typical members made.

Typical members did occasionally mention other congregational activities, mostly aimed at learning and discussing ideas. Whether it was attending Sunday school or a book group, if they were active in adult education activities, their focus was more cognitive and their attendance more occasional than we saw among the most spiritually engaged. Some of the typical members also admitted that they do not know very much about their tradition or that they are pretty sure they do not agree with everything they do know. James Dupree recalled the UCC slogan "God is still speaking" and said, "I think I identify with most of the beliefs. It's a pretty liberal church so that I can go there.... I don't really know what their platform is on a lot of things." Atlantan Mark Fuller did know that his Presbyterian heritage included the doctrine of predestination, and he specifically mentioned that he did not believe in that.

In spite of having fewer stories about intimate groups that share learning and spiritual growth, typical members were just as likely to tell stories about the way their congregations care for them. The stories were different, however, in being centered mostly on times of crisis, rather than everyday support. Vicki Johnson recalled when she had recently had surgery, "I know this summer I had lots of folks [at St. Michael's] really praying for me." It was a discipleship group at the Vineyard Church that helped Meredith Jones through a series of deaths in her life, and Hank Matthews recalled that the rector at All Saints had been a real comfort to him when his father died. About a half a dozen others, similarly, mentioned the empathy and support they had received from a pastor in a time of difficulty.

Others told about the enjoyment and sense of identification they find in their religious community (what social scientists have come to call "bonding social capital"; Putnam 1995). Jessica Fletcher, for instance, said she likes the "hipster feel" at the Vineyard Church. John Travisano wondered aloud about people who have no church—"Who would you know?" And Gwen Mothersbaugh said that when they first moved to the community, they joined Grimsby Congregational, in part, to meet people. Perhaps that is one reason she now hosts dinners for new members at her house. She took a picture of her dining table and said, "I like to spend time with people at a table eating. Having conversation." When we asked her to tell us a story about that space, she said,

> Well, we had, um, new members come, potential new members, come to dinner with some of the deacons. And our pastor. And there was just, he's good at drawing people out, so there was such wonderful sharing back and forth. We all got to know each other in a significant way that wasn't false.

That story is striking for being one of only three accounts of typical members sharing meals with each other—no talk about parties or getting together for holidays or just going to lunch with church friends. Unlike the wide-ranging fellowship cultivated by the most spiritually-engaged, moderately spiritual people have fewer social ties, touching fewer parts of their lives.

One of the dimensions that is present is a concern for introducing one's children to a religious tradition. Among the most spiritually engaged, only one person told of a spiritual journey that began with concern for the religious upbringing of a child, but more than half a dozen of the typical members talked about what the religious community has to offer their children. Congregationalist James Dupree said, "I've always wanted my family to go to church, kind of like what I did...it's good to teach your kid. I think it helps kids for life, life skills." Amelia James is depending on her new church to help her raise her young son. "I want him to be a strong Catholic because I want him to be strong enough to stand up to the culture. And the culture is very anti-Christian right now." One of the things Andrea Valencia likes about her Pentecostal church is the "great stuff" they have for her kids, and Jennifer Hammond is tied to Grimsby Congregational in large measure by the fact that her young son loves Sunday school there.

Typical members also help keep their congregations running. More than spiritually engaged people (who do the teaching and leading of small groups), typical members told us stories about a different kind of leadership—balancing the books, managing property, and serving on boards. It is necessary work, but no matter how spiritually attuned the person doing it, it is still just necessary work. Very few of these stories were told with any spiritual inflection. People seem rarely to meet God in the congregation's boardroom.

The picture that emerges, then, is that typical members participate in their religious communities for ordinary and practical reasons as well as for the support and inspiration they find. Participation is important for reasons of gaining social capital and raising children. It is a community to which one can turn for help in a crisis, and it is a community where one can learn from sermons and be inspired by the music. It is less often a place where wide-ranging spiritual conversations take place. Worship is a matter of quiet comfort and individual reflection. Stories of seeking comfort were not especially common overall (in spite of what Karl Marx might have expected), but typical members were the most likely people to speak in those terms. As Mary Hage put it, "You know it's a comfort because it's a ritual." Others commented about the silence and peacefulness of special worship spaces, something they too found comforting. For people with typical patterns of spirituality, the specific comfort offered in times of illness, death, or tragedy grows out of the calm they find there in other times. The community is there when they need it, but it is not a community in which they are deeply enmeshed in ongoing everyday spiritual conversations.

On the Margins of Organized Religion

Religious communities were sometimes talked about as places of comfort even by people who are not currently involved. Michelle Winter is not attending services at her parish very often these days, but she said, "I find peace in church. When I find that something's going on with me, if I go to church, I find some kind of peace within myself." Ericka Lombardi is more clearly estranged from the Catholic Church, and when she does have to go, she says, "I certainly don't pay much attention to the readings or to the prayers." She does, however, create a certain peaceful, meditative space for herself. "I think I just have always taken that as my time for my own, my own reflection." Over one-third of our participants reported that they rarely or never attend religious services, but that masks a number of real differences among them. Most especially, it masks a difference between those for whom spirituality is at least somewhat important and those who have little interest. Twenty of the thirty-four who rarely if ever attend services are nevertheless open to some level of spiritual engagement and, in most instances, find themselves sitting on the margins of religious communities, not thoroughly disconnected. Nineteen of these we might call "marginal members," while one, Alex Polani, is spiritually engaged but not with any traditional religious community.[13]

Some of these people are still actively connected to their religious communities in ways other than attending services. Erika Lombardi has multiple connections to the Boston Catholic community and, with her husband, teaches Pre-Cana marriage preparation classes regularly; but she has no desire to attend regular services and does not consider herself a believer. Similarly, Patrick Zelinsky is active in the administration of Congregation Sinai but never goes to services. He reported that he originally joined a synagogue for the sake of his children but has little spiritual interest himself. Half the Jews in our study, in fact, fit this pattern. They attend for holidays and rites of passage but do not think of regular weekend attendance as necessary. Rebecca Klein, for instance, has taught in Hebrew School, loves being part of the Jewish community, and tries to make it to synagogue for special occasions, but she often feels uncomfortable in the weekly services because she does not know Hebrew and grew up in a nonobservant household. In addition, she confessed, "It's hard for me now that I have the shop. You know, my religion has become this shop." Her pattern of participation is actually quite typical for American Jews, where both membership and weekly service attendance is much less prevalent than in other religious groups in the American population (Wertheimer 2005).

Rebecca's need (or desire) to work through the weekend in her shop is typical of why some otherwise interested people do not attend. Other reasons for nonattendance included a recent move, a health problem that makes getting to church difficult, and a husband who does not go. National surveys have often found that life transitions and intermarriage are points where a change in affiliation or dropping out entirely may be likely.[14] For these and other reasons, some of our participants simply found themselves not routinely in the services of their religious community. Their own spiritual commitment was not entirely dormant, and one can imagine them returning at some future date. In the meantime, they may participate in some religious activities and maintain their sense of belonging, in spite of not being there for worship. But the absence of ongoing spiritual conversations in a religious community means that they have fewer interactions in which to tell stories that link everyday life to spiritual realities.

In some cases, what keeps people away is also their unhappiness with their congregations, their disagreement with their tradition's beliefs, or their disappointment at religious failings.[15] Religious failings were spectacularly visible in the world our Boston participants inhabited. The sex abuse scandals that have plagued Boston's Catholic Church might easily have come up often in our conversations, but only Erika brought them up. They were part of an entire pattern of things that make her angry at the Church.

> I guess anything related to sex in any way is a source of anger. Contraception in particular and the church is very popular in and growing in Africa and where they are discouraging the use of condoms where AIDS is rampant, is terrible.

For Larry Waugh, the issues were about both race and his status as a gay man in the Catholic Church.

> So, the gay thing came. And, uh, I didn't feel quite—you know, I was still going to church, but it just doesn't quite work. You know, it just doesn't quite work. So I left going to that church. And then also the church I was going to decided they would sell the church and move because the area was turning Black. I didn't agree with that. I said, how can you be hypocritical? I just thought it was very hypocritical for an organized religion. So I left that church.

Other Catholics said they think priests should be able to marry, that women should be ordained, or that the Church is wrong about abortion or homosexuality. The Pew Religious Landscape Survey found that "two-thirds of former Catholics who have become unaffiliated...say they left their childhood faith because they stopped believing in its teachings" ("Faith in Flux: Changes in Religious Affiliation in the U.S." 2009). Participants in our study who grew up Catholic were, in fact, disproportionately likely to be among the nonattenders (see Table 4.2). Like Larry and Erika, most were still moderately committed to living a spiritual life and still maintained a sense of identification with the Church, but they could no longer find a place for themselves in Catholic parishes.

Questions about belief extended beyond the Catholic Church. Grace Shoemaker wonders whether she really believes the things she says in the creeds that are recited on Sunday at All Saints, and for a variety of reasons she is rarely there. Not everyone who disagrees with religious doctrines, however, stops attending. Some of the most committed members agonize over things they think their religious communities are doing wrong. Their stories contrast to the accounts heard from marginal members, however, in the relative agency they exercise in addressing those disagreements. Too many ties bind them to the community to allow an easy exit, and those same ties provide resources for fighting back (or at least for commiserating). As Michele Dillon (1999) has written about loyal Catholics who fight the Church from the inside, sometimes the very ideas of the tradition itself can be used by the loyal opposition to argue for change. For people less engaged in spiritual life or already on the margins, however, few social ties bind them to the community, and differences over beliefs and practices are a natural way to tell the story of leaving.

Sometimes the stories of marginal members tell of a more dramatic moment of reckoning. Lily Mattison made it through college with her faith more or less intact, but it was not easy.

> When I went to college and I took history lessons on the Bible, I started realizing that the Bible wasn't really authoritative, and that was problematic for me. And when we started reading things from Paul, I felt he was very misogynistic. And of course in college, I was a huge flaming feminist and it really bothered me.

The defining moment for Lily, however, was when her mother died an agonizing death from cancer.

Table 4.2 Adult Participation by Childhood Traditions

					Childhood Affiliation				
Current Participation (any tradition)	None	Various	Conservative Protestant	Mainline Protestant	Black Protestant	Catholic	Jewish	LDS	Neopagan
Attend rarely or never	100%	22%	47%	23%	22%	44%	55%	0	0
Attend 1–3 times per month	0	56%	29%	32%	56%	24%	22%	0	100%
Attend weekly or more	0	22%	24%	45%	22%	32%	22%	100%	0
Total number of cases	N = 1	100% N = 9	99% N = 17	99% N = 22	100% N = 9	100% N = 25	100% N = 9	N = 2	N = 1

It all fell apart like an onion, like you were peeling the onion away. And there was these things you didn't believe in, until you get to the very bottom, and you're, like well, that will be the core of faith—and it wasn't there. And she died. A month after she died I said that I didn't believe in God anymore.

Now, as a graduate student, she is finding most of her life's meaning in the ideas and people in her academic world, but there are a variety of ways that she remains attuned to a spiritual dimension in life.

Failure of belief was not the most common story for Protestants, however.[16] Protestants who found themselves in a state of religious limbo were most likely to land there because their churches failed to care for them. Shirley Glazer has a moderately active spiritual life, but she is not attending church much at all. There are multiple reasons, but one of them is the way her Atlanta Presbyterian church has treated her.

And so this church that I've belonged to for four years...four thousand members. I am—I came in at the cusp of losing [my husband]. No support really. And I don't mean to sound sour grapes. It's just an observation on their priorities. And so there really were no phone calls around that, no reaching out, no "How are you doing?" no "Gee we're starting a group support; would you come?" [Since] I missed this past year I thought I'd just sort of slack up on my pledge amount. I thought, well, I haven't been going; I just might not make that second half of my pledge this year. Four letters. [You got four letters? we asked.] Four letters. [Really?] Three telephone calls.... I have not been back or given any more, and it's not an angry decision; it's just that's not really where I want to spend my time.

Liz Thompson has suffered from depression off and on in her life, and, she said, "I felt like in my times of need the church wasn't there for me. I then just became so depressed that I stopped going altogether." She is reasonably satisfied with Centre Street Church in Boston. "You know it is a very nice old traditional church. Enjoying the preaching. The sermons are usually very good. Seeing a lot of people in one place all intent and focused on the same thing. I always enjoy the music." "Would you say you feel a strong sense of connection to the congregation?" we asked; and Liz replied, "No, hence my irregular attendance."

Disappointment, disaffection, and disbelief can, then, sometimes drive a wedge between otherwise spiritually interested people and the religious communities they might participate in. A little more than half of the non-service-attenders remain somewhat interested in spiritual life, and about half of those are still marginally connected to their religious communities. Most of the rest maintain whatever spiritual practice they have on their own, outside organized religion. They may read books, attend an occasional seminar, surf the web, or just pray or meditate more or less regularly. Interestingly, only one person—twenty-something Polly Baxter—admitted that she preferred watching services on TV, rather than attending megachurch Deer Valley in person. This group of marginal members has not substituted any form of "electronic" or on-line church for in-person attendance. Whatever spiritual interaction they may have is shaped neither by media-based communities nor by the traditionally designated religious organizations of American society. They are essentially without a spiritual tribe.

The Spiritually Disengaged

Of the thirty-four participants who are currently inactive in any religious community, the remaining fourteen are nonaffiliates and likely to stay that way because they also have little or no interest in spirituality or religion. They are neither spiritual nor religious.[17] John Lehman, a middle-aged Boston computer programmer, told a classic secularization story, speaking of himself in contrast to people in the past.

> Religion, for them, was very important. Whereas, for us, it is not so important, because we have other institutions. We have schools. We have hospitals. We have moral, legal institutions. Society has evolved.

More commonly the crisis in belief is more personal than evolutionary. The story we heard from Lily Mattison hints at an underlying theme in many of these stories—at some point in the past, religious belief or a religious community failed. Lily lost her mother, and Gordon Johnson lost a young child.

> My firstborn child died at six and a half. She had a brain tumor. I did all the things—like my wife's uncle was a preacher, so he said we should fast. So I did that. But I also looked at the reality of it. Your chances

for—I mean there are miracles, or there are said to be miracles, but the reality is if you have a brain tumor your chance of surviving is very slim. It does happen but it's very slim. So I do question.

Alicia Waters is now a successful president of a nonprofit organization in Boston; but in the past, she has struggled with mental illness, and she recalled that "when I was very sick, I mean I was taking my daughter [to the parish]. But, you know, people did not really reach out to me." Two of our gay participants said that they could not imagine being out and being in church. And some of our inactive participants had unpleasant memories that went back to childhood when they were "dragged" to church or encountered unfriendly or intimidating religious people. There were, in other words, unhappy stories that spanned a lifetime, and people who told such stories were much less likely to be regular religious participants today than were those whose memories are more positive.

Whether these unhappy incidents or differences over beliefs actually caused disaffiliation is not clear. Few people were as unambiguous as Charlotte MacKenna in naming a moment and a cause for leaving the Church. She talked about how much she disagreed with the Catholic Church's stance on birth control, and as she was telling the story, she said,

> I think I will tell you exactly when I decided not to go back to church.... Just came to me just now. Talking about birth control [pause]. I was twenty, and once I had—once I started having sex I stopped going to church.... I just remember that now. I made a decision—because up until then, you know, you are a virgin, you go to church, you are holy, you go to stupid confession, and tell all your stupid sins. I said there is no way I am going to confession and saying I had sex with blah, blah.... There is no way I am confessing that because that was my choice. I am an adult now, I am twenty years old, and I am not going to confess that.... and that is when I stopped going to church.

It is possible that narrating disaffiliation seems to call for identifying reasons, that is, giving an account (Mills 1940). Those who have left religious communities draw times of unhappiness and disagreement into the story of how they came to be nonreligious. However the unhappy events have unfolded over time, they are part of the story of disaffiliation.

Another of the common elements in disaffiliation stories were the upheavals of the college years—sometimes because new ideas threatened old ones but just as often because being away from home, with new things to do, broke old routines. For Barbara Robinson, it was also "the sixties." "We just didn't go anymore," she said. "I was in college and, you know, and that was, uh, Black Power Movement, and it was the Flower Child Movement, and it was a fun time [laughs]. Lots of stuff was going on, and it [church] wasn't important to me anymore." For others the turning point was marriage. Catholic Mary Poulsen is now seventy-five, but she remembered vividly that her intent to marry an Episcopalian created conflict with her parish priest and precipitated her exit.

> He was so nasty.... They do everything they can to discourage this thing.... You're going to be at a side altar, which is heart breaking to a girl on her first marriage.... And we were going to go for three sessions. After that one session I said, Herman, I'm not going to put you through this. We'll get married in the Episcopalian church.

John Lehman remembered fondly his attendance at Mass with his father, but he married a Jewish woman and quietly quit attending Catholic churches not long thereafter.

Thomas Miller, a "consistently inconsistent" Jew, married a Methodist woman he met in Catholic high school. "Is one religion right to the exclusion of others? Doubtful. But they're all religions; as long as they're not teaching ignorance and hatred," he said. He went on to say, however, "My wife got good things out of her religious education, and I did also, and it was just a matter of how to impart that to the children and how to work with society which does have various religions and churches." He was not unusual among these nonaffiliates in voicing some appreciation for what religion can do for others, for children, or for themselves earlier in life. Greg Bradley, a middle-aged Boston social worker, said, "I'm glad I had the basic values" taught in the various Sunday schools he attended from time to time in childhood. A young Boston researcher, Matthew Smith, admitted, "Well it's kind of also a force for, I guess, advancing humanity morally.... So I almost think people almost need a religion to function full happy lives and whatnot. Yet they're all fairy tales, and I can't believe in them myself." Similarly, Gordon Johnson is happy to support the participation of his wife and daughter at Cornerstone Baptist, but he feels no need to attend himself.

A few of the nonaffiliates mentioned that they had done some exploring of religious alternatives at some point in their lives, and by far the most likely destination was Unitarian Universalism. Some came away wondering what the point was in going to a church that was "sort of a church" or "just like a meeting," as they described it. Others did see a point, even if they did not make ongoing commitments. Daphne LeCompte and her husband had taken their son to Unitarian Sunday school in Atlanta, and she talked about a recent return visit. "It was quite pleasant and I kind of thought—this is going to sound really awful—I said, wouldn't it be good to have a place where when we die we have a place to have our memorial service." Jocelyn Frederick, a young health researcher in Boston, had a more proximal goal. "When I first moved...to Boston, I was having trouble meeting people, so I actually went to a Unitarian Church for probably a month or two. Churches are good ways to get close to people, but I just didn't have time for it in the end." Jonathan Snow, an Atlanta teacher, is a convinced nonbeliever, but at one point when he was feeling burned out by teaching, he actually considered becoming a Unitarian minister. "But eventually I could tell that it was kind of like Unitarians celebrate all religions equally, and I'm sort of more, like, suspicious of all religions equally."

All of these nonaffiliates are, like Jonathan, deeply skeptical of all forms of religion and spirituality. They are more likely to use Extra-theistic terms to talk about spirituality, if they do at all, but they mostly live their current lives with little reference to any form of spiritual presence and without any engagement with a religious community.

People who arrive at this destination do not all start from the same places. Some attended regularly as children, others very little; childhood attendance itself (at least among our participants) explained very little of the adult patterns we observed.[18] People were likely to stay within the broad religious tradition with which they were raised,[19] but there have been as many twists and turns along these Americans' religious paths as we find in the population as a whole—in and out of participation, in and out of different religious communities. There was, however, one distinct set of paths—an exodus from conservative Protestant and Catholic upbringings, echoing similar trends documented in national surveys ("Faith in Flux: Changes in Religious Affiliation in the U.S." 2009). Eleven of the twenty-five people who reported being raised Catholic now attend rarely or never, as did eight of the seventeen people raised in conservative Protestant churches (see Table 4.2). It is interesting to note that these are traditions that have dominated their respective regions. Baptists in the South long enjoyed a pervasive influence that was sometimes compared to the presence of the Catholic Church in its European and immigrant heyday—the "Catholic Church of the South." And Catholics in Boston were legendary for their presence. In 2010, they still constituted nearly half the population and three-quarters of the religious adherents in Boston (Association of Statisticians of American Religious Bodies 2012). But as the cultural power of each of these traditions has diminished, people have been freer to declare their independence. What they have not always done in the process is leave behind either their basic sense of identification or whatever spiritual inclinations they may have developed along the way.

Leaving and Staying—Organized Religion and the Spiritual Life

Just as today's patterns were not set in childhood, neither are they shaped primarily by factors of class, gender, or education. People who are better educated and better off are no more nor less inclined to attend infrequently; and the men in our sample were as likely to be devoted participants as women. On these patterns our participants are not significantly different from national trends (Putnam and Campbell 2010). That we also found no difference by region or ethnicity is, however, unusual, since most studies find that participation is greater in the South and among African Americans.[20] Life-cycle, on the other hand, does seem to play a role. The oldest people in our sample were slightly more active in their religious communities, while the youngest cohort—as expected—was the most likely to be completely uninvolved. But within the younger cohorts, being a parent made at least moderate participation more likely. People who are married to an opposite-sex partner who shares the same religious tradition are the most active, while people who have an unmarried partner are the least religiously active. In other words, many of the traditional normative patterns can be seen here—being married, sharing a religious tradition, and parenting are all related to rates of religious participation.[21] We will return to this intersection with family life in the next chapter; it is important here because it signals a key social dynamic at work in everyday spiritual life. Conversations that span social domains, including the space between congregation and household, are critical vehicles for spiritual narratives.

The range and focus of spiritual conversation is the mechanism that links individual spiritual quests and organized communities. Those we've called "spiritually engaged" not only participate more often in their congregations but also have intimate conversations there about everyday life, depending on the community when they are making decisions. They are more likely to talk about the friends they have in their religious community, and they are more likely to be married to someone who attends with them. This is a pattern, in other words, where spirituality is deeply embedded in close social relationships and overlapping domains. It is also a pattern more common in conservative Protestant and Mormon congregations, where frequent attendance, developing friendships, and ample programs of spiritual development are the norm, and where the dominant form of spiritual discourse is Theistic. But spiritually engaged people are present in all the other religious traditions, as well. In other traditions, the spirituality being nurtured ranges across the Theistic and Extra-theistic categories, with many of these people recognizing both the presence and action of God and the spiritual dimensions of nature, community, and lives well lived.

The thirty-five people we have called "typical members" span a fairly broad range of religious and spiritual affinities. They generally like the worship and fellowship they find in their congregations, but they are much less likely to be involved in the kinds of small group education and nurture that sustain a conversation linking faith with everyday life. Instead they point to the music and preaching they hear on Sunday as their primary sources of inspiration. This pattern, too, is found in every tradition, but it was especially common among our mainline and Black Protestant participants. Churches in the Black traditions certainly maintain programs and expectations for adult participation in Bible study and devotional activity, but the disproportionately affluent middle-class African American participants in our study seemed especially likely to cite their busyness or the distance to church to explain their less regular participation. They simply may not be typical of other Black Church members, but they may also represent the now-recognizable trend among African Americans that "religion has increasingly become a middle-class affair" (Putnam and Campbell 2010, 276).[22] Mainline White churches, similarly, have long struggled to convince their busy middle-class adult members that education is something that continues past confirmation. Both of these traditions pride themselves on good music and preaching, and these are the mainstays of the spiritual connections between them and their "typical members." These are members who can draw on the stories they hear in sermons and the images in the hymns they sing, but their range of opportunities for active conversation is limited. Their own stories do not get told in this spiritual context, and they hear fewer everyday spiritual narratives from others.

The nineteen "marginal members" maintain at least some spiritual openness and individual spiritual connection, but they rarely if ever attend religious services. This was actually the norm for the Jewish participants in our study. Regular participation in synagogue life is not expected and tells us little about a person's sense of connection to Jewish life as a whole. All the Christian traditions, on the other hand, expect participation but have their fair share of marginal members. Most have drifted to the margins and tell stories of disbelief, of communities that fail to care, or of disjuncture between their lives and the churches they have known. These are not, for the most part, "secularization-style" stories. In fact, the *non*-college-educated people in our study were especially likely to be in this marginal category. These are, rather, failures in the relationships and conversations that constitute a spiritual community, a failure to connect the vicissitudes of an individual life with the spiritual resources of a faith tradition. These people are not the fully disengaged, but like that group, there are few active conversations in which it is possible to speak of spiritual realities and everyday life in the same breath.

All but one of the spiritually disengaged began life in a family that encouraged at least sporadic religious attendance, but at various points along the way they have left religious interest aside. To the extent that they recognize or practice any spiritual connection it is more likely to be an Extra-theistic one. While the youngest people in our study were the most likely to be nonattenders, they are not actually the most likely to be among the truly disaffiliated. That honor belongs to the baby boomers. Having dropped out in the sixties, more than a few have simply not ever returned.[23] What all of the disaffiliated share, however, is a way of telling their religious story that highlights the pains of the past. They may acknowledge some fond memories or positive benefits in previous participation, but they also remember the nasty characters and boring hours, the silly beliefs and meaningless rituals, the hypocrisy and the cultural pressure to conform. Where others found connection and inspiration, they felt alienated and unmoved.

Today's American culture makes room for all of these religious narratives, with widely varying relationships between individual spirituality (or lack thereof) and religious institutions. Far from discreet "religious" and "spiritual" institutional domains, the robust religious organizations of the United States are prime sources of the production of the spiritual experiences most prevalent in the culture. And those who are estranged from those organizations find themselves also largely disconnected from alternative spiritual communities and mostly uninvolved in individual spiritual pursuits. Without spiritual tribes, they tell few sacred stories. What remains is to ask what difference any of this makes beyond the private lives and religious communities whose spiritual contours we have now mapped. It is time to look at the domains we do not automatically label "religious" to see where and how spiritual and religious dimensions shape them.

5 EVERYDAY LIFE AT HOME

Everyday life doesn't get more everyday than the routines of household life. The people with whom we live and the places where we eat and sleep form a foundation around which most people build the rest of life. As people delineated the chapters of their lives in the initial conversation we had with them, courtships, marriages, divorces, births, and deaths in the family were among the most consistent markers on their life's journey. When they took pictures of the important places in their lives, 80 percent of them took at least one shot in and around their homes. And diary entries were filled with stories of relaxing Saturdays at home, frustrations with teenagers, and even tales of washing dishes and ironing clothes. While people may spend many hours and invest much of their sense of identity in their occupations or other commitments, there is still something fundamental about the place we call home (Pratt and Fiese 2004). If we are to understand the degree to which religion has a place in everyday life, this is the place to start. If we are to understand how spiritual tribes are constructed, households have to be part of the picture. While we did not intentionally sample based on household type, our participants are a fairly close approximation of the distribution found in the larger population (see Table 5.1), running the gamut from married-with-kids to people living alone to grandparents caring for a grandchild to a same-sex couple with their daughter. The stories from this wide range of everyday living arrangements can give us new insights into the intersection of spirituality and family life.

Navigating everyday life in the household revolves around the axes of time, space, and relationships, and on each of those dimensions we will look for where spiritual stories are heard. The routines of everyday life and the cycles of a lifetime are sometimes merely mundane and sometimes infused with religious meaning. The spaces of the household can be both sacred and ordinary; and relationships with partners, children, extended family, former spouses, and roommates may or may not also include divine actors. As we

Table 5.1 Household Composition

	Percentage in the Study	Percentage of U.S. Households*
Single, living alone	23.0%	27.5%
Single, with children	6.0%	9.6%
Unmarried partners, with children	2.0%	
Unmarried partners, no children	4.0%	5.4%
Married couples (including same sex)		
With children under 18	25.0%	21.4%
With children 18 and over	7.0%	28.2%
Without children at home	20.0%	
Unrelated adults (roommates)	12.0%	8.0%**

*Source: Bureau, U.S. Census. "S1101. Households and Families: 2006–2008 American Community Survey 3-Year Estimates." http://factfinder.census.gov/servlet/STTable?_bm=y&-geo_id=01000US&-qr_name=ACS_2008_3YR_G00_S1101&-ds_name=ACS_2008_3YR_G00_. Accessed November 15, 2010.

**Combines unmarried family households without children under eighteen and other nonfamily households.

paint the contours of everyday household life, we will look for sacred presence, absence, and the mixing of the two. In the 1,064 household stories that were analyzed, I noted who (if anyone) besides the teller was involved and whether it was a routine event or something special (in the past or in the future). The stories often involved intersections between household life and other social domains—work, consumption, religious community, neighborhood—and that was noted, as well. In addition, the emotional and spiritual content of the story was categorized and coded (see Appendix 2 for additional detail). We will be able to see, then, how different kinds of household stories, told by different kinds of people help us to understand whether and how spiritual life is present at home.

Rather than asking people to give us a general assessment of how important religion is in their households or a calculation of how much time they spend on spiritual activities, we simply asked them to tell us stories about the people, places, and events that are both memorable and ordinary. When people generalized about their families, they sometimes made grand claims: "Everything to do with my daughters and my wife and the house and work revolves around my religion and the love we have for each other," said Francis Parker, a devout Boston Catholic. While he talked about the family's involvement in church, a majority of the stories he told about his household—about sporting activities, working around the house, and the like—were told with no specific reference to any spiritual dimension. Conversely, Rachel Halpern, a Jewish mother living in suburban Atlanta, said, "I wouldn't say in everyday life that we go through and—I'm doing this because I'm Jewish; I make this decision because I'm Jewish. I think it just depends on what it is." Yet she told us story after story about the decisions they have made and the routines of daily life in which sustaining Jewish identity and tradition were at the heart of the matter. Overall assessments are important, then but the stories tell us a good deal more about what is happening on the other side of the front door.

The Places of Home

From a room in a college fraternity house to starter apartments and small first homes to large, lovely houses set in idyllic locations, our participants occupy a wide variety of spaces.[1] Whether a luxurious house in a fancy suburb or a simple in-town apartment, households are defined, at least in part, by the spaces the occupy. Energy and resources are expended and considerable symbolic meaning is attached to where one lives. Finding places to live was, in fact, a central theme in many of the stories people told about turning points in their lives and, almost always, the location of other family members played a role. Meredith Jones, a young mother who is a member of the Atlanta Vineyard congregation, recalled the decision to move to Atlanta from Florida, closer to family: "We were moving two and a half hours from our parents, which was great." They first moved into an apartment but as their son grew, they had the opportunity to buy a house. "We decided to pull all of the test scores and stuff for the schools. Because wherever we went, we knew we'd be there for a while. And [this] elementary had the top—I mean, *the* top test scores. So we decided that we would move here." American status aspirations, along with the pull of a family network, shaped her story about the place they now live.

Of all the stories about finding housing, about half were told in just such matter-of-fact terms, reflecting rational calculations and cultural norms. Some of the most spiritually engaged hinted, however, at something more going on in the process. Jessica Kingman was just looking to share a simple apartment in Boston. A casual friend mentioned that a roommate was moving and that Jessica could move in, if she wanted to. "She never told me that it was across the street from the church! It was right within what I could afford. When I pulled up here, I literally—like my face dropped. It's like those little signs in your life." Shirley Knight was equally convinced that the house she and her partner had built was more than just a mundane place to live. "To me this was very sacred space, even before we started building this house. We would come out, and on the full moon, standing like in the driveway up there, the moon comes up over this ridge." As a Neopagan, it was important to her to be close to the sacred forces of the earth; this was a good place for a house. Grace Shoemaker took a picture of her house (Figure 5.1) and told us,

> My husband and I both have felt that God put us here.... It seemed like everybody that was living around here took notice of the children, and were so loving and kind. It was almost like we had—God had put all of these guardian angels around us to help us with these two kids.

Each of these women draws broadly on both Theistic and Extra-theistic vocabularies of spirituality and participates in a religious community, and each finds that the geography of household life has been defined, at least in

FIGURE 5.1 "God put us here."—Grace Shoemaker

part, by the presence of spiritual forces.

In and around the physical structures in which people live are specific spaces that are sacralized, as well. Michelle Winter is a mother of two and a member of the same Boston Catholic parish as Jessica, although she has become an infrequent attender. She told us that she intentionally displays a variety of religious objects in her home—a picture of Jesus, Bibles, old wooden rosary beads, and the pictures her husband loves to take of old churches. Steven Kahn, from Temple Beth Torah in Atlanta, describes his home as "a very Jewish home," similarly noting the various religious symbols that are present. Laura Henderson took a picture of her living room (Figure 5.2), describing it as "the heart of my home; it is the heart of my heart." It includes "one of my paintings over the mantle and my crow totems on the mantle and my brooms on the fireplace." Bessie Connors is a sixty-something Southern Baptist in Atlanta who spoke in her diary about the "spot in my bedroom where I would kneel and pray every day," noting that when she feels that her life is not pleasing to God, she "would walk around that spot. I wouldn't even step in that spot on the days that I felt like I wasn't worthy." Drawing on the

FIGURE 5.2 "The heart of my home."—Laura Henderson

sacred symbols and practices of very different religious traditions—Catholic, Jewish, Wiccan, and Baptist—these people bring a spiritual presence into the spaces where they live.

Such specific designation of sacred space was noted by only half a dozen of our participants, but several others talked about gardening as an activity where they lose themselves in something more than ordinary (cf. McGuire 2007). They also pointed to the results of their work as spiritual signs of the earth's goodness. Walter Green, an active Southern Baptist, more than once began his diaries like this: "This morning I'm sitting out here on our side porch overlooking a beautiful green forest, hearing the birds sing. It's so peaceful and so quiet, and we feel so blessed that we have this beautiful home and this beautiful place to live."

Not every special household space was sacralized, of course.[2] Pointing to one of her photos, Mary Hage, an active member of St. Agnes Catholic parish in Atlanta, said, "It's small, its home, it's cozy, it's me. It's a fantastic neighborhood. I have trees." Erika Lombardi, a disaffected Catholic in Boston, said of a photo of her home, "It's a happy place for me in my house. It makes me happy 'cause it's sort of old things that I bought a long time ago, and more recently, something I bought with my mother, something I bought with my husband." For many, the spaces are made special by the relationships symbolized there—artwork done by a child, a gift from a husband or grandparent. This attachment to the places of home was by no means confined to Catholics (or to women) and was spread rather evenly across people with all kinds and levels of spirituality. Nor is it confined to people with high incomes and especially luxurious places to live. Carolyn Horton has a modest household income but lives in an intentional community where several dozen adults and children spread out over multiple houses and often share communal meals. She described both the space and the meals as things she loves, that make her life meaningful. Household space is often meaningful, but those meanings do not always carry spiritual significance.

Household spaces were also sometimes the sites of tension, conflict, and unhappiness. Some of the stories we heard about the places where people live were stories about the less happy sides of household life. Sometimes it was a minor irritant like mice in the attic or more major issues like a tree falling through the roof. No one had more of a horror story than Alicia Waters, a fifty-something head of a nonprofit organization in Boston. She took the risk of inviting her sister's young adult son to stay with her while he was trying to get off drugs and get his life straightened out. Her reward was a major flood caused by his negligence and a subsequent fire from sloppy repairs. Most household tensions were less dramatic but almost no one told a household horror story in a way that connected it with any religious or spiritual presence. It seems that when things go wrong around the house, God gets neither blame nor credit. When the spaces of home are narrated in happier terms, about a third of the stories were spiritually meaningful. Happy or sad, the spaces of home only occasionally escape their mundane materiality.

The People of Home

Space, of course, is not the sum of what defines a household. All the wise sayings agree that a house is not a home without the people in it, and those people are likely to be among the most important influences shaping a person's sense of identity and meaning. As we asked participants to tell us about their everyday lives, the members of their households often figured prominently in the stories. Spouses and partners, children, grandchildren, and roommates are recurring characters in the everyday tales we heard. Several of our participants (twenty-two of them) lived in single-person households, something that is increasingly common across different seasons in a lifetime, as people find themselves between significant relationships. That does not mean that they are untouched by relationships with kin, however. For most of a century, students of family life have assumed that households are increasingly small and decreasingly multigenerational.[3] But whether single persons, empty nesters, or parents with their one or two children (the most common patterns), beneath the demographic surface are the pervasive ongoing connections between households and the extended families of which they are a part (Bengtson 2001).

Every person who participated in this project told at least one story about a person from their extended kin network, someone not living in their household but related by blood or marriage. Most stories came without prompting, in the context of the pictures people took and in the stories they told about everyday joys and struggles. When we asked participants to name the handful of people they feel closest to, 70 percent of them named at least one member of their extended clan. Their grown children and grandchildren, their own parents and siblings but also the spouses and children of those siblings were part of the circle. Many live near enough to be part of the face-to-face interaction of the household but mostly people talked about communicating by phone (not, interestingly, via email and text). Many of the stories we heard were about holiday gatherings, but most were not. They were daily and weekly routines of calls to parents, routine meetings for Sunday morning coffee with siblings, and daytrips to see grandmother. Family is simply not limited to those in the household.

About half of all the kinds of relationship stories we heard were told in completely secular terms, situated in the ordinary scheme of things. In these narratives, people were brought together, negotiated their relationships, took care of each other, and sometimes drifted apart with no named guidance or inspiration from religious or spiritual sources. The other half of the stories, however, included elements of spiritual presence, of shared ritual, of a divine hand. The stories of household relationships, like other household stories, can be both sacred and secular tales.

The majority of stories about these household and family relationships were about the routine happenings of everyday life, rather than about any-thing special; but even the routines could evoke strong feeling. The dynamics and emotions of family life are the stuff of drama and legal conflict, happily ever after and tragic endings. Over two-thirds of the stories we heard were told as satisfying and joyous accounts of relationships past and present; but that means that a substantial minority of stories provided a glimpse of the darker sides of family life. In our initial interview, we were not often invited into the most intimate and painful corners of the household. But as the proj-ect progressed, through conversations about the pictures participants took and, especially, into their recording of oral diaries, the level of intimacy grew noticeably deeper. Worries and conflicts were sometimes confided to the digi-tal recorder as if it were a trusted friend. The picture that emerges from our data, then, includes a healthy slice of both the joys and sorrows of living in families.

Finding, Keeping, and Losing Partners

One of those ubiquitous getting-acquainted questions is "So how did you two meet?" The mythic narrative of meeting, falling in love, and deciding to spend life together is a story we learn about as soon as we hear our first story-book tales. While the plotline often takes a number of twists and turns, it is nevertheless a powerful trope in Western culture, and about a quarter of our participants included a courtship tale as part of their initial life history nar-rative. Listening to how they told the story, we see that questions of religion and spirituality were often present, more so than in routine household stories. Of all the courtship accounts we heard, almost two out of three were shaped at least in part by religious or spiritual considerations.

For a number of our participants, it was important to find a spouse of the same religious tradition or to figure out how to work around the reality of being religiously different. Samantha Bailey identifies herself as Wiccan and said she was probably first attracted to the man who became her husband because he, too, was actively exploring Wicca and other pagan beliefs. Over the years, their beliefs have diverged somewhat, but "they're pretty much along the same lines. Yeah. He does not identify himself as Wiccan, just pagan." Sylvia Carter, a Jewish young adult who is still looking for the right partner, talked about having dated Christian guys, in some cases seriously, but finally concluding that she really did want "someone who is raised Jewish who has that sense of culture, community—but I don't want him to be any more observant [than I am]." Margi Perkins is a deeply spiritual and very active Catholic living in Atlanta. Her husband, on the other hand, has always been a Southern Baptist. Happily, they have overcome that difference.

> Now he is completely supportive; he comes to church every Sunday. He's Southern Baptist but he has not been in a Southern Baptist church in twenty years. He comes here to church every Sunday with the children. This is a Southern Baptist who prays the Hail Mary with my children. So, I have no problem with that. If he would come to the faith I would think that was wonderful. I pray for that but it's something that he has to be called to do. I don't want him doing it just because he thinks it would really make me happy. I want him to do it because it will really make him happy.

The question of Catholic/Protestant unions raises far less anxiety today than would have been the case in the past.[4] Jewish intermarriage, on the other hand, remains controversial, even as rates soar.[5] Margi's and Samantha's emphasis on religious accommodation are typical for those whose religious identity and practice are quite central in their lives, while Sylvia's desire for a co-religionist partner is unusual for someone who is otherwise spiritually disengaged. But Sylvia's experience also makes clear that finding a religiously compatible person is often an important part of the partner selection process, even when the issue is making sure the person is not *too* religious.

Within the broad streams of moderate and liberal American Protestantism, homogamy is on the decline (Sherkat 2004), and most of our mainline Protestant participants simply did not talk about their courtship experiences in religious terms. Nor did our African American Protestant participants. They told about meeting at work or at school, about falling hopelessly in love or about patient courting—a process more of the head and heart than the soul. On the other end of the spectrum, all but one of our LDS participants is married to a fellow Mormon. They either grew up in the Church together and never considered marrying outside the faith, or they converted together as adults. For a faith in which families are not just temporal but eternal, courtship and marriage are inevitably defined in sacred terms.[6]

Once having made a match, relationships are sustained by all the intricate ways in which lives become intertwined as well as by the special moments and practices that reinforce the bond. Our participants talked about celebrating anniversaries, entertaining the friends they share, and setting aside weekend time to relax and catch up. Those whose religious and spiritual lives were most active were likely to see those activities in religious terms or focus them on religious activities. Mark Fuller talked about how much he and Leah enjoy entertaining, including friends from their Presbyterian church with whom they share grace before the meal. For those who are less personally engaged in spiritual pursuits, nurturing a marriage is no less important but not so clearly linked with spiritual life. Rebecca Klein's children are grown, and she happily reported, "It's like my husband and I have rediscovered each other.... We share our history but we, like, we want a future." Jennifer Hammond talked about putting together a list of the twenty reasons she loves her husband as part of her twentieth anniversary gift to him. Rebecca is Jewish, and Jennifer is a Congregationalist, but neither is particularly invested in a religious community. Both are simply pursuing good practices for keeping the marital flames alive.

But sometimes marriages are tested by unexpected life changes, by illness and financial setbacks, by infertility, and by a host of other situations that hold the potential for clashes large and small. Crises resolved become the building blocks for future strength and the stuff of stories joyfully told. Stephen James and his wife suffered through six years of infertility, miscarriages, and even an ectopic pregnancy and emergency surgery. When their son was born, he required special care for nearly a month; but on the other side of all that, theirs is now told as a story of prayers answered and family commitment strengthened. Erika Lombardi and her husband traveled a considerable distance down the road of infertility treatment, too, and finally concluded that the physical and financial toll was just too great. They explored adoption but decided that was probably not a good possibility for them, either. Coming to terms with being childless has been a struggle, but it is a struggle they seem to be handling together. While they consider themselves quite thoroughly nonreligious, they nevertheless have a deep and lifelong set of connections to Boston's Catholic community. When they were going through the infertility treatments, Erika reported that they "had full support actually of my nun friends and of the priest that we knew from the young adult group." In spite of never attending Mass themselves, Erika and her husband teach in the Church's Pre-Cana marriage preparation program, and they always share their struggles around childlessness with the new couples. The people and programs of the Church have been critical players in their marriage, even without their own participation in religious rituals or their belief in Catholic dogma.

In the midst of a crisis, as the script is still being written, it is less clear how the story will be resolved. Catherine Young is struggling with her own high ideals for what a Mormon wife and mother is supposed to look like. When her infant daughter does not behave well in church or wakes up in the middle of the night, Catherine finds herself cranky and irritated. Worse, the strains of her husband's start-up business and her adjustment to full-time motherhood are taking a toll on the marriage.

> We have been talking about it and Bryson described it that what we basically were giving each other were leftovers of our energy. Like he would go to work, and he is putting everything into work, and . . . I give that all away to friends or to Sarah, and then when we get home together at night we just kind of have nothing left to give to each other. We haven't prioritized our time and energy to be able to have anything left.

Catherine and Bryson have ample religious guidance and strong norms from their religious community to guide them, but that does not make the stress go away.[7] Looking back, people with an active faith almost always interpreted their relational crises in religious terms, while otherwise nonspiritual people did not. For one conservative Protestant man, divorce represented a spiritual failure he still struggles with; a nonreligious woman, by contrast, talked about how it was her therapist who helped her get through a similar difficult time.

The family challenges faced by Amelia James are all the more formidable for the gap between her own religious commitments and her husband's. While religious experiences and commitments have become more and more important to her in recent months, her husband is uninterested. In one of her diary entries, she talked about an experience of healing that she described as "probably one of the most important experiences I've ever had. . . . The only problem with that is that Terry—I didn't tell him about this. I don't think that he would understand." In our initial conversation with her, she had confessed that money was a "sore subject between my husband and I because we think of it completely differently." Their financial struggles, she later reported in her diary, led her husband to ask her to resume birth control.

> I had a huge, huge fight with Terry today.... We recently had a scare, thinking I was pregnant again, and we really can't afford another child.... Terry asked me, you know, what are the chances of you getting back on the patch. I said none! I will not go on birth control! It is, you know, against my religion. And he tried to argue with me about it, saying how, you know that nowhere in the Bible does it say anything about birth control.

What she then recounts in her diary is a heated discussion that included arguments about permissible forms of birth control, worries about the side effects of the pill, and the importance of Catholic teachings—none of which convinced her husband. The conversation ended in tears and a slammed door, and despite her husband's subsequent willingness to let the issue go, she is convinced that they will have to talk again. She ended the day's recording by saying, "I feel absolutely horrible about [hurting Terry's feelings]. And I don't know how it's going to get fixed. But I don't want to lose him. I really, really don't want to lose him." Her own strong religious commitments, not matched by his, make this a story with a very uncertain ending.

Between the Generations

Over the course of human history, one of the primary functions of an adult household was to produce offspring. The birth control revolution of the last half century—notwithstanding resisters like Amelia—has substantially altered that fact. Still, the presence of children—past, present, and future—occupied the narratives of over half our participants. Just over a third (37 percent) of them are currently raising children (and in one case a grandchild), but others reminisced about now-adult children or speculated about the future. Their stories, on balance, reflected more of the joy of parenting than its frustrations but the worry and frustration was there, as well. Fully a third of the parenting stories we heard (somewhat more than the other household stories) were tinged with the conflict, fear, and sadness that sometimes mark the life of a parent. We will look at the role of children in various aspects of household life in the pages that follow, but we begin here with what our participants had to say about the basics of their children's presence in their lives, the work they were doing to shape their children's lives, and the way all of that is affected by various community institutions.

As with so much else about household life, the presence or absence of any spiritual content in the parenting routine is largely determined by the level of individual spiritual engagement of the parent who is telling the story. Those who are personally engaged in spiritual life and those who attend services more regularly were more likely to talk about their interactions with their children in religious terms—to see them as gifts from God, to participate in religious training and rituals with them, to pray for them. A disaffected Catholic such as Charlotte McKenna, on the other hand, told a wide range of stories about her young adult children (one of whom is still living at home), and neither church going nor any hints of spirituality ever entered the picture. She mentioned in passing that her sons had gone to CCD classes, but they are no more involved in church today than she is, and she figures that religion will have little bearing on their choices of marriage partner and future childrearing.[8]

Unlike Charlotte, parents who are themselves spiritually engaged often told stories about including prayer, Bible reading, and other religious activities in the family's daily routine. Andrea Valencia talked about the bedtime routine of reading a story and then kneeling by the bedside with her children for a prayer. In the past they have watched cartoons designed to teach biblical and moral lessons, and she frequently quizzes them on Bible knowledge. Catherine Young took her recorder along while she was shopping in preparation for their Monday night "family home night." As she explained it, "the [LDS] Church encourages families to get together, take time, have a spiritual thought, maybe even do a little game together and have a treat together and just take some family time on Monday night to learn more about the gospel and to spend quality time together." Pam Jones and several others had more modest routines, such as saying grace "as a family." These three mothers are each active participants in a religious community—Pentecostal, Mormon, and African American Baptist, respectively, and each talked extensively about her own spiritual life. Their communities have provided resources for bringing religious practice into their children's lives, and their own commitment has made that a priority.

The values parents talked about were not always overtly religious, however. Nora Cole is Jewish and not especially spiritual herself, but she does want her son to appreciate the beauty in the world around him—even on their daily drive to school (Figure 5.3). As she showed us the pictures she took, she said,

FIGURE 5.3 "We are often stuck at this traffic light, and this is the courthouse building.... I just like the way it lights up."—Nora Cole

> This is a building we go by in Salem on the way to taking my son to school, and we are often stuck at this traffic light here. Every day. And this is the courthouse building from the late nineteenth century, and I like the building, and on a good morning like this, uh, the morning light hits this side and it kind of glows.... I just like the way it lights up, and I point it out to my son every time. I say, "See the light on that building. Isn't it pretty?"

Jennifer Hammond (a member of Grimsby Congregational) has strong feelings about the sense of privilege and entitlement that exists in her community, and she is already thinking about how to teach her young son about money. "I want him to understand that things have value and that things—you know, he shouldn't just have everything." Nora and Jennifer are somewhat active in their religious communities but not especially engaged in everyday spiritual practice themselves. They are communicating their Extra-theistic sense of spirituality in the moral and aesthetic lessons they teach their children.

Parents who are less religious have to figure out how to navigate the pervasive presence of religion in American culture. Mostly our nonreligious participants seemed willing to let their kids explore, but it sometimes meant awkward conversations at home. Robin Mitchell and her wife Colleen adopted Alexa from China and are enormously proud of her ("She's a cool chick!"). Robin also described her as a "little bit of a believer." "She's asked me in the past, you know, like well, how you pray and what are you supposed to say or do. So rather than denigrate it, I'll say, well, you know, just think about the things that are important to you and, you know, if you believe in God, then you can tell those things to God." Robin and Colleen are very unlikely to cultivate Alexa's interest on their own, but they have a hard time avoiding the conversation.

Beyond the household, the most ubiquitous presence in the lives of children and parents is school, and on balance what we heard about school was about as likely to be a matter of anxiety as of satisfaction. Certainly there were triumphs and joys celebrated, but when children struggle at school, those struggles are often brought home. Olivia Howell's son is just four but his impulsive behavior has been causing trouble in his preschool, so she was thrilled to report one day in her diary, "He's had no time outs almost all week." These kinds of difficulties seemed to be just as prevalent among highly religious people (like Olivia) as among others, although people like Olivia were more likely to pray for divine comfort and assistance. Pam Jones, for instance, told us that she and her husband were praying about whether their daughter should transfer to a more challenging private school.

> Last Sunday was the first day in a while that we all could get to church. So we went and hadn't seen people in a while. Clearly, my daughter has grown up in that church, and when several different families—they wanted to know how old she was, what grade she was in. Each and every one of them was saying exactly what my husband and I have been telling her about school; that, you know, now she's in the eighth grade; next year it's high school and it's serious. It's time to buckle down and do the best we can and make sure you're in the best school—it's all a big step in the process of getting into the right colleges. After the third person said it, I looked at her and said, "Lindsay, I didn't put any of these people up to this!"

It is indicative of the social class position of our sample that we heard more stories about choosing the right school than about surviving a bad one. Cynthia Gardner was even willing (and able) to take the risk of moving cross-country so her son could be in a school that would meet his needs. "He's severely learning disabled and he started [this] school at thirteen years old. He did not know the alphabet. He could not read at all. And [now] he's getting straight As in college, carrying eighteen units!"

In addition to parents and schools, children are often nested in circles of neighbors, friends, and extended family members. Andrea Valencia took a picture of what she had labeled "The Bus Stop." "That's where our kids meet us, and that's where all us moms hang out and gossip. And I've made a lot of really good friends there at the bus stop." They share information about what is happening at school and in the neighborhood while they look out for their children. Michelle Winter has help from her parents, who live downstairs in their typical Boston two-family double-decker. She acknowledged that "it can be hard to have someone's parents downstairs or upstairs but it works out well. It really is a partnership. She helps me. I help her.... She [pause] is a good role model for my kids. I think they enjoy hearing about her growing up or her coming to this country. They're very proud of my mother." This satisfying sharing of life with an older parent was the exception, however. More common were stories about the struggles of tending to aging parents.[9] Greg Bradley recounted his trips to New Jersey to help his sister move their father into an assisted living facility where his dementia could be monitored. He was one of several who told stories about the reversal of roles when parents are the ones who need care. For these people, the events of the day recorded in their oral diary might begin with thinking out loud about who will be on duty to watch after Mom.

The stories we heard often reflected, in fact, a sense of family fragility. These are certainly not the world's impoverished and endangered families. The threats they faced were far from the realities of disease and malnutrition and war that disrupt the lives of millions of families around the world. The disruptions facing these households ran, instead, a gamut from divorce to drug addiction to various forms of illness, disability, and death.[10] Especially in oral diary entries, we heard about the disruptions of sick infants, ER visits, and even the miseries of orthodontia. And at least half a dozen of the parents in this study had also experienced a young child's serious illness or death. Unlike the routine crises, these stories were very likely to be told in a spiritual mode, but that does not mean that faith was always enough. Recall that Gordon Johnson left his faith after the death of his young daughter. For others, crisis was thoroughly interwoven with faith. Jen Jackson's baby was not yet out of the woods, but when she began her second round of oral diaries, six months after the first, she was excited to report that the baby's failure to thrive had just been diagnosed as a problem with food allergies. "And she's, she's going to be fine, and so I just praise God for that, 'cause the last six months have been really difficult and really taxing on me and my family, my marriage, just so many areas of my life." Even when the children are grown up, parents still worry and often remain involved as they confront divorce and job loss, alcoholism and addiction. These stories of grown children, by contrast, almost never included references to spiritual sources of support. Once out of the nest, the travails of adult children seem to be merely tales of worldly woe.

The relationships between the generations impinge on household life in other ways, as well. While the grandparents in our study were unanimous in their delight at spending time with their grandchildren, relationships in the other generational direction were not always so happy. Some parents and siblings from families of origin as well as the occasional "step" relative were not altogether welcome guests in the household. That seemed especially true where significant religious differences have developed over the years—differences in either generational direction. Neopagans from evangelical families had especially dramatic stories, but so did other evangelical parents. "The attitude of my children is something I will never understand. Or my grandchildren," said Mary Margaret Sironi, an eighty-seven-year-old member of Center Street Church in Boston (a large evangelical congregation). "If you don't teach them they're not going to know. And I feel that my sons missed that boat. And so I really don't blame the grandchildren.... Their parents didn't think that was important."

It would be misleading to end on that note, however. On balance, households with children seemed to be places of a good deal of joy and satisfaction. Births were often noted as the start of a new life chapter—usually looked back on as a good one. Similarly, for Robin and Colleen, adopting Alexa redefined their family. "So Colleen and I have been together for twenty-two years. In 1999 we adopted a daughter from China.... So now we, uh, have a family of three." The commitment to being parents was, for many of our participants, a deeply spiritual one, both requiring and calling forth new capacities. James Dupree looked back on Abbie's birth and said, "When we had Abbie, I had no idea what life would be like. I thought that I was groovy; I thought I had lots of love in my heart. But you don't really know—because I didn't know about sacrifice; I didn't know about sleep deprivation. The true nature of love is sacrifice.... Get up and get a cup of coffee for somebody, give them a glass of water, all the way up to sacrificing—bringing your parents into your home when they're older, whatever." Mark Fuller, neurology resident and father of a six-month-old son, summed it up well:

> The big thing I'm doing right now is, other than work, is still trying to deal with the enormity of having the little boy around. Things are rapidly shifting from—okay, how can we meet his basic needs? to Oh my

goodness he's turning into an actual person! Is he going to be a good person? Hope he's going to be a good person. How's he going to learn how to be good; he's watching me [laughs]. And realizing that [pause] my father said on many occasions that he thought parenthood taught him a lot about the relationship between God and man, and I see why.

["How so?" we asked.] Because you want them to do the right thing. You want them to be good. You want them to be kind. You want them to care for people. You want them to be principled and you can't make any of that happen. You do what you can and make sure you love them even when they mess up, but they're not in your hands.

Clocks and Calendars

Households, then, are never quite as simple as they might seem if we look only at the list of who lives there. They include constantly shifting relationships both inside and outside their four walls, and each of those relationships is shaped by the rhythms and constraints of time. Mark Fuller's story detailed how each day in a complicated two-career household required navigating work, daycare, and all the necessities of survival. These are the kinds of stories that were more likely recorded in an oral diary entry than remembered and marked in an interview. But throughout their participation in our project, people narrated their lives in ways that often centered on time—ordinary time and extraordinary time, sacred time and profane time. As the touchstone of everyday life, households are shaped both by the people in them and by the rhythms imposed by clocks and calendars and Blackberries.

Day In, Day Out

The morning alarm's sound finds most people "at home," and the routines of life begin with activities in preparation for the obligations of the day ahead. Harris Crosby and his wife Megan both work for an Atlanta broadcast company and have a young daughter. Here's how Harris describes the routine.

I get up at 5:30, every morning, Monday through Friday. And, um, while Megan's getting ready I come in here and I have a protein shake and take a big handful of vitamins. And then I get my gym stuff together and get my truck loaded up. I sit down for about fifteen minutes and read what of the paper that I can. And then at 6:25, 6:30ish I get Amy up so she can get to see her mommy before mommy leaves for work. I get Amy dressed. We have a little bit of time up here. I usually read her a book or she's knocking stuff over or something. I don't know. And we spend a little bit of time together and then we get in the truck and we drive over to [the daycare center]. And then I drop her off there and make sure she's all set to go. Then I go to the gym four days a week and I work out until about 9 o'clock. Then I hit the shower, and my heels have to hit the sidewalk at 9:30, and I drive from there to work. And I get there about 10 o'clock and I read in... [he continues with a description of his day at work]. And then I usually come home and I do whatever chores I have to do when I get home, which is usually water the tomato plants, and take the garbage up to the curb, or take the cans back from the curb. Bring the mail in. Uh, do laundry. Something like that. And then we eat dinner. And we're horrible, we eat dinner in front of the TV with Amy. And then give her a bath; one of us gives her a bath; the other one tries to clean up. And then the opposite one reads her a story or something and puts her to sleep. Then we sit up and, you know, we used to like stay up till 2 in the morning. Now we stay up until about 10 and that's late!

Studies of household labor (e.g., Sayer 2005) would tell us that Harris is a remarkably involved father (and that he may just be overestimating how much time he spends on parenting and household chores), but the daily mix of household upkeep, childcare, work, and tending to relationships is typical among middle-class American families.[11] Like other spiritually disengaged participants, Harris's daily routine shapes his life, and it is not something he thinks of as religious, transcendent, or especially meaningful. He did joke, however, "It's not very spiritual but.... have to do a lot of praying I guess and hope the Lord helps us with potty training."

In the context of everyday household routines, prayer can be, in fact, just about that mundane. Participants with more active connections to religious and spiritual life often told us about praying for everything from school exams to traffic jams. For Melissa Parker, the rhythms of the day are punctuated by prayer.

I drop the kids off and pray that we have a safe day; that the kids are focused at school; that Daddy is safe—because my husband leaves early, he leaves first—that Daddy has a good day at work and a safe day at work and that we all make it back home together.

Melissa is a very active member at New Beginnings Church in Atlanta, an African American church that encourages this kind of everyday spiritual engagement. Across religious traditions—Catholic, mainline Protestant, conservative Protestant, LDS, and Wicca—some of our participants adopted prayers and rituals that could be incorporated into routine daily household life.

Even for spiritually engaged people, though, some things really are just routine. As devout Andrea Valencia mused in her diary one night, "Another day is over. I'm getting ready to go to bed and it's so late again. You know I've come to learn that there are two things in life that never, never end: dishes and laundry." Just mundane household chores. But even washing the dishes caused Cynthia Gardner to reflect as she was

> noticing the rainbow colors in the suds. Thich Nhat Hahn refers to it as being in the moment, to be in the moment; and that's a great Buddhist thing is to be in the moment. But I think for me as a Christian, being in the moment is also when I can really be aware of God.... feel the warmth of the water on my skin, and to see the colors in the soap bubbles, to hear the squeak of the clean plate. And when I can really be in that moment there is a peace comes over me that isn't there when I'm frantic and working and obsessing and worrying and always doing.

Here as elsewhere, Cynthia draws both on her Episcopal sensibilities and her Buddhist study and practice even in the everyday routines of housework.

The nature of everyday household routine is neither inherently secular nor inherently sacred, then. People disconnected from spiritual and religious traditions rarely talked about daily routines in sacred terms, while people with at least some religious attachment described their bedrock routines in ways that mixed secular and sacred.

Eating Together

Like all the other daily routines, cooking and eating is sometimes sacralized and sometimes not. Nothing says "family" in the popular imagination quite like the kitchen table, and almost a third of our participants took pictures of just that spot (Figure 5.4). While a shared sit-down meal may be a disappearing phenomenon in U.S. households, stories about meals played an important part in what our participants told us about everyday household life. About half specifically mentioned mealtime routines, shopping for groceries, and choosing what to eat. Lily Mattison was a twenty-eight-year-old, recently married student when we interviewed her, and she told us a lot about the way she and her husband are dividing up the tasks. Despite recognizing it as stereotypical, she confessed that she loves to cook. One night when she was doing her oral diary, she said, "I made a really good sandwich tonight.... It means a lot to me to be able to cook something healthy for the ones that I love."

People who were married were far more likely to take note of meals than were people living alone or even people living with other partners; and if there were children in the household, meals were even more likely to show up in stories about everyday routines.[12] Jennifer Hammond is the mother of an adopted preschool son, Aidan, and she talked extensively about her love of cooking, her routine of baking bread, and how menus have changed since SpaghettiOs and mac-and-cheese entered the family repertoire. Even when the children are much older, perhaps no longer in the household but nearby, gathering the family for a meal often defined the best moments that people told us about in their diaries. Barbara Robinson and her husband have one young adult son at home and another who is living nearby. Recounting the events of her day, she recalled,

FIGURE 5.4 "We always grew up, like, eating dinner together."—Jessica Wilson

My oldest son came over...and my husband was cooking on the grill and...my children love my husband's cooking....So we sat down; we had dinner. And I love this. I love having my family surrounded around me. And I love dinner time. I love to have them at the table; eating and enjoying our meal.

These stories are told as examples of the everyday joy of family life, with no special religious or spiritual intent or significance. Meals are a critical part of the glue that holds these households together, and that glue can work without any specifically religious content. As with many other things, the spiritual meaning is in the person more than the practice itself. Individual participants in our study who were otherwise not attuned to spirituality and not involved in religious communities were just as likely as the more spiritually engaged participants to emphasize the importance of meals, but they almost never described mealtime in spiritual terms. For others, more attuned to spiritual practices, saying grace was one way that meals were sometimes sacralized. James Dupree took a picture of his family at mealtime and told us, "We're saying grace. We always sing, 'For health and strength and daily food.'...So you get a chance to bond as a family, hold hands as a family, stop for only twenty seconds, maybe even ten—sing a song and remind yourself [to say], 'thank you, Lord.' So it's a good ritual. Rituals make your life deeper and more meaningful." A simple prayer of grace provides a moment of acknowledgement that routine meals can have a deeper significance.

For two of the religious traditions we included in our study, food is more than just an important element in a happy household. Latter-day Saints and Jews were much more likely than other participants, in fact, to talk about food as they told stories about everyday household life. Here the sacred meaning of food comes from the tradition and not just the person. Both groups have extensive dietary rules that become, for the observant, a marker of religious membership and a daily reminder of one's religious allegiances. The LDS official website, introducing teachings of the Church, explains,

He [God] revealed a law of health, called the *Word of Wisdom*, to Joseph Smith in 1833. The *Word of Wisdom* prohibits the drinking of alcohol, coffee and tea, and the use of tobacco. It also implies that we not use illegal drugs or abuse prescription drugs. The *Word of Wisdom* also encourages us to eat plenty of the fruits and vegetables that are in season, plenty of grains and a moderate amount of meat. It reminds us to eat these things "with prudence and thanksgiving." ("God's Commandments" 2010)

Catherine Young said, "I mean we just try to take really good care of our bodies. We believe that they are temples for each of us, and we just try to put good things in them. And there are some things that we avoid because it is part of the *Word of Wisdom*." She and her husband Bryson not only pray at every meal but also shape the meals themselves according to Church teaching.

Sam Levitt and his wife, on the other hand, do not see fully eye-to-eye on keeping kosher. "I would probably keep a kosher home if my wife would let me get away with it [laughs], and she just doesn't go that far with me." Meals are nevertheless important to them. "My wife and I have dinner together every night unless one of us has a meeting or something.... It's a routine and it's an expectation." When we asked about Friday night, he said, "Yes, every Friday night we do it. I actually buy dinner—not as special as I would like it to be...[but] she'll do the candles and the blessings and we do the lengthy Kiddush. And when we were just in Israel, we bought yet another set of candlesticks that she picked out, which I always love to see." Since our participants came from a Reform temple in Atlanta and a Conservative synagogue outside Boston, it is perhaps not surprising that none of them are strictly observant, but even in deciding where they will draw the lines, they were shaping household routines in dialogue with religious traditions they wish to see continue. Kitchen tables are key sites where spiritual and everyday overlap, where sacred and secular are negotiated on a daily basis.

Walking the Dog and Feeding the Cat

Over a third of our participants, with no prompting from us, made sure that we knew how important their pets were in the everyday life of the household.[13] They mentioned acquisitions and deaths of pets as milestones in their lives. They took pictures of their pets, and some even regaled us with tales of pets in their oral diaries. The presence of pet stories seemed to have few demographic contours—not education or income or gender or even parental status. In fact, only a very few of the stories we heard involved children and pets together. Pets were much more often mentioned by empty nesters and by single adults either living alone or with roommates. Rather than having pets *for* the children, people seemed to be having pets *instead*. And in almost every story we heard, pets were extolled as sources of great pleasure and contentment. "So if you got a box full of puppies, it's almost impossible to be depressed. It just makes you smile," said Bill Hamilton, a forty-year-old Atlantan who lives alone. Seventy-three-year-old William Pullinger, a retired engineer and empty nester, pointed out that his two-mile walks with the dog are good exercise for him. Those walks were a routine he included in his oral diaries: "The temperature today was beautiful. It was in the fifties, and so I decided to take a walk with my dog Goldy. Goldy is a ten-year-old Vizsla. She's my constant companion. Whenever I go riding in the truck she must go with me. She loves everybody. The sweetest dog we've ever owned." Thomas Miller, who lives nearby on Boston's North Shore, actually took his recorder along on one of his excursions with his dog, narrating as he went: "It's a very beautiful little walk here, and I'm with my dog Rusty, my poodle, who carries with him a stuffed animal." Miller is the father of three school-aged children but the dog is his.

Bill, William, and Thomas were among the least spiritually engaged of our participants, although William attends Grimsby Congregational fairly frequently, and Thomas is a member of Congregation Sinai. Also in the minimally spiritual camp was Steve Sims, a thirty-something single man, living with roommates in Atlanta. He told a long dog story that stretched from his interview through multiple diary entries. He had adopted a previously neglected dog and slowly worked to earn its trust, but after the dog inflicted injuries on others, he reluctantly concluded that it would need to be put down. He agonized over what he described as a moral dilemma, not convinced that humans should have such power over other living things. It was clear that Steve found something inspirational about this animal. When he described his most important routines, he immediately named "walks with my dog. And I would call it like meditation time or just—sometimes it's actual meditation." Bill Hamilton is even more disconnected from religion or spirituality but he noted that that box of puppies would not only make a person smile but would also put "you in touch with something that's bigger than you." Said Larry Waugh, an inactive Catholic, "I truly believe that my dog and my roommate's dog were godsends—were little angels put in our lives in a moment when we needed it." The furry members of their households provided a small window on a spirituality these men otherwise rarely encounter.

The role of animals in spiritual life was not just found among those outside traditional religious institutions. The most conservative of our participants, oriented dominantly to Theistic spirituality, were less likely to talk about pets at all and rarely attributed any spiritual connection to them, but those attuned to Extra-theistic spiritualities were likely to tell pet stories and to make spiritual connections to what they observed in those pets. Laura Henderson told us, "I try to come home at night and walk the dogs, and not only does that help with the stress but it connects me with the earth again," she said. "Allows me to get out and breathe the air and listen to the little animals scampering around and just see what She [the Goddess] has there for us." Her fellow Circle member Emma Cooper likes the routine of feeding and caring for her cats because it connects her to long generations of women who have cared for living things. The most prolific tellers of pet tales, in fact, were those who combine Theistic and Extra-theistic ways of thinking about spirituality. Across Catholic, mainline Protestant, and Jewish communities, we heard people describing pets as signs of transcendence in their everyday household lives.

Some of the most religiously active participants included pets in their practices of spirituality. Jessica Kingman is single and Catholic and works at home, so she is able to incorporate a prayer break into her routine.

> So when it was five of 3 and I was getting extremely frustrated with what I was doing, I joyfully (little laugh) walked away from the computer and went to get some peace, and knelt down—and grabbed my dog who comes with me all the time—and we kneel in front of Jesus and Mary and Saint Joseph and set about prayers for about fifteen minutes.

Theresa Collins showed us the picture of her front gate and told us,

> This is coming out where I come out of the house, through the front gate there and head up that street every single morning…that's just the beginning of my life every single day. It's where I start my prayers. I usually, I mean, I usually come out, I close the gate, and I say, "Good morning, world," and then I start my prayers. And Digby and I walk up the street, and then we usually head right over to our favorite walk, over to the ocean and back (Figure 5.5).

Digby is a collie, and Theresa had already talked about what an important part of the family he is but she also joked that he was "the Lord's dog—'the Lord is my shepherd, and the collie is his dog!' And it makes me very happy to have the Lord's dog of all the dogs I could have."

The connection between Theresa's spiritual life and her dog was further affirmed by her faith community itself. On the first Sunday in October, in celebration of St. Francis Day, dogs are welcome in the church service at All Saints Episcopal and receive a blessing from the priest. But Theresa and other dog lovers do not have to wait for that celebration. "On Thursday morning, Thursday at 9 a.m., there's a little holy communion in the chancel…which

FIGURE 5.5 "I thank the Lord every morning, every day, every time I take this walk."
—Theresa Collins

is a wonderful service. It's attended by maybe ten to twelve people. It's also attended by the Reverend Wilson's, um, Spencer, who happens to be a black lab. And it's also attended by my collie, Digby, who lies quietly in the pew with me. Even though he's only two years old, he mellows down the minute he gets into church." Sam Levitt was similarly attached to his dog and similarly made sure that the dog was included in the spiritual life of the household. "We would always say it's Friday night, let's welcome Shabbat and say the prayers. And the dog is always part of that, as well, and he knows that he gets to eat some challah, and I hold him, so that's a nice part of it as well." Officially sanctioned religious rituals intersect here with the routines of household life and draw into their circle of significance the four-legged creatures along with their human caretakers.

Juggling Work and Family

The routines of everyday household life are, of course, not isolated from the many other domains people inhabit, and few institutions have a larger impact than the labor force (Hochschild 1997; Schor 1991). Half of our participants told us stories about the present and past ways that jobs have intersected with the life of the household. As we listen to those stories, it is critical to remember that the people who agreed to participate in our study were disproportionately in management and professional jobs (or retired) and had a relatively high degree of autonomy in their work. A more blue-collar group of participants would surely have added a broader range of concerns; but even so, half of the work-and-household stories we heard reflected worry, unhappiness, tension, and conflict more than the happy and satisfying emotions of many other household routines.

Sometimes it is the job itself that is unsatisfying and a source of stress that finds its way home. Amelia James, unlike most others in our study, lives in a financially strapped blue-collar household. She is a twenty-eight-year-old mother of a toddler, who is working a full-time job, while also trying to start a home-based business. One of her diary entries reflected both her frustration and her hopes:

> I'm trying to start up this side business so I don't have to work full time.... Once the business is successful, which I know it will be—it's the type that is not going to take five years to be successful; it will take less than a year—I'll be able to quit my job and give him [her son] all the attention in the world.... I won't be exhausted all the time with him.

She felt the pressure even more because her husband had gotten laid off and only recently started working at a new job. "So you know it's been a really hard road the past couple of years financially, and we're just coming out of the woods now." To manage their jobs and childcare, Terry and Amelia work alternate shifts and just sleep when they can. Through the ups and downs, Amelia's church has prayed for her, and she says, "I'm trusting God that everything will be taken care of." A few of our professionals complained about their jobs, as well. Not surprisingly, Mark Fuller, a neurology resident, felt overworked and taken advantage of. But the jobs most of our participants held were much less likely to take this kind of toll on family life.

More commonly, family worries were about whether, how, and when to make the next career move. Many of the courtship and early marriage stories we heard involved happy memories of meeting at work or moving together to a first job for one or both. Marriages that have survived seem to be ones where the partners remember the early work-family negotiations as having been successfully concluded. Margi Perkins recounted a series of moves she and her husband (both broadcast professionals) made, some of which meant they were working in different cities. When he landed a job in Atlanta, she eventually quit her job in Chattanooga, and they started a family. When her youngest started kindergarten, she started working as an assistant in a Catholic preschool, a job that she has come to like, both for the shared religious atmosphere and for the way it dovetails with her children's schedules.

Not everyone is so lucky. The tension of balancing work and family obligations was the most common theme in the stories we heard about household strains. Pam Jones is a buyer for a retail clothing store, and her work keeps her very busy. When we asked, "What are the hardest decisions you have to make at work?" she replied, "Do I leave now while this is unfinished—to come home and get dinner and homework done? I think juggling. How do I juggle is probably the hardest decision I have to make. You know, how much can I push my family by not being around, and how much can I push, you know, my job by doing things." Looking at photos of his grown children and their children, eighty-year-old John Travisano sighed and observed that he had probably not been as present for his sons as they now are for their children. It seemed inevitable to him that work interfered with family life. Nora Cole, a Boston architect by profession, admitted, on the other hand, that the household and parenting tasks she now does pretty much full time are not as exciting as the professional work she can only do part time while she is parenting.

Pam, John, and Nora are Protestant, Catholic, and Jewish, with varying levels of engagement with their faiths and typical work-family stresses. For each of them, faith communities and spiritual resources are absent in the stories they told (although religious participation may influence their work-family tradeoffs in ways they do not fully recognize (Edgell and Ammons 2007)). Each of them have had the luxury of some degree of control over their work and family juggling act by virtue of their occupations and relative financial privilege, but they still find the labor market a greedy taskmaster (Schieman and Glavin 2008). Sometimes other participants spoke of getting through these and other work-related stresses and strains with the help of their faith, but those spiritually infused stories were the distinct minority. We heard Amelia James's expression of trust in God to help solve their work, family, and financial problems, and others recorded in their diaries stories about the divine interventions they were praying for. More often, however, divine intervention in work-family dilemmas took a social and material form. Harris Crosby, whose rigorous daily routine we saw earlier, told us about their struggles to find daycare when their daughter was first born. The person they found was someone they met through their Atlanta Presbyterian church. Similarly, Margi Perkins's job as a preschool teacher came through church connections.

Only rarely did we see work, family, and spiritual life thoroughly woven together. Walter Green is a retired math professor but he and his wife opened a B&B, in part because, he said, "Ruth and I enjoy working together." But they also hoped that the inn would "provide a haven for people who were stressed out, where they could have quiet, pleasant surroundings, good food, conversation if they wanted it or none if they didn't." They even had the pastor of their Baptist church come and dedicate the building. "We wanted it to be God's house in some way," he said. "It wasn't that we overtly were trying to evangelize, but I think people knew that we were Christians." Family and spirituality were intermingled with work for other couples as they prayed together or as family members were actually involved in some aspect of the work itself.

The world of work routinely crosses the border into the world of the household, but the vast majority of those border crossings are described as ordinary events. The occasional crisis may evoke a spiritual opening, and the most religiously engaged persons may be intentional about making spiritual connections in the midst of the routines, but the work-family nexus is one that is infused with spiritual content by only a minority of our participants.

Time Off—Having Fun Together

The rhythm of daily household life is not entirely about sleeping, eating, and working. It also encompasses the fun times, the lazy moments, and the leisure activities that were often pointed to as the most joyous. With a sample skewed toward the affluent end of American households, we clearly heard more stories about European vacations and high-end sports than one might otherwise have expected. But we also heard stories about quiet evenings at home, nearby excursions, sports and games, and otherwise just being together. Studies of household time use would tell us that these activities are not likely to be happening every day. The amount of time families spend in "social leisure" has declined somewhat in the past three decades, but it has also gotten constrained into fewer days of the week and month (Bianchi et al. 2006, 105–11).

Most of our participants lamented not having enough time for leisurely relaxation, but when asked to take pictures of the important places in their lives or just to record a diary entry for the day, the occasional leisure activities were there. One of Julia Oliva's diary entries made this note: "Something that I did fun this week was, um, actually last night, Andy and I, after studying the whole day, we just played games. We play, um, Solitaire, Uno, I think Chinese checkers…it was so fun because I don't really get the opportunity to just be with him, and laugh and just relax." Without a high income and still working on professional certifications, this young Mormon couple cherished a simple and inexpensive evening of fun. Jennifer Hammond and her family have a much higher income, and her lazy day account included her young son's swim and gymnastics lessons in the morning, where she chatted with friends. Her dad dropped by later in the morning for coffee, and the family spent much of the day outside.

> The day was beautiful. We waited for the grocery delivery to come. We were outside in the back yard; Aidan was running around rediscovering all his toys from the previous summer, his sandbox, and getting out the chairs on the deck. Made lunch and sat on the deck.... After lunch my husband and Aidan went to the kite-fly in [a nearby town].

For many of our participants, evenings, Saturdays, and Sundays were times to rest and play with the members of their household.

The single most common kind of leisure activity we heard about was sports. Victoria Edwards and her husband ride a tandem bicycle. Matthew Smith talked about playing various sports with his roommates. Aidan Hammond was by no means the only child taking lessons or playing on community and school sports teams, and that often means that parents (and grandparents) spend part of their leisure cheering on the sidelines. Fishing, skiing, sailing, and even belly dancing were among the activities various of our participants shared with others in their households. Almost without exception these stories were told with no reference to God or to anything even vaguely spiritual. In spite of the way religion seems ubiquitous in American sports (Forney 2007), in these households sports are just sports. One mother said offhandedly that she hoped God would help her figure out how to make sure her child could take tennis lessons, and a Mormon couple talked about the discipline of exercising together as part of their spiritual experience. Beyond such passing glimpses of spirituality, however, household sporting activities are in the secular domain.

Often the household leisure routine included television and other media (Hoover et al. 2004). Robin Mitchell told us that her wife "loves watching TV and will watch crap happily, like Disney channel movies, and, um, I really am not that into that. So I will watch sports.... 'cause Alexa [their daughter] likes sports." Lily Mattison also talked about incorporating television into household leisure. In the case of Lily and her husband, it is "Mystery Science Theatre 3000." She owns tapes of every episode of all seven seasons. "And so we decided to watch them every weekend. We usually do watch them Saturday and Sunday, just a little bit each day." Like Robin, Lily and her husband are not involved in any religious community, so weekends are uninterrupted by church or synagogue, and television is a purely secular pursuit.

A few of the parents talked about media in less positive terms. Jen Jackson, evangelical mother of a two-year-old, screens even the Disney movies before she will let him watch. At his age, the cartoon violence is something she worries about him imitating. Melissa Parker had similar worries about her children.

> And me being a Black woman, trying to raise healthy Black children with a good self-image of themselves—TV is like my arch nemesis. I don't let my kids watch videos; I don't let them walk around with their pants hanging off their butts and all that crazy stuff you see on TV. I just can't stand it. And I think that TV just perpetuates a jacked-up image of Black people. And I just don't like it, because I know that I'm not like that. I was not raised like that. My friends are not like that; their children are not like that. But if you watch TV....

One of Jen's solutions is the children's video series "Veggie Tales," something Andrea Valencia mentioned, as well. This Christian cartoon series retells Bible stories ("Mo and the Big Exit") and legends ("Pistachio: The Little Boy that Woodn't") using vegetable characters and clear moral lessons. Andrea, Jen, and Melissa actively participate in conservative religious communities, and that participation is clearly connected to the moral work these women are doing in their consumption of television.

More often, television, movies, outings to the local museum or a restaurant, and all the other routine leisure activities we heard about were framed in ordinary language, reflecting mundane considerations of time and money and preferences, rather than moral choices or spiritual encounters. What people are able to do with their free time and how they feel about it is shaped by the economy and marital relationships more than by religious tradition or spiritual engagement. The happiest leisure stories came from people with the most comfortable incomes and with the long standing stable relationships and routines that come with age and marriage. A few single people, on the other hand, and people in unmarried partnerships talked about negotiating leisure activities as points of some tension. Jocelyn Frederick is a twenty-nine-year-old health researcher in Boston, who recorded in her diary, "My boyfriend and I had a conversation earlier about traveling, and it's funny how we seem to, without fail, pull out these things to talk about, which were the most different, and traveling is one of the major ones." Negotiating leisure is part of the process of building a successful household, and something Jocelyn and her boyfriend are still working out. Pam Jones, in contrast, talked about the beach house that is shared by her parents and various adult siblings and their families.

> The beach house to me just symbolizes family and fun. Because there is always people there, there is always family, always love, always fun. Playing games, eating too many meals, laughing, arguing, doing family things.... And it is just a home that we go to, and it is just a great place, a lot of fun, a lot of love.

Both financial resources sufficient to support a shared vacation home and a long-term stable marriage were critical to such happy and memorable vacation stories.

When vacations included these kinds of experiences of getting away, they were more likely to be described in spiritual terms than were other leisure activities. People unplugged from their usual routines in a way Victor Turner (1977) might almost have described as liminal. While disengaged from prescribed roles, people can experience something of a "peak" of intensified engagement with each other (and often with nature), and then reenter normal life with new insight and commitment. Vacations often include opportunities to encounter especially awe-inspiring natural environments, which also invite spiritual interpretation. Ann Rosa is a Catholic with a spiritual life that draws from both Theistic and Extra-theistic sources. She spoke of the "evocative" character of the Middle Eastern landscapes she grew to love earlier in her life. She pulled photos from an album to add to the ones she took for the project and said of them,

> They're of the Sinai Desert when we were there. We used to go a lot, and I didn't pick them so much for the people or what we're doing but for the evocativeness of the desert.... I love the solitude, the quiet and the grandeur of it.

Francis Parker, like a few other study participants, talked about taking his religious practice with him on vacation.

> My wife has this feeling that when we're on a trip we should try to get to church, even though the Church says you don't have to go if you're on vacation. Well, we like to visit other churches, and when we

go to visit a new church we like to light a candle.... You know, we go to Disney World and Magic Kingdom and all that with the kids, but I like going to the Shrine [the Basilica of the National Shrine of Mary, Queen of the Universe].

The presence of religious meaning and practice in leisure activity was certainly not the norm, but it was not completely absent. Those who told stories like this were, like Francis, people who are active participants in a religious community and people for whom spirituality is already an important part of life. In fact, attaching religious significance to leisure activities was much more common among participants from conservative religious communities than among any of the rest of our participants. While leisure may produce the occasional liminal moment that hints at a larger spiritual presence, the spirituality we saw most often was brought to leisure pursuits rather than generated by them.

Weekly Sabbath?

For most Americans, Saturday and Sunday are days when obligations to the workplace cease (or at least slow down) and when the rhythm of life shifts toward leisure and home. The designation of those two days originates, of course, in religious observance—the Jewish Sabbath and then the Christian day of worship. The latter was institutionalized in the earliest days of European settlement in North America as Puritan church leaders policed the practices of the households in their charge, making sure that church services were attended and work set aside (Solberg 1977). Those strictures made their way into "Blue Laws," patterns of mail delivery (John 1990), and other cultural habits that still shape, albeit in highly diluted form, what can and cannot be done and sold on Sunday. Today no stern deacon is likely to reprimand the citizen who fails to make a Sunday church appearance, and the one holy day has been augmented (thanks to the labor movement) by a second day to make a "weekend" (Clark 2007). How we have come to understand these two days is now a peculiar mixture of work and pleasure, sacred and profane (Rybczynski 1991).

The intersection of religious observance with household life varies, of course, depending on the nature of the household and the regularity of the observance. A third of our participants live alone or with roommates, so questions about religious participation require little interpersonal household negotiation. Another third rarely or never attend services, meaning that their household calendar is uninterrupted by religious attendance. For the third of our participants who do attend services more than occasionally and also share a household with other family members, one of the questions to be addressed is where and how often they will worship. Eighty percent of those who regularly attend shared a single place of worship with the others in their household. Among the most spiritually engaged people in our sample, this was almost uniformly the case. Even individuals who were personally quite attuned to spirituality were less active in religious communities when their spouses were not on the same page. Julia Oliva, for instance, is the only one of our Mormon participants who is not married to a fellow Mormon, and she is also the only one who does not attend services regularly.

The other Mormons, by contrast, describe church participation as a "way of life" and told stories about Sunday services, about Monday family home nights, about visits from their spiritual guides, and about various other church-related activities—all of which were *family* activities. The intertwining of church and family is very visible in a story Catherine Young recorded in her diary.

> I went to another activity for my church tonight that was just for the women's group. So I left my daughter home with my husband, and I had made me a quick dinner and just made him a plate of the thing that I had made for dinner and I went to the activity. And it was fun and nice to be there with the women....I got home and my husband had written me this cute letter thanking me for the dinner that I had made him.

Jen Jackson is heavily involved with the Atlanta Vineyard Church and took her husband there on one of their first dates. A marriage and three children later, they are all involved in multiple activities, and pictures of the christening of their most recent addition were among the shots Jen collected for our project (Figure 5.6). Similarly, Dr. Walter Green, a Southern Baptist in Atlanta, thinks of church as something "we" do. He matter-of-factly reported in his diary, "It's Sunday afternoon, June 3, 2007. As is our custom, we went to Sunday school and church this morning." Mormons and conservative Protestants were the most likely to have religiously homogamous households and also very likely to find the overlap between home and church to be quite broad. As we have already seen, religious communities provide a lively arena in which spiritual conversations take place. When the entire household participates, that arena stretches, overlapping everyday life at home.

FIGURE 5.6 "Lots of family came. This is when he started praying for the baby."
—Jen Jackson

The overlap is not always present, of course. Others, especially Catholics, presented a much more mixed picture. In a number of cases spouses differed considerably in their degree of religious involvement, even if they were part of the same tradition. Where both were equally active, the overlap between household and religious community was considerable. Frances Parker and his family, for instance, have been active at St. Sabina's in Boston. "My oldest daughter and I used to be Eucharistic ministers at the church. The middle girl was in the choir with my wife. My younger daughter became an altar server, and she did that until she got into high school." By contrast, Michelle Winter is a deeply devout Catholic but has diminished her church attendance. She and her two sons have been very involved with parish and school activities in the past but, aside from an occasional Knights of Columbus activity, her husband does not attend. She is now drifting toward his style of participation. Gordon Johnson almost never attends Cornerstone Baptist, either; but his wife and daughter, like Michelle and her children, are more active than he is. And Theresa Collins has made her peace with the fact that her husband is much less involved at All Saints Episcopal. In each case, less active husbands were willing to have their wives take the children and participate as much as they like.

Other households with one nonattending spouse were not so happy. Vicky Johnson made a good-faith effort to join her husband at a large evangelical megachurch in Atlanta, but she has since returned to Catholicism and attends St. Michael's by herself. In the midst of a fairly fractured family, she actually relishes that personal spiritual time and space. Amelia James, the young Catholic mother we met earlier, has no such peace about her husband's lack of religious participation. That he does not share her beliefs or her openness to religious experience has become a source of alienation and conflict between them.

Those unhappy situations were less common than the pattern of either common participation or successful accommodation to different preferences.[14] Equal participation sometimes meant, as we have seen, equally high involvement and a strong overlap between home and congregation. It also sometimes meant a shared lack of participation. Stan Morris and his wife made sure to have their children christened and enjoy having everyone together for holidays but actually spoke very little about Grimsby Congregational. Rebecca Klein noted that all her children had been bar mitzvahed, but she otherwise had very little to say about their local temple. Instead, she remarked, "My husband and my house and my children are my soul."

What we heard from Stan and Rebecca is typical of a pattern that is widespread in our sample and in American culture. Stan wanted his children christened; Rebecca made sure hers had a bar mitzvah. It really is true that many people join for the sake of the kids.[15] Half of those who are or have been parents told stories about religious participation that included their children. Jane Baker's own upbringing in the Black Church had given her a foundation, but she had drifted away until she knew she was going to be a parent herself. "Initially she was the reason I got back into church, because when I got pregnant I wanted to make sure my daughter had that kind of foundation that I had. So that's when I rejoined, reconnected with the church." Daphne LeCompte is only minimally interested in spirituality, but they tried Unitarian Sunday school for a while when their son was younger. For many parents, religious participation is an important component of their task. They hope it will lay a moral and civic foundation, but they also frame it as a choice their children will eventually have to make for themselves.[16] In the end, many of them also hope, as Olivia Howell put it, that the religious community will be an extension of the care and nurture of the home. "The kids have been really well loved and taken care of and they know they have several sort of sets of grandparents and people who they trust. So if something happened we know that they would take care of them"—a particularly striking statement for an African American family in a predominantly Euro-American Baptist church.[17]

Parents, then—if they are married—are more likely to make at least some commitment to participation than are their unmarried and nonparent counterparts. While parents are still in the midst of raising their children, ironically, overall frequency of attendance is lower, even among the most spiritually committed individuals. The sheer time factor seems to intervene to dampen what would otherwise be more active participation (cf. Edgell 2005). When households have children in them but there is no married heterosexual couple at the center, cultural pressures push in the opposite direction, entirely away from congregational participation. Unmarried parents were less likely than any of the rest of our participants to be involved in organized religion. Charles Curlew is still active at Brookfield Baptist, but he talked extensively about how inadequate he feels as a divorced father. When Shirley Glazer's second husband died and she was again single, she too found herself uncomfortable in the churches she attended.

> I currently have not found a church where I feel welcomed.... I can go, and have many times, to [Downtown] United Methodist church, and I will not be spoken to unless I reach out and do all of the initiating. So it's cliquish; that's my perception. That's my selective perception. And then it's all couples. It was painful there for a while that it is a couples, family church; and so it was no singles, no singles to speak of. So I just found that difficult.

But no matter what the household composition and stage in the lifecycle, religious participation is still strongly linked to the individual spiritual commitments of the person. The link between parenthood and religious participation may be a strong cultural push, but a much larger piece of the story is simply the degree to which our participants are, in any way, spiritually engaged. Those that are most serious (about a quarter), whether or not they are married or parents, interweave some degree of religious participation into their routine household life. Those who are not at all spiritually engaged (not quite a fifth) establish households where weekends are for movies and relaxation, not service attendance. So long as there is (non)religious agreement in the household, the only times they have to worry about religious participation are when holidays, weddings, and funerals may take them into the religious worlds of their friends and families. For the half in the middle, who embrace a typically moderate level of religious and spiritual involvement, stages in the lifecycle are among the factors that explain whether the rhythms of household life include routine (or even occasional) attendance at religious services.

Holidays

Just as the household routine is occasionally punctuated by moments of leisure that range from goofing off to trips to the Sinai, so that routine is also punctuated by the annual cycle of holidays. Many of the days circled in red on the cultural calendar are days that are normatively focused on households and families. We asked each of our participants about their favorites among the holidays, and Thanksgiving and Christmas were hands-down winners. In both cases, the overwhelming majority of the stories we heard were happy accounts of times with extended families, reenacting traditions, and feasting together. Perhaps not surprisingly, stories about Christmas were especially likely to be framed as religiously significant. Theresa Collins spoke of

> … going to Church a lot. We went to church three times. Well, this year it was Christmas Eve—we went up to Christ Church to the Christmas Crèche to see my granddaughters who were in it and to enjoy the service. Then we went to [another] church at 6 o'clock, and then we went to the 10 o'clock service at All Saints. So we go to church a lot at Christmas. I love it. I just love it.

Gwen Mothersbaugh is part of the Congregational Church not far from Theresa's Episcopal parish, and like Theresa, she is a grandmother. One of her diary entries reflected the wild mix of meanings and emotions that was often present in these stories. Christmas is, she said, "a busy time of year when the awe of the Christ child's birth is coming closer. And when the mayhem of grandchildren opening gifts is coming near. And all those expectations that people have, um … hoping that you can find the right gift to show your love to somebody and, uh, or maybe to make points, I'm not sure what it is. But, it's a time that is full and challenging and wonderful." A few of our participants worried about the overcommercialization of Christmas. Jen Jackson talked about limiting her shopping and rationing out the gifts her children would receive. Her conservative Protestant values strongly emphasized the religious meaning of Christmas over its cultural and commercial impact.

Christmas is, however, such a cultural and commercial fixture in the United States that one does not have to be religious to love it. The oral diary we received from Robin Mitchell, one of our most nonspiritual participants, included this entry: "I love Christmas. I love the holiday. I enjoy the lights. I particularly like the songs. I think the story is very sweet, and from what I know of Jesus, which is very little, he sounds like a basically decent guy. So

I like getting people presents and love Christmas trees and reindeer. I just really enter the whole thing; I just think it's so fun." Daphne LaCompte is equally uninterested in the spiritual dimensions of Christmas but talked about enjoying the traditions surrounding putting up a tree and decorating it. Others simply talked about this as a particularly happy family time, loving the excuse to do lots of shopping or enjoying the fine music that is performed at the Christmas season. Even a couple of our Jewish participants admitted that there were parts of the Christmas ritual they routinely embraced.

For other Jewish participants, however, Christmas could be a real trial. Rachel Halpern recounted the double insult of receiving a Christmas ham from her husband's boss! Another, whose sibling is intermarried and pays little heed to Jewish traditions, remembered how uncomfortable it was to be with that branch of the family at holiday times. Differences in religious commitments accounted for most of the less happy stories we heard about holidays. Religiously disengaged adult children sit uncomfortably at the family table for Easter dinner. Evangelical siblings sometimes point out the error of the nonbelievers in the family.[18] But sometimes, the difficulties of the holidays are simply inherent in the dysfunctions of family life. Polly Baxter, a single young adult in Atlanta said, "Holidays are so hard, because our family does not get along. I kind of, like, dread them." These kinds of stories about holiday difficulties were actually most common among our participants who were living with unmarried partners. Like the working out of vacation styles, working out joint holiday arrangements may be among the rough spots that have to be worked through on the way to a strong relationship.

Christmas elicited a wide range of stories—secular and sacred, happy and painful. The range of stories was different for the other holidays. When Mothers' Day, Fourth of July, Valentine's Day, birthdays, and the like make their way into the lore of the household, the stories are likely to be happily memorable. And without widespread cultural rituals that continue to link them to religious meanings (in spite of what they may have meant at their founding), they were much less likely to be interpreted by our participants through a spiritual lens.[19] The same is the case for Thanksgiving. Often mentioned as a favorite family holiday, the sentiments of the day were warmth and gratitude that can exist without specific religious rituals and meanings. Indeed the ritual of football watching may be as prevalent as the ritual prayer of blessing. People who are part of a religious community and who are themselves spiritually attuned may bring those religious sensibilities to any holiday, of course, but the typical holiday storyline—even for Thanksgiving—neither elicits nor requires spiritual elements. At least some American cultural holidays have indeed been secularized in practice.

There are holidays, however, that remain sacred. Easter for Christians and the High Holidays for Jews are distinctly sacred moments on the household calendar—even if the person in question is not feeling especially religious as they roll around. "I don't believe in God right now. I do like the Jewish holidays though," said Sylvia Carter, a thirty-year-old student in Atlanta. Mark Fuller is thirty-four and in the midst of his residency. He noted the arrival of Lent in one of his diary entries and talked about it as an important season but one he just could not find the energy to observe that year. Elizabeth Evans, on the other hand, immediately named Easter as her favorite holiday. When we asked why, she replied, "Well, because it's the resurrection. It's what Christianity is all about. I mean, if there hadn't been the resurrection, you know, there probably wouldn't be Christianity." The High Holidays evoked similar stories for Jews about the importance of showing up for services at the temple or synagogue. Passover, on the other hand, is normally celebrated at home, and Rachel Halpern talked about how the religious meanings of Passover are embodied in the physical acts of preparing, eating, and telling the story (Figure 5.7). She took a picture of a holiday table to show us.

FIGURE 5.7 "This was for Passover.... I love our dining room and I love entertaining."
—Rachel Halpern

This was for Passover. The Passover table. And I thought I did a pretty good job. It's actually not even everything. The table was so full by the time I had everything on it—but I just thought it was really pretty.... I love to cook and set up and do everything, and I was really proud of the table and the way it looked.

From time to time, then, household routines are interrupted by a cycle of holiday traditions, at least some of which, in some households, may be infused with sacred meanings.

Whether they are or not is largely a product of the religious and spiritual commitments people bring to them, but some holidays seem to have a spiritual power of their own, amplified by the surrounding culture and active religious communities. There are readymade scripts and symbols, things to buy, and events to attend. The presence and absence of spirituality in household holidays is both a matter of individual inclination and effort and a matter of cultural expectations and traditional religious lore. In the end, from time to time, the mundane spaces of dining table and living room can become sacred spaces, and the round of everyday profane activities is marked by liminal time, often shared with family.

Sacred Stories in the Household

Stories about household spaces, people, and times are mostly just mundane everyday stories that neither require nor evoke any particular religious explanation. Dogs get walked, dishes get washed, and everyone gets off to work or school. Still, 45 percent of the household stories we heard contained at least some spiritual content. Prayers are said as the dog is walked, the goodness of God is celebrated in the warmth of the dishwater, and God's protection is invoked on the comings and goings of the household. Stories included divine actors, marked people and places as sacred, and described activities in terms of religious traditions and spiritual realities.

Some aspects of household life were more likely to evoke such meanings than others. Spirituality was more likely to be present when stories only concerned the household itself, rather than its intersection with work, leisure, school, and the like. There is at least some evidence, then, that households are domains in which actors have the ability to create a sacred realm, if they choose. Where the rest of the world impinges, that ability may be constrained or dampened. The constraints are not, however, easily traced to social location. Sacred household stories were just as common in Boston as in Atlanta. They were only very slightly more likely to be told by women than men. Ethnicity made no difference, and people with incomes above $60,000 told *more* sacred stories than did those who were less well off. Parents, married people, and people under fifty were the source of more sacred stories than people in other life stages and circumstances. The only hint that secular influences might be diminishing the sacralizing of household life is the fact that more educated people told fewer spiritual stories. Those with less than a college degree included spiritual content in nearly two-thirds (62 percent) of the stories they told, while only 42 percent of the stories told by those with a college degree or more took religious elements into account. The fact that our sample considerably overrepresents the latter group means that we probably underrepresent the degree to which ordinary Americans see their everyday household lives in religious terms.

How that spiritual dimension opens up in everyday household life is a matter of both intention and connection. As we saw in Chapter Three, many spiritual practices take place in the household. People who are intentionally pursuing a spiritual life often do so at home. This chapter has made clear that connection is important, as well. Religiously homogamous households become part of the spiritual tribe. Religious participation and the conversations of religious communities help to create sacred stories that migrate across institutional boundaries into households. Fully half of all the household stories told by regular attenders made reference to religious or spiritual realities, compared to only a third of the stories told by people who are religiously inactive. But that difference masks the even larger contrasts between the more and less spiritually engaged participants. People for whom spiritual life is very important narrate the stories of everyday household life in spiritual terms at three times the rate of those who say spirituality is unimportant to them—even when they attend services at the same rate. Within every religious tradition, individual spiritual engagement matters. Tradition itself matters, as well. Conservative Protestants and Mormons were the most likely to talk about the spiritual dimensions of their household life. But even in those traditions spiritual virtuosi were more thoroughly immersed in the sacredness of everyday household life than were their less spiritually engaged fellow church members. Personal spiritual engagement is intimately tied, then, both to involvement in a religious community and to the extension of that spiritual tribe into the everyday life of the household. Which comes first is hard to tell.

Spiritually engaged people tell the stories of their household lives and their stories of religious participation in terms that freely mix spiritual realities with the secular routines of everyday life. For them household life is often sacralized. Here in a domain in which they have a good deal of control, they redefine mundane routines in spiritual terms. As we turn to other arenas of modern life, the presence or absence of spirituality may be less firmly in the hands of the individual actor, no matter how spiritually engaged they are.

6 NINE TO FIVE: SPIRITUAL PRESENCE AT WORK

Karl Marx pictured work as machine-like drudgery, at least until workers got the power to reshape it on their own. In contrast, Max Weber wrote about a high divine calling that early Protestants took with them into their worldly vocations.[1] The everyday truth of the matter is probably somewhere between those two extremes. Sociologists have paid a great deal of attention to work—as do most ordinary people. In recent decades, sociological analysis has centered on big, "macro" questions of how labor markets are structured and the "micro" questions of how power is distributed in work organizations. We have asked how workers gain human capital (training, skills, credentials) and how employers compete for as much as possible of that human capital at the lowest possible cost. We have also looked for how work is fundamentally structured by dynamics of gender, race, and class: how workers seek recognition and reward and fairness within the overt and covert structures of inequality in the workplace. Questions of inequality and power have dominated both the macro- and the microanalyses, in contrast to the "functionalist" analyses earlier in the twentieth century, in which sociologists asked how bureaucratic "rationality" divided up and compartmentalized tasks in the most efficient manner possible.[2]

All of this research has helped to reveal the large structural constraints that shape employment opportunities, but fewer researchers have looked at what the everyday experience of work is about, how work intersects with other life domains, and what sense of meaning or purpose workers may bring with them. A variety of ethnographic studies of particular occupations have provided us with some insight into the everyday experience of working, but comparative ethnographic data are rare.[3] This study will certainly not suffice to fill that gap, but even with a relatively small group of people, concentrated in the middle and upper-middle classes, the stories collected for this project are powerfully suggestive both of the way work is experienced differently in different sectors of the economy and of the complex ways in which work is not a self-contained domain that operates exclusively on its own logic.

As we listened to our participants talk about their work, there was both joy and worry, high calling and pure happenstance, deep attachment and deep frustration—often in the same person talking about the same job. In addition to knowing what job they do and how much money they make, our narrative analysis will go much deeper. The initial interview generally provided the life course overview—a look at the big decisions and the most memorable moments in a person's work history. We also asked about challenges, frustrations, and satisfying aspects of their current (or most recent) job and began to get a fuller picture. But it was the oral diary exercise that afforded many of our participant's opportunities to talk in detail about what they were doing at work. Some of them took the recorder with them and talked during off moments. Others kept the recorder in the car and reflected on the day ahead (or just completed) during their commute. And still others simply turned to what was happening at work whenever they picked up the digital recorder to talk to us. What we have is not any sort of "time diary" of how work time is spent (e.g., Sayer 2005) but a narrative diary of work stories, selected by the participants themselves. Of the seventy-eight participants who completed at least one round of diaries and are currently in the labor force, all but ten recorded at least one account of an everyday happening at work.

Altogether, across our various interactions with them, our participants told 851 stories about their work. From dental assistants and bookkeepers to engineers and business owners, we heard about learning new skills, tackling computer bugs, staffing and scheduling problems, sales awards and successful grants, and the thrill of designing a piece of the lunar rover. Each of those stories was coded to identify what combination of actors was involved and the primary theme of the story (see Appendix 2 for additional detail about coding). Was it about the work itself, money, training, bosses? Was it about relationships or spaces or schedules? As with all the other stories, we also noted the emotional tone of the story and the degree to which it represented the person's own agency. We looked for what sort of spiritual or religious elements (if any) were referenced and whether it was about a recurring event, a crisis or special occasion, or something that happened in the past. Each of those aspects of the 851 stories can be counted and compared and will inform the analysis of the chapter, but counting and comparing will be in the service of understanding the narratives of work we heard from our participants. As much as occupations shape who we are, the box we check on the census or the survey tells only a small part of the story. Each occupation is constrained by the organizations and the economy of which it is a part, but the day-to-day experience of working is also about the spaces people occupy, the people who surround them, and the sometimes mysterious way the work itself can be both exhilarating and mind numbing. As people told us stories about their work, those stories were complicated and multidimensional. This chapter will examine the who, what, where, and when of the stories, listening especially for the times when the presence of religion and spirituality can be recognized weaving through the texture of everyday work life.

The Basic Occupational Picture

As we have noted before, our sample overrepresents people who are well educated and relatively well off; and that can be seen in the occupations in which they work (see Table 6.1). Only one person we interviewed was unemployed at the time of the study, although several others were outside the labor force by virtue of retirement, full-time parenting, or still being in school. Those that were in the labor force were virtually absent from the blue-collar occupations, so we will hear only occasional stories about the physical rigors of work or the recalcitrance of machines or the insecurities of being at the bottom of the hierarchy. As we recruited participants, these workers were less likely to be available for and interested in this study, and that leaves a gap that simply cannot be filled in their absence. Future explorations of work and spiritual life will be needed to provide a picture of the working world of those who populate the factories and fields and highways, asking how spirituality might or might not be present. Sociologists have certainly not ignored working-class life, but rarely have they asked those working people about what role their faith plays in the everyday world of making a living.[4]

Our participants are primarily middle class, but those in "pink-collar" and sales jobs were often just barely getting by, with household incomes well below the overall national average. Theirs is not so much hard physical labor but labor that is highly constrained, underpaid, and often uncertain. We will hear a good deal about the world of offices and stores and computer terminals where nearly a quarter of our participants keep the books, sell the goods, and keep life organized for the businesses that employ them. These are people who are often very good at jobs they enjoy, but they are also subject to the vagaries of low wages, incompetent managers, boring tasks, and reorganizations that can cost them their jobs. Some of them, as it turned out, are also artists.

Table 6.1 Occupations of Study Participants

Occupational Sector and Distribution in the U.S. Civilian Labor Force	Occupational Distribution of Study Participants		
	Full time Employed	Part time or Retired	Average Income
Blue-collar workers (16.5%) van driver, housecleaner	1	1	$20–40,000
Pink-collar workers (21.0%) secretaries, bookkeepers, office managers, dental assistants	9	3	$40–60,000
Salespeople (11.4%) retail clothing, industrial parts, bar supplies	9	1	$75–95,000
Artists (1.9%) photographers, writers, visual artists	6	2	$50–70 000
Medical professions (5.9%) doctors, nurses, opticians, epidemiologists, bioresearchers	15	3	$65–85,000
Service professions (7.3%) teachers, social workers	14	2	$75–95,000
Business people and executives (19.3%) high-level managers, financial officers, software designers, engineers, business owners, and lawyers	20	2	$80–100,000
Not in the labor force students, homemakers, unemployed	0	7	$35–55,000
Not included in this sample (20.0%) construction, farm and forestry, manufacturing	0	0	n/a

Source: U.S. Census Bureau. "S2401. Occupation by Sex and Median Earnings in the Past 12 Months (in 2008 Inflation-Adjusted Dollars) for the Civilian Employed Population 16 Years and Over."
http://factfinder.census.gov/servlet/STTable?_bm=y&-geo_id=01000US&-qr_name=ACS_2008_3YR_G00_S2401&-ds_name=ACS_2008_3YR_G00_. Accessed November 15, 2010.

Eight of our participants identified their primary vocations as writers, musicians, photographers, and visual artists, although not all of them earned their money primarily from their art. In fact, we will listen as some of them struggle with whether they can take the leap into making their art their primary source of income.

Given that our locations were Boston and Atlanta, it is probably not surprising that almost one in five of our participants has a connection to health professions and biomedical research. Boston's biotech industry and Atlanta's Centers for Disease Control and Prevention (CDC) will be the backdrop for some of the stories we hear. But so will the hospital corridors where nurses care for patients and the offices where doctors at various stages of their careers think about what it means to do the work they do. We will listen as they wrestle with the power they do—and do not—have.

A roughly equal number of the people in our study work in other kinds of helping professions, shaping lives more than physical products. Some were in social work, and others worked in educational roles that ranged from private school headmaster to preschool teacher. Some jobs were fairly tightly structured and full of paperwork and regulations, but all called on their occupants to use their own learning to enable others to navigate life's challenges.

The largest single occupational sector among our participants encompassed the jobs where the wheels of the economy are ever turning. Whether writing contracts, designing buildings, overseeing quality control, or running a small business, these are people who have a fair amount of autonomy in their work but are also subject to the whims of markets and mergers. They work in a world of bottom lines and products that must find a niche in the market. Their own ingenuity and hard work can bring financial success and acclaim, and it can also affect the lives of the people who work for them or depend on their expertise. These were, not surprisingly, the households with the most affluent incomes.

Work over the Course of a Lifetime

As people narrated their life stories in our initial conversations with them, many marked early careers as a transitional time—uncertainty, multiple moves, and changes of direction before a path was chosen. Anyone who knows today's job market knows that people rarely make a single employment commitment for life; but even in the past, young adults have taken first (and second and third) jobs simply to get started. Sometimes those fumbling starts were remembered fondly by our older participants or at least valued for the good start they inadvertently provided; but just as often worry and uncertainty colored the accounts we heard, especially among those still in that starting out stage. Bill Hamilton is forty and had been a "poor rock climbing and canoe instructor" and a public school teacher (which he hated) before a chance meeting in Costa Rica resulted in his current job in a business distributing alcoholic beverages to Atlanta area restaurants. The business is going pretty well, but Bill has little attachment to it. Similarly, Polly Baxter is a twenty-something who has settled into a retail sales job, although she is not especially satisfied with it. Still, it is a step up from her first job on a "ranch" in Vermont, where her fellow employees seemed stuck in a party culture. "I knew that that's not what I wanted my life to be about," she said. Polly and Bill are members of Deer Valley Church in the Atlanta suburbs, but neither attends with any regularity; and religious belief was not a part of their decisions. They just had a vague sense of what kind of life they did and did not want to lead.

Jessica Fletcher is about the same age and a much more active conservative Protestant (at Atlanta's Vineyard Church). She recounted that she

> worked several different jobs but all the while still feeling like I'd reached a plateau and that it wasn't really, nothing more was going to happen there. Then my brother offered me a job to come to Atlanta to make a little more money, have a little more time and maybe just mature [laughs] a little bit more. And, so I was like, okay, well, you know, it's worth a shot.

Unlike Polly, she did think about her vocational journey in spiritual terms. She said, "You know, God's opening a window for me." Jessica Wilson is a bit older but has had a similarly rough start. She began her working life as a flight attendant for Delta, but as that industry got more and more untenable, she finally quit. She was well into her nurse's training program when we talked to her, but there were still decisions to be made. She was pretty sure she was going to want to work with children, for instance, rather than adult patients.

> I just feel like that's going to be my thing, which is good, 'cause I think a lot of people are like, ah, I don't know what I want to do. I mean I don't know that I am 100 percent going to do that, or that I know exactly what I want to do with them, like what area of the hospital to be in, but at least I kind of have an idea. It's better to, like, do a job that you like,

especially with nursing, with the people that you are compassionate for and about, and that—'cause otherwise I think you just get bitter and—I don't know—it's not fun, and you don't want to be there, and you just get burned out quickly.... I don't want to work all the time. That's why I'm being a nurse so I don't have to work all the time. But I want to...you know, have a normal life, a house and a car and a family. So I don't know, maybe I will have to work a lot.

Nursing is a matter both of compassion and of fun, of recognizing one's limits and of pragmatically seeking the American Dream. It is also, for Jessica, something into which she has felt spiritually led. "I have been led in the path to do this, and the people that have encouraged me to do it, and the encouragement I continue to get from people [at Deer Valley Church], just talking about it, I have to be okay with that for right now." In these start-up stories, as we will see throughout, the primary ingredients in a spiritual work story are participation in a religious community and personal spiritual commitment.

About half the "first job" stories we heard were false starts, but the others were more directly connected to the careers that followed. Still, despite a more clear "vocational" narrative, these kinds of stories were no more nor less likely to include religious or spiritual elements. Gordon Johnson rarely sees anything spiritual about his life, and work was no different. He is now retired from his career as a chemist. He majored in chemistry in college and when he got drafted in the 1950s, he managed to get placed in an elite scientific division that he then turned into a career of doing chemical research—first in weapons, then in food chemistry—for the military. Like most college-educated Americans who have put together a curriculum vitae or introduced themselves at a cocktail party, Gordon knew how to tell his career story. Appropriate training, hard work, fortunate opportunities, and steady advancement are the familiar themes. God is not routinely part of this public career narrative. Pam Jones is a much more involved member of Cornerstone Baptist than Gordon, but she talks about getting started in much the same way. "I took a part-time job in retail, and at the time helped to open a store on Newbury Street, and just got the bug." She enrolled in a management training program and worked her way up to her current position as a buyer for a major women's clothing chain.

Only among the most spiritually serious of our participants did we hear with any frequency vocational journeys that were shaped by spiritual contingencies from the beginning. Dr. Stephen James's career in pediatric medicine was one of those, as was Cynthia Gardener's work in the sales of biotech products. While she has had times in her working life that were less than happy, she loves what she does now. "I sell products to people in research. I'm an immunologist, that's my background, so I'm very comfortable talking to science people. I do a lot of training, a lot of troubleshooting. I help people write grants. I give seminars. I help people with experiments and I sell." She moved into this particular job from within her company, but it involved a transfer from California and—to her great delight and gratitude—provided for the education of her special needs son.

I don't believe in God being a puppeteer so we'll just leave that tension there. But yes, there is something about—I look at my life, and I have a son born to me with severe learning disabilities. I studied German and science in school, and—just, like, things come together. I was in the office…in California (I was doing tech support at the time), and I overheard the sales manager say, "There's so much business out in Massachusetts, we need a sales rep out in Boston in three to six months." This is in April, and I round the door, I said, "I want that job." He said, "I thought you didn't want to do sales." "Well I do. I do want to do sales" [laughs]. That was a big lie. I said, "I want my kid to go to this school." Well, to make a long story short my company paid to move me out here. His education was funded to the tune of $30,000 per year.… How can you say I am not where I am supposed to be? In a sense, how my whole life has funneled to this point to have the gift for my son and the gift to myself.

She and Dr. James each have high-level professional jobs they love, accomplishing work they see as significant. Both Jessica Fletcher (the administrative assistant working for her brother) and Jessica Wilson (the fledgling nurse) similarly see God's hand in the directions they have recently taken, but they do not yet have the kind of job security or satisfaction Cynthia and Stephen have. Their conservative theology encourages them to see God no matter what, but the jobs they have are not yet firmly established in a career story they look forward to telling in the years ahead.

Do these people think they have a "calling?" In the early 1990s, Robert Wuthnow found that about 30 percent of the American labor force agreed with a survey item that asked if they felt called by God into the particular line of work they were in (Wuthnow 1994, 69). Forty-six percent of regular churchgoers say yes, and if forced to respond to such a question, Cynthia and

Stephen would almost surely have been among them. They are spiritually serious and see God's hand in their professional choices. But that categorization hides the complexity of the story. As we will see, vocation is also very much about day-to-day moments in which divine purpose and personal work intersect. "Vocation" is a way of telling one's life story that goes beyond a single divine calling; training, hard work, opportunities, and advancement are still part of the narrative arc. If these participants in our study had to check off "important reasons" for selecting their line of work, all of those things would have been on the list.[5] If "God's will" is not the only reason they give, does that mean that they are merely mimicking the standard career narrative? I think not. To make decisions about work is not an either-or, secular or spiritual matter. All of these aspects of a career are present in their stories, but their own perception of a spiritual dimension in life means that the usual secular career narrative is not sufficient. As powerful as that account is in American culture, a few people like these add another narrative layer, weaving spiritual significance into the tale, especially at its key moments.[6]

Some, like college senior Phil Marini, recognize that their religious communities have taught them values that shape career choices. "Even since I was little," he said, "no matter what I wanted, it always involved helping people. That was somehow related to how I help people when I do stuff with church." Even Carlos Fernandez, who no longer attends his Catholic church, sees his vocational choice as shaped by what he learned there.

> You know when I look upon the profession I've chosen—pediatrics—I look upon it as—kids as a sort of a group that tend to be the underdog. They're not really respected in society. They can tend to be at the bottom of the heap lots of times. And so to be able to—specifically HIV-infected children are even more at the bottom of the heap. So to me the fact that I've chosen that is sort of a Christian ideal.

Vocational narratives shaped by religious formation were more common in the helping professions than in other sectors of the economy. Only a handful of business people or lower-level pink- and blue-collar people adopted similar narrative strategies. Some jobs, in other words, seem more amenable to interpretation as "vocations" in the religious or spiritual sense of that word. While Cynthia sees spiritual meaning in selling biotech products and Jessica Fletcher hopes that her move into her brother's company will allow her to mature spiritually while enhancing her resume, they are in a small minority among the inhabitants of the everyday business world. Most of their compatriots in business speak of their career histories in ordinary secular terms. Spiritual stories about starting on a career path seem shaped both by the spiritual sensibilities of the teller and the way they and the audience understand the work in question. Some jobs are simply more plausible as spiritual narratives than others.

At the other end of the career trajectory, Stan Morris and his wife are planning toward retirement. He said that they will definitely work several more years to pay off the last college debts from their children's tuition. Then they will see where those children (and potential grandchildren) are living, try to balance his desire for peace and quiet with her desire for a big city, and decide when and where to retire. Just as he saw no spiritual significance when he "fell into" the work he has done as a business analyst, so he expects to make the move to retirement in a similarly rational way. Neither his occasional participation at Grimsby Congregational nor his (minimal) personal spiritual engagement enters the equation.

Other retirees used retirement as a transition to work that they found more meaningful.[7] Mary Poulsen and Mary Hage both took early retirement packages from big businesses and were not sorry to leave the corporate world behind. Ms. Poulsen now works part time doing work she hopes will help people in financial difficulty, and Mary Hage has launched a whole new career as a professional storyteller. Marjorie Buckley was happy to do less of the manual labor that had supported her most of her working life and to turn her attention to regular volunteer work at the LDS Family History Center. Jim Childs and his wife now help lead tours of a religious retreat center (Figure 6.1), while John Travisano spends much more time volunteering with his St. Vincent DePaul Society. Mary Poulsen is the outlier among this group of Catholic, Baptist, and Mormon active retirees. She rarely attends church and is not spiritually active; her retirement work is guided more by her own internal sense of life's meaning than by spiritual or religious considerations. All the others are regularly engaged in religious communities and at least moderately serious about cultivating a spiritual dimension in life. For them, retirement offered an opportunity for faith to trump the structures and demands of the labor market.

The Necessity of a Paycheck

On the way to retirement, everyday working lives are often shaped by attempts to balance financial need and job satisfaction—what sociologists of work might call "extrinsic" and "intrinsic" factors. Samantha Bailey is an artist and

FIGURE 6.1 "My job I guess is to take the people through when they come in."
—Jim Childs

photographer and very in touch with the spiritual side of life and work, but she admitted,

> I do weddings to pay the bills. And I'm not really interested per se in doing weddings, but I do to keep the work up. Sometimes it's very frustrating for people to not see me as an artist [laughs]. They see me as someone there to take the pictures, and that's very frustrating for me because I'm trying to do more than that.

Samantha's Neopagan spirituality shapes her view of the kind of work she would like to do, but the realities of the market shape the work she has to do. Amelia James's conservative Catholic faith is radically different, but she, too, finds herself between what her spirit wishes for and what the checkbook demands. She worried aloud in many of her diary entries about the unstable employment situation she and her husband found themselves in and how frustrating it is to have to work all the time at multiple jobs, rather than being able to afford to be a stay-at-home mom. "You know, I'm very traditional. I'm very conservative and I, the, um, religious Christian ideals are important to me. The traditional female role, I think is a beautiful thing." Her picture of Christian gender roles defined any workplace labor as non-sacred.

More typical was Melissa Parker, a forty-one-year-old active member of Atlanta's historic African American New Beginnings Church. She likes selling real estate, but she is not yet making enough money to meet the household budget. In her oral diary, she articulated the dilemma:

> I'm trying to decide if I should continue with trying to be a full-time sales associate, selling new homes, or if I should just go ahead and get a job. It's hard to decide because looking for a job is a job.... And if I am going to do that, I feel like I am cheating myself out of giving real estate a 100 percent try. You know, I prayed about it. I asked God to help me, to show me, you know, where I should be, what I should do. And I just, right now I really don't know. I know that there is money to be made selling real estate. But my financial situation just won't allow me to go for months and months without some type of pay. So that's my dilemma. Should I stay or should I go?... So, you know, my faith will, I'm sure, help me to make the right decision through prayer and just being patient. I guess right now what I need to do is be still and wait for God to tell me something, show me something.

Samantha and Amelia were clear about the conflict they perceived between a given kind of work and the spiritual ideals they held. They do the work because they have to. Melissa likes what she is doing, but without a more steady income, she may have to give it up. Like most of the other spiritually engaged people who talked about such dilemmas, her faith was part of the story, but not the ultimate definer of the direction the story would take.

People without active religious and spiritual connections faced similar dilemmas in equal numbers, but for them the calculus is exclusively a worldly one. Erika Lombardi has a law degree, but is not working in a firm. Instead, she works from home reviewing real estate legal documents (and as a substitute teacher on the side). "Anyway it's boring. It's a living. It's fine," she said of the legal work. Jocelyn Frederick, like Erika, is among the young adults in our study who have little interest in religion or spirituality and do not see their work through that lens. She, too, found herself in a frustrating job with an unpleasant boss and not enough pay. She compensated by doing a variety of other odd jobs to save for the condo she wants to buy. By the time we saw her the second time, to talk about her photos, she had made a move in the direction of changing her money-and-satisfaction equation. She had landed a new position and negotiated for a better salary. Whether resigned to a boring job or seeking out a better one, stories like these—told by people without strong religious attachments—are focused on human effort in a human system.

The vocational decisions of our most secular participants were shaped by the internal logic of career development and the exigencies of needing a paycheck, but they were also sometimes shaped by a strong sense of a person's own internal moral commitments about what is worth doing and why. The relative value of money was at the heart of it for some of them. Steve Sims was very clear about what guides his work:

> I think the thing that probably irks me the most is seeing people perform tasks or do things strictly for monetary reward, for a financial reward. I think there's way too much of that in our culture.... I work as an optician. My goal on a daily basis, no matter which patient I'm dealing with, no matter what insurance they have, is to provide them with the best vision possible.

Robin Mitchell has a similarly strong ethic about her work. She is a financial planner and takes enormous pleasure in helping people—especially women—use money well. She also talked about how there are lots of corners that can be cut that would make her much richer if she cut them. In one case, she recalled, "I realized the right thing to do was to tell him [to] put it all in Putnam and then bring it over. Well, 1 in 100 advisors would probably tell him to do that. But I sacrificed my $5,000 so that I would retain a sense in my heart of having integrity and being a good person." Neither a Theistic spirituality nor an Extra-theistic recognition of spiritual forces in the world makes sense to Robin or Steve, but they share with most of the rest of our participants an Ethical spirituality, and it is that grounding that guides their work decisions and how they balance vocation with financial necessity. The dictates of the market do not have the last word.

Doing the Work

The everyday experience of working has been more the subject of journalists and photographers than of sociological inquiry in recent decades (Halford and Strangleman 2009). Studs Terkel famously set out to listen to the voices of ordinary people and rendered their stories of working in his book of the same name (Terkel 1972). His was a tale told with deep lament about the search "for daily meaning as well as daily bread" (xi), a search made difficult by the nature of the work done by the Americans he interviewed in the 1960s and 1970s. People treated as robots and disposable objects were to be found, he said, "in the office as well as the warehouse; at the manager's desk as well as the assembly line; at some estranged company's computer as well as some estranged woman's kitchen floor" (xiii–xiv). Like Terkel, we took our recorders to homes and offices and coffee shops to listen to the stories of working life, to try to map out the salient social contours as they were reflected in those stories. How are the computers and managers' desks and sales floors defined and shaped by the people in them?

Sociologists who have studied work have often taken a more distant view, charting the macroeconomic forces shaping the labor market, sometimes missing how those trends are experienced by workers. Even studies that presume to tell us about the "meaning" of work include long batteries of questions about money, available leisure, prestige, and job security. The "intrinsic" meaning of work is captured only by questions about whether it is interesting and well matched to one's skills and abilities (Wray-Lake et al. 2011). Survey constructors seem not to imagine that one might work for reasons related to some larger good. If anything outside the "iron cage" of rational calculation were going on, many sociologists of work would be largely blinded to its existence by their own tools.[8]

The surveys are not wrong to point to questions of autonomy on the job and the structure of particular occupational sectors. What we heard from our participants reflected, both implicitly and explicitly, those very real social structures of work; but the stories also sometimes reflected an additional dimension provided by a spiritual perspective. The workplaces where these activities took place vary enormously in how tightly they are structured, the degree of autonomy workers have, the balance of physical to mental labor, and a host of other factors.[9] And each of those things may affect the degree to which the work itself is seen as having religious or spiritual significance. Where there is little room for the individual worker to shape the work, perhaps it is perceived as both impersonal and profane, outside the domain of any spiritual intentions. Where the focus is profit and productivity, perhaps there is less room for a religious sensibility to shape how the work is done. If Weber (1958) was right that modern capitalism no longer needs the moral underpinnings of a "Protestant ethic," then we might expect to hear little in everyday work stories about things that go beyond the logic of bureaucratic rules and the bottom line. Because these factors may play out differently in different segments of the economy, it is useful to compare work experiences across those sectors, listening for hints about how the structure of the job affects the way spirituality does or does not appear in the workplace.

Products and Profits

Twenty-two of our participants were in management or professional-level positions in firms that ranged from the insurance industry to law offices to a landscaping business. What they shared was a world of work that is oriented to the capitalist economy, with all its potential for success and failure. While they might have a good deal of discretion about how they do their work and a good deal of influence over the outcomes, they also live in a world of markets and regulations and bureaucracies—all the things that characterize the modern economic system. Their stories only occasionally took those structural forces explicitly into account, but neither did they routinely speak of work as having deep personal and spiritual meaning. They were less likely to talk about the work they do in spiritual terms than were the workers in any other sector of the labor force. Most of the stories sounded like Daphne LeCompte's account of her job as a corporate communications officer (Figure 6.2).

FIGURE 6.2 "There's been a lot of reorganization at work."—Daphne LaCompte

> What's going on in my life right now? I wouldn't exactly say that I'm in chaos, but to a certain extent I am. There's been a lot of reorganization at work, and we've been bought out by a very large company. My job description ostensibly remains the same, but I'm feeling a lot of outside influences and having to work with combinations of people who I'm not that comfortable with.

On a lighter note, Alicia Waters, who is the executive officer for a large non-profit, recorded in her diary one day, "Everyone at work seemed happy to have me back. We had an educational seminar that went well, and I felt really good about helping other people with some needed information." Alicia and Daphne are equally detached from any spiritual or religious engagements in life, and their accounts of their work lives were unsurprisingly secular.

But so were most of the other stories told by business people. Among those with modest levels of religious involvement and/or spiritual commitment, about a quarter of the stories we heard introduced some sort of non-secular sensibility into accounts of work life, but most of those (as we shall explore below) were focused on relationships in the workplace rather than on the work itself. Only the most spiritually serious among our participants talked about the way their faith informs what they actually do.[10] Most of these stories remained fairly general. Andrew Hsu talked about praying for the ability to focus on accomplishing the tasks at hand; Julia Oliva was praying for confidence as she started a new job; and Nora Cole's description of her work seemed to follow her Jewish emphasis on *tikkun olam*.

> I like to feel that I have done something constructive in the world. That I've made life better somehow for somebody and that I haven't hurt other people along the way. So, I like doing architecture because it makes the world look better and makes people's lives work better.

When asked how he makes decisions in his landscaping business, Lawrence Urban said, "prayer and experience." Some of these same people also talked about the occasional time when the demands of the workplace conflict with religious obligations, such as expectations that they work on the Sabbath or on Sunday. Protecting sacred time from the encroachments of work was one of the ways religious business people asserted a spiritual counternarrative. When an individual worker carries a strong spiritual sensibility into the world of business, then, they recognize the presence of something more than rational calculations, but even they do not routinely talk about what they are doing in religious terms, and the stories they tell interweave the sacred and the mundane—prayer and experience. The narrative of the business world is the dominant one, punctuated only occasionally by the spiritual perspectives a few professionals and managers bring with them.

There are, of course, visible exceptions within the American corporate landscape. Chick-fil-A closes its franchise outlets on Sunday, and many businesses have corporate chaplains, accommodate religious observance in the workplace, and otherwise invite religion into the world of business. As Lake Lambert III (2009) documents in *Spirituality, Inc.*, "spirituality at work" is a recognizable movement with many different manifestations. There are shelves full of books, dedicated journals, and consultants who will advise managers on how spirituality can improve work satisfaction. Systematic analysis is, however, in shorter supply than the advice. What the stories of our participants suggest is that the everyday work of keeping American corporations running is not likely to yield easily to sacred reinterpretations. There may be more spirituality *at* work than spirituality *in* work.

Science and Medicine

Six of our participants spend their working lives in biological and health research labs of various sorts—two at CDC and the others at labs in both Boston and Atlanta. The accumulated stories they told provide an interesting window on the world of research and the conditions under which this most "secular" of pursuits can and can't be sacralized. Matthew Smith and Jocelyn Frederick are both in their twenties, both without spiritual connections, and both fairly dissatisfied with their work. Matthew works on injectable microparticles but described himself as a bit of a slacker at work. He said, "I think people can tell themselves, 'Oh, we make people's lives better; we're producing something that's going to help with the kind of outcome of disease state or something like that.'" That is not a view he finds particularly convincing, however. Jocelyn simply said that her job analyzing medical survey data was not one she wanted to stay in for very long. It is no surprise that neither she nor Matthew saw anything about their jobs as spiritual.

They stand in contrast to Charles Curlew, an active member of Brookfield Baptist and a statistician at CDC. He has settled into a satisfying career and is the sort of active research scientist who worries about the backlog of journal articles he has not yet read and the article reviews he owes. One day he told us in his diary about an article he had just published describing "a mathematical statistical approach that would enable them [researchers] to save hundreds of thousands of dollars" in estimating chemical levels in a population. What he had also told us is that he had a regular morning prayer routine that involved vowing to work that day "as unto God."

> There have been many mornings that that prayer has also expanded into my working on this particular problem that I just talked about, where it looked like there wasn't a way to solve that problem. . . . And so there were many times when I would be praying about how to solve a particular problem related to a computer program or related to a mathematical derivation and that's pretty much the way I work. I'm in constant dialogue with God about what I'm doing and really many times see God leading me to answers, giving me insights, leading me to other research papers that I might not have found on my own.

For Charles, there is nothing in the science that is inherently alien to his spiritual life (or vice versa). He does not leave his faith at the door of the lab (cf. Ecklund 2010). As with other kinds of work, it is often not the nature of the work, but the sensibilities of the person that shape whether and how spirituality is present.

The doctors in our sample, on the other hand, sometimes found the work itself to evoke a spiritual sensibility.[11] They certainly told stories about the mundane side of medicine (Figure 6.3), but they also pointed both to the overarching meaning in their work and the moments of transcendence along the way. Carlos Fernandez is a doctor and the other CDC researcher, a specialist in pediatric AIDS treatment—a commitment we have already heard him describe in religious terms, even though he himself is no longer especially religious. Steven Kahn is Jewish and moderately active in his religious tradition. He made no explicit links between choosing to be an ob-gyn doctor and his spirituality, but the way he described his work, it might not be such a stretch: "In my mind, there is nothing better than delivering a baby," he said. "It is such a wonderful experience. Every time I do it, I can't believe that a baby's being born. It never gets old." Stephen James gets the harder, high-risk cases. He is deeply committed to his faith and talked about the spiritual reasons for his devotion to increasing access to medical care and to treating high-risk infants. He insisted that his success in working with families who may very well lose their babies depends on faith.

> I need to bring something to that—that makes it clear that I can only do but so much. I can't do that unless I have that same hope

FIGURE 6.3 "Every morning the in-patient team talks [here] about how we can help these people."—Mark Fuller, M.D.

myself.... And I found that I did have that hope; it was there. It's part of why I do what I do. I know that through God so much is possible.

He works creatively at the intersection of his skills, his acknowledged limits, and his confidence in God. Like Charles Curlew, Dr. James brings a strong individual religious and spiritual engagement into his work, but there are hints here that even without that individual religiosity, medicine may sometimes evoke a certain awe that pushes some of its practitioners toward transcendence and moral meaning.

The link between science and transcendence was also made by one of the scientists who is not herself religiously engaged. Carolyn Horton talked about her biological research work (and her art) in Extra-theistic spiritual terms. Her bread and butter job is in a botany lab, but she said,

My work is as an artist, I've always been fascinated with living things and also geology but just things of nature; organic forms and stuff that are very small. Oftentimes I'm interested in stuff that you don't see except through a microscope because one thing I'm fascinated with is that there are all these patterns that keep recurring in lots of different areas of nature, completely unrelated areas of nature. Like, the way a tree branches, mathematically, has similar patterns to the way a river branches or the way lightning branches or those kinds of things.

That fascination with patterns in nature, which she gets to observe in the lab, also showed up in the pictures she took for this project. They included "little critters" on the beach and vast expanses of sky and clouds. She finished showing us the pictures with the declaration, "That's my collection of sacred places." When spirituality is taken to include a sense of awe at the complexities of nature and of life and death, the work of scientists and physicians may sometimes be experienced as spiritual work.

The Artists' Way

Carolyn's stories about her work evolved over the course of her diary entries to include her reflections on whether she could move toward doing her art full time.

> I'm sort of thinking I'm going to take off the golden handcuffs of having a full-time job that I don't l like so much, but that kind of pays the bills, and try to start up a business of my own. It's really frightening. But it's very energizing....I think that there's a way for me to use my talents and, you know, make a decent living out of it. I don't really want to be famous, and I don't really want to be fabulously wealthy; I just want to make a decent living doing something that I do well.

Her struggle to balance her love for art with the necessities of making a living was a familiar refrain among the ten people who defined at least part of their vocation as an artistic one. Six were working full time at their craft, two part time, and two trying to break in. James Dupree is one of the lucky ones. He is an independent composer and choral director, and he describes being a musician as "fabulous." "To be able to be a musician and make money, to make a living out of it," he said, "it's just a blessing and a half!"

Among our artists, stories about getting into the profession were joined by stories about the everyday routines of photo shoots and contracts and jam sessions. Like other workers, artists live in a world where the structures and narratives of business and production shape much of what they describe. But more than most other workers, they also tell stories where the mystical and sacred side of life appears. When sociologist Robert Wuthnow began to explore the emergence of spirituality in American religious life, he chose artists as the focus of his analysis. He points to the way artists often attempt to "capture some partly understood mood or experience" that tries to express "spiritual connectedness and spiritual wholeness" (Wuthnow 2001, 9). Alex Polani is the most prototypical spiritual seeker among our participants, and we have noted his descriptions of the transcendence he experiences in his music. Rebecca Klein picks up the refrain, as well. She is marginally connected to her Jewish community and teaches art to at-risk students, but she also runs a small boutique in an artsy North Shore (Boston) community. She described how much she loves creating a space in which women can help each other dress beautifully. It is more than selling clothes. It is the communal "effervescence" and the beauty that emerges as person and clothing find each other, and some of the women she has met have become more than customers. She and three others are about to start a women's group "of women who are in their, you know, sixty or over, who are looking for what it is that we want to do for the next twenty or thirty years of our life." Rebecca described the experience of one of the women who had temporarily relocated to the community.

> She rented a house by herself. She's married; raised two children but decided that she needed some time to find her spiritual self. She came to [this community]. So for the last six weeks she's been discovering herself. She's lived near the beach, she's walked the beach, she's written poetry. She's used the ocean as her spiritual outlet. There are two other women also who have used [this community] in this way as their spiritual place, and they've been coming into my shop and I've been having these unbelievable conversations.

Like Carolyn and Alex, she speaks of an Extra-theistic spirituality in the world, and that spiritual dimension is thoroughly intertwined with the artistic work she does.

Others of the artists would agree with Carolyn or Alex or Rebecca about the mysterious sense of connection and awe that characterizes artistic creation, but they were also likely to name a specific connection to the divine. James Dupree's understanding of music was thoroughly spiritual, "'Cause music is directly right from God, and if you can stay in the music, you're just like—phew—you're living your life right there with God." He is an active member of Grimsby Congregational and cultivates his individual spiritual life—and writing and performing music are part of that picture. Emma Cooper is a Neopagan and experiences much the same thing in her writing (Figure 6.4).

FIGURE 6.4 "This is where I write.... I've got a lot of things on my bulletin board, a lot of goddess images for inspiration."—Emma Cooper

Anything I do with reading or writing is spiritual to me. Again, even if I'm not consciously thinking of it. Like, I think my work is very part of my spiritual life.... I write mainly nonfiction for kids and mostly social history.... Like all my books I'm really, really conscious of integrated religious history, and it's a real mission to me and actually is a big part of my spiritual path. Because, in a sense, it's part of bringing the goddess back into consciousness. But it's also so hard to separate it all out because it's all so intertwined to me [pause]. But that, to me, is like a religious mission.

While the most spiritually serious among our business people or researchers might manage to bring faith with them into the workplace, little about the structure of the work itself seemed to open up windows on spiritual life for people who did not already have faith commitments. Among the artists, on the other hand, even the less spiritually engaged seemed to encounter something more than mundane matters of production and sales in what they did.

Cubicles and Deliveries

The work stories of artists stood in vivid contrast to the stories of those who occupy the support positions that keep organizations and commerce moving. The vast majority of the stories told by drivers and bookkeepers and clerical workers were about aspects of their work other than the work itself—the people, the money, the customers. When they did turn their attention to the tasks they perform, it might be to report on skirting the unreasonable demands of the boss or about frustrations with the organization's priorities. Jessica Kingman likes doing sales, but her current job simply is not very challenging, and Charlotte McKenna admitted that when business is slow at the store where she works to supplement her photography income, she spends time surfing the web. Not all of the work is boring, of course. We heard a few stories about a moment of pride in learning a new skill or accomplishing an assigned task well.[12] Liz Thompson talked about the challenges of driving a public transit van in Boston—not only the crazy drivers, but the snow-clogged winter streets and the worn-out equipment that breaks down and leaves her and her handicapped passengers stranded. Liz sees the overall mission of her job as a worthy one, but she certainly sees no spiritual direction in the way the bosses run the operation.

When religion and spirituality appear in these stories they are largely either as a criterion by which to judge the ethical character of the work or as a resource for mitigating a difficult work environment through prayer and patience. Other research has pointed to ethical decision making as one possible impact of spirituality in the workplace (Giacalone and Jurkiewicz 2003), but making judgments about difficult issues at work is not something we heard much about from these workers; they have little autonomy for making such judgments. They did, however, sometimes worry out loud about the very nature of the jobs they do. Alexis Nouvian wondered if it was really a good thing to be a personal shopper helping rich women buy expensive clothes. By contrast, Greg Collins was content with his low-level administrative job because it was located in a nonprofit drug and alcohol treatment program that he sees as doing a lot of good. The nature of the job and the nature of the organization both count in the moral equation. What one is doing—filling out forms, paying bills, selling widgets—may not be inherently glamorous or evoke spiritual depth, but being part of a worthy organization can transform an ordinary job. Alexis and Greg share an Ethical spirituality that they call on to think about the worth of what they do for a living.

In each of the other occupational sectors, we have observed that the presence or absence of spirituality has been largely a matter of the individual inclinations of the worker in question. Here that is not the case. Actively spiritual individuals (like Alexis) were no more nor less likely than minimally spiritual ones (like Greg) to tell spiritual stories about work. The nature of these blue- and pink-collar jobs seems to discourage much storytelling about work at all; and when it happens, there are only occasional links between the routines of the workplace and the world of religion or spirituality. The sensibilities of the person do not change that fact. The inherent alienation of these jobs seems to have separated most of their incumbents from their own spiritual selves (Erikson 1986).

The "People" Jobs

Sometimes called "service professions," jobs like social work and teaching may take place in organizations that are as large and bureaucratic as any business. People in them may feel as constrained as clerical workers do, but their work is fundamentally different. The "product" they hope to produce is much less tangible, and the focus of the work is a person, not a material object or financial transaction. To spend one's life helping people and teaching children is likely to win a person admiration, and that admiration is reflected back in the deep joy many of these participants expressed when talking about their work. Barbara Robinson's description of facilitating adoptions is a case in point. "Adoptions are so rewarding. Oh, my God. Because you're finding permanent homes for children that doesn't have a permanent home. And when that adoption's finalized, it's so beautiful that you found a home for this child." Barbara has almost no connection to New Beginnings Church where she is a member and is not otherwise engaged in spiritual practices, but she knows that her job has meaning. Sam Levitt's sense of meaning, on the other hand, is deeply interwoven with his Jewish spirituality, even when he does not explicitly say so. He concluded our initial conversation by reflecting on the work he does as headmaster of a private school.

> So it's not whether the school exists, it's what it means in the lives of the people who are part of that school.... I'd like to be someone who helped people see what it means for communities... [to] give people a vision of what it could be. So not for the sake of that institution but for the sake of the people who then have a bigger view of what's possible.

As with many of the service professionals, even when the story had no overt spiritual or religious content, a deep satisfaction and sense of purpose shone through.

Education and social service, like other occupational sectors, are filled with everyday routines that may or may not be shaped by religious and spiritual sensibilities. A new unit of study needs to be planned; a new client's profile and needs have to be assessed; there are meetings to attend and reports to read and write and bosses to please. Most of these stories were recounted to us in pragmatic, secular terms—just the stuff of everyday work life, even in a profession that can lend itself to spiritual interpretation. Sometimes those everyday stories were told with a spiritual twist, however, and that came from the commitments individuals brought with them to the job. Elizabeth Evans is certainly a person who has brought a deep sense of faith to her lifetime of work in health education. She has a sense of gratitude for what she sees as divine blessing in her own life. "It's just humbling. I mean I have to be grateful. That's why, you know, I'm always trying to do something to, you know, pay back what He's given to me." What she continues to do, as she is moving into retirement from CDC, is to travel the world evaluating HIV interventions and educating women about their own health. Hank Matthews was in a similar life stage—nearing retirement—and similarly reflective about his work as a professor, helping his students learn to contribute to society. "Most of the time, maybe the small amount of good that you do, well you never really see it. But what's the admonition of the New Testament? Go about your business quietly? I'm a firm believer in that." Like Elizabeth, Hank has a basically religious view of the world that comes with him—quietly—to work. Neither talked about "using" religion to try to change the people they work with. This is not about proselytizing. It is about the way a spiritual understanding of oneself and the world shapes both a vocational choice and the everyday execution of that choice.

Not every story about helping was a happy one, of course. Sam talked about his continuing struggle to make his private school more than just a school for rich kids. Both Michelle Winter and Barbara Robinson talked about their frustration with the paperwork and bureaucracy that surround their social work jobs in Boston and Atlanta, respectively. Erika Lombardi was working as a long-term substitute teacher in a Boston middle school to supplement her freelance income from reviewing legal contracts, and she told unrelentingly unhappy work stories. Nearly every day's diary contained a new tale of the torments middle school students can inflict on substitute teachers, and all she could say was "never again." Like Michelle, she is a disaffected

Boston Catholic, but she had no sense of either greater good or of spiritual resources for coping. Rebecca Klein had some similar tales about her work as a temporary art teacher in an alternative school for kids with serious learning and behavioral problems. Unlike Erika, she found spiritual resources for confronting what was happening in her classroom and for deciding she would have to find another job. As she told us about what she had been through, she said, "I think it's all pretty spiritual. You know. I think forgiving yourself and letting yourself be who you really are and not feeling like, oh, I've failed here." Finding inner strength to deal with difficult situations was the occasion for prayer among several of the most spiritually engaged of our participants. Working with people, especially people who have difficult life circumstances and mental challenges, is not easy.

The everyday world of labor is, then, both secular and sacred. In some kinds of jobs, the window for sacred meaning and spiritual action seems fairly wide. Artists tap an imaginative dimension in which wholeness and transcendence are glimpsed. Doctors are witnesses to life and death. Social workers and teachers embody the virtue of compassion. The jobs themselves lend themselves both to a sense of vocation and to the possibility for everyday encounters with larger meanings and mysteries. Selling expensive clothing or balancing the books for an insurance company are a different matter—not to mention driving a van or scrubbing floors. If there is spiritual meaning present, it resides in the mind of the person doing the job, not in the job itself. Sometimes religious faith provides a critical edge to wonder about the ethical significance of the work being done. More often, the everyday experiences of spirituality are efforts at coping. Few call on religious or spiritual principles and communities as resources for critiquing the nature and structure of the work they do. In even the most insistently secular and the most spirit-numbing jobs, however, a few of the most spiritually engaged workers find ways to integrate their daily activities into the spiritual and religious story of who they are.

The Social World of the Workplace

What happens in everyday workplaces is not simply the channeling of human resources and labor into organized and efficient output. It certainly is an economic exchange, lodged within a set of power relationships, but it is not merely that. As our participants talked about what happens at work, stories about relationships were nearly as numerous as stories about the work itself.[13] Across every occupational sector, nearly a third of all the stories we heard were primarily about the people involved, and that does not count the substantial number of stories (almost 40 percent) about the work itself that were themselves collective stories—not what *I* do but what *we* do. Understanding the sociology of the workplace is more than understanding bureaucratic positions and economic struggles; it is also about how sociality shapes this domain in which people spend so much of their lives. Lynne Pettinger's research is one of the helpful recent calls for attention to job-related friendship and general "sociability" (Pettinger 2005). As she points out, conversations among co-workers weave constantly into the spaces between official work requirements. Some non-task-related interaction may be intense and intimate, but most is something of an interactional pastime. Drawing on Simmel, she asserts that this nonserious chatting forms the very fiber of the social group (Simmel 1949). Jokes, sports, the weather, and shared impressions of customers and bosses fill the time and are hardly irrelevant. Over the course of interviews, photos, and diaries, our participants told well over two hundred stories of job-related relationships; and more than any other kind of work story, these were shaped by spiritual sensibilities and religious dynamics.

Hanging Out and Making Friends

Among the most common kinds of stories about workplace relationships begins with a simple account of an enjoyable atmosphere created by nice people. In these stories, the sociability is clearly working, and sometimes the enjoyable atmosphere carries over into afterhours activities, as well. Matthew Smith is the researcher who described himself as largely bored and lazy on the job. One of the pictures he took for this project was from his company's New Year's Eve party, so we asked him, "Is it comfortable hanging out with other people from work?"

> Yeah. Yes and No. It kind of depends. There's always a lot of drinking, but yeah.... There's definitely a few co-workers that I hang out with here and there, like Friday night and [pause].... My department was pretty boring at first. Now there's more twenty-somethings.

Carlos Fernandez is a doctor at CDC, and his excursions with co-workers run more to tennis matches and work team charity projects than pub crawls. While the activities are quite different, both men work for employers who seemed to be encouraging workers to spend extracurricular time together. Among our participants, people (like Matthew and Carlos) who were not involved in religious communities seemed more likely to talk about this sort of casual downtime with co-workers.[14]

Some of these co-worker interactions eventually deepen into friendships, of course, and some of those friends showed up in the pictures people took. Mary Hage pointed to one of hers and said,

She's an awesome friend.
Interviewer: That's great. So that must make work nice too, then.
Mary: It does and I don't really enjoy the work as such. It's not fun, it's not interesting. We do foreclosures and bankruptcies, and it's the same old, same old. Every now and then there will be something unusual or amusing—but it's the people.

A quarter of our participants, of all spiritual and religious persuasions, named someone from work as one of their closest friends, and a handful of others noted that some of their lifelong friendships started in previous jobs. Early in her life, Elizabeth Evans did a stint in the Peace Corps and then returned to Africa to do health education. As she looked back, she said,

That was probably two or three of the best years of my life, because the teachers were just so hungry for any kind of information. It was so great to work with them.... They knew that there wasn't much money. There was just you and your, you know, supposed technical expertise that wanted to work with them. So, um, yeah I guess those are—I mean it was the friendliness, the collegiality.... Yeah, I really made some good, good friends, and, um, long-time colleagues.

She added that the daughter of one of those school superintendents "was here for six years, living with me in the '90s. And she got her degree in microbiology at Georgia State." It has been a while since her last trip to Abidjan to see that family, but she gets phone calls and text messages and hopes to get back within the year. Friendship and work have been a satisfying and productive combination for her over her career.

Occasionally, friendships even become something more. Harris and Megan Crosby met each other behind the cameras in their television news jobs. And William Pullinger told an old-fashioned tale of falling for the girl in the mailroom at his first engineering job. The Crosbys still work together, while William's wife followed the older pattern of retiring from the workforce to raise their children. These happy intersections of love and work (along with many unhappy variations) are ubiquitous in American culture.[15] But even when work relationships do not become intense or intimate ones, it is clear that the social dimension of work is central.

What about the Boss?

In contrast to stories about co-workers and even customers, relationships with supervisors were not the happiest stories in the workplace. Only about a quarter of our participants talked about manager-worker interactions, but three-quarters of those stories focused on shortcomings and failures in management that were causing distress. Sometimes the issue was the simple failure to acknowledge work done well; other times there were major ethical issues such as failing to pay taxes or hiring people under misleading pretenses. To the extent that individual workers are themselves spiritually oriented, they often responded to such distress and worry by praying. Recall Melissa Parker's worry over being able to make enough money to stay in her real estate job. It was not just the money that posed difficulties, however. The broker she worked with turned out not to be trustworthy, but before she fully realized how bad the situation was, she simply worried—and prayed. Her diary entry included this:

> So my broker is coming out today, and I've just prayed to God, because I know God can handle everything. I know He already got this situation under control and I'm probably stressing for nothing....Because I'm telling you if these people come out here today, this broker, if she comes out here with any kind of criticisms about, you know, me not calling people or whatever, not doing this, not doing that—because I know that I am doing everything that I possibly can—I might just snap. I'm just asking God to please help me because I don't want to leave my current broker on a bad note.

The question is not whether God will somehow intervene and change the way these bosses do their work but whether workers like Melissa will have the wisdom to endure and the confidence to stand up when the time comes.

On the other side of the desk, those who are themselves managers also talked about that part of their work. Sam Levitt talked about how seriously he takes the task of hiring teachers, and Andrew Hsu reflected in one of his diary entries about trying to hire the right people for his software engineering team. He was especially aware that the team was suffering because, he said, "One of my, the guys who works for me is a little resentful because he is underpaid significantly.... So I am just praying for wisdom as to see how to resolve that. I've been working with HR as well as trying to work with my boss." He will also, he said, use the brain God gave him. As with so much else in the workplace, the tasks of managers are shaped by the rational and relational demands of the job. But for religiously engaged managers, those secular forces are interwoven with the spiritual understanding they bring to their work.

The Challenges of Diversity

Both bosses and colleagues today form their workplace relationships in the context of greater ethnic and religious diversity than ever before. The stories we heard often reflected that reality. The friendship Elizabeth Evans shared with her African colleagues was not based on common religious (or ethnic) traditions. The family she described was Muslim, although the daughter married a Christian and had her children baptized. While Elizabeth, a moderately active Catholic, was certainly aware of these differences, there was never any hint of conflict in the stories she told. Similar patterns of friendship across difference were present in roughly a quarter of the work friendships we heard about. People were aware that their friends participated in a different religious tradition or that there was a religious-nonreligious difference, but in most cases that difference was treated as incidental to the friendship. Thomas Miller is Jewish but has spent a good deal of time around Catholics in his life. About one of his work friends, he noted, "You know, he's a pretty strong Catholic attendee." But this is not something they ever talk about at work, he said. Carlos Fernandez, as we have seen, is someone who has a strong sense of a religiously informed vocation, even though he is not religiously or spiritually active. He judges his co-workers based on the good and caring work they do rather than on their beliefs (which tend to be similar to his agnostic stance). Thomas and Carlos are not themselves especially religiously active, so perhaps it is not surprising that they are able to set religion aside as a potentially divisive factor in their work relationships. In fact, the least spiritually engaged of our participants were the most likely to describe their work friends as religiously similar—similarly nonreligious, that is.

Religiously dissimilar friendships were actually more likely among the more spiritually engaged. Jessica Kingman was among the most intensely devout persons in our study, but she named a Sikh woman as one of her best friends, someone who had formerly been a co-worker. People like Jessica, for whom religion is so central, are less likely to ignore religious differences among their co-workers, but that does not mean that they are proselytizing (although some are—to which we will return below). More commonly, two actively religious people find their differences to be enlightening. Steven Kahn is a Jewish doctor, and his nurse/office manager is a dedicated Christian.

[She] is, I think, fairly involved with her religion and her church. It's important to her. And she has shown great interest in learning about Judaism....Being my nurse has involved her, because I have to schedule the Bris ceremony out of the office...and I'm often juggling patients around. She has been helpful in terms of getting that accomplished....She is very interested in learning when I lead services, and she asks how it's going. We talk sometimes about the differences between her religion and my religion.

It is not surprising that these conversations were taking place in an Atlanta office. Our Atlanta participants were more likely to tell stories about religious conversations among people at work and more likely to say that they talk with their work friends about religion. Jessica is the exception among our Boston workers. More typical in Boston is Ann Rosa, who is an active Catholic. Her religious participation might come up in casual conversation, and she did not try to hide her commitments, but, she said, "I don't feel the need to talk about it. I don't identify myself that way, as an introductory kind of thing; it's personal." A privatized Northeastern sensibility does seem to contrast with Atlanta's more openly religious workplace. Privatization certainly exists, then, but not everywhere.[16]

That does not mean that people in either Boston or Atlanta are blind to the diversity in their workplaces. When people talked about the people they interact with at work, they often mentioned the ethnic, national, and religious variety they see. Jennifer Hammond's job in human resources requires her to make decisions about pay and benefits for workers in a global firm, so learning about the business cultures of Taiwan or China is simply part of her job. Andrew Hsu works with a team of software engineers that spans the international diversity typical of that field. And Mark Fuller described the various religious traditions represented in his neurology team.

There's Christian Orthodox, a lot of Jewish people, both residents and faculty. The Christian spectrum was from Episcopalian to very, very, very Baptist. I know there are at least two Muslim residents, and I believe some of the attendings are as well. It's really all over the map.

Religion was not, he said, a major topic of discussion or disagreement, but as people chat about what they are doing outside of work or about family events, religion was likely to come up. As more workplaces are populated by an increasingly global labor force—something certainly more likely in some industries than others—people are encountering an increasing level of diversity at work. Our interviews would suggest that most of these encounters tend toward the benign, casual, and even informative. As Putnam and Campbell have suggested, meeting "my pal Al," who "happens to be" a religion other than my own, may increase levels of acceptance of religious difference more broadly (Putnam and Campbell 2010).

One of the key dynamics at play in negotiating workplace religious differences, however, is the relative majority or minority status of the people involved as well as the larger cultural climate in which those differences are defined and the relative power of the parties doing the defining.[17] People who are part of a minority religious tradition either have to stay quiet or explain themselves. Mormons, for instance, have a number of lifestyle commitments that are difficult to hide. As Leonard Pickett explained,

> I mean we have a life that probably makes us a little bit unique from the general population.... So the mere fact that I'm in business; if I'm at a cocktail party, I don't drink. When they pour the wine I don't have wine. In the mornings when everyone's loading up on the coffee....

We asked if people notice and asked him to explain, and he said, "Yeah, absolutely." When they do, he tells them that he is a Mormon and expects that most people will know enough about his religion not to need much additional explanation. If they harbor any prejudices (which many Americans do),[18] they will likely keep those feelings to themselves so long as the group has to continue to work together. The American legal system protects religious minorities from the most overt forms of discrimination and harassment.

Our Neopagan participants were not so lucky, and they were often not sure that they would be accorded those minimum protections. Laura Henderson works in a large food company and describes her work strategy as being in "the broom closet."

> At my desk, during the day—I have several things on my desk—to people who would come round my desk and just look wouldn't know the difference, but, to me—because I can't come out of the broom closet at work—are very pagan. Now if I had a pagan friend come by, they'd

go, "ah" [claps hands]. But most people just think that I have a really interesting desk.... I can look at these images or look at these things and remember it's just a job. All I'm doing is selling dead chicken, you know.

Most of the people in the office simply do not know about her religious commitments, even though she has managed to create a space she herself can experience as spiritual. Among her closest work friends, however, she has tried to introduce this aspect of her life.

[Ruth] is one of my good friends at the office. She's one of the ones that know I'm a witch. She is not of this path at all. She is—I think she's Presbyterian and is pretty strong in her faith. But because of the business we're in and being the multicultural industry that we are, [she] is very accepting of anything and everything.

She is—cautiously—introducing her co-worker to an unfamiliar religious tradition. As relative equals in the workplace, they have some cultural space in which to engage their religious differences without obvious threats. Dr. Kahn is able to do similar cultural work educating a Christian nurse about his Jewish traditions because he can offset his religious minority status with his workplace authority as a doctor. Whether and how a religious minority person can introduce new religious ideas and practices into the mix of workplace sociality and friendship depends on sufficient cultural and workplace power to prevent backlash.

When Religion Is Intrusive

The stories were not common, but they were there. Someone in the workplace insists on talking about religion when others find it offensive. Or someone insists on interacting with others based on a set of religious rules that are perceived as too rigid to accommodate workplace diversity. Shirley Knight is one of Laura's Neopagan friends and is a nurse. Because she knows what it is like to be rejected for her beliefs, she tries to be tolerant of others, but, she says, "It's hard sometimes when you have a Bible thumper in your face, you know. And I just don't say anything." People who were not themselves interested in religion or spirituality were the most likely to mention this problem. In Boston, it was likely to be Catholics who were named as offensively rigid. In Atlanta, it was evangelical "Bible thumpers." Even when religious people were not trying to proselytize, others could feel the weight of their cultural presence. Daphne LeCompte talked about living in Atlanta as a nonbeliever.

> I feel pressure not to say I'm not religious because everybody in Atlanta—maybe not in Boston, but everybody—it's, like, "After church we went to dah, dah, dah." And sometimes when you have a meeting where people are—they're going to do an icebreaker, it's a project team—now tell us a little bit about yourself. And "Dah, dah, dah, and I'm very active in my church." And I think "Who cares?" I'm sorry. It seems like it's a validation, like, a holier than thou kind of statement. But I think there is kind of an understanding among a lot of middle-class, nonacademic Atlantans that church is a part of what they do.

Even in professional settings, when work teams get together, Atlanta's pervasive religious culture finds its way into routine conversations that are experienced as oppressive by people who are not themselves believers. And given the American distrust of "atheists" (Edgell et al. 2006), they may be as careful about revealing their nonreligious identity as Laura and Emma are about being witches.

On the other side of the religious divide, a few of our most religiously committed participants admit to looking for opportunities to introduce faith into the conversations they have with their co-workers. Andrew Hsu refers to himself as an "undercover corporate chaplain." He keeps a plaque with a scripture verse on his desk and makes a point to protect his Sunday time for a day of church activities. And in an industry of ninety-hour-a-week schedules, any routine time not working is noticed. Leonard Pickett is not only comfortable explaining to people that he is a Mormon; he hopes that they ask him to say more about his beliefs.

> I think that goes back to my experience as a missionary for two years. I did that for two years and I mean I never would ever push my religion on anyone, but when I'm asked about it, I'm absolutely totally comfortable sharing what our beliefs are and how I feel about it.

Other LDS participants talked about trying to reach out to co-workers and employees, as did a few Evangelicals; but the large majority of the spiritually serious people in the workplace are not there to try to convert anyone. Because this is an important part of their lives, it may come up in conversation, but only a few see the workplace as a "mission field."

Where Faith Is Shared

Charles Curlew is one of those spiritually serious Evangelicals, but he said little about trying to evangelize his co-workers at CDC. What he has done is start a men's prayer group that meets each Tuesday morning, and having that group is important to him as a place to bring multiple threads of his life together (Figure 6.5). Such prayer and study groups are seemingly ubiquitous on the American work scene and sometimes touted by management experts as "affinity groups" that will improve overall workplace morale.

Organized efforts to bring workers together around spiritual pursuits are certainly worthy of note, but they by no means exhaust the ways in which religion serves as the basis for workplace friendship and sociality. Two-thirds of the work friends that were named by our participants were described as sharing the same or similar religious orientations. That is striking given the diversity of workplaces; random sorting would not predict that degree of religious homogeneity in work relationships. It is also striking given that our participants did not always define those relationships primarily in religious terms or spend much time talking with each other about spiritual matters. Nevertheless, even in the workplace, where religious identity is not the most salient sorting mechanism, birds of a similar religious feather seem to flock together.

FIGURE 6.5 "Men that I work with, we get together, have lunch and...pray together."—Charles Curlew

Even if only loosely recognized or defined, spiritual tribes are being formed. Some sort of spiritual signaling is enabling people of similar spiritual (and nonspiritual) sensibilities to find each other. People who are themselves nonspiritual find other nonspiritual friends at work. All of those whose dominant spiritual discourse was Theistic (and named a workplace friend) could identify the religious identities of their friends. They could also identify the religious differences between themselves and the friends they named. Their spiritual sensibilities have been shaped by well-articulated religious traditions that help them draw definitional distinctions. But those distinctions are not boundaries—these are their friends, after all. People whose notions of spirituality focus on Extra-theistic meanings were broader in their definitions of who counted as similar and less likely to say their friends were religiously different. Larry Waugh is a marginal Catholic and said of his business partner, "Goes to church. Spiritual path. We talk about it occasionally." His own definition of spirituality includes both Theistic and Extra-theistic elements, so there is plenty of room for common spiritual ground.

For a few of our participants, the workplace itself was religiously identified. Margi Perkins found that to be a wonderful bonus in her Catholic preschool.

> The best thing about what I do now is, because it's a faith-based school, you're working with people who are kind of along the same lines as you. So it's not as stressful, because you're not dealing with people who don't have the same value system.

In the Jewish day school where Rachel Halpern works, there is a similar meshing of religious and work identities. One of her diary entries began, "Today at school we celebrated Yom Ha'atzmaut and it was Israeli Independence Day. I just really enjoy these days at school." In spite of the fact that she encounters intra-religious differences among different kinds of Jews (and between them and the non-Jewish principal), having a workday centered on Jewish learning and co-workers who share her values was something Rachel cherished.

Most workplaces, of course, are not identified directly with any religious tradition; and many are determinedly secular, like the state agency where Michelle Winter works. Still, shared religious sensibilities came out. Michelle may not be very active in her Catholic parish these days, but she has still been profoundly shaped by her faith and welcomes the times when she can talk with work friends about it. One day, she told this story in her diary.

Today I went out to lunch with [my friend] and another woman named [Agnes]. They're people that I have worked with but also know outside of work. And they're people that I feel like there's a different level of connection to. Some of the things that we share in common are family values, commitment to things, and also I think the fact that we find some peace in religion.

Michelle was not the only person to talk about the special bond among people of faith who find themselves working together. She is very clear that overt religious talk and practice cannot be part of doing her social work job. Religion has shaped the values she brings to the job, however, and she finds reassurance in the times when she can talk about those connections with others who share her faith. Here the spiritual tribe, not unlike Charles Curlew's prayer group, gathers around the edges of work times and spaces.

Most work relationships are probably mostly secular most of the time. Only about half of the stories we heard about the people at work were stories in which religion or spirituality played a role. Still, that reflects a substantial presence of spiritual dimensions being recognized as part of the everyday social world of work. A striking number were able to tell us whether their work friends were religiously similar; and where they were, over half said that they do talk about religion and spirituality. A substantial minority of the American workers in our study have found a likeminded person at work, and that relationship establishes the potential for conversations where work and spirit intersect. For at least a few, their shared spiritual focus even carries into the work itself, enabling them to work in sync. As Jen Jackson put it, "There have been people that I have really connected with. And I'm like, oh my God, this is awesome, I love this person. I could work with them every day we're just so in tune."

Bringing the Golden Rule to Work

Lest this suggest that spiritually attuned people are huddled in a corner praying with each other, an accurate picture of their role in the workplace could hardly be more different. The most common theme in their stories about workplace relationships was their attention to the needs and concerns of their clients, customers, patients, and co-workers. What they bring to work is a "Golden Rule" sensibility that demands that they treat others as they would wish to be treated. They want to help people who need help and treat others with respect. When our participants told work stories in which spirituality or religion was present, the theme was often one of mutual care, of putting people and values ahead of competition. In contrast, when people told work stories in a secular mode, those themes of personal caring were almost never there. The wedding of spirituality with human caring is something we will explore more fully in the next chapter as we examine the links between religious participation and community engagement. But work stories, too, were sometimes about "doing unto others as you would have them do unto you."

James Dupree, for instance, talked about taking time to talk with a secretary whose husband has multiple sclerosis. He inquired about how she was doing and told her Jesus was with her. The two of them already recognized a common religious language, and in this story they talked together about the comfort of knowing that God is always present. Praying for the troubles that co-workers are encountering is a common pattern among people who are the most spiritually engaged. Jessica Kingman came back from a meeting with her fellow sales associates and recorded in her diary,

> Looking back at the day the more things that seemed to stand out for me were these trials and tribulations that my co-workers were having. So, tonight before I go to bed and next couple of days I'm going to try to keep them in prayer that God will give them the strength they need for whatever they're going through.

These were concerns about family members, accidents, and unexpected illnesses—not directly job related but clearly impinging on the lives of her co-workers. Some of the stories we heard seem to hint that the more spiritually engaged of our participants attract the confidence of people who need advice and comfort. As Jane Baker mused, everyone in the office seems to talk to her—not only about doing their work but also about things going on in their lives. Bringing a Golden Rule sensibility to the office seems to be a way that the boundaries between work and the rest of life are blurred.[19]

It also weighs directly into the way people do their jobs. Michelle Winter's story about her lunch continued, "We talked about how much the religious plays a role in the people that we are....So much of what I believe and how I believe things should be is part of my religious piece." How she thinks things should be includes unrelenting advocacy for the children she is seeking to assist, but it also includes dismay over one co-worker who is cheating on his wife with another co-worker. In her diary, she mused at length about the hurt being caused and said, "I can't understand how anybody could do that." Jennifer Hammond recounted in her diary an incident with one manager wanting to see another manager punished. She tried to assure him that she took seriously the bullying he had experienced but urged him not to exaggerate the situation. In the end, "We talked about forgiveness quite a bit, which is kind of interesting. The sales manager is Christian and he and I have talked about religion in the past, and we talked about forgiveness." Relationships in the workplace are often fraught, often impinging on the ability of people to get things done. Bringing spirituality into the equation is certainly no guarantee of smooth sailing. The point here is simply that workplace relationships are often understood and enacted in ways that include life rules learned in religious communities, and they are negotiated in the context of an Ethical spirituality shared by many of the players on the scene, a spirituality that transcends specific religious traditions but is nourished by them.

Long before there is a crisis, Ethical spirituality suggests to people that life is better when treated with kindness. The everyday rigors of work are cushioned by the small moments that reassure and encourage. Jen Jackson's work as a behavioral therapist with severely challenged kids takes a lot of patience, and she talked about needing to have a coping mechanism, which for her is prayer. "You really need some kind of religious outlet to work in this field and not get burned out," she said, "or just be so angry and frustrated that you just quit." When others do not seem to have that support for themselves, she said, "[I] find myself just speaking to people and encouraging them. Like a lot of times just encouragement is more of what I end up doing than anything else. But I get encouragement because I'm able to pray and...so I can help somebody else." Harris Crosby's coping mechanisms fall more on the earthy side, including a penchant for the kind of jokes that allow people to deal with the relentless stream of bad news that comes through his television studio to be broadcast. As in many helping professions, a certain dark humor is common backstage.[20] Harris sometimes worries that he will get desensitized to the human pain being reported, but he also said, "If something's funny, God invented humor, laugh at it." He might almost have been echoing the old Irish saying "Laughter is the hand of God on the shoulder of a troubled world."[21]

A Golden Rule mode of interacting in the workplace also appeared when people were weighing the most serious questions their jobs put before them. Mark Fuller's diaries were full of stories about interacting with his colleagues and patients, none more stunning than the occasion when he had just declared a patient "brain dead."

It's one of the more odd things about neurology in general. From a legal standpoint, I can walk up to someone who is on a ventilator and whose heart is beating, and I can do a couple of little tests on them using my hands and a flashlight and some ice water, and write some words on a piece of paper, and whereas before they were alive, afterwards they are dead.

The legal power he has to declare that death has occurred is not something he takes lightly. He has no thought of measuring his decisions against some sort of religious dogma. Rather, his religious formation and spiritual sensibility have shaped an awareness that life, in all its complexity, is something to be cherished and death something that means more than just his signature on that paper, even if that is all the law requires.

Conclusion

There is really no such thing as "the workplace." Nor is it only "work" that happens there. Understanding how "religion" has an impact on employment requires that we deconstruct both sides of that question. The religion we have observed in these pages is only occasionally about doctrines, proselytizing, or even calling. "Religion" at work does include enough of a commonly recognized social identity that two-thirds of work-based friendships are religiously homogeneous. And it does include the very real way in which participation in religious communities shapes decision making, coping, and the presence of a Golden Rule ethical sensibility at work. Religious communities, in other words, help to shape spiritual practices and ideas about good behavior that carry over into many kinds of work situations. To the extent that a person has learned those practices and developed habits of spiritual sensitivity, that person is likely to be aware of a spiritual dimension in the narratives of everyday work life.

Some work is, however, more susceptible to such understandings. What makes it so is not so much the presence or absence of an individual's power to bring spirituality in as the nature and social definition of the work itself. Work that involves service to others lends itself to spiritual enactment even when the individual worker is not exceptionally religious or spiritual. Similarly, work that explores the realms of beauty and imagination seems to invite spiritual definition. And work that deals with the limits of human existence is often narrated as a spiritual pursuit.[22] In these kinds of work, the presence of spiritual understanding and practice emerges both from the experience of the individual worker and from the work itself.

By contrast, work in business and all its related enterprises as well as labor in what is euphemistically called "service work" is not likely to be defined by the people in it as a spiritual enterprise. Here Weber is right. Modern industrial capitalism no longer expects this kind of work to be animated by Protestant (or any other) ascetic ideals (Weber 1958). People who work in menial jobs as well as those whose primary ethic is the accumulation of profits rarely say that what they do is done to the glory of God.[23] Such jobs can still be spiritual pursuits but only insofar as dedicated individuals, supported by active participation in a religious community, look hard for the sacred content in what they do.

What they are likely to find, however, is not that the work itself is sacred. Rather, the Golden Rule ethical sensibility, itself a widely recognized form of spirituality, provides guidance for how people treat each other. We have heard stories here about hiring and fair pay as well as about a willingness to learn from others who are different. And we have heard about an openness to human connection that transcends the functional requirements of the job. It is often in "random acts of kindness" that the sacred is present in the domain of work. To ask about "religion" and "work" requires that we pay attention to the way both secular narratives of career and marketplace and spiritual narratives of human concern and greater good are interwoven in any given story. The causal influences are constantly being negotiated in the everyday places where people experience what work means in their lives.

7 EVERYDAY PUBLIC LIFE: CIRCLES OF SPIRITUAL PRESENCE AND ABSENCE

We have now followed our participants through their everyday routines of household and work and have seen the ways in which their spiritual engagement shapes and is shaped by the particular social domains in which they are present. We have seen the spiritual tribes gathered in religious communities and in households and even in loosely tied networks of recognition and caring that form in the workplace. It is now time to follow people into their neighborhoods, communities, marketplaces, and larger public arenas to hear how, if at all, stories about those public places are inflected with a spiritual accent, how, if at all, spiritual tribes gather there, as well. Here we will listen to their stories about everyday routines but also their reflections on what the world *ought* to look like. How do they name the world's ills, where do they draw the boundaries of concern, and how do they identify the necessary moral virtues for living in the world? Do the stories about what they actually do grow out of or contradict the vision they describe? What activities and organizations embody their moral concerns?

Raising these questions allows a new look at very old questions. Does spiritual engagement mean worldly withdrawal—a basic Marxian assumption? Are people who are most actively engaged in spiritual practices and religious participation too busy with other-worldly concerns to pay attention to public life? Do religious organizations absorb all the social energies of their participants, leaving nothing for the larger community? Do highly religious people think that only God can change the world? We will look for the limits that may be present on the power our participants perceive themselves to have and the constraints they experience. Is the world of politics and the market—even (or especially) for the most spiritually engaged people—perceived as a world where elites and impersonal forces are in charge and religious power is mute? What our participants say about changing the world and what they report about their activities will provide an intimate look at the place of religion in everyday public life.

We asked each of our participants, in our initial interview, to talk about what a better world would look like and to describe things they routinely see that they judge to be unethical or wrong. The things they would like to see change ran the gamut from everyday acts of meanness or bullying to the traumas of war and terrorism. Throughout the interviews as well as in their diaries and descriptions of their photos, we heard additional stories—a total of 637 of them—that provided direct and indirect access to their moral sense of the world. They talked about how things ought to be, how people ought to behave, people they consider admirable or despicable, and what they do to try to live up to the standards they set for themselves. These "morality tales" were coded for the focus of concern, for who is deemed responsible, and for how change might be possible (see Appendix 2 for additional detail on coding). Some of these stories are about specific social domains that are within the range of a person's face-to-face experience, while others concern the state of the nation or the earth itself. In each case, we will look for the presence and absence of a spiritual dimension in the concerns that are expressed as well as the role of religious institutions in making things better (or worse).

Similarly, we will assess the stories about what people are doing in those larger arenas of public concern. When people talk about their everyday lives, work and family are more dominant sources of memorable stories than is political activity or other public participation. There were comparatively fewer stories about everyday life in neighborhood, marketplace, charitable organizations, and politics—404 in all. Here again, we carefully categorized each story based on who the actors are, what kind of action they are undertaking, the focus of that action, and the balance between human and divine agency in making things happen.[1] From neighborhoods and cities to far-flung crusades fueled by the nightly news and the internet, where and how does civic action enter the routine of everyday life? A few of our participants were quite politically active, and several are invested in community charitable activity, but many of the stories about this larger world simply asserted basic rules to live by, guidelines that people hoped might create the bigger changes. That basic moral compass is where we will begin.

Rules for Living

As I noted in the first chapter, I have been asking members of religious communities what it means to them to be part of their religious tradition—to be a Christian or a Jew—for two decades, and the answers remain remarkably the same.[2] When challenged to sum up what it means to live a good life, no answer was more common than the very answer reportedly given by Jesus to a similar question. Jesus began his answer by reminding his hearers that the greatest commandment was to love God; but he went on, quoting the Torah: "A second is like it: 'You shall love your neighbor as yourself'" (Matthew 22:39, quoting Leviticus 19:18 NRSV). American church- and synagogue-goers enthusiastically embrace this very pragmatic answer to what lies at the core of faith. What people name as definitional to their religious identity is rarely a doctrine or even a spiritual experience. What they name is a way of living. Similar appeals to mutual caring can be found in nearly all the world's religions.[3] In a variety of subsequent research, I have documented that "serving others" and "living one's faith every day" are the defining moral center of religion for well over half of the participants in America's religious communities (Ammerman 2005b); and as we saw in Chapter Two, Ethical spirituality is a common cultural discourse in the conversation about what spirituality is.

What the participants in this project make clear is that this basic moral injunction is so pervasively recognized in American culture that it was cited by those outside religious communities as often as by those who are religiously active. Camilla Hart is a member of Cornerstone Baptist, a Black church in the suburbs of Boston, and she summed it up this way:

> It's how you live your life and what you do for others, too. How you help other people. Helping other people—to be that role model, mentor, teacher, helping that person who's sick. Just being as good a person as we can be.

But our disaffiliated participants said similar things, even referencing religious traditions as the source of these teachings. Recall (from Chapter Two) Robin Mitchell's description of Jesus as a "John Lennon type" whose teachings were worth paying attention to, even if Christianity has since done a pretty bad job of exemplifying its founder. Even those, like Robin, who are not involved in a religious community draw on these culturally available religioethical resources to guide their moral lives. Loving and caring for others, being compassionate, and setting aside selfishness were guiding virtues espoused by participants across the religious and nonreligious spectrum.

Where are these virtues practiced? Many of those who talked about this way of living illustrated it with stories about how they relate to their friends, family, and co-workers. We have already seen how a Golden Rule sensibility shapes relationships at work, but in other friendships, as well, relationships need to be built on taking time to listen, being truly empathetic, and helping each other in difficult times. Being a Christian, James Dupree said, means "being sympathetic and empathetic. Sympathetic, not working from your ego, working from love, working from your heart. God is the center." He went on to tell about a particularly troublesome member of the musical group he leads and concluded, "So my thing is just forgiving him for that. That's where he is." The stories we heard about putting the Golden Rule into practice were often, like James's, recognized in the breach. Aimee Ralston is a young member of Cornerstone Baptist, and she pointed to a person in her photography class: "She's very critical of people and she doesn't take the time to find out why they are the way they are. She just, you know, cuts them down. And I think by being in a church environment all your life you sort of maybe pay attention more to people and who they are on, like, an individual basis, not just going off first impressions, that kind of thing."

Many of the everyday life stories we heard about how people chose to live their lives and how they hoped their actions would make a difference in the world reflected what they identified as spiritual disciplines that allowed them to reach beyond themselves and to act with compassion. Altogether, half told at least one story about something they do to help others, something explicitly seen as an expression of their spirituality. Phyllis Carrigan is a middle-aged member of St. Sabina's Catholic parish in Boston, and she was struggling financially when we met her. As she reflected on the important routines in her life for her oral diary, she talked at length about the people she is teaching. She recounted sharing clothing and a box of Valentine's chocolates with an immigrant man she was teaching English. Later, talking about continuing to make charitable contributions even when she herself is hurting, she mused that you "can't out-give God." All of this was for her a Lenten story. Her spiritual discipline for the Lenten season was to turn her own anxiety about work into good deeds for others. "I need to practice what it means to really trust God, that God will provide your future in everything." Theresa Collins, from All Saints Episcopal in Boston, also had a story about the spiritual discipline of living compassionately. On her daily prayer walk with her dog, she often meets a woman who seems to be lonely and perhaps in need of help.

> There's this funny little woman who walks around here. She carries a bag, a shopping bag, and she, she's a strange little person, and I've seen her for years.... So I've made a conscientious effort to be a good Christian, um, and to try and develop a relationship with her.... Just being friendly, trying to, you know, be a good Christian.

Being friendly even to a difficult person is as much a part of her spiritual practice as the prayers she recites from the Book of Common Prayer.

Loving one's neighbor is not always easy, and most of those who talked about the challenges of putting it into practice recognized that their religious communities helped to reinforce their spiritual commitment to hard relational work. It was also clear, however, that churches and synagogues do this both by their positive examples and injunctions and by their ample opportunities to practice forgiveness (Jones 1997). The religiously active people in our study were very aware of the imperfections in their communities, pointing to hypocrisy and jealousy as well as to more spectacular failures such as embezzlement and sexual abuse. At Brookfield Baptist, the level of tension was obvious in the stories various members told us, and Olivia Howell's diaries were full of reflections on how she was struggling to get along:

> I had to find a level of forgiveness that before then was not, you know, had eluded me. I mean I had to actively work at forgiving someone... for doing something that was really wrong. I mean what she did was just not right. It wasn't, and you know, and she knows it.

She went on to talk about recognizing that she is certainly not perfect herself:

> And what I found is that people have forgiven me without my even knowing that I had injured them or offended them. And so here I was on that other, I was on the other side of that.... And when we seek forgiveness, it should be provided, because we're all in the same boat.

"Doing unto others" includes mutual forgiveness, and it is required in religious communities no less than elsewhere.

Among those who are *not* regular religious participants, rules of life were sometimes grounded quite differently, derived from American culture more than from any religious tradition. Theirs were moral stories with heroes who are strong and independent, hardworking and creative. For Larry Waugh, a former Catholic, the philosophy he tries to live by is straightforward: "Keep your nose to the grindstone, behave, and everything will go well for you. You know, and kind of, basically that, you know, you'll be taken care of. But you've got to work for it and you've got to work hard for it." As an artist, Catherine McKenna's version of that philosophy is to value playfulness, imagination, and beauty and to encourage it in those around her. There were, in fact, many variations on life philosophies that grew out of Extra-theistic spirituality.

Alex Polani, the young Boston musician and spiritual seeker, was trying to ground his life in enlightenment.

> It's really like an inner journey and an experience of life and awaken-ing.... I'm just talking about self-awareness and enlightenment. All the mystics have actually said we all have the same potential.... The tendency is always to put the power outside of yourself, which is what religion has done, and that's kind of what pulled me out of religion.

Other nonaffiliates talked about reading and learning in a similar light. The answer to how to live is found inside the self, not in external authority.

For this population, where moral codes are fundamentally individual, the highest value of all is to be tolerant and nonjudgmental, to honor the sacred worth of the individual person. Jonathan Snow is unaffiliated and has a school-aged son. We asked what kind of world he hopes his son will inhabit. "Open and tolerant and peaceful," he said. "Free to think about things like this and pursue your own beliefs, all that kind of stuff." Larry Waugh put it in the negative—what people should *not* be is "judgmental.... [Why can't we] try to understand someone else's religion or point of view?" The single most distinctive moral refrain among those who are not active in traditional religious communities was the problem of religious intolerance. As people outside the bounds of America's religious cultural establishment, they are especially sensitive to the need for a greater measure of tolerance.

Numerous studies over the last several decades have confirmed that these sensitivities are not misplaced. Americans in general, and especially religious Americans, distrust nonbelievers and put them near the bottom of the list of groups whose rights should be protected. As Putnam and Campbell (2010) summarize their own and others' evidence, "Religious Americans are less stout defenders of civil liberties than secular Americans" (484). That would not surprise Laura Henderson. She talked about all the misconceptions she encounters in her Southern community, often hearing her Wiccan path char-acterized as "Satanist." In contrast, she said,

> One thing I do like about this path is that we seem to be very tolerant. We don't necessarily like what other people say about us, but we're very tolerant because we've been so prejudiced [against] that we're very tol-erant of what people pick as their religion. It just simply doesn't matter to us. As long as you're a good person and you follow something, that's sort of what we care about.

Similarly, Carlos Fernandez, an Atlanta doctor who no longer routinely participates in the Catholic traditions of his upbringing, said,

> The ideal would be that people would get along and would be willing to listen to other people's opinions and, you know, have that tolerance for the way other people think, the way other people live. And not necessarily feel as if, you know, just because I think this is the way it should be that everyone has to think the same way.

Of the thirteen people who mentioned tolerance as a guiding moral virtue, only one was a regular participant in a Christian congregation.[4] Nonaffiliates, marginal members, and people in Jewish and other religious traditions bring to the public table, then, a special sensitivity to the problem of exclusion—a moral concern often absent among their actively religious Christian neighbors.

The guiding virtues our participants identified, including this emphasis on tolerance, are dominated by variations on the Golden Rule theme, couching the rights of others in "do unto others" terms. Some give the Golden Rule a particularly theological flavor, a few frame it in justice terms, and a few think about obeying rules and laws; but each of those is a variation on an injunction to put the needs of others ahead of selfish desire.

The primary rival to Golden Rule moral guidance is the contrary advice found in the American credo of individualism, the advice to do what is best for the self (Bellah 1987). While the tolerance we heard about often took the needs of others as its focus, it also sometimes carried a distinctly individualist live-and-let-live tone. Barbara Robinson talked a lot about taking others into account, but when she reflected in her diary about how she raised her children, she said,

> I raised them to be independent thinkers, to, when you're ready to leave this home of mine, of ours, they will be ready and prepared for the outside world, because the outside world is not all good. But they needed the tools to be able to survive. First was education. And working hard. And to be able to...stand up on their own two feet.

Individual effort and individual enlightenment produce an internal moral compass that will guide each person to respect the other. Among those who are not active in any religious community, that American individualist credo was a close rival to the Golden Rule as a guide for living with others in the world.

Among those who regularly attend religious services, individualist virtues were cited much less often. Sam Levitt is an active member of Congregation Sinai, and his assessment is this:

> I think we live in a world in which—I think American culture is about as individualistic and isolationist as you can be. I think that the pendulum has swung all the way to one side…so religion to me brings us—is a communitarian expression for me, a group of people who I'm involved with in an ongoing way, a community that I have some strong allegiance to, responsibilities for, and I contribute financially to. And to me it sort of balances the dominant culture which I find is destructively anticommunitarian and individualistic.

His tradition, like the other religious traditions in this study, places limits on the individualism touted in the larger culture, encouraging members to add the needs of others to their moral equation.

Religious participants not only adopt a more communitarian moral outlook but also seem to get a stronger sense of the possibility that one should and can commit oneself to trying to live by these principles. Sometimes people told stories about how life should be with no expectation that they or anyone else could live up to those standards. Notice that both Larry and Carlos issued their pleas for tolerance in a "Why can't we?" mode. Polly Baxter was straightforward in her assessment. We asked whether she ever thinks about what a better world would look like, and she responded, "No, because it makes me sad. Because I know it's not going to happen." Statements of powerlessness like this were not common, but when they occurred, they were more often in the stories told by people like Polly (and Larry and Carlos) who are not religiously active. As we look more closely at what people are actually doing in pursuit of a better world, that question of power and powerlessness will be a critical one. What are the factors that empower action that goes beyond merely hoping for the best?

Changing the World Nearby

When people told stories about acting in the world, they often began near at hand, with things they had reason to know something about. Sometimes they looked no further than friends, co-workers, and fellow congregation members, but when they began to expand the circle, they thought about the needs in their own communities and the things that could and should be done to make those communities more humane. When they made this move from moral rules to moral action, the Golden Rule was again their guide, leading them to speak of "helping the needy" and service to people "less fortunate." American culture is saturated with calls to assist victims of disaster or provide Christmas toys for the "neediest cases." Americans have a fraught history of attempts to define just what constitutes a worthy recipient of aid,[5] but we have little doubt that the person who helps is to be admired.

Among the stories we heard about building better local communities, "helping the needy" was a common theme, but especially among those who are regular participants in religious communities. Church and synagogue participants told stories of charitable deeds that provided individual comfort to others in the community, often making direct links between loving neighbors and loving God. John Travisano told several stories about the people he visits as part of his parish's St. Vincent de Paul Society. "Spiritually," he said, "making these home visits.... It is something to be able to talk with these people at length and understand their problems and be of assistance and try to do God's work and help them." Fellow Catholic Jessica Kingman routinely works in a ministry to homeless men and told stories about conversations with her homeless friend Jeff—taking him to the emergency room when he was sick, sharing medals from Lourdes with him, praying for him. Sam Levitt's spirituality includes charitable giving.

> Giving away money is a high value among Jews—and time. So being charitable in general.... I think charity is a subset of loving-kindness. And so my wife and I every fall sit down and go through the lists of potential charities. We save all those envelopes you get inundated with during the year...and then we decide....And we give away—I don't know if it's 10 percent of our income but it's something approaching maybe 5 or 8 or even 9 percent of our income every year. And my wife is always surprised by how much we give away, but we both end up feeling good about that.

Sylvia Carter is much less devoted to a Jewish way of life, but she has nevertheless absorbed this particular Jewish emphasis. "I don't make a lot of money but I try to donate what I can to the hurricane and the tsunami, like that." Practices of charitable living are part of what Jewish spirituality means for many Jews, channeling the injunction to serve others into concrete financial commitments.

In the everyday ameliorative work of community service, the importance of religious communities and spiritual engagement is significant. Only a third of nonaffiliates told stories about local volunteer work, compared to roughly half of all those who have a congregational affiliation. Some of the marginal members, in fact, presented an interesting picture. While they rarely attend services in their congregations, some of them are actively involved in social service activities that the congregation facilitates. Jim Childs rarely attends Deer Valley Church, but he goes with a church group one Saturday a month to provide a meal for people who are homeless. Carlos Fernandez said,

> Lately I felt I wanted to get more involved with what the Catholic Church is doing, and one of the things that found me more involved was the AIDS Ministry....I thought that if I could have sort of an active role in the community in doing something useful, as opposed to just going to church, that I would feel much better about, you know, going to church.

This health-related work, organized by St. Michael's parish, provided Carlos a logical way to be connected to the community but also to the church.

Charles Curlew is a much more active church participant at his Southern Baptist Church in Atlanta, and he too depends on the church to help him serve his community. He is especially drawn to working with the many new immigrants who live nearby, at least some of whom have found their way to the church. He says,

> I really feel like it's not just something [where] I'm going to that place to get something for myself in terms of worship or fellowship or seeing other people but really looking for opportunities to minister to other people, to be the presence of Christ for other people, to get to know who they are and what their needs are and see if there's any way that I can help them meet their needs.

Hospitality and charity are the personal virtues implied in what he says, and his church is the primary arena in which he practices these virtues; but he is attuned to the needs of immigrants in his neighborhood, as well, providing transportation and other assistance from time to time. Others among the most spiritually engaged could be found working on programs to provide

FIGURE 7.1 "I went particularly looking for a church that gave back to the community."—Jennifer Hammond

better access to health care and education, serving on the boards of charitable organizations, volunteering at soup kitchens and in hospices, mentoring troubled children and teens, and dozens of other activities (Figure 7.1).

All of the people who routinely attend religious services linked their stories about community service to the teachings of their faith. Often they spoke of specific teachings, but just as often what came through was the extent to which the community itself modeled and enabled the moral ideals they held. The norms and rituals of these spiritual tribes are the context in which community action sometimes takes shape. People inside these tribes stand in significant contrast to the least spiritually engaged people, not only in how they tell moral stories but also in the degree of moral agency and action they exhibit in their local communities. What is happening inside the congregation is spilling over into action in everyday public life.

That sense of moral agency may be related, at least in part, to one of the key consequences of the U.S. system of voluntary religious participation. Voluntary organizations require the energy and leadership of those who participate in them, and the more active people are, the more likely it is that they will be called on to organize and lead. The result for many people is the development of what political scientists have called "civic skills" (Verba et al.

1995). These skills involve especially the arts of communication, planning, and decision making that are necessary for public actions such as letter writing, participating in decision-making meetings, planning and chairing meetings, and giving presentations or speeches. These skills are often learned in school and on the job, but they can also be learned through participation in voluntary organizations. Every club that plans a special event, every society that needs officers, and every congregation that asks its members to teach classes and chair committees provides opportunities for the development and exercise of civic skills. Indeed, research on civic skills suggests that the same person who learns to write letters to missionaries and collect money for new hymnals can use those skills to participate in local and national political life. What the stories we heard suggest is that active congregational participation and leadership produces both the skills and the sense of agency that extend into a broad and active engagement in the world.

The institutional infrastructure on which all of this depends comes from the fundamental organizational commitment of local congregations to the business of building what Robert Putnam has called "bonding social capital" (Putnam 2000). Given the American way of organizing religion, congregations are places of belonging that are bigger than the family and into which one does not have to be born. My earlier research has outlined the basic institutional patterns that constitute American congregational life, built on a foundation of "fellowship" activities aimed at creating a family-like atmosphere for their members (Ammerman 2005a). They are places where people take care of each other, teaching by example a repertoire of caring practices. They supply food, childcare, job assistance and in-home visits to the elderly in their midst; and we heard stories about this from our study participants. Catherine Young recounted how her LDS sisters in the ward brought in meals after her daughter was born:

> I was just so thankful for people's love, and they were so willing to do that for me. I just didn't have any idea how helpful it would be because it really did give me extra time not to worry about that, but to focus on being a mom.... It is just funny how things like that can just bring so much love into your life, and also it makes you want to be able to do that for other people.

Service inside the community, in other words, models the virtues of common good, accountability, and mutual care in ways that benefit the society as a whole.

Another organizational reality that gives congregations their impact in local communities is their significance as nodes in the voluntary organizing network. In part due to the weak American welfare state, there is both need and opportunity for voluntary service provision; and U.S. congregations are critical players in mobilizing collective energies. The larger of them may organize their own locally run programs of community service.[6] As we have studied congregations all over the country, however, it has become clear that a great deal of what they do in the community is not done through the mechanism of beginning their own individually run programs. Far more common are complex networks of organizational partnerships—connections that include everything from informal coalitions among congregations to financial and in-kind support to religious and secular nonprofit agencies locally and around the world (Ammerman 2005a). Almost three-quarters of the congregations we surveyed in the late 1990s had at least one substantive connection to a community organization that provides service and enrichment to the local public. Sometimes congregations are providing the space, money, and other resources to make the work possible; but they are also very likely to be providing volunteers. Both the congregation-based programs and the partnerships provide a mechanism through which individuals can pursue the moral imperative to "help people in need" and to "make the world a better place."

Facilitating community volunteering is something that is especially common among mainline Protestant and Jewish congregations (Ammerman 2005a), but among the participants in this study, it was Catholics who told more stories about getting involved in their neighborhoods, both through parish organizations like the St. Vincent de Paul Society and the AIDS Ministry at St. Michael's as well as through the things they learned and saw modeled in their churches. When we asked college senior Phil Marini about his future plans, he talked about how excited he is to be headed for work at a Jesuit Boys Home in Chicago. He has been active in both academic research on homelessness and parish-based opportunities to serve, and he mused, "I learned stratification through soup kitchens before I learned it in Soc class, so that always had a lot to do with what I want to do. Even since I was little, no matter what I wanted, it always involved helping people. That was somehow related to how I help people when I do stuff with church." My earlier research found that 60 percent of the individual members surveyed claim that they participate in community service organizations at least a few times a year, and 75 percent claim that they at least occasionally provide informal service to people in need (Ammerman 2005b). Other national research has found similar results. Controlling for all the expected other social factors that might influence volunteering, people who participate in congregational life are simply more likely to volunteer in the community than are people who do not attend services (Putnam and Campbell 2010). Doing good for people in need is part of what congregations and their members are expected to do.

The role of congregations in encouraging and facilitating local community service is considerable, but there are ironies in this story. People *outside* congregational life talked about wanting the world to be a better place, too; but they were more likely to express a desire for long-term solutions that would go beyond charity. They spoke in terms of building respect, advocating better government services, and reducing violence. They talked about the collective, governmental, and structural changes that might make a long-term difference. Theirs was a critical political perspective that was less often present among the actively religious. An ironic consequence of that perspective, however, was that the moral stories they told about their local communities were more often framed in terms of what "everyone" should do than in terms of what "I" or "we" should do; and they were less likely than their religiously active neighbors to be directly involved in any concrete effort to pursue those community betterment goals. They spoke of making occasional gifts to charity and participating in community fundraising events, but regular civic and charitable participation was not common in the stories they told. Jocelyn Frederick was one visible exception. She participates in the local Hunger Walk and is a regular Big Sister volunteer.

> I have been doing that for over a year. I have a twelve-year-old who I do activities with every couple of weeks. I'm actually going to see her this afternoon.... I do that and I'm really committed to that. I was doing a program where they put volunteers in homeless shelters to play with children, family shelters, but I just had too much that I was doing, so I stopped that.

Like Jocelyn, Alicia Waters is also unaffiliated and a Boston resident, and she is an even more dramatic exception to the pattern among other nonaffiliates. She has a special concern about access to mental health services and organized a successful nonprofit organization that she now runs. For a few nonaffiliates, everyday activism in local communities is a central thread running through their life stories. For the majority, however, seeing the need for long-term structural change has not translated into public action, charitable or otherwise.

Everyday Neighborhood Life

Stories about volunteering in the local social service sector stand in contrast to the stories we heard about the most immediate "public" most people encounter—the streets and sidewalks of the neighborhood in which they themselves live. Here the stories are largely about choices made for one's own benefit. Good school districts, convenience, and beautiful surroundings were the backdrop for stories about important moves that had shaped people's lives. Jonathan Snow even confessed that he intentionally chose a "blue" neighborhood where he could be surrounded by more politically liberal people (cf. Economist 2008). Quiet streets, Boston's seashore, and Atlanta's spring flowers were themes heard, as well, often as participants recorded their daily diary entries (Figure 7.2). As someone especially attuned to nature, Laura Henderson was effusive in her descriptions of both the beauty she sees during her daily commute into Atlanta and the secluded beauty of the rural location where she now lives. It is indicative of the middle-class character of our sample that only one person—elderly Mary Margaret Sironi—mentioned living in a troublesome neighborhood. Her HUD-operated apartment building in Boston had gone through management changes that worried her. Otherwise, when people told stories about their own neighborhoods, they were largely happy accounts, not stories of people in need.

FIGURE 7.2 "It was very beautiful and very peaceful."—Lily Mattison

Taking a daily walk, often with the family canine, was an occasion for a number of stories, and several people noted that these walks also provide opportunities for making at least casual connections in the neighborhood. Robin Mitchell told about taking their dog to the local dog park and how it was a good place to get acquainted with new people. Nora Cole and Alicia Waters both host Fourth of July parties each year to make connections in their respective Boston neighborhoods. Nora is mostly uninvolved in her local synagogue, and Alicia and Robin are unaffiliated; there is nothing spiritual about what they are doing in their neighborhoods. Theresa Collins's morning walking and praying stands out as the exception to the usual secular pattern. The intensely spiritual character of her relationship to her surroundings is uncharacteristic of the stories most people told about their neighborhoods. With few exceptions, neighborhood is a mundane space in the everyday lives of the people we talked with.

A few of our participants told stories about more organized forms of neighborhood interaction—condo associations, zoning hearings, and neighborhood associations—and they too were largely secular narratives. To the extent that everyday life included meetings with such groups, they were occasions for frustration more often than satisfaction. On that, Elizabeth Evans was the exception. In one of her diaries, she recorded this:

> I went to the third of a series of community meetings concerning development [around a nearby busy intersection]. I have enjoyed these meetings; kind of gets my juices flowing for the community organization kinds of things that I like to do. It was very interesting; I learned a lot and always a good crowd of people.

Although Elizabeth is a typically active Catholic, she did not make any real connection between this community organizing work and her faith. Carolyn Horton, on the other hand, is unaffiliated, but did make a connection between her spirituality and her commitment to building community.

> Community has become very important to me. Right now I live in a co-housing community.... I just have this sense that knowing your neighbors and caring about your neighbors and being in each other's lives is something natural to being human. And the way that we live in this culture of, like, driving a car into the garage and going into your house and watching TV and, like, what's that guy's name across the

street?…So I try to build community in a lot of different ways; it's really important to me. So that's a part of, I guess, almost a part of my spiritual life, really.

Stories about neighborhoods were not especially common overall, perhaps reflecting exactly the sort of individualist and isolated focus Carolyn decries. When these people think about everyday life, they do not situate themselves primarily in a local neighborhood.[7] Where neighborhood stories did emerge, they were more often told by people who are not involved in religious communities, suggesting perhaps a trade-off in where social capital is built and invested.

That Carolyn or anyone else thinks that neighborhoods could be spiritual spaces runs counter, of course, to the notion that cities are rational, planned, ordinary human creations. The reality is that spaces do get sacralized in a variety of ways. Whether an impromptu memorial erected after a tragic death or the religious buildings that punctuate the landscape, urban spaces often include reminders of the sacred. Even civic monuments and sports arenas like Fenway Park are treated as pilgrimage sites, and many neighborhoods still bear the marks of the religious communities that built or shaped them.[8] Tourists visiting from the outside may be more likely to note these sacred spaces than are the residents who inhabit them every day.

Jewish and Catholic communities have historically been linked to the geography they occupy. Observant Jews must live within walking distance of their place of worship, and Catholics have been religiously obligated to join the church that defines the geographic parish where they live. The most consistent linking of neighborhood and religion we heard, in fact, came from Jewish participants who commented on the degree to which theirs was or was not an especially Jewish neighborhood. Wendy Simmons is not terribly involved in Temple Beth Torah, but it is important to her to raise her children with a Jewish identity, and that influenced where she and her husband chose to build their home. As more Jewish families moved into the area, she was more than a passive observer.

I, with one other Jewish woman, said, "Why don't we do—since, it's such a transient city—why don't we send flyers out to all the Jewish families and see if they would like to do breakfast in the clubhouse and everybody bring a dish."…We were about 10 percent Jewish in that community. It was such a great idea, because very few people even have their parents fly in for the holidays.…It was wonderful. There were so many kids.…Everyone brought a dish and it was really nice.

While Wendy's community was becoming more strongly infused with a Jewish identity, Michelle Winter was lamenting the demise of the Catholic institutions that had once defined her Boston neighborhood.

> Today I was driving, and I happened to be near a church that I was a member—actually my parents were baptized; Anna, Daniel, and I was baptized at. And they recently sold the property, and they started to take—all the stained glass is gone. The statues are gone. They have now started to rip up the stone that was in front of the church. I was saddened when I saw how much they're just taking it apart....I made my first communion there. It just had been such a part of my childhood. It's now going to be gone...to know that the church I was baptized in, made most of my commitments to, are gone; my Confirmation is now...it's being taken apart bit by bit and sold to make way for more modern things....I can remember there was a school attached. The school's been closed for an awful long time—but how we would play there. May Day, we'd be outside and we'd decorate our boxes and have a parade and no one...my children certainly won't know that atmosphere.

It is perhaps understandable that Michelle's connection to her local parish is now so tenuous, even as her life is still marked by her deep Catholic sensibilities.

For Protestants and others, neighborhood and place of worship have never been so closely tied, and today most of our participants simply talked about their neighborhoods as their individually chosen places of residence rather than as a religious imperative. While congregations are intensely involved in connecting their members to local communities, the communities in question are not usually their own neighborhoods (Farnsley 2003). If anything, religiously engaged people are less attuned to their own neighborhoods as significant social spaces. Unlike nonaffiliates, they fill their lives with relationships and commitments elsewhere. Where one lives, for affiliated and nonaffiliated alike, was shaped by economic and aesthetic meanings more than religious or spiritual ones.

Morality and the Marketplace

If we heard few stories about neighborhoods, and few of them were spiritual in their orientation, there were nearly as few who talked about the everyday world of commerce and who linked their faith with how and where they spend their money. If they talked about the moral principles that should guide their interaction with the marketplace, the most common theme was personal responsibility for spending wisely. Congregationalist Jennifer Hammond talked about starting to teach her son about money. "You teach them some portion goes to charity, some portion goes to short-term spending, and some portion goes to savings. So that they get the concept early on of giving so that it becomes routine." Mormon participants talked about the obligation to work hard and pay your bills. As Leonard Pickett said, "Lorraine and I don't spend a lot of money on toys. We live a fairly simple life." And Southern Baptist Walter Green laughed as he illustrated the point: "Normally when we eat out around here we go to Crescent Garden Chinese buffet, and it costs us $16 for the two of us because we're senior citizens—and that includes beverage, includes dessert." Among the most spiritually engaged, like Leonard and Walter, these frugal habits were described as things encouraged by their faith. Indeed, people who are participants in a religious community were much more likely to talk about this sort of economic moral obligation than were people who are not religiously active. Across all the Christian traditions, at least a few of the people who go to church seem to take from that participation a moral imperative to use their money with their faith in view.

A variation on the stories about good uses of money, heard among unaffiliated people as well as religiously active ones, was an antimaterialism refrain. Jessica Fletcher, a young member of Atlanta's Vineyard Church, recorded a long reflection on materialism in her oral diary:

> It's something that I think that is a real problem in modern Christianity is the concept of materialism. You know, most people shrug their material gifts off, because, you know, we are always told to use our gifts for the betterment of others, for the spiritual fulfillment of our brothers and sisters. And so, you know, I think a lot of people justify the big house and the big car...but I don't really see too many people using their SUV's to witness to homeless people or, you know, I don't really see too many people using the eight spare bedrooms in their homes to house missionaries or, you know, take in underprivileged children. So, you know, I just, I feel like I don't have much, but I feel like if I were given much, that I would accept the greater responsibility of using those, you know, to further God's kingdom.

Our nonattending study participants were as likely to talk about the problem of materialism as were the active congregational members, but they were more likely to talk about the problem as endemic and not solvable. As Christmas approached during the time he was doing oral diaries for us, Greg Collins contemplated the idea of buying and receiving gifts with some dismay:

> I walked around and looked, the more I looked—and it was like, God, I've got so much stuff, and it's just stuff.... It seems really counterproductive. It seems like it's leading me in the wrong direction.... I really feel like life is complicated when you have a lot of stuff and that it would be much simpler if I had gotten rid of some of this stuff.

Greg is a disaffected Catholic who rarely attends his Atlanta church, but he is committed to doing something to simplify his life. Although there is no apparent overarching moral philosophy that informs his distrust of "stuff," he has the nagging sense that material goods are not leading him in the right direction. About a third of our participants expressed some moral conviction about materialism and/or the need to spend wisely, but about a third of those voiced that concern with a sense of resignation. Greed is rampant, they said. It would be good if it were not, but that is just the way of the world.

So how *did* people talk about shopping? About one in five of our participants recorded at least one shopping story in an oral diary, and some recorded more than one. Being a consumer is clearly part of everyday life for most Americans. Whether spending a Saturday morning at Borders, picking up household gadgets at Target, or shopping for bargains at Goodwill, spending money was part of routine—and often treasured—activity that ended up recorded in oral diaries. About half of our participants did not express any moral opinion about money, and unsurprisingly their accounts of shopping excursions were told exclusively in secular terms. Even those who had talked about the moral dimensions of their consumption were unlikely to narrate a shopping trip in spiritual terms. In some cases, in fact, accounts of shopping stood at some distance from the ideals they claimed. Alexis Nouvian (a member of South Street Presbyterian) spoke eloquently of being grateful, that what we have is enough and far more than what people in other parts of the world enjoy. Still she also told us about relaxing on a day off by shopping for clothes and make-up. And Pam Jones, from Cornerstone, admitted to feeling guilty about how much she enjoys shopping. The fact that both women are employed in retail clothing trades clearly complicates matters. In only a couple of cases did we hear stories that consistently maintained the connections between faith and spending, articulating a moral vision of money and carrying that into actual consumer decisions. Undoubtedly such connections existed in decisions we did not hear about, but as participants narrated the stories they found memorable and worth telling, shopping was largely a matter of whim and necessity.

Spiritual life was more likely to intersect with the world of commerce around a restaurant table than at a display rack or cash register. Going out to dinner or meeting friends for lunch, even stopping at a favorite Dunkin Donuts or Starbucks, were often noted among the memorable moments in a day or week. The majority of these stories were about the delight of spending time with family and friends and the joy of good food—happy and meaningful, but not sacred. A significant minority, however, were stories where the world of faith and the religious community extended into those culinary spaces. Sometimes it was a chance meeting of someone from the congregation, but more often the meetings were planned. Ann Rosa took a picture of a local diner where she and her friends often go after Mass on Sunday (Figure 7.3).

It's a wonderful diner. It was started in the 1950s. Joe was the owner. He was so surprised. He said, "Why are you taking a picture inside of my diner?" We go there at least once a week, usually for Sunday breakfast after Mass with a friend.... My best friend, we sit there and

FIGURE 7.3 "We sit there and we really, really have wonderful conversations."—Ann Rosa

we really, really have wonderful conversations. And it's the atmosphere that lends itself to that.... It's just a simple diner. It doesn't have fancy stuff, it just has basic stuff, and somehow to me that blends itself into those deeper conversations better than a fancy restaurant.

["So do you ever have conversations about the homily or anything like that?" we asked.]

Actually, it's funny because after the 8 am Mass, Cabot's fills up with St. Sabina's people. We talk a lot. Actually Barb and I, we not only talk about the homily, we talk about just all kinds of things, just everything.

Those who are regular participants in religious communities or otherwise have an active spiritual life were more likely than not to carry that spiritual life into the stories they told about gathering with family and friends over food and drink. Those otherwise outside religious and spiritual life, on the other hand, did not tell their dining out stories as spiritual tales. The world of the cafe can be sacralized, but it does not in itself invite spiritual encounter.

As people told us stories about money and spending, at least a few of them noted that the marketplace is often a cruel institution, dividing its rewards in corrupt and unfair ways. It was a concern heard in the stories of the religiously active and inactive alike. Steve Sims is no longer involved in any organized religion, but he grew up Catholic and recalled,

I saw a lot of people in the communities that I grew up in when I was going to Catholic Church who were debt collectors, who would take people's houses from them. They'd go to church on Sunday.... I saw a lot of hypocrisy.

By implication, people in religious communities *should* care about economic justice. Olivia Howell would probably not disagree. She remains very active in her Southern Baptist Church.

[I'm] thinking how we, as Christians, aren't where we should be, like, as a Christian community, and how it really should be. Like, in this community alone I just can't believe that we tolerate the poverty and the sickness and just the pain that people go through.

Olivia is unusual in recounting stories that explicitly linked her faith, her experiences at church, and her concern for economic justice. Among our participants, the few spiritual stories we heard about economic justice came mostly from conservative Protestants like Olivia. Vocal national critics of economic injustice and materialism are more likely to come from the mainline Protestant, Catholic, and Jewish leadership, but there are only dim echoes of that among these grassroots members. Messages of justice have gotten through, but grassroots members rarely articulate them as religious imperatives. Elizabeth Evans is an active Catholic and worked at the U.S. Centers for Disease Control and Prevention in Atlanta. She had a long list of moral ills she tries to address in her work, work that is often situated in overseas contexts of corruption and greed. For her, gender inequality, economic inequity, and dishonesty are all "social justice stuff" that concerns her. But in spite of her Catholic tradition's social justice teachings, she said, "I mean the church just didn't get some of these things." Like most Americans, few of our participants credited their churches or synagogues with teaching them economic justice (Wuthnow 1994) or identified the effects of hearing about these issues in weekly services (Wuthnow 2002). People in our study who are regular religious participants of any sort were much more likely than nonparticipants to identify poverty, access to health care, unjust immigration laws, and other social and economic justice issues as worthy of their concern. The power of the progressive message shows up in those concerns. Something about being in liberal religious communities seems to make a difference in how they see the world, but nothing in their discourse would tell the listener where their concerns came from.

Thinking about the deep-seated problems of income inequality and economic exploitation often drove people to express despair over ever being able to make a difference. Daphne LeCompte is an ex-Catholic and is still a Canadian citizen, but she told us,

> One of the things I think of is I'd like to be a [U.S.] citizen so I could be more active, more of an activist. But I don't know what form it would take. But it's all a drop in the bucket. I don't think there's much—much of what we do makes us feel better but doesn't necessarily have an impact. I think that's one of the things I liked about tutoring. That one on one—you can only do it one person at a time if you want to do some good. That's often the way to do it.

For people both inside and outside religious communities, local direct action was a place to see results in fighting poverty, but the feeling of powerlessness was hard to keep at bay. Religiously active people maintain a sense of agency

through their active charitable volunteering; a robust religious infrastructure of voluntary opportunities helps them avoid the despair and be at least a
"drop in the bucket."

The Bigger Picture—Seeking Social Change

Many of the stories people told, then, were about issues near at hand. The
everyday public action that happens in the marketplace and the neighborhood was action that was largely unproblematic and overwhelmingly non-
sacralized. The collective public action that is organized to alleviate nearby
suffering was, by contrast, highly sacralized. But what about the issues that
cannot easily be addressed by local voluntary assistance and issues about
which there is significant public disagreement? Practices of interpersonal love
and charity were the most common forms of spiritual engagement with the
world, but there were also stories that involved more active efforts to attack
the roots of the world's ills. For some, the path toward activism begins with
a kind of theological and spiritual frustration at all the things that are wrong
in the world. Francine Worthington, one of Theresa Collins's fellow parishioners at All Saints, said,

> [In Afghanistan] we have lost over 3,000 of our troops there and
> 10,000 badly maimed. Those are Americans, just for starters. I think
> it gives one pause in their belief system because the question "Why?"
> is always there. I pray on Sundays that the men who are guiding these
> events will be helped to seek another path, another course.

For her, it was not just prayer on Sunday. She noted in her diary that she and
her husband were considering going to Washington for a march in opposition to the "surge" in the Iraq war, although his health made a local protest
a more likely move. At age seventy, she might seem old for such things, but
this linking of spirituality with social action was more common among the
older participants in our project. Those who were younger, especially those
with children at home, were less likely to tell stories about being involved in
social activism.

More than three-quarters of our participants talked about at least one
national or global issue that concerned them, and roughly a third of all the
stories about making the world a better place had to do with political and
social issues that extend beyond local communities—from animal cruelty to

ending war to caring for the earth. Talk about these larger issues was as common among the most spiritually serious as among the most spiritually disengaged, among the active religious participants as among the nonaffiliates. Across the board, less than half of the stories about big social issues were told with any spiritual or religious import. By contrast, two-thirds of the stories about nearby civic concerns were interwoven with the practices, teachings, people, and places of religious and spiritual traditions. When the circle of care is drawn more broadly, the connections to spirituality seem to be more tenuous.

The things people care about included the really big issues like war and peace. Atlanta Presbyterian Harris Crosby said a better world would involve not "spending a lot of money on wars or something like that. A little more focus on like curing diseases, stuff like that, uh, not so much focus on oil." Nearly a third of our participants talked about the immorality of war in general or the Iraq war in particular, but fewer than a quarter of those stories included any religious or spiritual connections. Catholic Margi Perkins was the rare person who talked about her concern in terms of the "preciousness of life" and grounded that in her faith. As we interviewed people in 2007–2008, the issues of the day—the Iraq war, torturing prisoners—appeared in the stories we heard. Those who were involved in religious communities were slightly more likely, when they raised such issues, to make some connection to their faith, but those connections were still rare. These "big issues" were being pondered by our participants but not often as spiritual concerns.

Nor were religiously engaged people any more likely to report that they were active in seeking to respond to the "big issue" moral concerns they raised. On average, religiously active people were no *less* socially engaged than unaffiliated people but no more so either. There was often a sense of powerlessness or wishful thinking in the big issue stories we heard. Jennifer Hammond is a typical Congregationalist church member and fairly engaged politically, but when she reflected on what a better world would look like, she said, "So, that would be what I'd like to see. World peace." Then she laughed ironically and said, "Sounds like a beauty pageant." Lawrence Urban is not especially active in politics, although as a Boston Mormon, he travels in the same circles as Mitt Romney and occasionally gets pulled toward the political arena. His vision of a better world is clearly a spiritual vision that pushes him toward evangelization more than politicking. "Wouldn't it be wonderful if everybody on this earth had unconditional love for each other? All of the little bumps and all of the little things that happen, they wouldn't blow out of proportion. They wouldn't lead to world wars. All of this is foolishness, these wars. I know we must strive to teach the Gospel." Faced with local community issues, religiously active participants, as we have seen, are more engaged, putting voluntary energy to the task of addressing the issues they care about; but that mobilization effect does not seem to carry over into the national and international political arena.

That does not mean that religious communities never make connections to national and international concerns, but when they do, they follow the charitable model they have learned for local engagement. They look for ways to make a direct impact in places where there are needs. Church-organized work groups, for instance, have participated in rebuilding the Gulf Coast following Katrina, something Hank Matthews, from All Saints, talked about supporting through his local Episcopal Diocese. His North Shore neighbor Stan Morris, from Grimsby Congregational, actually went along on a work trip to the Gulf. He also told us about his daughter's trip to Honduras with a group from church. They worked with Habitat for Humanity on building a house for a needy family. The members of Centre Street Church in Boston are also very globally aware, thanks to their church's strong history of support for international mission work. When framed as mission work or as concrete assistance to people in need, national and international concerns do get brought into the discourse of religious communities, and those communities do serve as agents of mobilization—but rarely so when the issues are framed as political.

Caring for the Earth

Environmental concerns were an interesting partial exception to this political rule, occasionally mixing spiritual, political, and voluntary action (cf. Kearns 1996); but more often concern about the planet lacked a spiritual cast. People *outside* religious communities were half again as likely (compared to active religious participants) to include care for the earth among their list of concerns; and not surprisingly, they almost never saw this as a spiritual matter.[9] Thomas Miller said that in a "better world" people would be "more sensitive about their environment. We try to live more in tune with it and minimize waste and minimize destruction of the planet; maximize sustainability of the planet." He said that he was both optimistic that human beings have the capacity to do this and pessimistic when he looks at the human history of war and greed. He is not active in his local synagogue, and his Jewish tradition did not figure into how he framed the issue. Sustainability was simply a moral goal to be pursued by people of good will. As the Pew Research Center reported in 2010, "Religion has far less influence on opinions about environmental policy than other factors do. Just 6% say that their religious beliefs have had the biggest influence on what they think about tougher environmental rules" (Pew Forum 2010).

Whether the spiritual element was present was dependent on the religious involvement of the person telling the story. Religiously active participants, when they did talk about the environment, were very likely to see the issue as a spiritual one. Stories about taking care of the earth were more frequently heard among mainline Protestants than among conservatives or Catholics, but Andrew Hsu was among the most specific about the link between faith and action. He thinks his fellow Evangelicals should pay more attention to environmental issues and proportionately less to other hot-button concerns. He is a very serious conservative Christian, and he said,

> In things from, like recycling, which is part of environmentalism and stewardship of the environment, to ranging from that to being honest, and to ranging from worshipping God and service, love to my fellow humankind. I would say faith informs, I hope, every part of my life, or I aspire to that.

Stories from religious participants often included practical actions such as recycling. Having such a concrete way to respond was one of the reasons environmental concern was much more likely to be linked with direct action than were issues like corrupt politics or violence against women. In Andrew's situation, the theological notion of "stewardship" is directed toward a specific global issue—the environment—and linked to practical action—recycling.

In a quite different religious community, our Neopagan group, the theological ideas were different, but the link between ideas and action was no less strong. Nearly all the Neopagans we talked to spoke of the earth as a mother and of care for the earth as a religious duty. As Laura Henderson put it, "It's an earth-based religion. I try to think of that and how that affects—what I do affects this earth every day." She and most of the others who placed the environment in their circle of public concern were very likely to talk about that concern in active terms. They might not be able to prevent global warming, but they were doing their part to recycle, to reduce their carbon footprint, and the like. They could draw on a range of cultural messages, secular organizations, and practical strategies to lend agency to this moral concern, but in some religious communities environmental action has been sacralized, as well.[10]

The Hot-Button Issues

Environmentalism as a Neopagan religious concern is not, of course, what first comes to mind when one mentions the link between religion and politics. What Americans are likely to think of first are precisely the hot-button issues Andrew wishes we would pay less attention to—abortion and homosexuality—the issues that have been at the heart of the political marriage of conservative Protestants and the Republican party (Putnam and Campbell 2010). But despite the hot-button character of those issues, neither subject came up in more than a handful of our conversations about everyday life. Four of our twenty conservative Protestants and an equal number of our twenty Catholics named abortion as a moral evil they hoped to combat. Five conservative Protestants also named gay marriage and "the gay lifestyle" as immoral. In each of these cases, people were clear in describing their passion for the cause as rooted in their faith and in the teachings of their churches. If we had asked directly about these issues, there is reason to believe that Catholics and conservative Protestants might have voiced conservative positions in greater numbers. Sixty-three percent of Evangelicals and 42 percent of White Catholics report, for instance, that they think abortion should always or almost always be illegal (Pew Forum 2010). After a generation of political organizing with abortion and gay marriage as touchstones, there is a clear conservative political culture in many conservative religious communities (Bean 2009). Well over half of Evangelicals and Catholics report that their clergy are active in speaking out on abortion, and 53 percent of Evangelicals say that religion is the most important influence on their opinion on this subject (Pew Forum 2010).

With these issues clearly on the national agenda and so closely tied to conservative religious cultures, we might have expected them to show up when people were asked to talk about a better world or to describe things about today's world that concern them. It is hard to tell whether their relative silence represents disagreement with their church's position or simply the open-ended character of their conversations with us. Our initial interviews included direct questions about politics and public engagement; and photos and oral diaries provided opportunities to capture everyday commitments to political action; but in only one story from one participant did actual activism on these conservative causes come up. Mary Hage, a sixty-five-year-old Catholic in Atlanta, talked about the right to life vigils in which she participates and took a picture of her group in front of the church with their sign (Figure 7.4). For some small handful of conservatives, religious teaching and religious organizational structure combine to shape a moral passion and

FIGURE 7.4 "This is a group in the Church to which I belong. We are an arm of Georgia Right to Life."—Mary Hage

provide mechanisms of engagement, but we uncovered much less activism than might have been expected.[11]

On both gay rights and reproductive rights, in fact, the moral conservatives in our sample were outnumbered by pro-choice and pro-equality supporters drawn from the ranks of mainline Protestants, Catholics, and Neopagans. Mainline Protestants sometimes described this as something they learned from their churches and their faith. Cynthia Gardener has started an Episcopal version of PFLAG and regularly speaks before the state legislature and in school antibullying programs. Full legal rights for gay people is something she is passionate about. As she said, it is not fair that only "one of my sons has all these legal rights and privileges—federal and state rights and privileges—there's over a thousand of them—and my [other] son's denied that simply because of what I feel is the way he was created by God; the way he was born." As much as her passion is fueled by her conviction that God's creation of her gay son is a good thing, she is also aware of the imperfections in her church. "There's a lot of hateful speech going round church also. We have a bishop in New Hampshire [Gene Robinson] who is gay and lives in an openly gay relationship, and it's really divisive in our church. It's all split our church apart. It's been horrific." Although the Episcopal Church is officially gay affirming, there are still pockets of conservative resistance. For Catholics, on the other hand, taking a liberal stand on sexuality issues was done in conscious opposition to the Church's teachings, and it fueled much of the anti-Church passion expressed in the stories we heard. "Look at the HIV/ AIDS situation and all the stigma and discrimination by the Church," said public health researcher (and active Catholic) Elizabeth Evans. "This whole thing, you know, related to homosexuality.... There's no dogma on that, but calling homosexuality something that's disordered—You know, I can't— based on where I am, I can't buy that."

These religious pro-gay advocates were joined by unaffiliated Robin Mitchell. She is involved in a number of political causes and active on the board of GLAD (Gay & Lesbian Advocates & Defenders), which won the marriage case in Massachusetts. Talking about that work, she said,

> I love public speaking, so just this weekend, uh, I had the opportunity
> to speak in front of a crowd of almost 1,000 of our donors, and uh,
> I just love that. I couldn't wait to go on, just go to behind the podium
> and enjoyed, enjoyed doing it. I was able to, and you know—again it's
> all about, for me, trying to capture some of the passion I feel about
> the world and activism and whatnot. And then have the pulpit from
> which....

At that point, she stopped herself to wryly observe that if she were just a believer, she might have wanted to be a minister in a church. This work for her community is a passionate commitment for her and not unlike the practices others named as spiritual.

Making connections between these contentious social issues and one's faith was not, however, a matter of how salient spirituality is or isn't or how often one attends services in some generic religious community. This is not a matter of "more" or "less" religion but which religion. Religion has its effects in the particular religious messages and communities in which people participate. While conservatives seem to hear a clear message from their religious communities about what they should oppose, not many of them take action on those issues. Mainline Protestants seem to have heard either silence or mixed messages, leaving space for some to link faith and pro-rights activism, while others do not.[12] Catholics heard consistent messages, but ones they often had to reject or work around (Dillon 1999). Only the stories of the Neopagans sounded a consistent theme of gay inclusion and reproductive choice as part of what it means to pursue their spiritual path.

Spirituality, then, does show up in public life. To the extent that specific issues have been publicly linked to religious ideas and communities (as abortion and homosexuality have), those communities sometimes produce a storyline about faith and politics, about the need for believers to be actively involved. But even that storyline seems not to dominate the visions of most of the conservative Protestants who live with it, and it is being actively rejected by most Catholics. More common, however, is a simple disconnect between spiritual life and social advocacy. When there is no widespread public identification of specific political issues with a religious tradition, participants in that tradition are much less likely to talk about their social commitments in spiritual terms. This is true even if the tradition in question has ample theological resources for such conversations. If we were to take the theological writings of Catholics, liberal Protestants, African American Protestants, and Jews as our guide, we would expect a lively engagement in efforts to save the planet and bring about social and economic justice. And we would expect the members of those churches and synagogues to talk about their work in the world as expressions of the faith they learn about in their religious communities, but that is rarely the case. There is some evidence that environmental concerns and economic justice concerns do resonate with a significant minority of people in those traditions, and at least some of that minority talks about their social concern in religious terms, voicing a collective commitment and being spurred to action by and through religious organizations. But when it comes to the biggest, toughest issues, like war and peace, nonaffiliates are just as likely to be concerned; and neither religious nor nonreligious people were convinced there was much to be done.

Doing Politics

Responding to any of these issues is likely to involve some sort of political action, and when we turn from issue advocacy to politics in general, the overall mood shifts into a darker space. It was in the realm of politics that our participants were most likely to express resignation and frustration over the status quo (see Table 7.1). While they might have a wide range of national and international social concerns, the idea of addressing those concerns through political action was less than appealing. Fully a third of all the political action stories we heard either were full of worry, fear, sadness, and frustration or were told with the implication that no action was possible. The other side of that picture, of course, is that two-thirds of the political stories we heard were told with satisfaction and committed passion.

Looking more closely at political activity stories, we see that only a small number of our participants were completely disengaged from the political

Table 7.1 Political Stories and Spiritual Engagement

	Spiritually and Religiously Disengaged	Marginal Members	Typical Attenders	Spiritually and Religiously Engaged	Total
Stories characterized by fear, frustration, worry, and sadness	23%	25%	13%	13%	17%
Stories characterized by resignation or ambivalence	41%	17%	10%	12%	16%
Stories characterized by commitment and satisfaction	36%	58%	77%	75%	67%
Total number of political stories	N = 22	N = 36	N = 62	N = 52	N = 172
Stories per person	1.6	1.8	1.8	2.0	1.8

Table 7.2 Political Engagement and Spiritual Engagement

Political Engagement	Spiritually and Religiously Disengaged	Marginal Members	Typical Attenders	Spiritually and Religiously Engaged	Total
Antipolitics	17%	6%	3%	10%	7%
Vote only	42%	44%	31%	33%	37%
Stay informed and talk about politics	25%	12%	16%	19%	16%
Local or issue-based involvement	0	25%	31%	24%	24%
Electoral activism and more	17%	12%	18%	14%	16%
Total number of persons	12	16	32	21	81
No information	2	4	3	5	14

process. For a few, like John Lehman, political disengagement seemed to be part of a general pattern of withdrawal. He told us he had not voted in the last ten years. "I guess I've become somewhat of a social hermit in the last ten years," he said. "So I'm not involved in any civic association. I'm not involved in any social club. So why is that? I don't know why that is. It's just what it has become." Polly Baxter, on the other hand, was very clear about why she is not involved: "I think the government is whacked out of their mind. I don't think anyone is especially fabulous, and I think they're trying to infringe on our privacy. But am I actively doing anything about it? No." Jessica Wilson is a fellow church member at Deer Valley (an Atlanta megachurch), and she confessed, "Hate politics, can't stand it." When we asked whether that was a conscious decision or just apathy, she said, "Both. I don't think there's anybody worth voting for, and then I think, well, maybe I should vote for the lesser of the evils. But I just feel like, if I'm going to go vote, I really need to know who I'm voting for, and I don't put the time into it, so I don't know." Jessica is among the most spiritually engaged of our participants, and that makes her an exception in this antipolitics chorus, which is dominated by the less religiously active people like Polly and John (see Table 7.2). This also seemed to be a matter of generations. Both Polly and Jessica were under thirty-five, and it was their age mates in that younger cohort who were the most likely to talk about being disengaged from politics.[13]

The most common political story was "voting, but nothing more." Like the complete rejection of politics, this minimalist involvement is more common among the spiritually disengaged than among the religiously active. They were more likely to talk to us about politics in negative or alienated terms and less likely to talk about doing anything more than their basic civic duty. "I vote but I'm not involved. I just do my own reading and I don't talk about it with anyone, really. So, no, I've never been very involved with politics," reported Shirley Glazer, who is a member of South Street Presbyterian but rarely attends. Ex-Catholic Charlotte McKenna actually comes from a political family in Boston, but she describes herself as just an observer. She votes but nothing more.

A significant minority of our participants edged a bit closer to the political arena by intentionally staying informed. They told stories about paying attention to the news and talking about politics with their friends and family. Barbara Robinson said she is addicted to NPR and CNN. Eric Patterson is a student and recorded a story about watching the presidential debates with his university friends. Emma Cooper says she always watches the news, and

Rachel Halpern said staying informed about politics is important to her. Barbara is religiously and spiritually disengaged; Eric is a marginal member of the Vineyard Church; Emma is an active Neopagan; and Rachel is a spiritually serious member of Temple Beth Torah. Where one stood on the religious and spiritual spectrum seemed to make little difference in whether political information and talk was part of everyday life.

Stories about voting and the electoral process were almost always told in matter-of-fact secular terms and almost never as spiritual or religious tales. If there is a secular space in public life, it is surely the voting booth. For a few, there seemed to be a hint of religious duty in their electoral participation, but it was never made explicit; and no one talked about their religious tradition as a direct source of their voting behavior. But that does not mean that there are no traces of religious influence in how people vote or even whether they do. Both American Jews and African American Protestants have a long history of religiously informed political engagement, and among our participants, these were the most likely to include stories about political activism in the accounts of their everyday lives.[14] Camilla Hart noted, in fact, that one of the reasons she initially liked Cornerstone Baptist was that she occasionally heard about politics at church. Three of her fellow Cornerstone members specifically mentioned working on Deval Patrick's gubernatorial campaign in Massachusetts. Whether or not they told the story of their activism in spiritual terms, it is clear that the political culture of their Black Baptist church makes it more likely.

At least in a few instances, the links were more direct and explicit. Religious organizations were playing a direct role in supplying the information that was being consumed and facilitating political action. Hank Matthews says that he enjoys reading the *Anglican Digest* because "it has political views similar to mine. So one always likes to read that one is affirmed, that other people are thinking similar sorts of things." This is especially important to him, however, because, he says, "We are called to our Christianity not as individuals but collectively." The Catholic tradition has been especially strong in its advocacy of just such a communal sense of faith and responsibility. John Travisano is now retired and says, "I stay very much informed, particularly the church's aspect.... I'm a member of the network thing which is in Washington, and they're supposed to be nudging our Congress and so forth." At Centre Street Church, by contrast, the political diversity of the evangelical community was on view. Bethany Armstrong is actively committed to various progressive causes and talked about avoiding political conversations with many of her church friends who are more conservative. Andrew Hsu recounted a time when those divisions were especially apparent:

> We invited a speaker over to Centre Street Church. He goes to another local area church, and he is involved with politics....he's a Democrat...I guess the leadership of the 30s Ministry, one of the guys knew him and told him not to, you know, spout off his radical views, and he still did.

The radical views in question were about gay rights and this candidate's support for marriage equality—a source of contention in this evangelical community.

The religious and spiritual dimensions of political life were most visible in the stories people told about the issues they are supporting (or opposing). John Travisano not only stays informed but is also very active in voluntary social service and in lobbying for various justice issues.

> That's why I got involved with the justice [committee] because I think from that end we could probably do a lot more and make our legislators and people aware of the problems....the living wage, the minimum wage, and all these type of things. What we're doing is helping, but somehow the government's gotta get—we've got to get the government more behind doing these things....The bishop is going to be in Washington this next—I think in early March, and he's gonna speak before Congress and outline some of these things. The effort's somehow gotta be there to change some of the things that will make a big difference in a lot of people's lives.

The range of issue activism was broad. We have already encountered Mary Hage's right to life vigils, but the other side of that issue is just as passionately pursued by Anna Cook, who strongly links her Wiccan practice to supporting women's rights of all sorts. Andrew Hsu volunteers for (conservative) James Dobson's Truth Project, and Stephen James organized a group that works for access to health care. We have also already seen Cynthia Gardener's activism on behalf of both marriage equality and disability access. While these activists run the gamut of theologies and religious traditions, they are disproportionately people who are both active in religious communities and themselves spiritually engaged. The passion they have for religious and spiritual life translates into a passion for social issues, as well.

The most visible exception to this pattern of links between political action and spiritual engagement is Robin Mitchell. A secular Jew, with no spiritual or religious interest, political action *is* her spiritual passion. She speaks of her financial planning business as especially meaningful because it serves the gay and lesbian community. She stays up to date through the internet on what is happening to LGBT people in other parts of the country and the world. She and Colleen were in line at the Cambridge courthouse the first day it was legal for them to get married in Massachusetts, and she is active in GLAD (Figure 7.5). She helped get out the vote in the 2008 New Hampshire Democratic primary and worked the phones for Deval Patrick. When we asked about any special clothing she wears to express the important things in her life, she told us this:

> During political campaigns, I really, um, am committed to wearing my little buttons. So it's like a big deal for me to be wearing my Deval Patrick or Howard Dean or whoever it is, um, so that's kind of part of my basic activism.... I've had many cars and most of them by the time I, you know, turn them in, you can't see the car for the stickers. So, yeah, I'm really into kind of, you know, this notion of the power of one and the power of democracy, individual ability to shape change. And to start dialogues, you know.

FIGURE 7.5 "This is where Colleen and I got married."—Robin Mitchell

Robin stands out from all the other spiritually neutral participants in having made this intense commitment to working for change. For most of the religiously disengaged people, politics was of little interest. They live outside the networks of religious voluntary organizations in which activism was more common and have not made their own. But not Robin. She has made her own networks, seeks her own information, and has invested her formidable passion for justice in a wide range of political action.

Conclusion

There are places in the everyday public realm that are largely untouched by any hints of transcendence or spirituality. The neighborhoods in which people live are largely seen through the lens of choice and comfort. The places where they spend their money are routinely secular, as well, even when they may otherwise opine that materialism is a bad thing. These routine elements of the middle-class habitus have their own mundane logic, and it is not a religious one.

When asked to think about change, however, the stories are different. How and whether people seek to make the world a better place is a question that intersects in multiple ways with how and whether they are engaged in religious participation or serious about pursuing a spiritual life. Most basically, local congregations are among the most important institutional sources for moral education and for voluntary engagement in local community social service. The pervasiveness of local congregations and their network of affiliated organizations make them powerful players in social service delivery, and the institutional patterns that shape congregational life in the United States mean that they are expected to provide opportunities for worship and religious education, for fellowship and mutual care, and for service to the broader community (Ammerman 2005a). Each of these functions has important implications for the public lives of their participants. Worship rituals set out visions of possible worlds; fellowship provides spaces for debate and discernment and moral modeling; and the network of voluntary organizing facilitates engagement in pursuing public goals in the community. The result is that religious participants have a comparatively fuller vocabulary of public concerns and a more robust means of engagement in pursuing those concerns. Their moral energies are turned toward cultivating virtues of kindness, hospitality, charity, forgiveness, and service to others. These virtues are both elements of personal character to be exhibited in home and congregation and ways of being in the everyday world that extends to work, voluntary organizations, and far-flung communities in need.

Those outside traditional American religious communities are certainly not without moral sensibilities and public concerns, and they are especially aware of the need for religious tolerance. Their better world would be one where there is more freedom to be different. They are more likely to talk about individual rights and individual worth as their moral guide, rather than focusing on the more other-directed Golden Rule ethic that dominates among religious participants. Since they lack the ready voluntary infrastructure provided by local congregations, however, they more often expressed a sense that nothing can be done about the problems they see. When they do engage in action in pursuit of their public goals, it is more likely to be political action or monetary contributions than voluntary service.

Political action was, in fact, rarely the subject of overtly religious or spiritual reflection. To the extent that people brought social and political issues into the realm of their everyday lives at all, the stories they told seldom had spiritual plots or characters. The hot-button issues were there but only dimly. Just as important as supposedly religious issues such as abortion were concerns about economic justice, the environment, and gay rights. It is possible to see traces of religious traditions in the particular issues participants emphasized, but they rarely made those connections themselves. Like most Americans, they do not want their religious communities to be dominated by politics, but there are subtle ways in which the conversations of a particular spiritual tribe are resonant with some social issues and not with others.

Most of our participants were moderately socially concerned, tried to stay informed, voted, and left the active work of politics for others. A handful of them *are* politically active, however, and several of them act in ways that they clearly linked to their spiritual commitments and religious communities. As the everyday world extends into the complicated world of civic and political action, spiritual convictions can sometimes be present, sometimes embodied in the organized action of religious communities. But at this macrolevel, spiritually infused plotlines mix with all the other stories being told and often disappear in their midst. Spiritual narratives of public action are much more likely to be told and noticed when the subject is meeting local needs than when the focus is political contention over national issues.

8 BODIES AND SPIRITS: HEALTH, ILLNESS, AND MORTALITY

Not long after this project got underway, as I was just beginning to read transcripts and was continuing to be in conversation with researchers in the field, a fellow sociologist asked me one of those predictable questions: what surprises are you finding? It was so early in the study that I almost demurred, but there was one theme that seemed too prevalent to ignore. When people talked about everyday life they were very likely to talk about health and illness. And when they talked about health and illness, there was very likely to be a spiritual dimension to the story. Now that all the data are in, and all the stories have been analyzed, that impression has been borne out. While stories about health and illness are not as numerous as stories about households and work, they are certainly part of the narrative structure of daily living.

Some questions in the initial interview elicited stories about everyday routines of diet and exercise or about medical crises that were critical turning points in life, but the interview was not intentionally oriented toward health questions—nor were the instructions we gave participants for taking their pictures or recording their oral diaries. It is striking, then, that when people were largely in control of the subjects they addressed—especially in the photo elicitation interview and in the oral diaries—so much of their attention turned to health, physical activity, illness, and death. Over all the phases of the project, our ninety-five participants told a total of 463 stories that were categorized as stories about health, illness, and death. Well over half of those stories came out in the conversations after the initial interview. Invited to talk about everyday life in informal and more intimate genres, stories often turned to the body—the participant's and those about whom they care. And a full half of all those stories, no matter the context in which they were told, were stories where spirituality, faith, religious communities, and the divine were part of the telling (see Appendix 2 for details on how stories were coded). That is a higher proportion than in any other domain of everyday life. My initial impression was right—people are remarkably likely to talk about health in spiritual terms.[1]

My sociologist friend, however, was surprised. Isn't medicine the ultimate scientific challenge to faith? Surely it is easier to see the divine in human relationships or in one's moral life than in the rational calculations of health regimens and drug dosages. Like the early sociologists who saw science and religion as competing explanations for the physical world, he was pretty sure science had won and pretty surprised that so many in the American population seemed not to have gotten the memo. In contrast, people who study religion have long known that questions of health and healing are never far from the concerns of theologians and ordinary believers.[2] People who study health behavior would not have been surprised, either. One of the fastest growing fields of health research addresses the multifaceted question of the role of spirituality.[3] Google those two terms, and you will get an enormous number of hits, even if you are searching just within the "Scholar" database. Far more numerous than sociological studies on that list are studies within the health professions themselves, all seeking to understand whether spirituality or religious participation make people healthier or perhaps can even account for actual "healing"; and if so, how does it work? Questions about spirituality and health are by no means esoteric.

Whether spirituality is good for you is not the question here. The everyday stories our participants told provide a unique window on *how* people think about health, both their own and others'. The stories they told us were analyzed to identify who the actors are, what kind of health practice or illness event is the focus, when it occurred, and the emotional tenor of the telling. This allows us to see where health is a routine concern of everyday life and when it interrupts the flow of life, demanding attention, however reluctant. We can also see whose health matters and how people draw the circle of care. And just what role does faith play in relation to the interventions of medicine? If science and religion are not playing on opposing teams in these stories, how do these Americans give an account of the ways in which they freely and fully engage both spiritual and medical practices in tending to physical bodies?

Eat Right, Exercise, and Take Care of Yourself

Mothers say it, as do doctors and the media—get regular checkups, eat healthy, exercise. And judging from the stories we heard, a fair number of people are trying to do just that. Theirs is not a passive relationship to their bodies and their health. No matter how much faith they have, health is not something they leave to the gods. Taking care of themselves is an active and multifaceted pursuit that begins in the realm of preventive maintenance. Routine medical visits were part of the "everyday life" we heard about in daily oral diaries. Not everyone told stories about going to the doctor for regular checkups and screenings, but several did. Mary Poulsen actually took a picture of the Harvard-Vanguard clinic where she goes to the doctor (Figure 8.1), and James Dupree recorded a story about the day he took his daughter for a doctor visit and then treated her to lunch. Mary is religiously and spiritually inactive, while James is quite the opposite, but neither talked about these routine medical visits in spiritual terms. Even for Andrew Hsu, one of the most spiritually engaged participants in the study, a visit to the dentist is just a visit to the dentist. Going to the doctor is something you do to take care of yourself, whether you are a religious person or not.

Sometimes these visits are not routine, however. They are reminders that bad news can follow, and on those occasions the bigger questions can emerge

FIGURE 8.1 "Where you go for your checkups and stuff."—Mary Poulsen

into consciousness—even for the least spiritual among our participants. Alicia Waters is one of those. She went for a routine bone density scan and saw how much the images had changed over time. She recorded in her diary that day,

> I will have to use all of my coping strategies to remain calm until the results are in. These strategies are going to the gym, getting massages, and talking to people. Wish I could just turn it over to a higher power, but I'm not very good at this. Medical issues scare me.

Elizabeth Evans confessed to some apprehension, as well, but as an active Catholic, her coping strategies also included prayer:

> I started the day with Mass, as usual. And then from Mass I went directly to DeKalb Medical Center to have my annual mammogram....Each year I go in and just assume that everything's going to be normal. But, you know, everybody starts their journey that way, thinking the same thing. And I just wonder if my luck's going to run out some day. I have a friend from church who's being treated at DeKalb right now actually, for very severe breast cancer. She's had both chemo and radiation. Don't know if she's going to make it very long; but anyhow, couldn't help but think of her today, and just be thankful that I can access this test with the insurance that I have. Pray for the best, and wonder each time actually what I would do if I was told that I had to come back for, you know, a more severe diagnostic mammogram, or they found a lump, or whatever, how I would react.

As we will see throughout this chapter, prayer is not a magic formula. People rarely claimed that prayer would protect them from "luck running out." What it seems to provide here is a measure of calm and optimism. Still, sometimes the tests come back with unwelcome results, and dealing with that uncertainty is part of interacting with the medical system (Cadge and Bergey 2013). Elizabeth and Alicia both dreaded that possibility, but both kept their appointments. Getting screened is something you do.

Attention to the body is also present between visits to the doctor. As we will see, exercise is a big part of that, but so is diet. About one in five of our participants specifically mentioned the dietary rules they try to follow, including a couple who confessed to routinely breaking them. We already noted in our discussion of household meals that specific religious guidelines define dietary practices for Latter-day Saints and Jews. Mormon prohibitions on alcohol and caffeine are part of a larger concern with caring for the body, a concern that is seen as a religious duty and is taught in sacred texts. As we heard from more than one of them, "The body is a temple." We heard the same sentiment from Alex Polani. As a serious spiritual seeker, Alex includes physical health in his vision of spirituality. "Again, you're talking to someone that is really passionate about spirituality so—I'm a health freak so I eat a lot of healthy foods," he said. He talked about the wonder of living in a physical body and of his fascination and excitement over how a natural, whole-food diet could allow him to be healthier and more alive. For at least some spiritually engaged people, both in traditional religious communities and in the larger spiritual milieu, disciplined eating is a spiritual practice.

Disciplined eating was also strongly present as a purely secular practice among our least spiritually engaged participants. Taking charge of one's diet was a common theme in their health stories, much more common than in the stories of the more religiously and spiritually active people (especially those not in traditions with specific dietary rules). The most secular of our participants told about spending time learning about staying healthy. They were likely to mention reading books about health and attending classes or checking out websites to learn more. With only one exception, these were college-educated people, people accustomed to seeking information and using it to shape their own lives.[4] Jocelyn Frederick described herself as a "compulsive label reader" in her search for a healthy diet. Others read about nutrition and trans fats and the politics of food, and at least some of them have stopped eating some or all meats. Learning about and experimenting with healthy eating is part of the pattern of life that prevails among those whose worldview is the most decidedly this-worldly. They seek information and take charge.

Rational calculation and rational action are involved here, but so are a deeply satisfying sense of personal well-being and intimate connections with families and tablemates. Recall Lily Mattison's story about how cooking a healthy meal for the people you love is one of life's deeply satisfying practices. Food and eating are a central ingredient in personal and social identity for everyone. Shared meals can be both mundane and meaningful. They are shaped by secular habits and intentions in the secular corners of the world no less than by religious sensibilities where religious traditions prevail.

Sometimes concern about food was also a concern about controlling weight. While secular participants were especially attuned to good eating practices, they were neither more nor less worried about losing weight. A substantial handful of our participants—without exception, females—worried aloud about dieting. Some noted that once the pounds are on, it is hard to get them off. Others talked about how it is harder to do as one gets older, and Catherine Young was worried about still feeling fat after the birth of her daughter. Melissa Parker is a forty-year-old clerical worker, and when we asked her if there were any special lifestyle commitments she has made, she said,

> The food—I'm working on that. You know, I know that I don't take care of myself the way I should. I don't eat right. And my weight will go up and down, up and down. Like I'm as big now as when I was when I delivered my children. That's too big. And just health-wise…I know I have to do better. And I guess I need to pray about that more because I pray about everything else.

Melissa is an active participant in an African American church in Atlanta that has a health ministry, but she is not part of it. Many Black churches, like hers, have become important conduits of health education and intervention,[5] but Melissa had not taken any active steps—with or without church help—to change her diet. Starting to pray about it may be a first step toward naming a healthy weight as something of spiritual significance. Women like Melissa who were spiritually active tended to link their efforts at weight control to their spiritual lives, while women with a more secular orientation did not. Describing weight as a spiritual problem only happens to the extent that a woman already brings a spiritual view of the world to her everyday life.[6]

Avoiding other unhealthy habits, on the other hand, does seem to be shaped by specifically religious ways of life.[7] Mormons, of course, are especially notable for their shunning of alcohol, tobacco, and recreational drugs, while Matthew Smith—one of our secular participants—admitted to indulging in those very things perhaps a bit too often. In the same breath as his admission that a recent story on NPR had made him think he should start eating a more healthy diet, he also said, "I'll smoke here and there, I'll drink here and there and do drugs here and there." NPR was enough to make him think about his diet, but there were no authoritative voices cautioning him about his other habits. Jessica Fletcher, on the other hand, reflected in her diary about giving up smoking:

> When the appetite or the river overflows and gets out of control, it is a—it brings death and destruction along with it, and you know. That's something that I've—I love metaphors—and that is a metaphor that I've been using a lot lately, because I've just noticed that my appetites for a lot of things in life have gotten out of control quite literally. And

I—and with that I was able to, I'm able to overcome smoking—with the help of that metaphor and with the help of, with the help of the Lenten season, I was able to give up smoking.

Existing research would indicate that both her private spiritual life and the support of her religious community may be important if she is to succeed in kicking the habit.[8]

The medical community takes note when religious organizations help people to maintain healthy lifestyles and avoid risky behaviors. These are effects probably best documented for adolescents but also present in the adult population. Whether through explicit teachings (as with Mormons), through organizing health education and outreach (as is common in Black churches), or simply providing a community of emotional and social support for healthy behaviors and coping, religious organizations generally get a thumbs up from epidemiologists.[9] Even prayer is a practice medical researchers have examined, although with inconclusive results.[10] The turn to "alternative" medicine in recent years also has had a strong spiritual component. While spiritual forms of healing were not common themes, we did hear stories from a few people who routinely call on the spirits for protection and health. Shirley Knight, a member of the Neopagan group described her practices:

I find myself doing more natural things before I go to the doctor. Even though I'm a nurse—I practice Western medicine—I try to do more holistic and alternative medicine. Before I did my last knee surgery I did Reiki. I did a lot of natural remedies. Like the tiger balm and the emu oil, and certain elixirs that people have said this will help this, and this will help that. And they do for a while. I'm not saying they cure me, but they certainly don't do any different than just giving me a pill that masks the symptoms.

Joshua Roberts, who goes to church with Jessica, is a musician who is convinced of the powerful mystical qualities of music, qualities he is convinced have physical roots and physical effects. He took a picture of the gym where he routinely exercises because all of these things—physical, musical, and spiritual—are of a piece for him. "Physical stimulation elevates the mind to a higher level of consciousness," he said. "You know that's what I've been studying on my studies of nervology and music. You know I think I remember telling you that I did my undergrad thesis on music physics." Mainstream Christian and Jewish teachings rarely include things like nervology or elixirs, but many people both inside and outside those communities avail themselves of a wide range of spiritual resources they call on to stay healthy.[11]

Others, especially those not otherwise spiritually engaged, simply look for ways to bolster mind and body in everyday pampering and stress reduction. Erika Lombardi loves to sit in the Jacuzzi after a hard day at work. A couple of other people mentioned getting massages, and two women took pictures of their hair salons. As Charlotte McKenna said, "This is my one little luxury.... I've been going there for twenty-eight years.... When I'm in there, I just feel fabulous. It's my one luxury. I even have my nails professionally done. I spend a hundred dollars, and it's my luxury, that's why it's really important to me." Is she healthier because she gets her hair and nails done? Who knows? But for many people feeling good about the way they look provides an important boost in self-esteem. Rebecca Klein's boutique caters to exactly that body-spirit connection. When she showed us pictures of the store, she told about getting a call from a friend who had bought a pair of shoes there.

> She was just going on and on how they were magic shoes for her and how people would come up to her and ask her where she got them, and she feels that—she just feels so amazing. And I do, I do believe that when you dress, you know, it's like little boys when they become Superman in their Superman outfit, you know [laughing]. It's the same thing for older women. Or for men, you know. It's like, it gives you a feeling of well-being and that you're beautiful.

There may be reasons to worry about tying well-being to consumption and beauty. Absent other efforts at self-care, and in the midst of a culture that ties women's value to a narrow definition of physical beauty, cosmetic activity alone is hardly a sign of health.[12] Still, Rebecca's philosophy seems to lean more toward a beauty that begins on the inside. She went on to say, "Women are so obsessed with their bodies, you know, and I believe.... Eat right, eat for health, but don't get all upset about—with the way you're looking. Be healthy and then you'll be fine. Then you'll be the way you're supposed to be."

Stories about being healthy ranged across accounts of routine medical care, disciplined dietary choices, and finding ways to relieve stress and enhance subjective well-being. More common than any of those, however, were stories about getting exercise. We have already seen in Chapter Three how exercise is sometimes a form of spiritual practice, but it is also sometimes just exercise. One way of talking about it is as likely as the other, and the spiritual dimension of exercise was as likely to be noted by people who are not conventionally religious as by those who are strongly committed to religious and spiritual practice. Bill Hamilton resisted talking about *God* in his stories about rock climbing, but he definitely talked about the physical experience as *spiritual*. Describing one of his pictures (see Figure 3.5), he said,

> This is me climbing up a route in El Dorado Canyon. It's one of my favorite climb pictures taken by a friend of mine... and it's a beautiful, gorgeous day. It's just such a physical thing where your physical and your mental all comes together. You're in a Zen-like state, you're just in that moment—no future, no past—you're just happy to be alive.

This is, in fact, one of the places where an expanded definition of spirituality allows us to recognize activities as religious that would not otherwise be counted as such. The people who made this link between physical activity and spiritual growth—whether religious participants or not—were people who were proficient in an Extra-theistic discourse about spirituality, in talking not just about exercise but also about the spirituality of beauty, connection, and meaning.

Linking spirit, mind, body, and nature was also something we heard in the stories of some of our most spiritually engaged participants. Vicki Johnson talked about the sense of healing she felt in walking outdoors after her first heart surgery. Showing us one of her pictures, she said, "This, out of my window—this is the cure." Vicki is Catholic, but we heard similar links being made by mainline and African American Protestants, as well. Being healthy often means precisely this link between natural surroundings, spiritual centering, and physical activity (Figure 8.2). Exercise is not always done outside and is not always spiritual, but sometimes it is both.

Whether spiritual or not, about a third of our participants marked exercise as an important part of their own everyday efforts to stay healthy. They told stories about playing volleyball and mountain biking, teaching aerobics and playing tennis, gardening and swimming, walking and therapeutic horseback riding. Walter Green, a devout Southern Baptist and former math professor, was seventy-seven years old when he was participating in this study, and he started his diary one morning with characteristic mathematical precision:

> Got up at 6:11 this morning and spent forty-five minutes doing stretching exercises and calisthenics. I try to do this at least two times a week, preferably three. I don't like to do exercises. I'm not sure that anyone does, but I do feel better when it's done; and I can see that I'm

FIGURE 8.2 "This is not too far from my house where I went riding."—Alex Polani

increasing muscle tone and strength, both of which are good. It's hard to balance time among all the things that you are supposed to be doing these days, but taking care of our body and being as strong as we can is good.

Like most of the health stories, this one is about regular routines of activity that are undertaken in large measure because both trusted authorities and one's own body give evidence that they are beneficial. We want our bodies to be healthy and to last a long time, so we exercise. As Thomas Miller, a secular Jewish lawyer, put it, "I intend to have a long life. There's a lot of stuff I enjoy, and there's a lot of stuff I want to do, and I can't do it if I'm not fit." Perfectly rational—sometimes exercise is just exercise. Like much of everyday life, the reasons and the stories range from the mundane to the sublime. Staying fit, like other aspects of staying healthy, is neither necessarily a sacred duty nor inevitably a secular enterprise; but in a surprising number of stories, caring for the body evoked more than mundane concern.

When Things Go Wrong

As participants unfolded their life stories in our initial conversations with them, about midway through, if they had not already talked about any crisis moments, we asked, "Have you ever had a time in life where you've faced serious difficulties, some sort of crisis, maybe the death of somebody, or financial crisis?" What often followed was a story about a medical challenge, their own or someone dear to them. We also heard about medical emergencies and chronic problems in the day-to-day stories recorded in oral diaries. From childhood tumbles to adult bouts with the flu to ongoing concern for fragile parents, the vulnerabilities of human bodies were never far from everyday consciousness. The vulnerabilities of the human mind appeared, as well, with reports of depression, attention deficit disorder (ADD), addictions, and bipolar disorder. These psychological difficulties rarely came out in the first interview, but were elaborated as people extended and deepened their relationship with us in the project.

Nearly half the stories we heard about physical ailments were the sorts of issues everyone deals with and are eventually forgotten. Some of these stories were significant enough to make it into the initial interview's life account—childhood dyslexia or ADD, for instance—but most were recounted in daily oral diaries. When asked to say how one's *life* has gone, these ailments are not part of the story. When asked to say how one's *day* has gone, the "migraine from hell" or the bug that has been going around are often at the top of the list. Older adults confessed to their growing list of routine complaints, even as they expressed gratitude to be doing as well as they are.

Given the relative economic comfort of most of our participants, even the working people were largely confident that insurance would pay and that they could manage the time away if it was necessary. For the few who had lesser means, sickness was more of a worry. Andrea Valencia recorded this story at the end of a tiring day:

> I can feel a cold coming on now and I can't have a cold because I have to do my two jobs. Not going to get myself worked up and I'm not going to go back on that cycle. I'm just going to say, it's going to be okay; God will provide. God will take care of me and my kids.

It was not so much the physical illness itself that drove her to invoke divine protection as the realization that the family's livelihood was so precarious. Three out of four stories about routine illness had no such urgency and were told as ordinary mundane accounts. They needed neither divine explanation nor divine intervention. Even among the most spiritually aware people, daily physical complaints are simply not God's problem.

Lives Interrupted

The episodes that were serious enough to make it into a life story were another matter. Even the least spiritually engaged people sometimes recounted times when physical challenges interrupted life and drove them to prayer. For Charlotte McKenna, it was an injury about a decade earlier.

> I was forty-seven, I was injured, and I was in a lot of pain for nine months [sigh] and I kind of, like, had to work it through then. I mean I had help, I had to have help from counseling, but then just kind of kept doing a lot of praying just to get me through it—take me out of this pain, don't want to be in this physical pain. If I can just be out of the physical pain I can handle it. I was doing a lot of praying; that helped.

Praying in the midst of serious illness was a break from Charlotte's usual more secular view of the world. By contrast, it is just the sort of thing we would expect to hear about from a devout Southern Baptist like Walter Green. He recalled having chronic pancreatitis for fifteen years, when he finally had an endoscopy.

> They found that I had a cyst on the pancreas, which they thought might be precancerous, and they also discovered some lymph nodes that they didn't like the looks of. So they suggested, rather casually, that I have a Whipple operation, which means major surgery on the pancreas, which was done at Emory.... This happened in May of 1999, and it was on May 22nd, and we'd been reading our Bible through that year, and that morning before I was taken to surgery about 6:30, I'd wakened probably 6 o'clock. I did my daily Bible reading, and the passage was Psalm 118, I think it is, verses 17 and 18. Which says, in effect, God has chastened you severely but he has not given you up to death. Because I didn't know when I went in the operating room whether I was going to come out the other end alive or not. I called Ruth immediately...and I shared the verse with her.

Like the stories of others with active spiritual lives, Walter's is a tale of medical expertise, good fortune at finding a problem in time and having good doctors and good hospitals, scientific details that reflect the curiosity and empowerment of an informed patient—and the special confidence that came from a spiritual message received by way of his routine practice of Bible reading. His story was at once both scientific and religious and, in his case, had a happy ending.

People who are not otherwise inclined to see life through a spiritual lens narrate medical crises differently. Two of the most vivid examples both involved back injuries, subsequent surgeries, and long recuperations. For Wendy Simmons, it happened in her midtwenties, not long after she got married.

> Something happened to my back. Finally, after about six months of being in and out of hospitals, we found out what was wrong with my back, and I had surgery, and I ended up being in bed, pretty much flat on my back, for a good year and a half. During that time, my husband left. So my parents were taking care of me, my sister, and my grandparents.... I was definitely in a very severe state of acute depression at that time. Just nothing could lift my spirits.

Like Wendy, Larry Waugh was not an active part of a religious community when his crisis came, and like Wendy, calling on spiritual resources was not part of the story.

> I was like twenty-five years old and was working at the airlines and hurt my back; had two back surgeries. Was out of work for about, almost a year.... That was a tough part of my life. Being [in my] twenties, being scared if I could walk.

Wendy and Larry have multiple continuing medical issues that have given them plenty of reason to be pessimistic about their physical bodies. What is striking here is simply the contrast between stories told as unmitigated times of suffering and stories told as trials from which the teller has emerged to remember the spiritual blessings along with the pain and anxiety. The suffering itself does not account for the difference; rather, it is the spiritual perspective the person brings to the experience.

For spiritually disengaged people as well as marginal members, even hitting bottom in a cycle of addiction might or might not induce spiritual reflection. As a younger woman, Alicia Waters had had a major psychological crash that was also accompanied by addiction issues. She lost her job and her marriage and even lost custody of her daughter for a time. In the recovery process, she participated in Alcoholics Anonymous but never quite took to the notion of a higher power.

> Well, I mean if you go to two AA meetings a day and you're getting, trying to get sober and, um, yeah, it was the closest I think I came to almost being won over.... So I often felt, you know, I mean you can't spend your first year in AA without somehow getting into it, and feeling a little guilty that you're not getting into it.

We have already heard Alicia musing that it might be easier if she *could* turn things over to a higher power, but that is just not something she can do. Bill Hamilton gave a similarly nonspiritual account of his addiction treatment, as did Larry Waugh. In spite of the strong spiritual component in much addiction counseling, these are people who entered with few spiritual inclinations and seemed quite capable of exiting as stronger people, but spiritually unpersuaded.

Greg Collins's story is different. In our first conversation, he talked about a time in his life when he was living very self-destructively, including drug use. He had been raised Catholic, but as a gay man he no longer found the Church a good place to be. But he had not lost his sense that God could be a real presence in the world, sometimes a very strong one.

> [It was] the night I hit my bottom and realized that... or came to terms with the fact that I was addicted to crystal meth and that I needed help. That I had tried for a long time to quit on my own and just could not do it. And that night I had this—another one of those "Come to Jesus" meetings between me and God, one of those knockdown, drag out fights. And I was very aware that he was there. Because it was—the result of that was I was finally able to ask somebody for help.

Since that time, he has continued to participate in twelve-step programs, and he decided that his photos for the project should somehow reflect the importance of that in his life (Figure 8.3). He struggled to figure out how to take a picture of something that is supposed to be anonymous and finally settled on a picture of a poster found on the wall of the room where they meet. "These are the twelve steps. I'm a member of the twelve-step program.... That's sort of the core of my spiritual life now, is the work that I do through a twelve-step program." The Church is no longer his spiritual home, but he has found a new one.

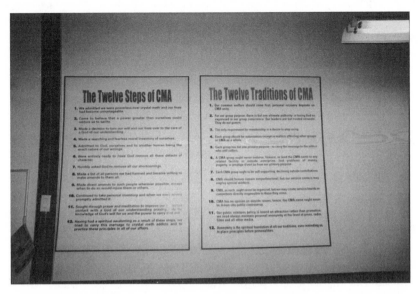

FIGURE 8.3 "Any room that you go in for the twelve-step program they always have on the wall the twelve steps and the twelve traditions."—Greg Collins

It is interesting that only one active religious participant (out of sixty-one) talked about battling addiction, while five of the thirty-four nonaffiliates and marginal members included addictions as key parts of their life stories. Rates of addiction may, in fact, be lower for active religious participants.[13] For that or other reasons, addiction was not one of the routine ailments talked about by the most religiously active of our participants. Active religious participants were also less likely to talk about significant mental health issues. A couple of them mentioned minor or one-time episodes of depression, but only two talked about chronic struggles. For both, the cure was a combination of faith and therapy. When we talked with her, Jessica Wilson was thirty, a nursing student, and a member of evangelical Deer Valley Church in Atlanta. She told us in our initial conversation about the depression she suffered in college and that both her sister and her grandmother have had problems with depression, as well. She said that without her faith, she might have had no hope at all. Jessica then recorded three rounds of oral diaries for us, spread over most of a year, and in that time, she recounted her struggle. During the first round, a good friend had been diagnosed with terminal cancer, and that was both making her sad and putting her situation in perspective.

I have definitely had my share of being sad and depressed and hope-less.... I mean I don't know why I am sad, I have so much in my life to be thankful for and yet over different times in my life I have been just so unbelievably sad.

By the time she recorded the next round, she was really struggling.

> Today is Wednesday. I've been too, um—I'm depressed I guess—to talk the past few days. I wake up and I don't even know, like, I don't know what I'm going to feel like that day. And even before I get out of bed, I usually try to pray and to say, you know, "God, please, please help me to see You today and give me hope and protect me from evil and pain." And still like so many days I just feel, like, I wake up and I just can't seem to get out of whatever the darkness is, the heaviness, the sadness, the tiredness. And I just cry. I'm just wiped out. I'm worn out.

She eventually told her doctor that she was depressed, and he prescribed an antidepressant. She was ambivalent at first, wondering if her faith should be enough, if it was wrong to need this crutch. But by the time she made her third round of recordings, the medicine had taken effect. She was still a bit ambivalent but had also resolved that this was the right path for her.

> I don't know, at some point, I guess, God created medicine—um, or let us be smart enough to create medicine, and we should be smart enough to use it when we need to. Our bodies aren't perfect, and sometimes I feel like it's just being lazy, using the medicine, but if you actually have an imbalance and there is something wrong, there is technology and brain power behind some sort of cure or care that can help in whatever is wrong. Hopefully.

As a conservative Christian, it was important to her to come to a theological understanding of what she was doing, one that gave God the credit for making human beings smart enough to find medical cures. It was exactly the sort of mix of science and faith we heard so often among those who are religiously and spiritually engaged.

Stories about mental illness were both more common and more purely secular among those who did not, in general, bring spirituality to their accounting for life. We have already noted the strategies Alicia Waters has learned in managing what turned out to be bipolar disorder. She and others reported dealing with psychological issues with rational, medical, and strategic forms of coping. Robin Mitchell, for instance, described herself as a successful graduate of eighteen years of psychotherapy, and she had also taken herself off of her Zoloft after she quit therapy. She reflected in her diary one day, however, that she was not so sure that was a good idea.

> So, the past month or two I've been feeling kind of blue. Not really related to anything; a little irritable blah, blah, blah. So, I was debating what to do, because I'm turning fifty. Is it menopause? Is it that my wife is menopausal and particularly grouchy so that's making me grouchy? Is it that I'm really depressed? Is it that I'm just biologically depressed? Do I need to call my therapist? Do I need to call a psychiatrist? Do I need to call a gynecologist? And I had this full, unopened bottle of Zoloft, but I didn't really know how to go back on it. And I wasn't certain if I wanted to, because what is going on Zoloft? Is it like dulling your experience of the world so that you're not as bummed out by it? Or is it falsely making you a little cheerful, even though, if you had your wits about you, you wouldn't be that cheerful? Or is it just recalibrating those delicate chemicals in your brain so that you react normally to situations rather than with irritation or sadness?

After devising a strategy for beginning to take Zoloft again, she reported that she was feeling relieved, glad that the bumps in the road will be smoothed out a bit. Unlike Jessica, she needed no theological explanation for her strategy. Like Jessica, she trusted medical experts and pharmaceutical interventions. Despite the difference in their views of the world, their behavior was remarkably similar.

Looking for Answers, Looking for Comfort

People who went through a life-threatening crisis sometimes simply declared that being alive was a miracle. That was more common when their stories are shaped by a Theistic spiritual framework, where it was an active deity who was believed to have intervened. At age sixty, Vicki Johnson had already confronted a series of coronary traumas.

> The thing with the heart attack and the open heart surgery was really traumatic for everybody because that's not what I went in for. And my vessels just dissected, and one thing was happening after another. And it's just a miracle—a true miracle that I'm here.

At eighty-five, Marjorie Buckley was rushed to the hospital on Christmas Eve and eventually left with a pacemaker. As she tried to absorb all of this into her sense of God's plan in her life, she concluded that it was simply not yet her time to die. Both she and Vicki are active in their religious communities (LDS and Catholic, respectively), and both were convinced that God would use their traumas for some good end. They did not claim to understand how God intervened alongside the medical interventions that saved their lives, but their Theistic view of the world wrote God's presence into the story. Each now looks at life through a narrative of expectation—expectation that their lives and their experience of crisis will produce some greater good.

For Wendy Simmons, that greater good had already come around. Wendy's is a life full of more tragedy than any ten ordinary people might expect. We have already heard her story of a back injury and depression that interrupted life in her early twenties. But her youth had also been deeply shaped by the debilitating neurological illness that eventually took her sister's life; and she herself had, by the time she was forty-one, developed a seizure disorder. So when her daughter was ten (the age when Wendy's sister first developed symptoms) and started to complain about a twitch and then a pain in her eyes, Wendy took it seriously. "She's complaining. I'm not messing around. She's in fifth grade. She's going to be eleven. The pediatrician knew all about my sister, knew all about me." The doctor took the situation seriously, and within a couple of weeks they had discovered a massive brain tumor that surely would have killed her daughter if left untreated. "The only reason that we found out that Abigail had a brain tumor is because my sister died of Hallervorden-Spatz," declared Wendy. In her case, this was not a miracle wrought by God, but a miracle wrought by intelligent reasoning and human sensitivity. Hers is a spirituality more dominated by Extra-theistic sensibilities than Theistic ones. This connection between her sister's death and her daughter's life provided a deep spiritual life meaning to Wendy.

Explanations were not always the point, however. As much as people might ask a rhetorical "why?" the quest for understanding was not necessarily central to the story. Some people simply looked for ways to get through the day-to-day agony, and for some that relief came through spiritual practices. Larry Waugh gets acupuncture treatments and combines them with meditation but also works hard to keep up his regimen of antiretrovirals. Francis Parker has an astonishingly long list of critical illnesses—Addison's disease, ulcerative colitis, and now lung cancer—and mostly he just takes his pills. But he also routinely attends a Tuesday evening Mass for the healing of the sick. One night, he said, "God touched me," and he started feeling better. He does not expect his illnesses to go away, but something about that service provided both spiritual and physical comfort. Grace Shoemaker recounted a similar experience in her diary. She has muscular dystrophy and grieves at the activities she is slowly having to relinquish and the routine pain she endures. She has practiced Reiki healing for some time, but while she was recording diaries for our project, she went with a friend to a charismatic healing service and was called up to be prayed for.

> The minister touched me on the forehead and told me, or told God or whoever she was talking to, um, that the disease should be gone, and she touched me on the forehead, and I felt such a power go into my body. I almost lost my breath and the next thing you know I was on the floor. And they covered me. I just went right over. They covered me with a blanket and knelt down with me. My friend stayed with me. And I was awake but I was in such a state of peace. There were tears coming out of my eyes. I didn't even want to get up, and they prayed over me. They had their hands on me, and it was, it was a miracle. It was miraculous. And eventually I got up, and they said I had such a look of serenity on my face, and I felt so full of peace and calm. All of the tensions that were in my body when I had arrived was just gone. It was just gone. It was like this thin veil had parted and I had walked through. I felt wonderful, and um, and I went home and, you know, told my family about it and they were, they were really happy. I had a pretty good night sleep. I've had no pain, um, through the night; and this morning I slept late, and I woke up and I feel good. I feel peaceful. I think that's the best word I can use.

Grace is an Episcopalian, but her combination of Theistic and Extra-theistic spirituality allows her to draw from a wide range of healing traditions. Emma Cooper is a Neopagan with a congenital heart condition that has sent her through multiple crises, but she remembers with special fondness the time she experienced tuning her chakras to music, followed by chanting to Green Tara. She has maintained an attachment to that particular goddess since. Like Grace and Francis and Larry, Emma combines these alternative spiritual and healing practices with regular medical care. Emma took a picture of the view looking north from her doctor's office. "It is a beautiful view. Actually, that is a major part of my life too, 'cause having an artificial heart valve I go to the doctor a lot. So that's—yeah, definitely part of my spiritual journey is coping with that."

Facing one's mortality is clearly part of the story here. As Larry said about getting an HIV+ diagnosis, it was about "being scared to death. Immortality issues." His response stands in contrast to Mary Margaret Sironi's reaction to her doctor's assessment of her lungs—"terrible," he said. When he told her that even oxygen would not help but that he would run more tests, Mary Margaret admitted to feeling discouraged. But, she said, "God has been so good to me and has made me a happy person in spite of my physical body. But I really don't mind. I take one day at a time. I do what I can each day. Some days I cry a little. But I get over it because I know God's there taking care of me."

The presence and role of God in the midst of suffering is one of those perennial theological questions that human beings have been asking for a long time. This group of sufferers can perhaps tell us something about how Americans today are dealing with the need to place their situations into some sort of larger frame of meaning. Larry and Emma represent one strategy. Neither seemed to spend much time trying to find a cognitive explanation. They engaged spiritual practices that they experienced as calming and strengthening alongside their careful adherence to medical routines. Adding "alternative" health strategies has become, in fact, part of the medical routine for many. They and their health providers see both physical and spiritual dimensions to the healing process. What they have developed, then, is not so much an explanation for why their bodies are sick as a holistic understanding of health that incorporates both scientific Western medicine and other sources of healing.

Francis and Grace are not so very different from that pattern. They, too, take their pills, do their therapy, and seek out spiritual sources of healing. But each of them spent at least some time trying to see God's hand more directly in their situation. Grace confessed, "I don't even know if there's a God or what it is, but there's something that, no matter how bad it gets, something good comes out." Not only was she convinced that divine powers were bringing good in the long run, she also experienced God's presence in everyday health practices.

> Sometimes I'll write on a piece of paper, "Okay, God, why am I in so much pain today, and what am I supposed to do about it?" And then sometimes it will pop into my head, "Lay down, stupid. Lay down, take some Tylenol, and rest." You know, I'm not looking for a miracle, it's just these little simple answers will pop into my head.

Francis, too, looked for positive answers. "There's a reason behind it, and I try to look at it as something that's educational, something that's going to be okay." Here the role of God in suffering is both to point people toward a greater good and to provide day-to-day pragmatic coping strategies. Vicki and Marjorie had a similar conviction that God would bring good from their illness, but both of them—drawing exclusively on Theistic spirituality—pointed toward spiritual growth rather than this-worldly coping. The broader Extra-theistic spiritualities Francis and Grace employ shape a broader range of meanings. Theodicy in both cases means trusting God to have a plan, whether or not the contours of that plan are immediately apparent. The kind of spirituality at work shapes where the person looks for evidence and insight.

Sometimes, however, a divine plan seems out of reach and beside the point. The day Francis recorded that relatively optimistic note in his diary, he also noted the most memorable event of the day—getting a CAT scan and waiting for the results. The results, in fact, were not good, and the next day he related in his diary what happened when he and his wife learned that he had lung cancer:

> So Adele and I started crying and holding each other and saying it can't be, this is too much—too much for one guy to take on all this time. And, you know, start thanking God, praying to God that he'll take care of you and make you feel better and get rid of this. But I mean this is a knock on the head.

It simply seemed too much to bear, and they hardly knew what to ask God. A miracle would be nice, but having God "take care of you" may have to do.

Bethany Armstrong's medical saga was at least the equal of Francis's, and she spent a great deal of time agonizing over the place of God in her story. In her early twenties, she had suffered a complete physical breakdown that was diagnosed as an autoimmune disease. She was bedridden for a year and housebound for three subsequent years. She made progress for a few years after that, but then she was diagnosed with vasculitis of the central nervous system, something she expected to kill her in a matter of months. It didn't, but she is incredibly vulnerable. A flu bug she picked up at church put her in bed for weeks. A back injury slowed her down for months, and she still cannot work a steady job. When she told her life story, she wove into it the spiritual comfort she has learned to find (Figure 8.4):

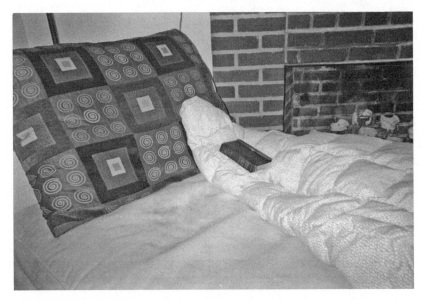

FIGURE 8.4 "I will feel a sense of His presence, a sense of sort of a soothing and a reassurance."—Bethany Armstrong

> The one thing that I can have wherever I am is God. The one thing that I can do, regardless of my energy level, is to pray. And I don't mean pray in a put my hands together and close my eyes and get on my knees necessarily, but to just be in—I want to say in conversation with God.

She also recounted one of the moments of relatively good news. A neurological scan showed that areas of her brain "that had 20 percent perfusion or blood flow are now at about 80 percent, so there's still a problem. There's still insufficient blood flow, but there's enough. It's not what it should be, but it's enough. And that, frankly, really surprised me." Her evangelical church friends said, "Hallelujah. Praise Jesus. That was just a miracle, healing." But, she said, "God did not make it all disappear. And that raises bigger questions, at least in my mind, of wow, what's the power? Is the power in what exists physically or is the power in what we believe and how we perceive it?"

A few months later, with a back injury and more chronic pain besieging her, she recalled in her diary, "About a month into it, I thought, okay, well, this is, you know, God's protective hand and I'm just going to have to find another way to manage the pain and to deal with my back.... So now it's been a good two months that I've been trying to, um, live with this, and make adjustments and it's just been very difficult." At the end of one of those difficult days, she recorded another diary entry:

Found myself just praying to God, sharing that this is a really hard day. I'm really tired and I hurt and there's so much that I want to do and there's a world out there. There's a world outside and I want to be a part of it.... I'm asking God why? What sense does this make? This is ridiculous. Do I—I've—I've prayed for so many years. Hourly doesn't even cover it. Please, just heal me. Now you're the creator of the universe; you could certainly cure chronic fatigue.... Surely you can fix it even if the doctors can't.

She prays for a miracle, but she also sits quietly with the frustration of her life. This is clearly one of those conversations with God she had told us about, and it fully reflects both her faith in God's ultimate power and her frustration with her suffering. Meanwhile, she also said, "I am thankful that I got good medical treatment and a good diagnosis and, um, that I have a compassionate doctor."

Many people told us that what got them through their difficult times was their faith, but faith rarely came with a definitive road map. It was more likely to include holistic practices of spiritual healing—including prayer—than the expectation of a physical miracle cure. It was more likely to be a general sense of confidence in the future than a claim that there is a definitive story that integrates past, present, and future. For most people, "faith" meant a sense of divine presence, a willingness to depend on a higher power and to expect that power to provide comfort and assurance of one's inner well-being. The explanations we heard for the suffering of life came with a strong dose of uncertainty. Why is my life like this?—I don't know. What will God do about it?—I don't know. What spiritually engaged people did know was that pursuing that ongoing conversation with God, even when they were frustrated, was what kept them well, in spite of illness.

When the Illness Is Not Your Own

Human bodies and their well-being are not just individual projects; concern for health and illness is one of the things that bind people together into extended communities of care. Stories about the physical struggles of family and friends were as numerous as stories about the participant's own health. And like those personal stories, they were framed both by the severity of the crisis and by the spiritual perspective brought to the telling. Health issues that have become a routine and manageable part of daily life may still cause worry and are sometimes the subject of prayer, but they enter a spiritual narrative that is already underway and do not disrupt or fundamentally change the way people already see the world. Cynthia Gardener is a deeply spiritual and active Episcopalian, and as she told story after story about her son's ADD and learning challenges, his psychiatric problems, and finally his life-threatening alcoholism, religious youth groups and her own spiritual practices were as much a part of the narrative as schools and treatment centers. Medical and educational interventions were intertwined in the telling with religious and spiritual support. Cynthia's deep spiritual engagement will probably continue to frame her interaction with and understanding of her son's ongoing struggles. Charlotte McKenna, on the other hand, is not especially spiritually interested and deals with her husband's PTSD as simply part of the household routine. Because of his need for peace and quiet, he sleeps odd hours, and she fixes dinner for him around midnight every night. She has shouldered this somewhat burdensome routine for many years, doing the necessary things to care for his physical and mental well-being—tasks undertaken with the same humane caring that shapes other parts of her life. Both Charlotte and Cynthia have been profoundly affected by the need to care for a family member with special needs, and each found ways to integrate that caring into her own life narrative—one strongly spiritual and religious, the other largely secular.

When the routines are interrupted, when spouses and children are more suddenly stricken or finally get relief, the situation is more likely to evoke a spiritual telling. One in five of our participants recounted such moments when the health of a loved one was seriously in question. Most of these stories were memories from the past, but several of them were remarkably in the moment, events that were unfolding as our project was happening. When we sat down with Emma Cooper to talk about the photos she took, she explained that she had intended to take a picture at her belly dancing class, but on the night when she took the camera with her, she got a call from her husband halfway through class begging her to come home immediately. She rushed him to the hospital, where he had emergency gall bladder surgery. She was obviously worried and frazzled, but she said, "I hadn't had any inklings, any premonitions or omens or anything." Her Neopagan beliefs (not unlike Walter Green's Bible verse) gave her confidence that things would be okay. William Pullinger is a New England Congregationalist and not normally very spiritual, by his own account; but his wife's suffering with a back ailment and the events surrounding her successful surgery were the single time he could think of when he was confident of God's involvement in his life. Why? Because someone at church took the initiative to grease the wheels so that his wife could get an otherwise hard-to-get appointment.

Anna we wouldn't consider an intimate friend by any means, but she knew Liz was suffering, and it turns out her niece was a—of course I prayed for Liz's condition often and frequently—but Anna has a niece who is a business manager for one of the best bone doctors at New England Baptist and so she contacted him. As I said, we'd been trying to get an appointment, and he would only see her in six months. You know, these guys are really busy…and Anna set it up so that Liz actually got the operation about three weeks later, and I can only think that God worked through Anna to help us. That probably did for my faith, probably more than anything in my life.

"Do you consider that to be miraculous?" we asked. "Yes. Absolutely," he answered. "I got my wife back." Crises and cures were not always a catalyst for spiritual changes, but sometimes they were.

More often, they were simply interpreted in light of the spiritual narrative already unfolding. Jen Jackson gave birth during the time she was participating in our project, and her daughter experienced a variety of difficulties over the next few months. Jen's Pentecostal faith was very clear in how she told the stories each day in her diaries.

Well, I feel like I'm really in a testing season right now [laughs]. Today I found out that my daughter had been overdosed with the medication she was prescribed by her doctor for reflux, and apparently the pharmacy, they put the wrong dosage on the box of medicine that she received….I'm very angry, upset, and frustrated about the situation. Very prayerful that the baby is going to be okay, and I believe that God is going to take care of my baby, and He's going to, you know, heal her little body and take care of her. We spent all night in the emergency room with her just hoping and praying that everything will be fine, and as of now the doctors have said that they think she will be okay. She's just going to be in pain for a little while.

The next day she reported,

Today was a better day. Went to the pediatrician this morning, and my baby is very blessed. The pediatrician said that the medicine that she was originally going to prescribe her was lethal in high doses, and it would have killed her [laughs] had it been misdosed. And I am very, very grateful right now, very thankful, and I just give all praise and glory and honor to God who spared my child and saved her life from, you know, my own hands giving her medication that she had been misdosed on. So I'm just; I feel just overwhelmed right now with emotion and gratefulness and praise and thanks to God, 'cause He's the only one who could, who could have spared my child's life.

And at the end of the week, she reported in again:

Well, I took my baby to church for the first time today.... I could not wait for, you know, everyone to see her and just to give God glory and praise and thanks, you know, because I mean, you know, I've had such a long week with this baby.

Jen is still very much depending on the medical system to help her daughter heal and eventually thrive, and she is angry and disappointed at the medical mistake that threatened her baby's life. This is very much a medical story, but it is also a story about affirming Jen's relationship with God. Like William Pullinger, she does not blame God for the suffering, but she does believe that God is present in the process of healing. In both these stories, faith communities also played an important role. Part of how God works is through the practical and moral support to be found among people in the congregation. We will return to that theme shortly.

The obligation to care for people who are sick is most directly felt within a household, but it also extends into the larger family circle, especially to aging parents.[14] For one in four of our participants, the health of parents was a matter of everyday concern. Among those in the middle range of their own lives (aged thirty-six through sixty-five), it was one in three who told such stories. Some of these stories were the kinds of life-defining episodes that appeared in our initial life history conversation—parents whose illness shaped a childhood—but most were more proximal stories faced as adults. Joe Silverman has been consistently engaged in a variety of spiritual practices over his lifetime, so praying for his mother in a time of crisis was not unusual. He recalled a time when she had oral surgery.

Well she didn't come out of anesthetic. She was in a coma and she had to go on a breathing machine and so for two weeks she was on a breathing machine. We didn't know if she was going to live or die. I remember every day I used to go to Georgia Baptist Hospital, go in the small chapel and pray for my mother to live. God, please let my mother live.

Well, she came out of the coma, she didn't have brain damage, and she did live.

Was God responsible? Especially given that when Joe later prayed for his wife to be spared, she still died? Joe's Reform Judaism tells him to pray, but it also tells him to ask questions, and he does both. He says he is not at all sure what God's role has been in these two very different outcomes. He offers neither definitive thanks nor blame. Carolyn Horton, on the other hand, is not a spiritual person, and her story about her sick parents was shaped by her concern and worry but not by any extraordinary religious or spiritual interruption in the secular way she understands life. Health crises in the lives of aging parents are, in most instances, simply integrated into an ongoing story—no more nor less spiritually significant than other parts of life.

The stories we heard in the context of photos and diaries brought the concerns about aging parents into the present, even when the parents were not close by. There were stories about falls and dementia and cancer and just general decline—inevitable vulnerabilities people expected and seemed resigned to. The few who reported that their parents were actually doing okay did so with a sense of relief and gratitude—but no expectation that this would last forever. These were not necessarily life-changing crisis stories, but they were the everyday entanglements that belie any notion that extended families have to be living next door to be involved in daily caregiving.[15] Carlos Fernandez is from Puerto Rico, and he took a picture of his mother when he was on a recent trip there.

> My mom is a real special person in my life as well. She's a widow; my dad passed away about 1990. And so she's been living on her own since then, and I really value the friendship, um, that we have. I pretty much call her every day to make sure she is doing okay. And luckily my brother lives not too far from there. He's also a physician, and he stops by every day on his way to work and checks in on her. But we have a real close relationship.

Carlos was by no means the only person to report regular phone calls and frequent visits. A handful were providing care at a closer range, as well. Debbie Rogers's diary entry, recorded on her way to work one morning, was typical.

> I'll talk to my mom this morning, which reminds me I need to call and get her—she's got twenty-four-hour help after breaking her arm,

and I need to get those hours adjusted. I think she can do without the nighttime daycare or a nighttime person, now.... She's made my brother promise that I couldn't put her in a nursing home and this is a whole 'nother dilemma about what would happen with her then, since she really can't come to my house. One, no one's ever home; and two, we have an upstairs bedroom for her, and since she's handicapped that just would not work. So here again is something to put into God's hands.

The pragmatic family negotiations about where parents will live and who will provide the care are everyday realities for the adult children of the millions of Americans who are among the frail elderly. In 2009, about 14.6 million Americans—or 37 percent of America's 39.6 million elderly population—had some type of disability. While some of these disabilities were relatively minor, many result in functional limitations in activities of daily living (ADL) (Aging 2010). In that same year, one in four U.S. households reported at least one person in the household had served as an unpaid family caregiver to an adult in the past twelve months (Caregiving 2009). Caregiving is a pervasive reality in American society. People who are involved in religious communities and who have an active spiritual life negotiate those realities no less pragmatically, but they are likely to tell the story as a spiritual one and to expect that their religious communities will be there to support them.[16] Just as religious participation proves advantageous for the elderly themselves, so their adult children seem to appreciate the support and comfort of a religious community where their care for aging parents is honored.

The Larger Circle of Care

Caring about the health of people beyond one's own family is indeed something that seems to be part of the culture of religious communities. Caring for household and extended family is something people do no matter what their religious inclinations; but more than one in four regular religious attenders told at least one story about a friend who was sick, while none of the nonattenders told caregiving stories that involved people beyond their extended families. Religious participants, that is, seem to draw the circle of care more expansively. They are aware of and tell stories about the physical difficulties of a fairly broad range of others, including people they know from church or synagogue. When Elizabeth Evans went for her mammogram, recall that she noted in her diary her concern for her friend with breast cancer. Thinking about friends in distress is also likely to include praying for them. In his regular daily prayer time, Walter Green prays for various people who are facing medical crises. In his diary one day, he talked about a church friend

> whose sister-in-law has been almost at death's door for a period of several months now.... It's just a very difficult thing. The husband feels that he cannot take her off of life support because he wouldn't know how to face her daughter and her family, and yet the financial cost, day by day, is very large and the doctors say there is no hope that she can ever get better. It's one of those decisions where we have to make god-like decisions, situations where we have to make godlike decisions, and we just don't know how to. So that has been a matter of prayer.

Sharing these difficult things with other church members, wondering together what should be done, and praying for wisdom—all part of what we might expect people of faith like Walter (a Southern Baptist) and Elizabeth (a Catholic) to do as part of their religious lives. Prayers for the sick are routine elements in worship services and are organized in many faith communities into prayer calendars and prayer chains (Figure 8.5). They are part of what binds the religious group together.

Prayers for the sick are, in many instances, as much symbolic ties as actual ones. Walter, for example, has never met the woman whose dying he is praying about, but he does know her brother-in-law and offers these prayers as part of that larger spiritual tie. Sometimes, however, spiritually engaged people seek each other out for more direct ongoing comfort and conversation. In the midst of her own suffering, Bethany Armstrong has spent a good deal of time with a church friend who has also received a devastating diagnosis of a degenerative disease. The conversation between these two young women has developed into an important relationship in which Bethany feels like she has something to give. She reflected, "It's hard to be vulnerable, even with your closest friends. But when we have those conversations, when you say, 'Tell me what's going on,' that's when our conversation is not about the nuts and bolts. It's not about unimportant stuff; it's about the most important stuff. It's about how do you make sense of this? How do you get through?" Having another person of faith with whom to ask that unanswerable question is itself part of the answer.

Things that are matters of prayer also sometimes become occasions for more this-worldly aid, of course. Help with household chores, rides to doctor

FIGURE 8.5 A prayer request being recorded for inclusion in Sunday worship.
—Nancy Ammerman

visits, and casseroles delivered during recovery are practices well institutional-ized in religious communities. We heard Margi Perkins, for instance, talk about being on the receiving end of her Catholic community's generosity when her husband had surgery, just as Catherine Young celebrated the tangible sup-port from her Mormon ward in the days after her daughter was born. On the giving side, Sam Levitt helped to make sure that his rabbi's special-needs son had all the necessary accommodations to thrive in the school Sam heads. And both John Travisano and Camilla Hart talked about spending time visiting and caring for sick neighbors. John, in fact, talked one day about seeing the lady across the street with a walker and discovering that she had recently been in the hospital. He was chagrined not to have realized that earlier, and he left his contact information for emergencies, if she should ever need it. John was practicing in his neighborhood the same virtues of caring that his involvement in the St. Vincent de Paul Society taught him; and Camilla simply mused that everything about her upbringing in a devout Black Baptist home had taught her to be a caregiver. As these stories suggest, the circle of concern extends out in many directions from the people who are active in religious communities. It is not just other congregation members who are prayed for, and it is not just prayers but practical assistance. In addition to stories about caring for neighbors, recall that we heard several people tell stories about praying for (and with) co-workers who were sick or had sick family members.

This concern about other people's illness seems to be a virtue that can be sustained even by people who are no longer very active but who were shaped in earlier years by religious participation. Among the infrequent attenders, Carlos Fernandez was one of the few to talk about tending to the physical well-being of friends and neighbors. He grew up going to Mass every week and to catechism classes, but what he said he mostly learned was

> the idea of sort of doing good for neighbor, sort of the Christian idea of helping those around you. So that's sort of how I—in a way that's sort of been a part of my everyday life in terms of the things that I've chosen to do, sort of trying to work with the underdog, you know, work in areas that I think people really need help and that no one else is going to really make an effort to make much of an impact.

His profession in pediatric AIDS research is clearly part of that effort to help the underdog, but it also came through in his stories about helping a co-worker who had had a stroke and in his admiration for another co-worker who had adopted a number of Russian orphans.

This long arm linking faith to the human experience of illness also showed up in Grace Shoemaker's diaries. Grace has not been going to church much and talked about not really missing it, but news she got one day changed that.

> I've been given some terrible news in the last twenty-four hours that a dear friend of mine has been diagnosed with a brain tumor. It's such a shock. It's unbelievable. She's been my friend since I moved into this neighborhood. She's lived here most of her life, and she's also a member of All Saints Church, and been a wonderful friend. She's almost like a combination of a mother, a sister, and a best friend. She's a little bit older than I am, and just seems full of wisdom and has always been there to help everybody. I don't know anybody that she hasn't helped in some way, even if it's just a hug, a smile, a word of encouragement, or fixing somebody a meal, just, she's just one of those people that follow the life of Jesus. She lives life the way Jesus would want us to live it.... This has been such a shock to me, and the first thought that came to my mind after I had registered what was happening was I need to go to church.... I have to pray. I'm sure that this Sunday we will go, and I will pray for her. And it's almost a need to be with the people

in church that know her.... Everybody in church knows her and loves her. So I think I need to be with all of these people and talk about her. Ask them, you know, if they've heard anything, or pray together with them—just to be with that group of people that love her as much as I do.

Not every physical crisis provoked this kind of response, but Grace's reaction eloquently expressed the mixture of spiritual, practical, and social solidarity that can be activated in religious communities faced with illness among their number and beyond.

Facing Death

When devastating medical news comes, those in the social community surrounding the sick person recognize that they may be about to lose one of their members and that they themselves are mortal. Acknowledging death as an inevitable part of life marked a variety of the stories we heard. The deaths of family members often signaled movement from one chapter to the next in people's life histories, although the deaths themselves were not nearly always elaborated. People simply bookmarked the story. Remembering people who have passed on or even thinking ahead toward one's own funeral was a theme that was sometimes noted without any significant existential reflection or attention to the potential spiritual questions it might raise. Erika Lombardi, a disengaged former Catholic, took pictures of her yoga studio and pointed out that it faces a cemetery. She described that as potentially creating "bad feng shui," but her own reaction is different.

I don't have an issue like with death, um, it's not something that scares me. So I—and I happen to like cemeteries. I find them to be very peaceful places and historical, historic types of places.... Sometimes we move and I mean you're looking out and there are these headstones. Sometimes there are flowers on the graves, and I notice, like, the flags for the veterans and so it's, it doesn't bother me, but I do, I think of it 'cause it's there.

Shirley Knight reported in her diary that she felt sad that day, thinking about her dwindling family. She and her brother had just returned from burying a cousin in Mississippi. She said that at forty-seven, she is starting to "feel like an orphan. Even though you know you're not, you feel like you're the elders in the family, and that's scary,... but death is, is still something that's really hard no matter how close or how distant a relative it is, because I think it makes us face our mortality, which is something I don't think any of us like to do." Shirley is much more active spiritually than Erika, but both told matter-of-fact stories about the presence of death in their lives. Shirley is not so much afraid of death itself as of the way it shifts the social and familial equations. Erika recognizes the social, historical, and even aesthetic significance of physically marking spaces to remember those who have died. Death can have these kinds of social significance without any strong spiritual dimensions being present.

That was not the norm, however. More than three-quarters of the stories about death and dying were also stories where the spiritual and existential realities of death played a role. Even the most spiritually disengaged sometimes mused about what they lose by not believing in an afterlife, and others thought about wanting a church funeral. Barbara Robinson, for instance, has not been active in her church for years, but she recalled in her diary one day a long conversation she had had with an old friend who is much more spiritual than she. Barbara spoke of visiting her family grave plots to pray but also about her own demise.

> I reflected on my experience and wondering, did I miss something all these years, not attending church? Um, I even thought about death, you know. When I die, do I want to be, um, laid out in some funeral home or do I want to be laid out in a church, in a home church with people, you know, that I have connected with and formed some kind of relationship, bond with, and have, you know, family. I don't know, I'm older and I think about stuff like that now. I never thought about death before. But all this sickness around me and the cancer I went through and my cousins having cancer a few years ago...so I think about it, you know. If I'm going to get sick one day and die..., where will people come to pay their last respects? And I don't want it to be in a funeral home; I want it to be in a church.

Others recounted spiritual experiences at the bedsides of people who were dying, experiences that defied their own usual skepticism. Shirley Glazer has an on-again, off-again relationship with her Presbyterian church in Atlanta, but the experience of losing her husband was a life-defining spiritual moment.

The moment he died was [pause]—it was an experience. You know, it was—Julian would have called it a vision, I think. Julian of Norwich, I'm referring to, would have called it a vision. And I'd never had one before but he [her husband] told me, "Now, before I die—after I die I want you to take my ring off and don't look down at me, look up, because I'll be leaving my body, and I'll be on my way to heaven. I don't know how that's going to play out, but that's where I'm headed." So, you know, a psychiatrist may tell me it was self-fulfilling prophecy or whatever, but I was in the room alone with him, and he died, and the machine went to flat line, and the nurse came in to confirm it, and she left. And I took his ring off and I just fell to my knees to dissolve in tears, and I can't explain it, but instead, I started laughing. And for maybe two minutes, I felt just an incredible heat over my body and a wave of sheer joy. Just absolute sheer joy. This is something like I've never felt before, and I just think I was being spoken to, somehow. "It's okay, this is what I'm feeling, and this is what's in store. I'm not with you physically but I will be spiritually. Don't worry about me. This is just a taste. Hold on to this when you need it." And then his last words to me echo daily. He said, "Be happy and live fully." Be happy and live fully. So, you know, I felt that in that room and I've never, ever lost the feeling of what that was like.

Like some of the other people who lived most of their lives outside religious communities and not especially in touch with spirituality, Shirley nevertheless described the experience of her husband's death in vividly spiritual terms.

There was another side to the link between death and faith, however. For several of our participants, the death of a loved one was too much to take, challenging their ideas about what God should be doing in the world as well as questioning the benefit of religious communities. If there is a God, why did my daughter die? That is a question Gordon Johnson asked and to which he got no reply. Greg Collins kept a keen sense of his own vision of God, but he also discovered just how far churches could be from that vision. He recalled in agonizing detail the horror of the early AIDS years and how many of his friends died and how cruelly they were rejected by so many in the community. His friend Sam had been especially abused by his parents, and when Greg gave the eulogy at Sam's funeral, he recalled,

Standing up there in a church, and I looked out and Sam's mom and his dad are sitting in the front row and all I could think about was how they had treated him, especially his dad. When I came down off the podium to go back to my seat, his dad stood up and wanted to shake my hand, and I just couldn't do it. It took every ounce of strength for me not to deck the guy.... The world has changed a lot since then, people don't remember how many guys in this country were literally put out on the streets, and they were taken in by other gay people. They were cared for because families wouldn't do it. Churches would not do it. Even today, the Black church doesn't reach out, doesn't take care of any of their people with AIDS. It's a taboo subject.

"That just cannot be God," he said. "That just cannot be God." In a variety of ways, deaths can highlight a disjuncture between old beliefs and new realities as well as between enduring beliefs and the communities that claim to embody those beliefs. The large majority of people who encounter death or think ahead to their own dying confront the experience in a spiritual frame of mind, but sometimes they are raising questions that find no satisfactory answers.

The modal storyline, however, is one where an existing spiritual narrative is extended to include the realities of death and dying. Existing stories and relationships, divine and human, incorporate an anticipated final chapter. Eighty-year-old John Travisano's thoughts about death were intertwined with his experiences in his parish and his own sense of physical and spiritual well-being. In one of his diary entries, he said,

> Father's homily was on mortality and... "are we ready when the time may come?" Naturally, it provoked a little interest in my part and thinking about where am I? And I guess, spiritually, and where my soul is today, I feel that I am ready. Hopefully when everything is balanced for what I have done and what I failed to do, etc., that I'll have the eternal reward in heaven and be with God. But I am not fearful. I guess one reason is that I don't think about death too much, uh, because at this stage of my life I'm still very healthy.... I know I can't lift as much as I used to, but I can still press ninety pounds and so forth. But anyway, spiritually I feel I am ready, should I be called tomorrow.

Sylvia Jameson's Southern Baptist world includes ample spiritual images and divine characters with which to populate stories about death, and she drew on those images when her own father was dying.

When my dad was very, very sick in the hospital, and he'd been through four years of dialysis and had two or three heart attacks, and you know, I just had to turn that over to the Lord.... And so I was at school teaching, and I had to leave the room for a few minutes…and I said, "But Lord, I love him, I love him so much." And it's like the Lord just spoke to my heart and said—and it was so gently—He said, "I know you do, I know you love him, but I love him more." And that just—(tearful) I'll never forget it. He just reassured me that—He gave me a picture in my mind of my daddy being small…and He just reassured me that He had always loved and taken care of daddy before he was ever even born or conceived and that He was going to continue to take really, really good care of my daddy.

Her conservative Protestant way of thinking about God is very personal, as is her way of telling this story about her father's death.

Hank Matthews's Episcopal world is less about a personal relationship with Jesus and more about the prayers and rituals that evoke a sense of God's spiritual presence and comfort. In his diary one day, he recounted the daily trips he was making to his mother's hospital room, where she had contracted pneumonia after surgery. Between that time and the next round of his diaries for us, his mother would in fact die; but at this point, she was hanging on.

The priest in charge of her parish has visited her weekly for a number of years now, and she's been to the hospital. She's anointed her, which I felt a sense of relief that that had been performed. And each day, when I see her, I do some readings from the Visitation of the Sick from our old prayer book, or some of the hymns that I know she knows, her favorites. Also yesterday, again, read the Litany for the Dying. This is a very spiritual time for me.

Hank is a fairly typical mainline Protestant churchgoer. He was not exceptionally focused on spirituality in his routine life, but he did have a reservoir of practices on which to draw. Like John and Sylvia, his way of coming to terms with death draws on the rituals, images, and spiritual relationships provided within a religious community. The point is not so much to arrive at a plausible set of beliefs about death and the afterlife but to draw on the sacred storylines already in place.

Conclusion

Death has always posed a mystery to human beings. As Clifford Geertz theorized, it is one of the "limiting experiences" that will always provoke a need for meaning (Geertz 1973). Precisely because we cannot know and cannot be in control, we often seek ritualized practices and spiritual accounts that provide order. Indeed, the experiences surrounding death were among the most predictably spiritual of all the experiences we heard about. For most of our participants, stories about death were extensions of the stories they told about life, the body, and illness, extending their spiritual narratives into the life beyond. But some otherwise less spiritually inclined people were pushed toward seeing a spiritual dimension when death entered their lives. While some struggled with the "why" questions, trying to find moral and philosophical sense in suffering and loss, for most it was more important to be able to ask the questions in the context of a shared community than to get a definitive answer, more important to believe that God was present than to know exactly what God might have in mind. The more religiously active the person was, the larger the repertoire of accounts and images they had to draw on, but the process for everyone was more relational than intellectual.

Nor was any of this a matter of pitting science against religion. Whether talking about their regular exercise routine or their parents' declining health, their own chronic illness or the death of a friend, these people were fully engaged with modern medicine and modern science. That was a constant. What varied was the degree to which they *also* understood their physical existence to have a spiritual dimension. That spiritual dimension was more likely to be there in stories about the end of life than in stories about eating right and exercising, more likely to be there in stories about crises than in stories about routine difficulties. Everyday routines, in other words, take on spiritual significance for people who are already spiritually engaged but are less often spiritual for people who rarely participate in religious communities and do not otherwise cultivate a life of the spirit. Most people simply integrated accounts of health and routine illness into the complex mix of mundane practices, spiritual care, and divine presence that makes up the account they give of their lives. When the question of health and life itself is at risk, by contrast, even the least spiritually active sometimes reach beyond mundane explanations, disrupting an otherwise secular narrative.

Everyday routines for staying healthy are especially likely to be viewed in secular terms by the most educated of our participants. As they talked about exercising and eating right, they brought their sense of informed empowerment to the task. But when difficulties arise, neither education nor any other demographic differences affect the presence or absence of spirituality. In the worst moments, pragmatic medical planning and intervention is joined by prayer and ritual and religious community. Physical bodies, in all their complications, are neither solely profane nor solely sacred but a complex mix of the two.

How people deal with those bodies is also not solely a matter of individual concern. One of the most striking aspects of the stories we heard is the degree to which caring for each other "in sickness and in health" is not only a matter of mutual family responsibility but also a matter of religious virtue and community connection. Caring for household members and caring for aging parents are understood by affiliates and nonaffiliates alike to be part of the obligations of family life. But people who participate in religious communities extend the circle of "brothers and sisters," not only to others in their congregations but also to the neighbors and friends they are taught to include in their attentions. The spiritual tribe they have created in their religious community is one that encourages them to include strangers in the circle of care. As we saw in Chapter Seven, religious participation matters for how people participate in the communities that surround them. The patterns we see in caring for the sick are reflections of those same patterns.

9 SPIRITUAL TRIBES: TOWARD A SOCIOLOGY OF RELIGION IN EVERYDAY LIFE

The stories we have heard—of work, health, family, politics, community, and caring—have invited us to step back from any easy assertions about the presence and absence of religion in a modern world. Indeed, they invite us to step back even from what we have often meant by religion. When a man reads psalms from the *Book of Common Prayer* to his dying mother, he is not making a bargain with God about his salvation or hers. He is not even really asking for supernatural assistance in any discernible way. When a woman finds common moral ground with her co-workers based on their shared faith (even though she hasn't been to church in months), "strictness" can hardly explain the religious social interaction at play. When a man faithfully dons *tallit* and *davens* every morning in his study, even though he is not sure he believes in God, doctrinal purity can hardly be the measure of the religion we are hearing about. And when all of these people tell us about the times they put Golden Rule compassion into practice in their communities, we have to take seriously that our definitions and measures are missing critical dimensions of the religious and spiritual lives of these very modern Americans.

Definitions are notoriously difficult, but by starting with stories we began to see the "family resemblances" that allow actions, relationships, motives, and meanings to fall within a domain we can recognize as religious. Mapping the discursive categories at work in how people talk about religion and spirituality allowed us to see that spirituality spans both Theistic and Extra-theistic ways of seeing the world and that both overlap significantly with what those same people take to be religion. While people in some religious traditions have a single dominant spiritual discourse, not all do. While people with no religious tradition often have little or no spiritual sense of the world, some do. Catholic, mainline Protestant, Black Protestant, and Neopagan communities, in turn, seem to sustain both Theistic *and* Extra-theistic understandings of spirituality.

However we are to define religion, it must include spiritualities of a variety of sorts. Scholars and popular culture often paint religion and spirituality as opposites, but the participants in this study who were most active in organized religion were also most committed to spiritual practices and a spiritual view of the world. There was good reason from previous research to expect this overlap. What we also discovered, however, was that the people who claim there is an opposition between being spiritual and being religious are, for the most part, themselves neither. They are, instead, engaged in a boundary-maintaining discourse that seeks to distance themselves from forms of religion they reject. Any attempt to map the empirical domain of religion and spirituality must reject the misleading effort to draw lines between individual and communal, spirituality and religion.

Recognizing the overlap between religion and spirituality has implications on both sides of that presumed divide. Simply abandoning the study of "religion" in favor of a presumably more inclusive "spirituality" is not an empirically defensible strategy, but neither is it possible simply to maintain existing measures of religious belief and belonging. For the large majority of people who make some claim to a religious sensibility or connection, the nature of their religiousness does not come in a neat package. In practice, accounts of religious belonging, tradition, belief, and spirituality are all implicated in each other, but not in ways that allow us to say that one thing comes before another. Some people have clearly articulated theological beliefs but few spiritual practices. Some have a clear identification with a particular religious tradition but rarely attend. Some are highly committed members of a local congregation but have little spiritual consciousness. Some know exactly what their theology says about moral and economic and political issues, but most do not. Some see the hand of God or the demands of faith in nearly every setting, but most do not. And while many of these things occur together in predictable ways, they constitute clearly separable strands in the religious narratives we heard. Neither a Weberian sense of religion as belief system nor a Durkheimian sense of religion as collective moral community nor a Jamesian sense of solitary experiences of transcendence is fully sufficient to account for how religion and spirituality find their way into everyday life.

Nor does the picture become clearer when we turn to what people do. Some engage in a rigorous round of spiritual practices that are taught by their traditions, but others experiment or do nothing spiritual at all. Recall the variety of things we heard about. While nearly everyone talked about prayer in one form or another, the habit of reading sacred texts was something cultivated only in some religious traditions and not in most. Beyond those two survey item staples, we heard about special clothing or dietary practices that are also particular to specific religious traditions with a long and fascinating list of other pursuits. Among the things on that list were:

- Consulting with dead ancestors as spiritual guides.
- Consulting with a living spiritual counselor or director.
- Going on a pilgrimage to Medadgorje or Lourdes.
- Having sacred images in a home.
- Keeping a journal.
- Participating in healing rituals for themselves and others.
- Wearing a cross or other religious symbol.
- Getting a tattoo or, in one case, growing dreadlocks as a spiritual journey.

In other words, there is a lot more spiritual activity happening than we know if we just count how many people say they pray and how often. We even miss the number of times that prayer is a simple "Help me get through this." Although that prayer for help fits Riesebrodt's (2010) picture of asking supernatural forces for assistance, many other practices are oriented neither to assistance nor to the supernatural. Asking what people *do,* rather than simply what they believe or where they belong, is a step in the right direction, but the spiritual activity we heard about is broader than many standard definitions of religion would include.

One of the perennial tensions in sociological discussions of religion is whether this plethora of practices should be taken as evidence for modern pluralist individualism or seen as the tenacity of tradition. What we have heard here is that spiritual practices were neither utterly individual nor strictly defined by collective tradition. There is a strong relationship between participation in religious communities and engaging in spiritual practices in everyday life; spiritual community and spiritual practice are in a dynamic relationship with each other. Within every tradition, there are people who are more and less active in pursuing everyday spirituality and more and less inventive in that pursuit. People draw on practices that they learn about from others, both inside and outside traditional religious communities; and occasionally they come up with something genuinely new (meditative mountain biking comes to mind).

Conservative Protestants and Mormons tend to have an exclusively Theistic orientation to spirituality and a well-defined set of prescribed practices, with relatively small (but not absent) spaces for individual variation. Other religiously affiliated people varied more widely in their spiritual orientation and practice. But surely we would not want to label one group more "religious" than the other. All are participating in a social arena in which spiritual cultural practices are being produced, talked about, and enacted. It is an arena with some recognizable clusters of practice, defined both by types of spirituality and by specific religious traditions, but no bright line defines some of these as religious and others not.

Are there, then, any threads running through all of this that allow us to identify something as religious? I think there are, and I want to reclaim two important words as descriptors of those threads. The first of these words is "sacred." Durkheim (1964) told us that religion has to do with "sacred things," and I think he was right. What I think he got wrong, however, is the notion that there is a sharp line dividing sacred and profane. For him, sacred times, objects, and functionaries were "set apart" and could be rendered profane by contact with people and things that had not been properly sanctified. I want to agree with Durkheim that sacred and profane are different ways of looking at and interacting with the world, but I want to blur the line he has drawn, suggesting that it is a continuum more than a dichotomy. From the first page of this book to now, we have heard stories that intermingle ordinary and extraordinary, that speak of mundane actions as religiously significant. A walk in the woods, caring concern for a neighbor, or a new job opportunity can be sacred actions in the world no less than attendance at worship or an hour of meditation. When people speak of their lives in spiritual and religious terms, a common thread that runs through those accounts is that there are things in the world they recognize as more than mundane.

But just what is that "more than?" To begin to tackle that, I want to reclaim the word "transcendence," but neither in its "otherworldly" nor its "supernatural" guise. Rational choice understandings of religion begin with notions about human desires for rewards and our willingness to "utilize and manipulate the supernatural" to get them, even if they can "be obtained only in a nonempirical (usually posthumous) context" (i.e., are otherworldly; Stark and Finke 2000, 277). Religion, for rational choice theorists, represents organized systems for bargaining with a nonempirical power for rewards that cannot be otherwise obtained. It is supernatural and otherworldly, or it is powerless to provide us with rewards, and we will abandon it for cheaper routes to pleasure. Riesebrodt's approach to religion removes some of the more crass images of bargaining for goods, but he still frames matters in terms of religious claims to "ward off misfortune, surmount crises, and provide blessings and salvation by communicating with superhuman powers" (2010, 72). That definition goes a long way in encompassing what most of the world's religious history has entailed.

However, the Extra-theistic and Ethical spiritualities we have discovered among our participants make clear that people often recognize a spiritual dimension in practices and experiences that have neither magical intent nor a location outside everyday reality. Recognizing the awesomeness of nature, the ideal of the inner self, the call of a life of meaning, or the bonds of human connection—all speak of some reality beyond the mundane self and its interests. Each taps a kind of transcendence, an effort to reach beyond a world that is merely ordinary. So, too, of course, do claims about the presence and actions of deities in the world. It is that *fundamental recognition of a "more than ordinary" dimension in life* that is the common thread running through all the spiritual stories we have explored. It is sacred and it is transcendent, and this sacred consciousness constitutes the domain sociologists of religion can and should be studying.

But do such apparently transitory engagements with a spiritual dimension in life have any social significance? Do they have the power to shape action in the world? Theorists and philosophers who have written about the modern world have often talked about the absence, shrinkage, or sequestration of transcendence. Rational scientific and systematically organized human action in the world have pushed any sense of enchantment to the side, along with whatever authority a sacred cosmos may have held over human action. It is an argument made well by Adam Seligman, but also found in the work of Charles Taylor (2007) and many others. Seligman says, "If that moral authority upon which the self rests is not conceived of in transcendent terms, its definition can only be immanent" (2000, 42). He goes on to argue that the self must "define itself in relation to something authoritative if it is to exist as something beyond a bundle of desires" (54), and it is essential that this moral ordering come from something external. Without transcendent authority, he says, we have no reliable way to call each other to account.[1] In this view, the kind of "something beyond" represented by Extra-theistic spirituality is too weak a mechanism to have social consequences. By appearing to ground religion only in individual experience, it seems to become a shadow of its former transcendent and authoritative self.

I am not, however, convinced. There are, it seems to me, both inherent moral strands in the Extra-theistic stories we heard and an implicit moral community in the connections generated and sustained in any common spiritual discourse. Spiritual stories about the meaning of life are not without the power to shape action just because they include no deities. The power and authority of spiritual claims is not, that is, a dichotomy based on the presence or absence of a supernatural authority. The capacity for moral community and authority should instead be seen as a continuum, allowing us to look for the conditions under which sacred consciousness is more and less consequential. How is a sacred consciousness related to communities of discourse and practice, and what effects does that variation produce? To what extent is it related to forces and beings that are understood to be superhuman, and what everyday difference does that make?

Sacred consciousness can, in other words, have significant implications for power, agency, and action. Life narratives always provide direction to action, supplying the plots for what is envisioned as possible.[2] Accounts are never merely accounts; they also shape reality. What matters is not only the shape of the narrative itself but also the nature of the conversation in which the story is told. We can ask not only about the effects of different visions of the spiritual world but also about the size, location, and cohesiveness of the spiritual tribe telling the story. When there are shared narratives about the availability of divine power to change the world, human action is often changed accordingly. Far from suppressing agency in deference to otherworldly solutions, as social movement research makes clear, shared spiritual stories have this-worldly power (Ganz 2009; Smith 1996; Wood 1999).

Sociologists seeking to understand religion unnecessarily limit the scope of our inquiry, then, when we insist that religion be contained in an authoritative, supernatural realm that is itself contained in recognized institutional boxes. Having asked a wide range of Americans to tell us about their everyday lives, the stories we have called "spiritual narratives" are distinct from the stories we have identified as mundane and ordinary. There is in these stories a consciousness of transcendence, a recognition of a sacred dimension that goes beyond the ordinary. It need not be embodied in a deity, although it very often is. It need not be systematized into a set of doctrines, although centuries of work by legions of theologians have provided ample resources. It need not be organized into legally recognized institutions, although the modern world has tended to try. It need not even have a name, although some forms of commonly used language seem inevitable in each society and time. When sociologists study religion, it is this sacred consciousness that is at the heart of our enterprise. Recognizing a wider range of variation will allow us more powerful explanatory models.

Religion in the Domains of Everyday Life

Sacred consciousness is not, then, something that comes in all-or-nothing, everywhere or nowhere, forms. I have argued throughout this book that we can identify social conditions that make such a consciousness more and less likely and social interactions that are sites of production for it. We can also assess the relative effectiveness of secular powers arrayed against it. By locating the stories we gathered across a broad range of everyday contexts, we hoped to provide a more nuanced picture of religion's presence and absence, and that has allowed us to undermine the sorts of either/or alternatives implied in secularization theories, to see where the mundane world is most power-fully disenchanted and where its interactions are suffused with more-than-mundane significance.

Household life has often been thought of as "private" and therefore per-haps more likely to be a sacralized space than other domains of everyday life. It is a space in which a small group of actors have relative freedom to include or exclude religious life. In fact, nearly half the stories we heard about house-holds contained at least some spiritual content. Stories attributed action to divine intervention, they described people and places as sacred, and they nar-rated activities in terms of and in relation to the religious traditions of which they are a part. But some aspects of household life were more likely to evoke spiritual stories than others. Where stories described the goings-on of just the household itself, spiritual meanings were more likely to be present than when the stories in question had to do with the intersection of households with work, leisure, school, and the like. Where the rest of the world impinges, the free space of the household is less likely to be described in religious terms.

Work is a key part of the impinging rest of the world, and here the picture is complicated. Stories about work were less likely to be told as spiritual sto-ries, but those that were spiritual emerged from three distinct social processes that provide critical clues to the way spirituality is implicated in otherwise mundane settings. One spiritual pathway into the world of work is the reli-gious commitment of the individual herself. Individuals who are prone to a strong sacred consciousness bring that consciousness to work. A second fac-tor at play, however, is the nature of the work itself, and a third is the interac-tional context of the workplace.

Starting with individual predispositions is predictable enough, but over and above individual characteristics, some jobs lend themselves to spiritual understanding more readily than others. Work that involves service to others or that explores the realms of beauty and imagination seems to invite spiritual definition. And work that deals with the limits of human existence is more often narrated as a spiritual pursuit. By contrast, work in business and related occupations as well as labor in what is euphemistically called "service work," was not likely to be defined by the people in it as a spiritual enterprise. People who work in menial jobs as well as those whose primary work is the accumulation of profits, rarely say that what they do is done to the glory of God—Weber's iron cage is, at least in this sense, alive and well (Weber 1958). Such jobs can still be spiritual pursuits but only insofar as dedicated individuals, supported by active participation in a religious community, look hard for the sacred content in what they do. Here we have macrosocial structures (occupations) and individual characteristics implicated in complementary and complex ways to define a given workplace situation as religious or not.

Between those macro- and individual factors lies, however, the third path through which spiritual elements flow into the workplace, namely the interactions of the workers. Listening to stories about work made very clear that there is a great deal more going on every day than merely an economic exchange of labor for monetary reward. Across every occupational sector, nearly a third of all the stories we heard were primarily about the *people* involved more than about the work being done or the power being exercised. And that does not count the substantial number of stories (almost 40 percent) that were about the work itself but were collective rather than individual accounts—not what *I* do, but what *we* do. Understanding the sociology of the workplace is more than understanding bureaucratic positions and economic struggles; it is also about how sociality shapes this domain in which people spend so much of their lives. As Pettinger (2005) points out, conversations among co-workers weave constantly into the spaces between official work requirements.

Over the course of our interviews, photos, and diaries, we heard well over two hundred accounts of job-related relationships; and more than any other kind of work story, these were shaped by spiritual sensibilities and religious dynamics. Michelle Winter, for instance, is very clear that overt religious talk or practice cannot be part of doing her social work job, but religion has shaped the values she brings to the job, and she finds reassurance in the times when she can talk about those connections with others at work who share her faith. Like Michelle, a substantial minority of the American workers in our study have made friends with a religiously likeminded person at work. They have thereby formed what might be seen as a transitory spiritual tribe. Their connection is not wholly defined by their spiritual sensibilities or pursuits, but those sensibilities are part of what binds them together. To the extent that such spiritual mini-tribes exist, they considerably increase the overlap between work and spirituality.

What also emerged in our stories is a picture of many places in the everyday public realm that are almost entirely secular. The neighborhoods in which people live, for instance, were seen through the lens of choice and comfort, not as sacred space. Surely many Americans think of their neighborhoods as extensions of their "parish" or as linked to the shul to which they walk for Saturday services. Some sacralize their streets for annual feast days, but most simply walk the dog and wave to neighbors they hope share enough of their view of the world to keep the property values intact. Similarly, the ways people spend their money are routinely secular, even when they may otherwise opine that materialism is a bad thing.

Political action was rarely the subject of overtly religious or spiritual reflection, either. In spite of the religiously infused political divisions in American culture, stories of everyday life rarely crossed into that domain. There are traces of the influence of religious traditions in the issues some participants emphasized over others—both occasional echoes of the culture wars and occasional adoption of a social justice agenda—but people rarely made direct connections between their religious lives and their political concerns. Most of our participants were moderately socially concerned, tried to stay informed, voted, and left the active work of politics for others; and they were unlikely to tell political stories in which religion plays a role. Whatever it is that has linked religious identities with political division did not show up directly at the level of everyday interaction.

When we turn from public political contention to other forms of public mobilization, the story is quite different. Voluntary charitable action in local communities was a place where the teachings and the practices of religious communities were clearly present. The religiously engaged stood in significant contrast to the unengaged, not only in telling more frequent stories about community problems but also in the degree of agency they exhibited in responding to those problems. Being part of a congregation constitutes a rather robust form of membership in a spiritual tribe, a membership that comes with both expectations and capacities. Other forms of civic mobilization clearly exist, but the sense of moral agency congregational members have flows naturally from the social capital, civic skills, and communication links generated in congregational life. Study after study has found that, controlling for all the expected other social factors that might influence volunteering, people who participate in congregational life are simply more likely to volunteer in the community than are people who do not attend services (e.g., Putnam and Campbell 2010).[3] Doing good for people in need is part of what congregations and their members are expected to do (Ammerman 2005a).

The effects of participation in an active spiritual tribe were also seen in stories about health and illness. Human bodies and their well-being are not just individual projects; concern for physical well-being is one of the things that bind people together into extended communities of care. Stories about the physical struggles of family and friends were as numerous as stories about the participant's own health. The obligation to care for people who are sick is most directly felt within a household, but it also extends into the larger family circle, especially to aging parents. One in four of our participants (one in three among the middle-aged segment) told everyday stories about the fragile health of parents. What we also heard in those stories was that people who are involved in religious communities and who have an active spiritual life negotiate all the everyday dilemmas of care no less pragmatically than their most secular neighbors, but they are likely to do so with an expectation that their religious communities will be there to support them.

Caring about the health of people *beyond* one's own family is also something that seems to be part of the culture of religious communities. More than one in four of the regular attenders told at least one story about a sick friend about whom they were concerned or whom they had helped. Among nonattenders we heard no stories that involved caring for people beyond extended families. Religious participants are aware of and tell stories about the physical difficulties of a fairly broad range of others, including people they know from church or synagogue but also occasionally including neighbors, co-workers, and other friends. At least in this sense, they seem to adopt others into their tribe, as people to whom they owe the obligations implied in the Golden Rule, whether or not those people share their specific religious beliefs or practices.

What about the matter of one's own health, illness, and even death? Have these central existential concerns remained religiously meaningful? Or has scientific medicine truly become the modern substitute for religious ritual? While medicine is seemingly a highly secularized realm, death has always posed a mystery to human beings. Indeed, the experiences surrounding death were among the most predictably spiritual of the experiences we heard about, even for otherwise less spiritually inclined people. The spiritual dimension was more likely to be there in stories about the end of life than in stories about eating right and exercising, more likely to be there in stories about crises than in stories about routine difficulties. Spiritual consciousness varies, that is, inversely with perceived human agency. In routine matters of health and wellness, the stories we heard started with modern medicine and modern science, intertwining whatever spiritual inclinations an individual might already have. In complex crises, even less routinely religious people narrated life in a spiritual mode. Physical bodies, in all their complications, are neither solely profane nor solely sacred but a complex mix of the two. To the extent that suffering and death are a human constant, we may expect spiritual practices, explanations, and the comfort of spiritual communities to continue to play a role.

In each of these arenas of everyday social life, then, the terms of action are largely mundane and secular—no particular surprise there. What people do in their households, at work, taking care of their health, or engaging in politics is largely narrated as a story whose characters are defined by routine roles and whose actions are aimed at practical ends. Indeed, I would note that this is probably not so different from the situation faced by most people in most times and places—much of life is simply not suffused with enchantment and probably never was (Douglas 1983). But neither are these everyday arenas devoid of spiritual meaning. Whatever we are going to say about the lines between sacred and secular, they are not drawn at the churchyard gate or synagogue door. Under some circumstances, people take their religious sensibilities with them in ways that shape their everyday behavior.

That does not mean that sacred injunctions then convert a secular place into a religious one. Nor is this the imposition of doctrinal or moral claims from religious communities on other sectors of life. It is also not about some mysterious generic force ("religion") that produces "effects," such as political attitudes or marital stability or even hard work. Our understanding of the presence of religion in everyday life is not enhanced by imagining a clear line between religion and everything else, a line that can be crossed in order to enlarge or contract the territory belonging to one or the other. What I am suggesting is that our modern preoccupation with identifying a distinctly "religious" domain has blinded us to the way the everyday world remains enchanted. A significant minority of all the stories we heard about everyday life were stories where sacred consciousness was present. Given the overrepresentation in our sample of people with college educations and high incomes, this is especially striking. We are not talking here about the "sigh of the oppressed creature" or the grasping of the uneducated for explanations. With a model of sacred consciousness that does not force respondents into either/or answers, we are able to see the presence of religion in places and situations that are *also* secular.

It is ironically the recognition of the power and presence of sacred consciousness that makes religion so often the object of state control and repression. Yang's (2012) account of the last sixty years of Chinese history is a vivid portrayal of the tug of war between the communist state and the myriad spiritual tribes that were never fully suppressed even under the most brutal sanctions of the Cultural Revolution. As he and others point out, every modern nation has sought to regulate religion.[4] Even presumably "secular" European states have found themselves embroiled in controversy when Muslim headscarves implicitly introduce a religious discourse into "secular" public space (Chambers 2007). Whether an officially recognized "state church" or simply the "tax exempt" imprimatur of the American Internal Revenue Service, no nation-state (despite what its constitution may say) truly allows free range to religious interaction.[5] Some have argued, in fact, that the very category "religion" is the modern byproduct of attempts to organize and regulate a form of association and interaction that posed problems for bureaucrats and professionals who had more "rational" aims in mind (Asad 1993). States have indirectly recognized the reality and power of spiritual conversations within all sorts of spiritual tribes. Household veneration of ancestors, modes of dress in public, communal exercise in a park—all can constitute unwelcome competition for authority. Sacred consciousness takes many forms and finds expression in many collective representations, large and small. Even in efforts at state regulation, we see the continued enchantment of everyday life and the intermingling of sacred and profane.

Explaining Religious Presence

One continuing theme in this research is that sacralizing everyday social spaces depends in significant part on individuals who bring religious sensibilities with them to those spaces. But that is surely not surprising. One of the dominant strands in what has been called "secularization theory" has argued that religion could survive the modern world as a certain form of individual consciousness. This was Luckmann's (1967) theory—he called it "Invisible Religion"—and it is essentially where Durkheim arrived in his essay on "Individualism and the Intellectuals" (Durkheim 1898 [1975]). Luckmann and the functionalists solve the problem of modern religion by positing "meaning" and "worldview" as quasi-religious human universals carried in individual consciousness. Religion disappears as a social institution but is replaced by individual worldviews and values (cf. Parsons 1964). Looked at from one angle, what I have described here are indeed individual people narrating the actions of their everyday lives, with some of those individuals more likely to weave a layer of spirituality into the fabric than others.

What the secularization theories do not make clear, however, is how that individual consciousness comes to be. How do modern individuals find themselves with a sacred consciousness in a world that is (according to this theory) increasingly devoid of religious institutions? Are they implying that it is actually constitutive of human being, sans social formation? Nor do functionalists clarify how we recognize a religious consciousness in a world without commonly shared religious symbols and cultures? What I want to suggest is that the answer to both those questions lies in expanding our understanding of the shape of collective religious life to include the wide range of spiritual tribes I have been describing in this book. That is made possible by recognizing the permeable boundaries of all institutions and the portability of the conversations that allow elements of identity to be shaped and carried across those boundaries. Sacred consciousness is neither confined to individual minds nor to self-contained religious institutions, but it is still social.

In making this argument, I want to undo a fundamental misconstrual of the nature of religious identity. Religious identity is not an essentialist social category. One of the things that narrative theories of identity make clear is that identities are always multistranded and intersectional. I am female, American, daughter, mother, wife, professor, baseball fan, Baptist of a certain sort, and quite a lot more; and in any given interaction, some combination of the stories of where I am in my progression through any of those identities may govern how I proceed. Which narratives are operative will depend on the particular combination of spiritual (and not-spiritual) tribes that is listening. What is odd about the way we have often understood religious identities is that we have assumed that they have an all-or-nothing character that few other identities are expected to have. By this account, one either is or is not religious. An action either is or is not spiritual. A place is either sacred or profane. And so on. What I am suggesting, then, is that even as we look at the presumably individual stories I have been describing, we should expect them to be *both* sacred and secular at once, continually evolving in multiple conversations.

I am building here on what George Herbert Mead (1934) and the symbolic interactionists first began to teach us about the way identities are constructed in interaction. As Berger and Luckmann (1967, 152) put it, "The most important vehicle of reality maintenance is conversation." We should, that is, be looking for the sites where conversation produces and is produced by the multistranded spiritual and religious identities taken to be present by those who are participating in these conversations. Spiritual narratives are produced in interaction, carried by conversants from one place to another, and redeployed and reworked in each new telling. This is not a simple "appropriation" of tradition into everyday life but a process of intersection and creativity. There is an intertwining of individual and communal. Religion is found in the places where individual agency and shared symbols intersect, where elements of socially recognized traditions meet the everyday situations of ordinary people. No part of social life is immune, although a variety of social powers can be brought to bear in suppressing individual and collective perception of sacred presence. Explaining religion's presence means looking for those conversations and interactions as sites of production, sites where sacred consciousness is being socially created and sustained.

Among the most important of those sites are the official religious institutions. One of the most striking results of this research has been the degree to which participation in organized religion matters. In nearly every systematic comparison we have attempted to examine, people who attend services more frequently are different in ways that go beyond demographic differences or differences based on the type of religious tradition or differences based on the individual's levels of spiritual practice and virtuosity. So when we ask about the sites in which spiritual discourse is produced, congregations and other organized spiritual groups are both obvious places to look and surprisingly downplayed in a culture and a discipline that have glorified the life of the individual spiritual seeker. When people do not have regular sites of interaction where spiritual discourse is a primary lingua franca, they are simply less likely to adopt elements of spirituality in their accounts of who they are and what they do with themselves. If they do not learn the language, it does not shape their way of being in the world. They can neither speak of—nor perhaps even see—a layer of spiritual reality alongside the mundane everyday world. Conversely, the more deeply embedded people are in these organized sites of spiritually infused conversation, the more likely they are to carry strands of that conversation with them. It's not that they have learned a set of doctrines or subscribed to a set of behavioral prescriptions—although they may have done both. It is that they have learned to "speak religion" as one of their dialects.

Within the bounds of a given religious community, then, people develop a way of talking about life that carries within it expectations about the presence of divine actors and the realities of mysteries beyond human comprehension and the normative goodness of "doing unto others as you would have them do unto you." As people chat over a potluck dinner or pray during a meeting of a women's group, the everyday stories they tell foreground spiritual interpretations. They come to think of sacred and secular as intertwined. What happens in these religious gatherings is not just a matter of otherworldly ritual and doctrinal teaching. What happens is the creation of a particular kind of conversational space. In some sense this is what Berger (1969) meant when he described modern religion as existing in "sheltering enclaves."

But it is more. These are not enclaves with high walls, where the sacred world is kept pure and well defended. Their ability to be powerful producers of sacred consciousness depends not just on their ability to evoke sacred reality in powerful ritual events or in coherent explanations of the cosmos. Rather, their power as sacred culture producers is in the degree to which they allow sacred and profane to intermingle. Recall that the people with the most robust sense of sacred presence in everyday life are those who participate in religious activities that allow for conversation and relationship. The conversations in which they engage inside the religious community are full of the stuff of everyday life, with mundane and sacred realities intermingling. People are going to the doctor and praying for healing, exchanging babysitting services and holding up religious ideals of family life, hearing sermons about the injustices in the world and mobilizing petition drives. That mixture is part of what makes those conversations portable. Congregations gain their potency as spiritual tribes, not through their exclusivity or high boundaries but to the degree that they create spaces for and encourage opportunities to imagine and speak about everyday realities through the lens of sacred consciousness.

Beyond the religious community itself, we do not live under a sacred canopy, so our interactions are not exclusively with others who share our assumptions about how to live. But what we have observed in this research is the presence of other forms of spiritual community and conversation, present in nearly every possible social arena. People move through life with a shifting cast of characters in a shifting array of institutional settings. The characters with whom they share the stage are not neatly compartmentalized, even if there is a regularity to who we meet where. Narratives from one part of life are drawn on and refashioned across those domains, and sometimes there are social occasions in which religious and spiritual assumptions enter the conversation. What we have seen in this study is that "the sacred" may be carried in individual minds, but it becomes real in conversations that can happen in sometimes unlikely places.

How are those conversational spaces created? Certainly we have seen that some social locations are more conducive than others. Households and health crises, charitable activities and serving professions—these are some of the everyday life places where the boundaries between sacred and secular seem to be most permeable. What I also want to suggest, however, is that we should pay attention to the nature of the relationships in which those conversations take place. Conversations require multiple conversants. A spiritually inclined person has to find another person who is at least open to talking about the world in terms that include religious dimensions. Certainly there are some

Bible-thumping Evangelists out there who will start a religious conversation whether the other person wants to listen or not. But mostly people of faith seem simply to be finding each other. We may not be surprised to find that roughly three-quarters of household partners share a common religious affiliation, but it is surprising that two-thirds of work-based friendships were described to us as religiously homogamous—not necessarily people sharing exactly the same religious tradition but people who think of each other as religiously similar. And in those religiously similar work friendships, people were more likely to report that they talk about religion.

This recognition and sorting process is, I think, a critical phenomenon for us to begin to understand more clearly. It underlies the title for this chapter and takes its inspiration from Michel Maffesoli's *The Time of Tribes* (1995). His is a postmodern argument about how societies can be held together, and I do not wish to rehearse or endorse his entire postmodern project; but his description of the shifting socialities of everyday life is helpful. "Neo-tribalism is characterized by fluidity, occasional gatherings and dispersal," he says (76). He notes that even in a complex social world of otherwise strangers, we recognize some others as people with whom we share a common bond, a set of customs, and shared sentiment. We use displays of clothing and body that are sometimes theatrical and sometimes subtle, cultural signals that allow us to recognize our fellow tribal members. Think, for instance, about the way we recognize neighborhoods as more or less attractive and the way that shapes our urban landscape (Brown-Saracino 2009; *Economist* 2008). Or think about what people call "gaydar," the ability to assess sexual orientation from various indirect visual and behavioral cues (Rieger et al. 2010). There are things we say about ourselves, more and less intentionally, by the very way we dress, walk, speak, and carry ourselves. What I am suggesting here is that religious identities can be part of the package of cultural cues that constitute the ever-shifting tribes of modern society.

It is worth pausing here to ask about the effects of religion's presence among the identity cues people present to each other in everyday situations. Some cues, distinctive dress perhaps, may signal that the participants come from very different spiritual tribes. Religious differences may then divide and alienate people who are otherwise sharing the same (otherwise nonreligious) social space. Much of recent anxiety about "religion and public life" comes from exactly this fear that difference is being unnecessarily introduced into a space that would better be left neutral. In other instances, however, religious differences may be bridged by the commonality of interaction focused in that same social space (Warner 1997). What people share in common may create a sufficient social bond to allow religious differences to be accommodated—but only if those differences are, in fact, recognized to be present. Putnam and Campbell (2010) note the increased tolerance that seems to result from interaction with "my pal Al" who "just happens to be" religiously different from me. So long as Al is a religiously anonymous co-worker, however, no religious bridging occurs. If we wish to understand religious difference, division, and tolerance, then, we will need to understand everyday religious identity cues and conversations no less than the pronouncements of officials and the proceedings of official interfaith dialogues.

We will also need to understand the corrosive way American politics has affected these same religious identity mechanisms. Especially since the 1990s, religious identities and political identities are increasingly aligned, with an increasingly wide chasm between left and right (Green et al. 2003; Putnam and Campbell 2010). Prior to the revolutions of the 1960s, denominational preference was much more likely to be influenced by social class position than by political party. Today, political cues are part of the cultural identity present in many local congregations (Bean 2009). People choose where to belong, or not to belong at all, based in part on what they see and hear about the political world (Hout and Fischer 2002). The conversations in local religious communities have become, then, part of the political echo chamber that keeps too many Americans from encountering, conversing with, and working alongside people who are outside their own political tribe. To the extent that religious identity cues help to reinforce that division, we are the poorer for it.

In the world of everyday life, sacred stories can be found, for good and ill, throughout the social world. There is much more to learn about how and to what effect sacred consciousness intertwines with mundane realities. Sacred consciousness is produced both in institutionalized spiritual tribes—what we recognize as traditions and religious communities—and in the shifting situational bonds of conversations among people who recognize some spiritual common ground. There is no single social location in which to look for religion. Still, different kinds of social location and connection matter. Different kinds of spiritual stories provide more and less powerful images of agency in the world. Different kinds of religious identity cues make cooperative interaction more and less likely. The sociological questions for analysis remain.

PARTICIPANTS AND THEIR RELIGIOUS COMMUNITIES

Sampling techniques are described in Chapter One, along with a discussion of some of the limitations of the sample. The quota sample employed by the project resulted in ninety-five participants distributed across most of the American religious and nonreligious spectrum. The Pew Religious Landscape survey allows us to compare their characteristics to roughly similar categories of tradition and attendance in the American population (see Table A.1). In broad contours, participants encompass most of that religious landscape in roughly representative numbers.

Recruiting participants who were religiously affiliated involved selecting religious communities from among the typical range of traditions and selecting clusters of five quota-designated participants from each. The congregations have all been given pseudonyms in the text. They include the following:

Mainline Protestant

- All Saints Episcopal, a classic New England, predominantly White parish, averaging up to one hundred in attendance in an affluent Boston suburb.
- Grimsby United Church of Christ, the other classic New England, predominantly White, congregation in the same Boston suburb—same social location, different theological and liturgical tradition. It is about twice as large.
- South Street Presbyterian is in an urban neighborhood of Atlanta. Predominantly White, it has an average attendance of about two hundred.

Table A.1. Religious Distribution of the Sample Compared to
National Population

Religious Tradition	Frequency of Attendance				
	Never	Rarely	Average	Often	Total
Number in study sample (target number Pew survey would suggest)	*Number in study sample (target number Pew Survey would suggest)*				
Mainline Protestant	14 (18)	0 (1)	2 (5)	9 (3)	3 (5)	14 (14)
Conservative Protestant	20 (26)	0 (1)	6 (5)	4 (3)	10 (11)	20 (20)
Catholic	20 (24)	2 (1)	6 (7)	3 (4)	9 (8)	20 (20)
African American Protestant	10 (7)	0 (<1)	2 (2)	6 (2)	2 (6)	10 (10)
Jewish	10 (2)	0 (1)	5 (5)	3 (2)	2 (2)	10 (11)
Latter-day Saint	5 (2)	0 (<1)	0 (<1)	1 (<1)	4 (4)	5 (5)
Neopagan	5(n/a)	0	0	5	0	5
All others	0(5)	n/a	n/a	n/a	n/a	n/a
No affiliation	11 (16)	11 (4)	0 (6)	0 (<1)	0 (<1)	11 (11)
Total in sample(total suggested by Pew survey)	95 (100)	13 (10)	21 (33)	31 (14)	30 (38)	95 (95)

Source: National figures calculated from the Pew Religious Landscape Survey (Religion and Public Life 2008). Our "often" approximates Pew's "once a week or more." "Rare" approximates Pew's "seldom" plus Pew's "few times a year," and "average" approximates Pew's "once or twice a month."

Conservative Protestant

- Center Street Church is a thriving evangelical congregation in the city of Boston. Predominantly White but with a noticeable international contingent, they average at least six hundred at their main Sunday morning service.
- Brookfield Baptist Church is affiliated with the Southern Baptist Convention and situated near the border between city and suburb in Atlanta. It is predominantly White but seeking to grow from its current one hundred or so attenders by reaching out to a more diverse set of neighbors.

- Atlanta Vineyard Church is a rapidly growing, mixed-ethnic charismatic congregation located in the city.
- Deer Valley Church is a nondenominational, predominantly White, evangelical megachurch, located in an Atlanta exurb, and attracting well over 2,000 each Sunday.

Black Protestant

- Cornerstone Baptist Church is a historic African American congregation affiliated with the American Baptist Churches, USA. Situated in an affluent close-in suburb of Boston, they average about 150 in attendance.
- New Beginnings is a historic African Methodist Episcopal church in a poor urban neighborhood in Atlanta. Attendance averages around three hundred.

Roman Catholic

- St. Felix, a mixed-ethnic parish in a Boston urban neighborhood, averages a hundred or so in each of several ethnic-specific Masses.
- St. Sabina, another mixed-ethnic parish, in a different Boston urban neighborhood, is slightly larger than St. Felix.
- St. Michael's, a large, mostly White parish is in a close-in suburb of Atlanta. Full of families, it draws 1,000 or more on a weekend.
- St. Agnes is a mixed-race/multiethnic parish in Atlanta that is not quite as large as St. Michael's.

Jewish

- Congregation Sinai is a Conservative Jewish congregation in suburban Boston. It draws up to 150 for special ceremonies but has a smaller core of regular attenders.
- Temple Beth Torah is a very large Reform Jewish congregation in a close-in suburb of Atlanta. It too has a regular core of a few dozen worshippers, with much larger crowds for special events.

Other

- A Neopagan circle of a couple of dozen members, is all White and mostly women. They meet in a rural area outside Atlanta.
- Cromer, Third Ward, a mixed-ethnic Latter-day Saints congregation averaging about 150 in attendance, is located in the exurbs of Boston.

CODING AND ANALYZING STORIES

Initial qualitative coding strategies began to be developed as the research team moved deeply into the data gathering. Amy Moff Hudec, Roman Williams, Melissa Scardaville, Tracy Scott, and I gathered in Atlanta at about the midpoint to begin to identify the themes we were hearing. The analysis, in other words, began to emerge in the midst of our interaction with each other and with our participants. By the time we finished gathering data in early 2008, had transcripts of all the interviews and diaries and field notes, and had catalogued 1,311 photographs, the sheer volume and depth of information was daunting. All 330 texts were entered into the qualitative data analysis software MaxQDA, allowing us to code and eventually sort the data to look for patterns in the stories. The original research team was joined in 2008 by Emily Ronald and Kevin Taylor, graduate students in Boston University's Religion and Society program, and we all became a team of coders, meeting in person and via Skype to compare notes as we developed the analytical structure we would use for our ordering of the stories. Coding was done in standard qualitative analysis style (Lofland and Lofland 1984; Miles and Huberman 1994), applying multiple and often overlapping thematic codes to whatever portion of text constituted a logical unit.

This initial coding laid the foundation for the next level of analysis. Different domains of everyday life were used as a primary organizing scheme for an initial sorting of the stories and organizing of this book. Within each domain, the primary unit of analysis for the second stage was the *narrative* itself. That, however, is not as straightforward as it might seem. People rarely told a story in a contiguous beginning-to-end fashion. They would begin and need to be prompted to elaborate. They would chase a rabbit. Or they would pick up new details and threads much later in the conversation. The first analytical task was simply identifying and naming the stories. Even this relatively small number of participants produced literally thousands of them, and the work on each of the chapters in this book began by cataloguing and naming the narratives to be analyzed.

A central question for each narrative was the presence or absence of "spiritual" or "religious" content. There were many ways for a story to be coded as pertaining to "religion or spirituality." It might directly mention a deity as an actor in the story. It might be explicitly describing an event as "spiritual" or "religious." It might be a story about a named religious tradition or group. It might be about a ritual or practice that the participant considered to be religious or spiritual. In other words, at this basic yes-or-no level, we included both commonsense identification of references to religion and an expansive identification of elements that the participant named as spiritual or religious, whether or not they fit typical cultural or scholarly designations as such.

A nuanced analysis of the meanings of "spirituality" is the subject of Chapter Two. All of the things described there—from references to mysterious happenings to references to ethical commitments or awe-inspiring natural beauty—were coded as spiritual if the participant identified them as such. Specific dimensions of religious practice—service attendance, fulfilling ritual obligations, activities sponsored by churches and synagogues, displaying religious objects—were included, as well. As I show in Chapter Two, the line between "religion" and "spirituality" is distinctly blurred, and one of the aims of this study is precisely to highlight that overlap. When participants made a point of highlighting what they saw as a difference, that becomes part of the story. When they are simply describing all the many ways in which they encounter nonordinary realities, the language of "religious" and "spiritual" will be used interchangeably and in tandem. These are categories that emerge from the stories themselves.

Having selected the text sections relevant to the domain of each chapter—households, religious communities, work, and the like—the cataloguing of stories began by establishing inductively the range of content on a variety of story elements.[1] For instance, what kinds of characters appeared in the story? The range in households included spouses and partners, children, extended family of all sorts, and so on. The range for work included co-workers, bosses, clients, and customers as well as friends and family. This detail allows us to see how the telling of spiritual stories may vary depending on what other characters are in the story.

Stories were also coded for the specific content or focus of the activity, but the range obviously varied by domain. For instance, when coding spiritual practices, the range encompassed all the activities described in Chapter Three. In coding religious participation, the range included music, preaching, other ritual activities, administrative work, care work, and the like. Among stories about the body, the focus ranged from exercise and other health practices to chronic illness and death. Again, the detail about what activities were being described allowed analysis of when and how human action was sometimes sacralized.

In some domains, other aspects of the stories were added to the analysis, as well. For religious participation, I coded for whether the story was about an activity in which the person had a leadership role. For religious practices, I coded for the range of material objects and settings that were described. For public activities, I paid attention to the form of political participation and the degree of agency being expressed as well as to the issue that is the focus of the story.

Across domains, stories were coded for whether the action was a one-time memorable event in the past, an ongoing routine pattern, or something anticipated in the future. Similarly, all stories across domains were coded for the emotional tone of the account. Was the story told with positive affects such as joy or humor, pride or satisfaction, or with negative affects such as anxiety or fear, sadness or frustration?

Each story, with codes describing its various contours, was entered in an SPSS spreadsheet. All the basic demographic information on the storyteller was added, as well, so that it was possible to compare stories across cultural locations and religious traditions, across gender and age and ethnicity, and along a variety of other lines suggested as the analysis progressed. From time to time, key differences are presented in the text via tables with numbers, but most of that quantitative analysis remains behind the scenes. When the text says that more stories of a certain type were religious or spiritual, the analysis behind the scenes was a comparison of means (t-test) or cross-tabulation (chi-square test) that showed the difference to be statistically significant. With several hundred stories within each domain, this statistical sorting has made it possible to note how stories are told differently by people in different social situations.

APPENDIX 3

RESEARCH PROTOCOLS

I. Demographic Data (completed by participant)

1. Are you male or female? _____
2. In what year were you born?_____
3. What is your occupation (or what was it before you retired)? _____

_____

_____

4. What is your highest level of formal education?
   [ ] less than high school [ ] high school diploma
   [ ] some post-high-school work
   [ ] 4-year college degree [ ] post-college graduate work or degree
5. What is your approximate total *annual* household income?
   [ ] under $20,000 [ ] $20,000 to $39,999 [ ] $40,000 to 59,999
   [ ] $60,000 to 79,999 [ ] $80,000 to 99,999 [ ] $100,000 or more
6. From what part(s) of the world does your family originally come? For example, most people who think of themselves as "White" have ancestors from Europe. (check all that apply)
   [ ] Africa [ ] Asia [ ] Europe [ ] North America (i.e., American Indian)
   [ ] Latin America [ ] Caribbean [ ] Pacific Islands [ ] Middle East
   [ ] Other _____
7. If your family has come to the United States in the last hundred years or so, about when did the first of them arrive? _____
8. Who lives with you in your current household? (check all that apply)
   [ ] no one, I live alone
   [ ] spouse [ ] partner (not married) [ ] other adult(s)
   _____ # children under 6 years old _____ # children 6–18 years old
   _____ # older children

II. Protocol for Initial Life History Interview

Guidelines followed by interviewers for semistructured initial conversations with participants.

Basic Contours

I'd like to start by asking you to tell me the story of your life—not everything, of course, but think about the major "chapters" and for each, tell me about the important things that were happening then, where you were living, what you were doing, who was important to you in that chapter of your life. And if you have been involved in religious groups and activities, include those, as well. But mostly I just want you to tell me about who you are.

Probes
1. Which adults (from your family), if any, typically attended this congregation with you?
2. Did you attend Sunday school and/or a religious youth group when you were growing up? [if yes] About how often did you do this?
3. Did religious participation have a major impact on your religious or spiritual life?
4. Is there a story you sometimes tell about going to church/synagogue when you were growing up?
5. Growing up, did you celebrate any major religious life rituals (baptism, bar mitzvah, etc.)?
6. Do you have any particular memorable experiences from your religious upbringing? Were there special people or places that were important to you?
7. If married and/or with kids, are they in the same religious tradition?

Faith

1. Today, how important is religion to you personally? Do you think your faith makes you a different kind of person? What would other people notice? How do you feel about letting others outside of your close friends and family know about your religious affiliation or ideas?
2. How has your faith changed over your lifetime?
   a. Was there ever a time when you weren't part of any faith tradition?
   b. Or times when you were much more involved than now or made a special commitment?

3. Have you ever faced a particularly difficult time, like the death of someone close to you or an illness or financial crisis? What happened? Have you thought about why you think it happened? Who and what helped get you through it?
4. Have you ever been mad at God?

Changes and Decisions

1. Have there been times when your life has changed in a fairly dramatic way? What happened, and what made it a major change?
2. When you have important decisions to make, what guides you? How important, if at all, are
   a. Your [spouse/partner]?
   b. Your other family and friends?
   c. The Bible? The teachings of your church or synagogue? Prayer?

Friends

Most of us have a few people that we are especially close to, that we could talk to about lots of things. These may be the people you live with or friends you see or talk to or phone or email with. So, I want you to think about the four or five people you feel closest to and write down their first name or initials on this pad, and I want to ask you a few questions about them.

a. How do you communicate with each of these people?
b. Which of these are family members?
c. [If working part or full time] Which of these are co-workers?
d. Which are members or regular attenders at your congregation?
e. Which set an example that helps you lead a better religious or spiritual life?
   [OF REMAINING] Set an example that does *not* help you lead a better religious life?
f. Which do you discuss religious matters with?
g. Which actively try to change your religious views or religious practices?
h. Which would you say hold religious views that are very similar to yours?
   [OF REMAINING] Very different?
   [OF REMAINING] Which do you not know if their religious views are similar?

Practices

1. Are there habits and routines that are important to you, that you try to make sure you do nearly every day? What makes them important?
2. Do you wear any special clothing or jewelry that says something about who you are?

3. Are there choices you have made about how you live (food, money, etc.) and what you do *and don't do* that have been important commitments for you?

4. Which holidays are most important to you each year? How do you celebrate them?

5. Are there traditional religious things (lighting candles, praying, reading scripture, etc.) that you do every day or nearly every day?

6. How often do you typically pray?

    a. At your family meals at home, how often does someone say grace or give thanks to God aloud before meals?

    b. [If they have children under eighteen living at home] How often do you
    Talk about religion or God with your children?
    Read the Bible or religious storybooks with your children?

7. Do you ever read any religious books or magazines or watch religious TV programs or movies or radio?

8. Do you have any other spiritual practices that you maintain, ones that are not part of a traditional religion? Where did you learn about them?

9. Do you ever think of things like exercise or being in nature as spiritual?

10. Have you ever experienced something that you would describe as a healing?

Beliefs and Values

1. What does it mean, to you, to be a [Christian]? Is there an example/story you can give me to illustrate that?

2. What do you think God is like? Is there a story about God that sort of "says it all?"

3. Are you the sort of person who thinks a lot about "big questions" like the meaning of life?

4. Have you ever had a time in your life when you have found it hard to believe in anything?

5. Do you like to have a really firm set of beliefs that you are sure about, or are you comfortable living "in the gray areas?" What makes you sure about the things you're sure about?

6. In your everyday life, what sorts of things do you see that you think of as unethical or wrong? What makes these things bad?

7. Do you ever dream about what a better world would look like, perhaps what you hope the world will be like for your kids? Can you describe it for me? What would have to happen for such a change to take place? Are there things you do to try to make that better world possible?

8. [Who have been your heroes/heroines at different times in your life? Why?]

Work

1. Do you currently hold a job outside the home? Can you tell me a little about what you do at work?

2. How did you choose your particular line of work?

3. Tell me about a time when you found your job especially satisfying? Especially frustrating? Can you tell me about a particular success story or great moment at work? Or a heartbreaking failure?

4. What are the hardest things you have to decide about at work? What helps you make those decisions?

Leisure, etc.

1. What kinds of things do you do besides work? (sports, volunteer work, arts, etc.) Tell me about a typical (game, volunteer session, etc.).

2. What television shows do you watch most regularly? Do you ever notice anything in those shows that you would describe as spiritual or religious? Do you find that agreeable or not?

3. Do you use the internet and/or email? What are your most common uses? Do you ever communicate with your religious community via email? Do you ever visit any religious or spiritual sites on the web?

4. Do you usually vote? Have you ever gotten involved in politics? What did you do? Why did you get involved?

5. Are there any other activities that are especially important to you?

Religious Involvement

1. How often have you been attending [church/synagogue/mosque/temple] worship services in the last year?
   a. Does your spouse/partner/children usually attend there with you?
   b. Are you an official member?
   c. What year did you start attending this congregation?

2. Think about a typical time you attended [church]. What is most memorable about being there? Can you describe a typical worship service for me?

3. Would you say that you feel a strong sense of belonging in that congregation? How close do you feel to the pastor or to the primary religious leader at your congregation?

4. If you were the leader of this [church[, what would you change about it? What do you like best about the way it is now?

5. How strongly do you identify with your [church] or [denomination's] beliefs? Are there things you disagree with? Things that even make you angry?

6. In the last few years, have you been a member or participated in any other [church]? Do you currently take part in any activities at any **other** [church]?

7. Are there any other religious organizations or groups that are important in your life?

8. Are you part of a religious small group? What does it do?

Religious Experience

1. Are there things you routinely see or hear that remind you of God (spirituality, etc.)?
2. Have you ever felt like you were exactly where you should be and doing exactly what you should be doing?
3. Have you ever felt like God (or angels or saints) was really present, directly helping or guiding you?
   a. or punishing you?
4. Do you think there are supernatural forces in the world? Are they good or evil or both? Which is stronger, the good or the evil? Is there a time when you've experienced this yourself?

Summing Up

What would you want to tell your grandchildren about your life? [Or what would you want people to remember about you?]

III. Sample Guidelines for Photo Taking

Think about the PLACES that are most important to you. They may be special because of what you do there, how you feel there, what you experience or remember there, or who you are with or think of when you are there. This might be your kitchen table, a favorite park or forest, a memorial or statue, your back porch, your church or synagogue, your desk or easy chair, the golf course where you play, almost anywhere. Often places will be important because of the people in them, so feel free to include people in your pictures.

In each place take one or two pictures. We're not looking for professional quality—just a snapshot that will capture the sense of the place.

Your camera will take twenty-seven pictures, but if you don't need that many to cover the places you want to record, that is fine. Please do try to take pictures of at least five or six places, however.

We will send you either a digital file or a set of prints (whichever you choose) of your pictures for you to keep, and we will keep a digital file that will be handled with the same rules for access and confidentiality that govern all the project's research data.

Discussion of Photos

After the photos are developed, the researcher will discuss them with the participant and will record the discussion on audiotape.

Sample Questions

- What is the story behind this picture? Tell me about where you were? What were you doing? Why is this place or person or group important to you?
- Tell me about who is in this picture? Why is this person significant to you? What is the person doing? Why was this situation important?
- Were there places you thought about photographing but didn't, either because they aren't nearby or for some other reason? Tell me about those places.

IV. Sample Instructions for Oral Diaries

This portion of the research process will allow us to understand your everyday experiences. Using a tape recorder, you will keep a verbal record of some of your daily thoughts and/or experiences. You may want to think of this as if you were keeping a diary or perhaps as if you were talking to a friend or family member and telling them stories about what's going on in your life.

With each story, try to include as much detail as possible: Where were you? Who else was there? How did you feel?

You may want to do this all in one session each day, perhaps in the evening or while you drive home from work. Or you may want to carry the recorder and talk about things as they happen during the day. Try to do at least a little every day. Each day's total journal entries should be approximately five to fifteen minutes.

The prompts below are meant as a guideline, but please feel free to talk about other things that you think are important for understanding your everyday life. Please try to respond to the daily story each day. In addition, each day, you may choose one or more of the other prompts to discuss. You are not required to tell all the possible kinds of stories! Simply use as many of these suggestions as you like as springboards for telling us stories about what is happening in your life this week.

Daily Story

As you imagine looking back on this day six months from now, what do you suppose will be most vivid in your mind? Even if nothing special seemed to happen, what were the ordinary things that happened that are the most important parts of your life right now?

Other Suggested Stories

1. Tell me a story about a recent accomplishment [at work/home/sports/ volunteer work/clubs]. What did you accomplish and why is this important to you?
2. In the past week, have you been thinking about an important decision you need to make about something [at work/at home/with other groups]? Tell me about this decision and what you think the possible outcomes might be.
3. Tell me about a time this week when you did something religious or spiritual. When and where was it, and what happened?
4. If you participated in any religious or spiritual group this week, tell me something about what happened there.
5. If you have a religious ritual you observe daily—for example, praying or meditating—tell me about what you do.
6. Tell me about an experience this week that left you angry or frustrated. Why were you unhappy? Was the situation resolved? How has this experience affected you since it occurred?
7. In the past week, have you faced any moral dilemmas? If so, tell me about those. Where did you face this dilemma [at work/at home/with your family or friends/ with a religious group/with another group]? What were you faced with? How did you deal with this situation?
8. Tell me about something you did this week mostly because you felt you had to, rather than because you really wanted to.
9. Think about the most significant relationship you have in your life at present. Tell me about something that has happened with that person this week (something you did together, a conversation or correspondence).
10. Have you interacted with your family at all this week? If you have, tell me about one thing you did or talked about and how it felt. How was this family time similar to or different from the way things usually are? If you have not had any interaction with your family, tell me about why you think that is.
11. Tell me about a conversation and/or an experience you had this week that reminded you of your childhood? What about the conversation/experience was reminiscent of your childhood?
12. Tell me about a recent experience where you tried something new.
13. Tell me about a movie or TV show or radio program from this week that you found especially inspiring or challenging. Did it make you think about your faith or your spiritual life?
14. Tell me about the music you've been listening to this week. Was anything especially memorable? What did it make you think about or feel that made it special?

15. Tell me about something you saw on the web this week (something you learned or a site you visited or a chat or blog or game you participated in). Was this something that "stretched" you, or did it reinforce the things you already think are important?

16. Tell me about a time when you did or heard or saw something that reminded you of God.

17. Did you spend time in any place that you see as sacred? Tell me about that.

18. Did you talk about politics or do anything political this week? If so, tell me about it.

19. Tell me a story about something you did for fun this week. Who was there? What did you do? What made it good?

20. Tell me about something that happened at work that made you feel really good (or really bad).

NOTES

1. "Pam Jones" is a pseudonym, as is "Cornerstone Baptist." All other nonidentifying details are as we found them.
2. The research was the "Congregations in Changing Communities" project, which resulted in my book *Congregation and Community* (Ammerman 1997d). The Golden Rule Christian concept was outlined separately (Ammerman 1997a).
3. Christian Smith and Melinda Denton (2005) observed this inarticulateness in the teens they studied and concluded that the teens were guided by a theology of "moral therapeutic deism." I'm not sure that does them justice.
4. Free riders are those who gain the benefits of religious communities without investing in them. This is one offshoot of rational choice thinking about religion (Iannaccone 1994).
5. The field of sociology as a scientific exploration of human behavior was shaped by the European Enlightenment context out of which it emerged as well as by the questions of modernization and urbanization that preoccupied nineteenth-century thinkers. As economic and scientific rationalization took hold, would the human spirit find itself in an "iron cage," as Weber (1958) worried? Or—alternatively—would it be humanely awakened from the haze of religious opiates, as Marx (1963) hoped? As totemic religions that held simple societies together faded, Durkheim (1964) wondered what would take their place? Golden Rule Christianity is not unlike the universalized values Parsons (1964) expected to replace religion, but here they seem stubbornly still linked with religious identity and participation.
6. The work of Roof (1993b, 1999) and Wuthnow (1998) was especially influential.
7. I have written an extended argument about the essentially political character of this rhetoric (Ammerman 2013). Portions of this section draw on that article.
8. From Berger's (1969) classic exposition of secularization and privatization to Bellah and colleagues' *Habits of the Heart* (1985), the received wisdom has been that the differentiation of modern societies has shrunk the domain of religion to sectarian "sheltering enclaves" and to individual consciousness, an argument

that echoes Durkheim's (1975 [1898]) observations from earlier in the twentieth century. Charles Taylor (2007) is but the latest to offer an account of modernity that places autonomous individuals at the core of the story and posits a resulting fragility of religious belief.

9. In reporting his summary of the religion/spirituality intersection, as seen in General Social Survey data, Mark Chaves laments that we do not know what people mean when they say they are spiritual but not religious (Chaves 2011).

10. Defining "everyday" is at least as difficult as defining "religion" and "spirituality." Influenced by Norbert Elias (1998 [1978]), I use the term "everyday religion" to point toward people who do not make a living in the domain of religion and toward social spaces that are not normally designated as institutionally religious.

11. Colleen McDannell (1995) makes a critical argument about the gendered character of the way scholars have identified "real" religion with ideas and institutions (both dominated by men) in contrast to materiality and practice (dominated by women).

12. We had in mind primarily the work of Iannaccone, Stark, and Finke (e.g., Iannaccone 1990; Stark 1996; Stark and Finke 2000).

13. Sewell (1992) calls this movement of schemas across institutional lines "transposability." The opposite theoretical position, positing clear boundaries, was typical of the functionalists who followed Parsons (1951). The notion of "fields" with their own logics is also fundamental to the work of Bourdieu (Swartz 1998).

14. Probably the most egregious overinterpretation of inadequate survey measures can be found in uses of the World Values Survey (Norris and Inglehart 2004). Wade Clark Roof provides a vivid account of what happens when survey questions meet the realities of a given individual's spiritual narrative (Roof 1999, 17–19).

15. This is but one of the many instances we will see of practices that are able to cross "fields," defying Bourdieu's notion that the logic of action (habitus) is specific to a given field (Swartz 1998).

16. There are many excellent sources on the role of narratives in social movements (Anderson and Foley 1998; Davis 2002; Peterson 1996; Polletta 2006; Tilly 2002).

17. Other theorists who have demonstrated the utility of thinking about social life as narrative include Coles (1989), Linde (1993), McAdams (1993), Rosenwald and Ochberg (1992), and Emirbayer and Mische (1998).

18. This is an argument elaborated in Ammerman (2003).

19. The notion that we use socially constructed "accounts" to guide our action is actually quite old (Mills 1940; Scott and Lyman 1968).

20. See Bourdieu (1979) and, among the many who have written on meaning-making, see Wuthnow (1987) and Geertz (1973).

21. The analysis of U.S. religious demography was based on the General Social Survey (NORC 2008). As we were completing our data gathering, a major survey of the "American Religious Landscape" enabled us to check and refine the estimates provided by the General Social Survey. It is those numbers that are used in Appendix 1, Table A.1, to compare our sample with the American population (Religion and Public Life 2008).

22. Eighty-two of the ninety-five completed the photo exercise, described below, and eighty did at least one week of oral diaries, while seventy-three completed a second round of diaries, as well. Because we were asking for a substantial commitment from them, we provided small cash tokens of appreciation as they completed each step of the process, totaling $210 for those who, in addition to the initial interview, did both the photos and two rounds of diaries.

23. Our methods are described in more detail in Ammerman and Williams (2012). Portions of this section are modified from that article. Thanks to Roman Williams for his work on photo elicitation methods, on which this section draws (see also Williams [2010]).

24. These life history narratives were elicited using guidelines gleaned from Atkinson (1998), Daiute and Lightfoot (2004), Josselson and Lieblich (1993), and Wortham (2001). See Appendix 3 for our full interview guide.

25. Among recent uses of visual methods in the sociology of religion are Shortell and Krase's (2010) neighborhood photographic surveys, which document religious collective identity in urban space, and Janet Jacobs's (2010) work on visual culture and religious memory in German concentration camp memorials.

26. Suzuki (2004) provides an overview of diary methodologies from language education and shows how the methodology has been expanded to use blogs. One would expect, in fact, that various electronic and social media will shape how these methods are used in the future. Both oral and video diaries have been used extensively by medical researchers, especially in seeking better methods of treatment for chronic illnesses (Rich et al. 2000; Rich and Patashnick 2002).

CHAPTER 2

1. All have multiple titles on Amazon.com's "top 25 books on spirituality" list (Amazon.com 2012).

2. One exception involved a large team of sociologists who were interested in having a more nuanced measure that could be used in health studies (Idler et al. 2003). It included experiential questions about feeling God's presence, finding comfort in religion, and the like, but remained largely theistic and traditional. Elsewhere Pargament and various colleagues have attempted to "unfuzzy" the concept of spirituality, but even after presenting a content analysis of participant-generated definitions, they proceed with analyses based on the more general questions of whether the respondent identifies as religious, spiritual, both, or neither (Zinnbauer et al. 1997). A more creative exception is the work of Italian sociologist Stefania Palmisano (2010), discussed below, whose survey included a long list of possible definitions of both a theistic and nontheistic sort.

3. The proliferation of "types" of spirituality appearing in the literature range from "workplace" spirituality to "Buddhist" spirituality. This definitional strategy is of little utility. As Moberg (2011) points out in his survey of current research, there is little conceptual coherence in this burgeoning literature.

4. An early version of this mapping was included in my keynote address for the International Society for Sociology of Religion (Ammerman 2010), and portions of this analysis appear in Ammerman (2013).

5. The criteria for this category are not derived from and are broader than recent discussions of practices of Christian spirituality (Bass 1997; Wuthnow 1998), although many of the activities they describe would have been coded here as practice-oriented definitions.

6. Factors were extracted using principal component analysis with varimax rotation and Kaiser normalization. Rotated component factor loadings for the three items were: .806 (God), .751 (practices), and .556 (mystery). This factor explained 18 percent of the variance.

7. Malinowski (1948) and others posited this in terms of a contrast between religion and rational science, and that continues to be a theme in how people talk about what religion is.

8. Geertz's writing about the nature of religion focuses on the explanations that emerge in the face of inevitable limits in human analytic capacities (unexplained happenings), powers of endurance (suffering), and moral insight (evil; Geertz 1973).

9. On pagans, witches, and other "effervescent" spiritualties, see Neitz (2000), Griffin (1999), and Helen Berger (1999).

10. See Voas and Bruce (2007) for a critique of the Heelas and Woodhead methods and counts.

11. Belief in reincarnation is often used, for instance, as a generic indicator of participation in "new age" spirituality, but Frisk (2010) shows that many who are active in "alternative spiritualities" do not share that particular belief.

12. The rotated component factor loadings for these four items were: .724 (meaning), .472 (connection), .700 (inner self), and .417 (awe). This factor explains an additional 15 percent of the variance.

13. This distinction is often present in theoretical discussions of the "autonomous individual" (e.g., Seligman 2000). Many European researchers emphasize the this-worldly, immanent character of these "new" nontheistic spiritualities (Frisk 2010; Heelas and Woodhead 2004).

14. There are now multiple journals publishing neuroscience studies of religious experience. One frequent contributor is Mario Beauregard (e.g., 2011).

15. McGuire (2008) offers a helpful feminist critique of the way the typical reading of "Sheilaism" ignores the public good of caring, and Schmidt (2005) argues similarly that the authors also ignore the deep liberal and progressive roots at work in making Sheila's story both possible and valuable.

16. Mainline Protestantism's ways of embracing the larger culture, including its orientation toward cultivating the self, are explored in a number of studies (Besecke 2001; Davie 1995; Ellingson 2001; Hoge et al. 1994).

17. This "baby boomer" cohort effect also shows up in Frisk's findings (2010).

18. The task of this book is in many ways remarkably like the work undertaken by participants in the Social Science Research Council's project on spirituality, political engagement, and public life (Bender and McRoberts 2012), a project inhabited largely by religious studies scholars, anthropologists, and historians more than sociologists. Both they and I are building on the "lived religion" tradition, although their focus is more inclined to dismiss the traditional and institutional dimensions of religion than I am. In their effort to set an agenda for the study of spirituality, one spin-off, the collection edited by Bender and Taves (2012), takes the turn of placing "valuing" at the center of analysis. What we value enough to set it apart as nonordinary, they say, takes "shape in tandem with practical and everyday actions that identify various institutions, ideas, or experiences as religious, secular, or spiritual" (Taves and Bender 2012, 2). My own project here does not depend on the question of "valuing." Rather, the focus here begins with how participants themselves use the particular discourses of religion and spirituality, finding in that discourse a common thread of nonordinary reality.

19. Factor loadings were: .832 (beliefs) and .771 (religious tradition). This factor accounts for 18 percent of the variance.

20. Alison Denton Jones (2010), similarly, points to how the use of the descriptor "religion" does political work for Buddhists in today's China. Some Buddhists claim the term as a way to protect the legal legitimacy of their practices, while others reject it because they are in routine interactional settings where the dominant meaning of "religion" is superstition. For them, the same practices of Buddhism are described as rational techniques and scientific learning.

21. There are many excellent studies of evangelical culture (Griffith 1997; Lindsay 2007; Marti 2008; Neal 2006; Smilde 2007; Smith 1998), including my own early work on Fundamentalism (Ammerman 1987).

22. This parallels Ecklund's findings from her study of elite scientists. They were extremely likely to draw a sharp divide between religion and spirituality and, if they were spiritual, it was very likely to be a nontheistic variety (Ecklund and Long 2011).

CHAPTER 3

1. Practice as a concept has its roots in Aristotle's term "praxis," meaning a practical wisdom that reflects on all human activity and that sets living well as its goal (Bernstein 1971). Marx's use of "praxis" begins, like Aristotle's, with "sensuous, human activity," social beings acting in conscious ways that reveal and challenge the social relations of production. This applies not only to systems of labor and production but also to all human social activity (Marx 1963). Here and throughout this section, I am drawing on ideas outlined in Emily Ronald's brief bibliographic essay written to augment work on this chapter.

2. Michele Dillon argues that Bourdieu is wrong in thinking that religious officials have all the interpretive power in defining religious practices. Lay people, she

says, use the tradition's own symbol systems to name the double-talk they hear (Dillon 2001).

3. Here I have in mind the furor over the Re-Imagining Conference in 1995 (Hoover and Clark 1997).

4. This working definition of practice is not unlike Swidler's notion of a "strategy of action" (Swidler 1986) or the theoretical statement on structure and agency worked out by Emirbayer and Mische (1998). The lived religion McGuire focuses on is encompassed, as well (McGuire 2008).

5. Throughout the book, comparisons between groups are made based on comparisons of means (e.g., the average number of stories about prayer told by one group of people compared to another group) and/or by cross-tabulating the presence or absence of a particular kind of story within the various categories of comparison. The text attempts to make these comparisons clear without including a barrage of numbers detailing the statistical tests themselves.

6. The General Social Survey reports 57.0 percent (NORC 2008); The Baylor Religion Survey counts 48.5 percent who "pray or meditate" at least once a day (Baylor University 2005).

7. A huge market exists for advice on how to have a strong prayer life. Historians and theologians write extensively about prayer, as well (Deweese 1986; Washington 1994; Wirzba 2005). The best recent ethnographic account of prayer is provided by Tanya Luhrmann (2012).

8. The Baylor survey found 33.4 percent who say they say grace at least daily (Baylor University 2005). Putnam and Campbell found 44 percent (2010, 10).

9. Prayer is one of the "great commandments" Mormons are encouraged to follow ("God's Commandments" 2010), although at least some confess that the ideals may be a bit more than a mere mortal can achieve (Barton 1987).

10. Prayers that ask for help (petitionary prayer) are clearly among the most common and transcend religious tradition (Carmody and Carmody 1990; Zaleski and Zaleski 2005).

11. Theologians often argue, in contrast, that this divide between private prayer and public action is not the ideal (Wolfteich 2006).

12. The General Social Survey data show that 27 percent of "mainline" and "liberal" Protestants claim to read the Bible several times a week or more, while 61 percent of "fundamentalist" and "evangelical" Protestants do (NORC 2010).

13. Steve would likely fit the category Tom Tweed calls "nightstand Buddhists" (Tweed 1998).

14. Colleen McDannell (1995) writes about Mormon garments as one of many ways material objects carry religious devotional meaning, and Pamela Klassen examines patterns of dress among African American women (Klassen 2004). These examples and those from this project demonstrate the broad range of distinctive religious clothing practices that go far beyond simply efforts to control female sexuality (Arthur 1999). Probably the most heavily researched item of religious clothing, in recent years, is the Muslim hijab (Chambers 2007; Peek 2005; Read and Bartkowski 2000).

15. Lynn Davidman writes about the many ways Jews create their own modes of observance (Davidman 2003).
16. A number of studies have paid attention to food as part of communal rituals and tradition building (Dodson and Gilkes 1995; Ebaugh and Chafetz 1999; Orsi 1985; Sack 2000). Sociological attention to individual spiritual food practices is less common. Griffith's work on Father Divine as well as her attention to evangelical dieting groups is a primary exception (Griffith 2001, 2004). Historians and anthropologists, on the other hand, have placed food much higher on the list of practices to be explored (Bynam 1987), and environmental ethicists and theologians have also taken up the topic (Jung 2004).
17. Southern Baptist Al Mohler (2010) and the Hindu America Foundation ("Take Back Yoga" 2011) agree that yoga *is* Hindu and that only Hindus should practice it.
18. See Bender's discussion of the history and current practice of yoga in the United States (Bender 2010).
19. From the Tolle website: "The realm of consciousness is much vaster than thought can grasp. When you no longer believe everything you think, you step out of thought and see clearly that the thinker is not who you are" (Tolle 2012).
20. The experiences they describe closely parallel the elements identified by Collins as part of an interaction ritual (being bodily co-present, barriers to outsiders, mutual focus of attention, and shared mood). It is not clear, however, that these particular musical performances sustain enough continuity to produce any group symbols, solidarity, or standards of morality (Collins 2004). While some theorists (Bauman 2007; Maffesoli 1995) point toward the ways in which modern solidarities (tribes) can be very fluid, it seems clear to me that consistency of interaction is a critical variable that substantially affects the likelihood that a shared ritual will produce a sense of identification and/or moral community.
21. See also Wuthnow (2001, 2003).
22. One Jewish woman spoke about her grandmother's presence, but the others who spoke of this kind of spiritual connection were African American, invoking a way of seeing the world with deep roots in African traditions (Chireau 2003; Fields 1985; Olupona and Gemignani 2007).
23. See, for example, Spiritual Directors International ("About Spiritual Directors International" 2011).
24. Pilgrimage is a venerable religious tradition that is being actively revived today (Eade and Sallnow 2000; Hervieu-Leger 2000; Post 2011; Rountree 2002).
25. Shrines for Mexican celebrations of Day of the Dead (*Día de los Muertos*) have become quite common, along with home altars kept by Hindu, Buddhist, and Vodou immigrants, the statues of the Virgin in Catholic front yards, and feng shui consultants. But Protestants are not immune, with their carefully displayed Bibles or religious art (McDannell 1995; Morgan 1998). See also Ritchie's photo documentation of family rooms (Ritchie 2010).

26. Bender notes that writing itself has become a common way to channel spiritual energy (Bender 2010). Journaling is recommended both by Evangelicals (Cepero 2008) and by advocates for Extra-theistic spiritualities (Johnson 2006).

27. Healing practices will be explored in more detail in Chapter Eight. Among the most important recent treatments of healing come from Meredith McGuire and Linda Barnes (Barnes and Sered 2004; McGuire 1988, 2008).

28. Her tattoo would probably not have marked her as odd within evangelical youth culture. Flory and Miller have noted the enthusiastic adoption of tattoos and piercings as part of what they call an "embodied spirituality" found in the postboomer generation (Flory and Miller 2000, 2007).

29. The role of reading in religious and spiritual life is a complex one. See, for example, Griffiths (1999) and Ronald (2012).

30. Clark and associates (2004) report that 68 percent of Americans have engaged in some sort of religious or spiritual activity online, but they include such things as ever sending a religious email or looking for service times. Closer to the practices we were asking about would be the 7 percent who have participated in prayer or the 21 percent who have sought information about celebrating a religious holiday.

31. The Lutheran journal *Word and World* devoted an entire issue to the automobile, but no one wrote about the spiritual aspects of driving. See for example (Forbes 2008).

32. This emphasis on nature is, of course, a recurrent theme in American spirituality (Albanese 1990), with recent additions of a website, professional association, journal, and encyclopedia on "religion and nature" ("Religionandnature.com" 2009). A few even argue for nature itself to be the focus of religion (Crosby 2002).

33. Among the few sources that pay attention to the link between exercise and spirituality are studies of Christian (that is, evangelical) weight loss programs, especially emphasizing the intersection of gender and conservative religion (Gerber 2009; Griffith 2004).

34. A good deal of literature has addressed the spiritual nature of this dance form (Crosby 2000; Dox 2005; Kraus 2010).

35. Orsi has written vividly about the embodied nature of Catholic practice (Orsi 1985, 1996, 2005). These are the sorts of embodied practices theorists such as Foucault and Bourdieu often had in mind.

36. See especially McGuire (2008). The continued presence of saints and miracles is reminiscent of the enchanted medieval world Berger thought disappeared in the face of the Reformation (Berger 1969).

CHAPTER 4

1. On Europe, see Davie (2000, 2002), Bruce (2002), and Norris and Inglehart (2004).

2. A detailed accounting of the affiliation and participation patterns of our participants is contained in Table A.1, Appendix 1.

3. Christopher B. James provided bibliographic assistance for the material in this chapter on religious participation.

4. I will use the generic term "congregation" in this chapter to include Catholic parishes and a Reform Jewish temple as well as Protestant churches. The sacred circle of the Neopagans will be described in other terms.

5. This suggests the importance of mimetic, bodily learning as a dimension of ritual (Bell 1997; Orsi 2005; Wulf 2006).

6. These discussions reinforce the point made by Heider and Warner (2010) that singing (and other shared embodied rituals) can be a powerful source of social solidarity. See also Mark (1998) and Warner (1997).

7. This suggests that the tradition of "narrative preaching" espoused by Fred Craddock (1979) is onto something.

8. This ritual structure of withdrawal and return is one of the basic elements anthropologists and ritual theorists point to in their analyses. See, for example, Durkheim's argument about the sacred as "set apart" and Turner's description of "antistructure" (Durkheim 1964; Turner 1977).

9. The National Congregations Study reports that 82 percent of conservative Protestant congregations, 79 percent of liberal Protestants, and just 61 percent of Catholic parishes offer adult Christian education of any kind. General Social Survey data indicate that 16 percent of Protestants and 7 percent of Catholics report having attended any religious meeting (beyond worship services) during the previous seven days (NORC 2009). Elsewhere, I note that the number of opportunities in Catholic parishes is simply not sufficient to provide for the huge numbers of people enrolled in those parishes (Ammerman 2005b).

10. Many have noted the importance of music in African American worship (Costen 1999; McGann 2002; Nelson 2005). Historian Christopher Brown argues that one of the secrets to the Reformation was Lutheran hymn singing (Brown 2005), and Linda Clark has written about singing in contemporary Protestant churches (Clark 1991).

11. Both Grimsby Congregational and All Saints are affluent churches in a very affluent suburban area, and it is clear that the middle-class tastes of these parishioners shape what they expect in church music. Tex Sample has written especially eloquently about these links between class, taste, and religious sensibilities (Sample 1996).

12. Kevin McElmurry's (2009) analysis of "River Chapel" is a brilliant exposition of how expert musicians, sound technicians, and multimedia artists accomplish just such a structured ritual experience.

13. Marler and Hadaway (1993) distinguish four kinds of marginal members. The largest group is "traditionalists" who would be there if they could. Next are liberals who just don't think attendance is essential; lifelong marginals have never attended regularly; and a small group of critics are marginal because they do not like what is happening in their communities.

14. The Pew Religious Landscape Survey ("Faith in Flux: Changes in Religious Affiliation in the U.S." 2009) is among the most recent and comprehensive studies of switching and disaffiliation. Earlier studies include Sherkat (1991), Bibby (1997), and Musick and Wilson (1995).

15. These would be the "critics" among Marler and Hadaway's population of marginal members.

16. Similarly, the Pew survey found "those who have changed denominational families within Protestantism are much less likely to cite beliefs as the main reason for leaving their former religious group." They instead cite the people and practices they grew to dislike ("Faith in Flux: Changes in Religious Affiliation in the U.S." 2009). Sullivan (2011) found that mothers living in poverty often had a strong personal faith and sent their children to church, but felt personally estranged from communities they saw as unwelcoming.

17. Eight of these fourteen were among those we recruited explicitly as "nonreligious and nonspiritual." Two of those ten recruits turned out to be, in their own ways, not so thoroughly nonspiritual after all. On the other side of the ledger, six of the people whose names appeared on lists of "rare attenders" in their religious communities turned out to be even more disconnected than the leaders in those communities knew.

18. Dillon and Wink's (2007) longitudinal study, following the same cohort of adults over four points in their lifetimes, documented a moderately strong correlation (.49) between adolescent religiousness and later patterns or religiosity. They noted, however, that "a large number of individuals who were highly religious in adolescence became less religious in adulthood and, conversely, a substantial number of nonreligious adolescents became religious later in life" (102).

19. The general retention pattern among our participants is not unusual, although the variations in ways of defining retention make comparisons difficult (Putnam and Campbell 2010; Religion and Public Life 2008; Smith and Sikkink 2003).

20. The General Social Survey finds that 46.1 percent in the South Atlantic attend more than monthly, compared to 37.5 percent in New England; 54.9 percent of African Americans attend that often, compared to 41.4 percent of whites (NORC 2009).

21. The link between religious participation and family formation is a long-observed one (Chaves 1991; Edgell 2005; Hertel 1995; Marler 1995) and extends far back in American religious history (Brown and Hall 1997).

22. Most previous studies of African American religious participation have either ignored social class differences or found no social class effects (e.g., Ellison and Sherkat 1995).

23. While most national data show the youngest cohorts attending at the lowest levels, the long-term effects of the sixties are also noted by Putnam and Campbell (2010).

CHAPTER 5

1. We did not have any participants who were without permanent housing, and because of the middle-class skew in our sample, none were living in seriously dilapidated housing.

2. The Family Room Project has documented the wide range of special objects, sacred and secular, with which people surround themselves (Ritchie 2010).

3. Recent research has begun to pay attention to intergenerational co-residence and the effects of expanded forms of communication (Tomassini et al. 2004; Treas and Cohen 2006).

4. Sherkat writes that "Religious homogamy remains strong in the US, although I find substantial decreases in homogamy among later cohorts, particularly for members of liberal and moderate Protestant groups. Intermarriage has also increased significantly among Catholics, however, even in the youngest cohort Catholic homogamy is nearly 60%." (Sherkat 2004, 620).

5. The National Jewish Population Survey (Kotler-Berkowitz et al. 2003) has documented intermarriage rates, and Moshe and Harriet Hartman (2001) provide a good analysis of the attitudes and debates.

6. On Mormon courtship patterns, see Moff Hudec (2013).

7. Much of the religion and family literature is focused on whether and how "religion" helps people navigate stress and shapes life transitions (e.g., Boyatzis et al. 2006; Mahoney 2010; Starks and Robinson 2007).

8. Like Charlotte's sons, the postboomer cohort is delaying marriage, having fewer children and later, and experiencing a much more unstable career trajectory. All of these things are having significant effects on their participation in religious communities (Wuthnow 2007).

9. Treas and Cohen point out that families are critical elements in the social safety net, and that support includes "the give and take of valued goods and services, that is, the social, emotional, instrumental, and economic exchanges engaged in by related persons over the life course" (2006, 118). This happens both through co-residence and through other routine contacts and is deeply affected by the national culture and welfare policies of different cultures.

10. It is perhaps not surprising that stories of family violence were not among the stories shared with us. That does not mean that such stories were not lurking beneath the surface (Nason-Clark 2004).

11. It would be more common to find a wife and mother picking up more of this "second shift" labor (Bianchi et al. 2006; Coltrane 2000; Hochschild 1989; Nippert-Eng 1996).

12. Time diary studies indicate that families are spending a decreasing number of hours on meals, but these stories suggest that the time they do spend may be weighted more heavily in memory than a mere "personal care" activity (Bianchi et al. 2006). See also Thomas-Lepore et al. (2004).

13. There is a very large literature on the health effects of pet ownership, especially for the elderly. Here our concern is closer to those who write about pets as members of the family (Power 2008; Serpell and Paul 2011).

14. Attending (or not attending) together is the pattern for roughly two-thirds of adults who have a spouse and/or children. Only about 15 percent report that they (or their spouse) attend alone (Edgell 2005, 48–49).

15. Whether or not they join for their children, it remains true that married couples with children at home participate in organized religion at higher rates than any other demographic group (Becker and Hofmeister 2001; Bendroth 2002; Brown and Hall 1997; Chaves 1991; Nash 1968; Rotolo 2000; Stolzenberg et al. 1995; Wilcox 2002; Wilson and Sherkat 1994).

16. Kevin Taylor is exploring how parents think about the values they want for their children and what role religious organizations play in supporting those parental goals (Taylor forthcoming).

17. This is in line with other research on the role of Black churches as support for families (Caldwell et al. 1992).

18. Singer Dar Williams provides an amusing picture of a pagan lesbian couple dropping in on an evangelical uncle in "The Christians and the Pagans." Kate McCarthy provides a more scholarly discussion of negotiations around family religious diversity (McCarthy 2007).

19. Leigh Schmidt's history of American holidays documents just how much religious culture and consumer culture are implicated in each other for virtually all our special days (Schmidt 1995).

CHAPTER 6

1. Marx's ideas are contained in a variety of essays (Marx and Engels 1959), while Weber's famous argument is in his *Protestant Ethic and the Spirit of Capitalism* (Weber 1958).

2. See Braverman (1974) for a classic Marxian understanding of the labor process, and Meyer and Rowan for an institutionalist reinterpretation of the "rational organizations" tradition (1991). Erikson (1986) points to the problems inherent in this bifurcation between micro- and macrounderstandings of work. Watson notes that research on work has continued to be undertaken in the service of understanding how to make it more efficient, although much of that research has moved from sociology departments to business schools under the rubric of "organizational behavior" (Watson 2009). He, along with others such as Halford and Strangleman (2009), argues for a reorientation in sociology that takes work itself more seriously.

3. A major exception to the absence of comparative ethnographic data is the meta-analysis done by Hodson (2004a). Among the classic single cases (in this case of the medical profession) is *Boys in White* (Becker et al. 1961).

4. Among the wonderful available explorations of working life—none of which ask about religion—are Ehrenreich (2001), Terkel (1972), and Whyte (1955). An exception to this pattern is Lamont's attention to religious differences in her study of working men (Lamont 2000). And Arthur Farnsley's *Flea Market Jesus* (2012) is a fascinating exploration of working-class spirituality.

5. Wuthnow's early 1990s survey on religion and the economy found that the top reasons checked on his list were money, the opportunity to use one's talents, circumstances, and being challenged (Wuthnow 1994, 49). These characteristics are similar to items others use to measure the "intrinsic" meaning of a job (Wray-Lake et al. 2011). The Baylor Religion Survey reported that "a quarter of working Americans reports that they often or always view their work as a mission from God. More than a third (36 percent) routinely pursues excellence in work because of their faith" (Baylor University 2011).

6. Many theologians have written about this spiritual dimension of work (e.g., Wolfteich 2001). Theologian William Placher (2005) notes, however, that Luther's teachings about the religious significance of ordinary labor no longer seem so appealing. Equating any single job with "vocation" has become problematic.

7. Retiring gradually, by taking on "bridge" activities, is very common (Cahill et al. 2006). We will examine patterns of volunteering in more detail in Chapter Seven.

8. A somewhat more robust definition of meaning is included in the "Meaning of Work" cross-national surveys. There the usual measures are combined with questions about the interactional context of work and the importance of a duty to contribute to society (Harpaz and Fu 2002). The study by Davidson and Caddell (1994) provides another contrast to the larger literature.

9. Organizational behavior research is replete with refinements on what leads to efficient and happy workplaces (e.g., Xanthopoulou et al. 2009), sometimes including spirituality as one of the variables (Kolodinsky et al. 2008). The classic work that elaborated on the nature and effects of workplace autonomy is by Melvin Kohn's (1969).

10. Similarly, Davidson and Caddell (1994) found that religious salience had a strong effect on the likelihood of viewing work as a vocation.

11. Grant and associates (2004) found that nurses often believed their work to be spiritual but still struggled to bring that spiritual sensibility overtly into the hospital. Cadge's research, on the other hand, found that people working in a neonatal intensive care unit were very likely to pray about their work, to engage in religious rituals around the deaths of their patients, and to honor the physical reminders of spirituality brought into the unit by families (Cadge 2013).

12. This emphasis on new skills is more typical of the aspirations of blue-collar teens than of those expecting to go to four-year colleges (Wray-Lake et al. 2011).

13. Hodson's (2004b) meta-analysis of workplace ethnographies suggests that a rich social life is common but more so for people in higher-level jobs.

14. Research on workplace relationships indicates that there is a tradeoff between family ties and workplace ones. It may be difficult for most people to maintain strong ties in multiple social spheres (Dahlin et al. 2008).

15. In popular culture, office romances are a frequent subplot in television series ranging from "Mad Men" to "Grey's Anatomy" to "House." The importance of relationships in the workplace has only recently been noted by sociologists—except as a distraction to productivity. Pettinger noted that the workplace friendships she observed often were romantic liaisons as well as more platonic relationships (Pettinger 2005).

16. Regnerus and Smith (1998) find that Evangelicals are now more likely than other groups to want their faith to be publicly relevant. Like much of the literature on "privatization" the question they addressed has more to do with politics than the workplace (e.g., Beyer 1990; Bruce 2002; Casanova 1994). In spite of the huge "workplace spirituality" literature in both management and theology, social scientists have done little research on this interactional dynamic, although Wald (2009) has provided a very good review of the legally contentious issues.

17. Yang and Ebaugh (2001) provide a helpful framing of religious majority-minority dynamics. King and associates (2009) examined the legal and social dynamics of religious diversity in workplaces across multiple national contexts but note that much more research is needed. Hicks's (2003) advice that "respectful pluralism" is the key is widely cited but little tested.

18. On views of Mormons, see Feldman (2008) and Putnam and Campbell (2010), and on the history of religious intolerance Neal (2010) provides a good overview.

19. Some businesses are institutionalizing this boundary-spanning activity by hiring chaplains whose job it is to do what comes naturally to Jane—listen to the life concerns of the workers around her (Lambert 2009; Miller 2007). This is also much of what hospital chaplains do, although they are also expected to deal with the weightier issues surrounding death (Cadge 2013).

20. On the notion of front- and backstage in social interaction, see Goffman (1959). The prevalence of "gallows humor" among medical professionals is such that a number of people have attempted to sort out when it might cross the line into something unethical (Watson 2012).

21. A small plaque with this saying hangs in my home, the gift of the late humorist and my dear friend Grady Nutt.

22. Geertz's definition of religion points precisely to these limiting conditions as the chaos religious symbol systems are designed to counter (Geertz 1973).

23. There are, of course, very visible exceptions to what we found. Bookstores are full of advice from religious writers about how making money is the Christian or Jewish thing to do (e.g., Lapin 2009; Richards 2010).

CHAPTER 7

1. Special thanks to Kyle Bozentko for his coding of the stories of political engagement.

2. I have since written extensively on this phenomenon (Ammerman 1997a, 1997c, 2001, 2005b).

3. Wattles provides an excellent overview of the similarities and differences among the teachings in the various religious traditions (Wattles 1996).
4. Studies of intolerance tend to indicate that more conservative religious groups are less tolerant (Ellison and Musick 1993; Froese et al. 2008). Wolfe's (2003) somewhat contrary read is that all of American religion has become remarkably accommodating, preferring to be seen as "nice" and not disruptive.
5. Among those who have written about these issues are policy analyst Mary Jo Bane and ethicist Fred Glennon (Bane and Mead 2003; Glennon 2000).
6. The literature on this phenomenon has grown quite large. See, for example, Chaves (1999), Cnaan and associates (2002), Farnsley (2003), Hall (2001), Pipes and Ebaugh (2002), and Wuthnow (2004).
7. The relative scarcity of friendship ties in neighborhoods is documented by Dahlin and associates (Dahlin et al. 2008).
8. Among the many who have written about sacralized spaces, Borer writes about Fenway Park (Borer 2008), and Grider analyzes spontaneous shrines (Grider 2006). Orsi has written vividly about a variety of sacralized urban spaces (Orsi 1985, 1999). And McRoberts (2003) analyzes the way urban congregations understand the relationship between themselves and "the street."
9. Actual support for tougher environmental laws does not vary significantly across religious and nonreligious groups, however (Pew Forum 2010).
10. The relationship between religious traditions, religious organizations, and environmental concern has been a growing topic for research (Djupe and Hunt 2009; Kearns 1996; Moody 2002; Pellow and Brulle 2007; Sherkat and Ellison 2007; Storm 2009).
11. As Munson demonstrates, even the congregations in which activists are located are often not themselves hotbeds of activism (Munson 2008).
12. Only 17 percent of mainline Protestants say religion is an influence on their abortion views, and only 39 percent say they have heard their clergy speak out on the subject (Pew Forum 2010).
13. Some national survey evidence indicates that there is a decline in civic engagement and loss of trust in the political process among younger cohorts (Syvertsen et al. 2011; Twenge et al. 2012).
14. Putnam and Campbell show that Jews and Black Protestants are the most likely to report politicking in their religious communities, while Mormons and Evangelicals are the most likely to report that they make an individual connection between their faith and their politics (Putnam and Campbell 2010, 439–40). Our observation is slightly different—Jews and Black Protestants are simply more immersed in political conversation, both inside their faith communities and beyond.

CHAPTER 8

1. Explorations of religion and the body have been increasing in recent years (Arthur 1999; Bender 2010; Gerber 2009; Griffith 2001; Heider and Warner 2010;

McGuire 2007). Cadge's (2013) research on "religion in the halls of medicine" asks how and where religion is present in elite research hospitals. While the doctors may not overtly bring religion into the picture, nurses, patients, families, and chaplains freely mix sacred practices and explanations with the scientific ones.

2. From American religious history to anthropological studies to "lived religion" studies of immigrants and women, it is apparent that the role of healing is ubiquitous in religious traditions (Badaracco 2007; Barnes and Sered 2004; Comaroff 1985; Espinoza 2004; Griffith 2004; McGuire 1988, 2008).

3. Research into spirituality and health has emerged in several disciplines, including sociology, psychology, public health, gerontology, behavioral medicine, and social epidemiology. Studies in this area look at not only how patients' spiritual beliefs play a significant role in shaping and framing beliefs about health and health care but also how spirituality impacts health outcomes (Ellison and Hummer 2010; Koenig et al. 2001; Pargament 1997). For instance, spirituality may help prevent cardiovascular disease and other conditions by encouraging better health behaviors, such as a better diet, more exercise, and less substance abuse (Powell et al. 2003). Scholars have even explored potential biological/physiological pathways through which spirituality may improve health (Seeman et al. 2003). As Cadge (2009) points out, however, these studies are often more revealing of the researchers' preconceptions about what religion is than of the mechanisms by which spirituality and health might be causally linked.

4. Education is one of the strongest predictors of health and healthy behaviors, such as a good diet, but there is still debate about the causal mechanisms linking the two. A college education may provide access to resources and information that make healthy dieting easier as well as psychosocial benefits related to social status and symbolic resources provided by higher education (Kawachi et al. 2010). Mirowsky and Ross (2003) focus on skills and abilities acquired through education, most notably effective agency or learned effectiveness, which encourage and enable personal control over a healthy lifestyle. Education, then, can be thought of as a root cause of good health because it allows individuals to take control of their lives in ways that foster better health.

5. Black churches' health education efforts have been targeted primarily to adolescents and have focused on issues such as sexual health and substance abuse (Billingsley 2000; Rubin et al. 1994). However, there are several successful examples of Black churches specifically addressing healthy eating and diet, such as the Black Churches United for Better Health project in North Carolina or The Body & Soul project, a collaborative effort between the National Cancer Institute and the American Cancer Society. That project found that Black churches were able to effectively improve members' diets through education efforts, pastor support, and other interventions (Campbell et al. 2007).

6. Excellent treatments of the link between religion and weight loss include Gerber (2011) and Griffith (2004).

7. The Adolescent Health panel study demonstrates, for instance, that both public and private forms of religiosity have protective effects on tobacco use, alcohol abuse, and use of marijuana (Nonnemaker et al. 2003).

8. The findings are decidedly messy on this topic. One attempt to sort out the vast literature on spirituality/religion and addictions found that 1,353 papers met the search parameters and were classified into ten nonexclusive categories (Geppert et al. 2007). Among the notable findings: an inverse relationship between religiosity and substance use/abuse was common, but the methods and definitions are so disparate that conclusions are hard to come by. See also Booth and Martin (1998).

9. One of the most innovative projects tracking religion as a community "health asset" is based at the University of Cape Town (IRHAP 2010).

10. Evidence for the efficacy of prayer as a direct medical intervention is inconclusive at best (Astin et al. 2000; Benson et al. 2006). Cadge (2009) provides a helpful review and critique.

11. Ritual healing is widespread in many religious traditions (Barnes and Sered 2004; McGuire 1988). In medicine itself, "complementary and alternative medicine" has become a recognized category of treatment (Sointu 2012).

12. A good deal of research has documented links between Western beauty ideals and sexist attitudes (Forbes et al. 2007). Those who work in the beauty industry, on the other hand, are likely to adopt just the sort of "look good, feel good" rhetoric Rebecca and Charlotte use (Sharma and Black 2001).

13. Attempts at rigorous testing of the relationship between religion and addiction treatment are somewhat mixed (Borras et al. 2010).

14. Cultural expectations affect caregiving and help to explain some of the differences in how different communities and populations respond to illness. Cultural values about reciprocity, filial obligation, and caring for older family members shape caregiving expectations, as do cultural perceptions about illness, particularly if a particular condition (such as dementia) is stigmatized (Dilworth-Anderson et al. 2002). Religious beliefs also seem to play a role in setting expectations for caregiving and for helping caregivers through the process, particularly among groups for whom religion is already culturally important to daily life (Donovan et al. 2011).

15. Extended family contact and care happens in many forms, not just in co-residence and face-to-face contact (Bengtson 2001; Kana'Iaupuni et al. 2005; Treas and Cohen 2006).

16. A number of studies have addressed the relationship between religious participation and well-being among the aging themselves (Black and Rubinstein 2000; Blasi et al. 1998; McIntosh et al. 2002). Providing care to a frail elderly parent has a profound impact on the adult child caregiver and his or her family, as routines are disrupted and emotional and physical strain takes a toll (Mancini and Blieszner 1989). Both spirituality and support from a religious community may help adult children cope with the stress of caregiving (Dilworth-Anderson et al. 2007).

CHAPTER 9

1. He goes on to argue that we can reappropriate a notion of transcendent authority in a postmodern world by maintaining a tolerant skepticism. Because the transcendent is utterly external and other, it is also unknown and unknowable, and we are all forced to remain humble in our assertions about how this transcendent authority calls us to live (Seligman 2000).

2. On this relationship between narratives and agency, see especially the work of Emirbauer and Mische (1998).

3. Recognizing this strong empirical pattern does not, therefore, "fetishize" the role of religious institutions, as Bender and McRoberts (2012) imply. To ignore it would be irresponsible.

4. Among the recent expositions of this relationship between religion and state power are Beckford (2003), Friedland (2001), Kuru (2009), Lu and Lang (2006), Moaddel (2002), and van der Veer and Lehmann (1999).

5. While Grim and Finke (2011) emphasize the "persecution" end of the scale, they also document the pervasiveness of both constitutional promises of freedom and state practices of regulation.

APPENDIX 2

1. Some narrative analysts engage this work by doing very detailed and nuanced analysis of a few highly elaborated stories (Riessman 1993). The method adopted here seeks broader and comparative analyses, taking smaller narrative units as the object and employing quantitative analysis in conjunction with qualitative coding. This is not unlike techniques used in content analysis. See Franzosi (2004) and Abell (1987).

BIBLIOGRAPHY

Abell, Peter. *The Syntax of Social Life: The Theory and Method of Comparative Narratives.* New York: Clarendon Press, 1987.

Albanese, Catherine L. *Nature Religion in America: From the Algonkian Indians to the New Age.* Chicago: University of Chicago Press, 1990.

Albanese, Catherine L. "Introduction." In *American Spiritualities: A Reader,* edited by Catherine L. Albanese, 1–15. Bloomington, IN: Indiana University Press, 2001.

Albanese, Catherine L., ed. *American Spiritualities: A Reader.* Bloomington, IN: Indiana University Press, 2001.

Allahyari, Rebecca A. *Visions of Charity: Volunteer Workers and Moral Community.* Berkeley, CA: University of California Press, 2001.

Amazon.com. "Top 25 Books on Spirituality." Accessed July 7, 2012. http://www.amazon.com/Top-25-books-on-Spirituality/lm/RVKK1AEH53XU4.

Ammerman, Nancy T. *Bible Believers: Fundamentalists in the Modern World.* New Brunswick, NJ: Rutgers University Press, 1987.

_____. "Golden Rule Christianity: Lived Religion in the American Mainstream." In *Lived Religion in America: Toward a History of Practice,* edited by David Hall, 196–216. Princeton, NJ: Princeton University Press, 1997a.

_____. "Organized Religion in a Voluntaristic Society." *Sociology of Religion 58,* no. 3 (1997b): 203–15.

_____. "Spiritual Journeys in the American Mainstream." *Congregations: The Alban Journal 23,* no. 1 (1997c): 11–15.

_____. *Congregation and Community.* New Brunswick, NJ: Rutgers University Press, 1997d.

_____. "Doing Good in American Communities: Congregations and Service Organizations Working Together." Hartford Institute for Religion Research. Accessed November 20, 2001. http://hirr.hartsem.edu/about/about_orw_cong-report.html.

_____. "Religious Identities and Religious Institutions." In *Handbook of the Sociology of Religion*, edited by Michele Dillon, 207–24. Cambridge, England: Cambridge University Press, 2003.

_____. *Pillars of Faith: American Congregations and Their Partners*. Berkeley, CA: University of California Press, 2005a.

_____. "Religious Narratives, Community Service, and Everyday Public Life." In *Taking Faith Seriously*, edited by Mary Jo Bane, Brent Coffin, and Richard Higgins, 146–74. Cambridge, MA: Harvard University Press, 2005b.

_____, ed. *Everyday Religion: Observing Modern Religious Lives*. New York: Oxford University Press, 2006.

_____. "The Challenges of Pluralism: Locating Religion in a World of Diversity." *Social Compass 57*, no. 2 (2010): 154–67.

_____. "Spiritual but Not Religious?: Beyond Binary Choices in the Study of Religion." *Journal for the Scientific Study of Religion 52*, no. 2 (2013): 258–78.

Ammerman, Nancy T., and Roman R. Williams. "Speaking of Methods: Eliciting Religious Narratives through Interviews, Photos, and Oral Diaries." In *Annual Review of the Sociology of Religion: New Methods in Sociology of Religion*, edited by Luigi Berzano and Ole Riis, 117–34. Leiden, the Netherlands: Brill, 2012.

Anderson, Herbert, and Edward Foley. *Mighty Stories, Dangerous Rituals: Weaving Together the Human and the Divine*. San Francisco: Jossey-Bass, 1998.

Arthur, Linda B., ed. *Religion, Dress and the Body*. New York: Berg Publishers, 1999.

Asad, Talal. *Genealogies of Religion: Discipline and Reasons of Power in Christianity and Islam*. Baltimore, MD: Johns Hopkins University Press, 1993.

Association of Statisticians of American Religious Bodies (ASARB). "U.S. Membership Report." The American Religion Data Archive. Accessed May 29, 2010. http://www.thearda.com/rcms2010/r/u/rcms2010_99_US_name_2010.asp.

_____. "County Membership Report: Suffolk, County." American Religion Data Archives. Accessed July 10, 2012. http://www.thearda.com/rcms2010/r/c/25/rcms2010_25025_county_name_2010.asp.

Astin, John A., Elaine Harkness, and Edzard Ernst. "The Efficacy of 'Distant Healing': A Systematic Review of Randomized Trials." *Annals of Internal Medicine 132*, no. 11 (2000): 903–10.

Atkinson, Robert. *The Life Story Interview*. Thousand Oaks, CA: Sage, 1998.

Badaracco, Claire H. *Prescribing Faith: Medicine, Media, and Religion in American Culture*. Waco, TX: Baylor University Press, 2007.

Bane, Mary Jo, and Lawrence M. Mead. *"Lifting up the Poor: A Dialogue on Religion, Poverty & Welfare Reform."* Washington, DC: Brookings Institution Press, 2003.

Barnes, Linda, and Susan Sered, eds. *Religion and Healing in America*. New York: Oxford University Press, 2004.

Barton, Eric. "Mormon Fatherhood: Can I Really Succeed?" *Sunstone*, January 1987, 34.

Bass, Dorothy C. *Practicing Our Faith: A Way of Life for Searching People*. San Francisco: Jossey-Bass, 1997.

Bauman, Zygmunt. *Liquid Times: Living in an Age of Uncertainty*. Cambridge, England: Polity Press, 2007.

Baylor University. *The Baylor Religion Survey*. Waco, TX: Baylor Institute for Studies of Religion, 2005.

———. "Wave III of the Baylor Religion Survey Examines How Religion Affects Individuals' Outlook and Well-Being in Tumultuous Times." Baylor Media Communications. Accessed July 24, 2011. http://www.baylor.edu/mediacommunications/news.php?action=story&story=100503.

Bean, Lydia N. "The Politics of Evangelical Identity in the United States and Canada." Dissertation, Harvard University, 2009.

Beauregard, Mario. "Neuroscience and Spirituality—Findings and Consequences." *Neuroscience, Consciousness and Spirituality 1* (2011): 57–73.

Becker, Howard S., Blanche Geer, Everett C. Hughes, and Anselm L. Strauss. *Boys in White: Student Culture in Medical School*. Chicago: University of Chicago Press, 1961.

Becker, Penny E., and Heather Hofmeister. "Work, Family, and Religious Involvement for Men and Women." *Journal for the Scientific Study of Religion 40*, no. 4 (2001): 707–22.

Beckford, James. *Social Theory and Religion*. New York: Cambridge University Press, 2003.

Bell, Catherine. *Ritual: Perspectives and Dimensions*. New York: Oxford University Press, 1997.

Bellah, Robert N. *Religion in Human Evolution: From the Paleolithic to the Axial Age* Cambridge, MA: Harvard University Press, 2011.

Bellah, Robert N., Richard Madsen, William M. Sullivan, Ann Swidler, and Steven M. Tipton. *Habits of the Heart*. Berkeley, CA: University of California Press, 1985.

———. *Individualism & Commitment in American Life: Readings on the Themes of Habits of the Heart*. New York: Harper & Row, 1987.

Bender, Courtney. *Heaven's Kitchen: Living Religion at God's Love We Deliver*. Chicago: University of Chicago Press, 2003.

———. *The New Metaphysicals: Spirituality and the American Religious Imagination*. Chicago: University of Chicago Press, 2010.

Bender, Courtney, and Omar M. McRoberts. "*Mapping a Field: Why and How to Study Spirituality*." New York: Social Science Research Council, Working Group on Spirituality, Political Engagement, and Public Life, 2012. Accessed December 9, 2012. http://blogs.ssrc.org/tif/wp-content/uploads/2010/05/Why-and-How-to-Study-Spirtuality.pdf.

Bender, Courtney, and Ann Taves, eds. *What Matters? Ethnographies of Value in a Not So Secular Age*. New York: Columbia University Press, 2012.

Bendroth, Margaret. *Growing Up Protestant: Parents, Children, and Mainline Churches*. Piscataway, NJ: Rutgers University Press, 2002.

Bengtson, Vern L. "Beyond the Nuclear Family: The Increasing Importance of Multigenerational Bonds." *Journal of Marriage and Family 63*, no. 1 (2001): 1–16.

Benson, Herbert, Jeffrey A. Dusek, Jane B. Sherwood, Peter Lam, Charles F. Bethea, William Carpenter, Sidney Levitsky, Peter C. Hill, Donald W. Clem Jr., Manoj K. Jain, David Drumel, Stephen L. Kopecky, Paul S. Mueller, Dean Marek, Sue Rollins, and Patricia L. Hibberd. "Study of the Therapeutic Effects of Intercessory Prayer (Step) in Cardiac Bypass Patients: A Multicenter Randomized Trial of Uncertainty and Certainty of Receiving Intercessory Prayer." *American Heart Journal 151*, no. 4 (2006): 934–42.

Berger, Helen A. *A Community of Witches: Contemporary Neo-Paganism and Witchcraft in the United States.* Columbia, SC: University of South Carolina Press, 1999.

Berger, Peter L. *The Sacred Canopy.* Garden City, NY: Anchor Doubleday, 1969.

———. *A Rumor of Angels: Modern Society and the Rediscovery of the Supernatural.* Garden City, NY: Anchor, 1970.

———. "The Desecularization of the World: A Global Overview." In *The Desecularization of the World: Resurgent Religion and World Politics*, edited by Peter L. Berger, 1–18. Grand Rapids, MI: Eerdmsans, 1999.

Berger, Peter L., and Thomas Luckmann. *The Social Construction of Reality.* Garden City, NY: Doubleday Anchor, 1967.

Bernstein, Richard J. *Praxis and Action: Contemporary Philosophies of Human Action.* Philadelphia: University of Pennsylvania Press, 1971.

Besecke, Kelly. "Speaking of Meaning in Modernity: Reflexive Spirituality as a Cultural Resource." *Sociology of Religion 62*, no. 3 (2001): 365–81.

Beyer, Peter. "Privatization and the Public Influence of Religion in Global Society." In *Global Culture: Nationalism, Globalization and Modernity*, edited by Michael Featherstone, 373–96. London: Sage, 1990.

Bianchi, Suzanne M., John P. Robinson, and Melissa A Milkie. *Changing Rhythms of American Family Life.* Rose Series in Sociology. New York: Russell Sage Foundation, 2006.

Bibby, Reginald W. "Going, Going, Gone: The Impact of Geographical Mobility on Religious Involvement." *Review of Religious Research 38*, no. 4 (1997): 289–307.

Billingsley, Andrew. *Mighty Like a River: The Black Church and Social Reform.* New York: Oxford University Press, 2000.

Black, Helen K., and Robert L. Rubinstein. *Old Souls: Aged Women, Poverty, and the Experience of God.* New York: Aldine de Gruyter, 2000.

Blasi, Anthony J., Baqar A. Husaini, and Darrell A. Drumwright. "Seniors' Mental Health and Pastoral Practices in African American Churches: An Exploratory Study in a Southern City." *Review of Religious Research 40*, no. 2 (1998): 168–77.

Bochner, Arthur P. "Narrative's Virtues." *Qualitative Inquiry 7*, no. 2 (2001): 131–57.

Booth, Jennifer, and John E. Martin. "Spiritual and Religious Factors in Substance Use, Dependence, and Recovery." In *Handbook of Religion and Mental Health*, edited by Harold G. Koenig, 175–98. New York: Elsevier, 1998.

Borer, Michael I. *Faithful to Fenway: Believing in Boston, Baseball, and America's Most Beloved Ballpark.* New York: New York University Press, 2008.

Borras, Laurence, Yasser Khazaal, Riaz Khan, Sylvia Mohr, Yves-Alexandre Kaufmann, Daniele Zullino, and Philippe Huguelet. "The Relationship between Addiction and Religion and Its Possible Implication for Care." *Substance Use & Misuse 45*, no. 14 (2010): 2357–410.

Bourdieu, Pierre. *Outline of a Theory of Practice*. New York: Cambridge University Press, 1979.

_____. *The Logic of Practice*. Stanford, CA: Stanford University Press, 1990.

Boyatzis, Chris J., David C. Dollahite, and Loren D. Marks. "The Family as a Context for Religious and Spiritual Development in Children and Youth." In *The Handbook of Spiritual Development in Childhood and Adolescence*, edited by Eugene C. Roehlkepartain, Pamela Ebstyne King, Linda M. Wagener, and Peter L. Benson, 297–309. Thousand Oaks, CA: Sage, 2006.

Brasher, Brenda. *Give Me That Online Religion*. San Francisco: Jossey Bass, 2001.

Braverman, Harry. *Labor and Monopoly Capital: The Degradation of Work in the Twentieth Century*. New York: Monthly Review Press, 1974.

Brown, Anne S., and David D. Hall. "Family Strategies and Religious Practice: Baptism and the Lord's Supper in Early New England." In *Lived Religion in America: Toward a History of Practice*, edited by David D. Hall, 41–68. Princeton, NJ: Princeton University Press, 1997.

Brown, Christopher Boyd. *Singing the Gospel: Lutheran Hymns and the Success of the Reformation*. Cambridge, MA: Harvard University Press, 2005.

Brown-Saracino, Japonica. *A Neighborhood That Never Changes: Gentrification, Social Preservation, and the Search for Authenticity*. Chicago: University of Chicago Press, 2009.

Bruce, Steve. *God Is Dead: Secularization in the West*. Oxford, England: Blackwell, 2002.

Bruner, Jerome. *Acts of Meaning*. Cambridge, MA: Harvard University Press, 1993.

Bynam, Carolyn W. *Holy Feast and Holy Fast: The Religious Significance of Food to Medieval Women*. Berkeley, CA: University of California Press, 1987.

Cadge, Wendy. "Saying Your Prayers, Constructing Your Religions: Medical Studies of Intercessory Prayer." *Journal of Religion 89*, no. 3 (2009): 299–327.

_____. *Paging God: Religion in the Halls of Medicine*. Chicago, IL: University of Chicago Press, 2013.

Cadge, Wendy, and Meredith Bergey. "Negotiating Health-Related Uncertainties: Biomedical and Religious Sources of Information and Support." *Journal of Religion and Health*, forthcoming 2013.

Cahill, Kevin E., Michael D. Giandrea, and Joseph F. Quinn. "Retirement Patterns from Career Employment." *The Gerontologist 46*, no. 4 (2006): 514–23.

Caldwell, Cleopatra H., Angela D. Greene, and Andrew Billingsley. "The Black Church as a Family Support System: Instrumental and Expressive Functions." *National Journal of Sociology 6*, no. 1 (1992): 21–40.

Campbell, Marci K., Ken Resnicow, Carol Carr, Terry Wang, and Alexis Williams. "Process Evaluation of an Effective Church-Based Diet Intervention: Body & Soul." *Health Education & Behavior 34*, no. 6 (2007): 864–80.

Carmody, Denise L., and John T. Carmody. *Prayer in World Religions*. Maryknoll, NY: Orbis Books, 1990.

Casanova, Jose. *Public Religions in the Modern World*. Chicago: University of Chicago Press, 1994.

Cepero, Helen. *Journaling as a Spiritual Practice: Encountering God through Attentive Writing*. Downer's Grove, IL: InterVarsity Press, 2008.

Chambers, Paul. "Contentious Headscarves: Spirituality and the State in the Twenty-First Century." In *A Sociology of Spirituality*, edited by Kieran Flanagan and Peter C. Jupp, 127–44. Hampshire, England: Ashgate, 2007.

Chatters, Linda, Robert Taylor, Kai M. Bullard, and James S. Jackson. "Spirituality and Subjective Religiosity among African Americans, Caribbean Blacks, and Non-Hispanic Whites." *Journal for the Scientific Study of Religion 47*, no. 4 (2008): 725–37.

Chaves, Mark. "Family Structure and Protestant Church Attendance: The Sociological Basis of Cohort and Age Effects." *Journal for the Scientific Study of Religion 30* (1991): 501–14.

———. "Religious Congregations and Welfare Reform: Who Will Take Advantage of 'Charitable Choice?'" *American Sociological Review 64*, no. 6 (1999): 836–46.

———. *American Religion: Contemporary Trends*. Princeton, NJ: Princeton University Press, 2011.

Chireau, Yvonne. *Black Magic: Religion and the African American Conjuring Tradition*. Berkeley, CA: University of California Press, 2003.

Church of Jesus Christ of Latter-day Saints, The. "God's Commandments." Accessed November 9, 2010. http://www.mormon.org/commandments?gclid=COn3q_2v lKUCFdJL5Qodfwk6Qg.

Clark, Cindy D. "The Autodriven Interview: A Photographic Viewfinder into Children's Experience." *Visual Sociology 14* (1999): 39–50.

Clark, Krissy. "A Weekend History Lesson." American Public Media. Accessed July 13, 2007. http://weekendamerica.publicradio.org/programs/2007/11/24/a_weekend_history_le.html.

Clark, Linda J. "Hymn-Singing: The Congregation Making Faith." In *Carriers of Faith*, edited by Carl S. Dudley, Jackson W. Carroll, and James P. Wind, 49–64. Louisville, KY: Westminster/John Knox, 1991.

Clark, Lynn S. *From Angels to Aliens: Teenagers, the Media, and the Supernatural*. New York: Oxford University Press, 2003.

———. "Religion, Twice Removed: Exploring the Role of Media in Religious Understandings among 'Secular' Young People." In *Everyday Religion: Observing Modern Religious Lives*, edited by Nancy T. Ammerman, 69–82. New York: Oxford University Press, 2007.

Clark, Lynn S., and Jill Dierberg. "Digital Storytelling and Collective Religious Identity in a Moderate to Progressive Youth Group." In *Digital Religion*, edited by Heidi Campbell, 147–54. New York: Routledge, 2012.

Clark, Lynn S., Stewart Hoover, and Lee Rainie. "Faith Online." In *Pew Internet & American Life Project*. Washington, DC, 2004.

Clark-Ibáñez, Marisol. "Framing the Social World with Photo-Elicitation Interviews." *American Behavioral Scientist 47* (2004): 1507–27.

Cnaan, Ram A., Stephanie C. Boddie, Femida Handy, Gaynor I. Yancey, and Richard Schneider. *The Invisible Caring Hand: American Congregations and the Provision of Welfare.* New York: New York University Press, 2002.

Coles, Robert. *The Call of Stories.* Boston: Houghton Mifflin, 1989.

Collins, Peter. "Congregations, Narratives and Identity: A Quaker Case Study." In *Congregational Studies in the UK,* edited by Mathew Guest, Karin Tusting, and Linda Woodhead, 99–112. Aldershot, England: Ashgate, 2004.

Collins, Randall. *Interaction Ritual Chains.* Princeton, NJ: Princeton University Press, 2004.

Coltrane, Scott. "Research on Household Labor: Modeling and Measuring the Social Embeddedness of Routine Family Work." *Journal of Marriage and Family 62,* no. 4 (2000): 1208–33.

Comaroff, Jean. *Body of Power Spirit of Resistance.* Chicago: University of Chicago Press, 1985.

Costen, Melva W. "African-American Liturgical Music in a Global Context." *The Journal of the Interdenominational Theological Center 27* (1999): 63–110.

Craddock, Fred B. *As One Without Authority.* 3rd ed. Nashville, TN: Abingdon Press, 1979.

Crosby, Donald A. *A Religion of Nature.* Albany, NY: State University of New York, 2002.

Crosby, Janice. "The Goddess Dances: Spirituality and American Women's Interpretations of Middle Eastern Dance." In *Daughters of the Goddess: Studies of Healing, Identity, and Empowerment,* edited by Wendy Griffin, 166–82. Walnut Creek, CA: AltaMira Press, 2000.

Dahlin, Eric, Erin Kelly, and Phyllis Moen. "Is Work the New Neighborhood? Social Ties in the Workplace, Family, and Neighborhood." *Sociological Quarterly 49,* no. 4 (2008): 719–36.

Daiute, Colette, and Cynthia Lightfoot, eds. *Narrative Analysis: Studying the Development of Individuals in Society.* Thousand Oaks, CA: Sage, 2004.

Davidman, Lynn. "Beyond the Synagogue Walls." In *Handbook of the Sociology of Religion,* edited by Michele Dillon, 261–75. Cambridge, England: Cambridge University Press, 2003.

Davidman, Lynn, and Arthur L. Greil. "Characters in Search of a Script: The Exit Narratives of Formerly Ultra-Orthodox Jews." *Journal for the Scientific Study of Religion 46,* no. 2 (2007): 201–16.

Davidson, James C., and David P. Caddell. "Religion and the Meaning of Work." *Journal for the Scientific Study of Religion 33,* no. 2 (1994): 135–47.

Davie, Grace. *Religion in Modern Europe: A Memory Mutates.* Oxford, England: Oxford University Press, 2000.

_____. *Europe: The Exceptional Case: Parameters of Faith in the Modern World.* London: Darton, Longman & Todd, 2002.

Davie, Jodie S. *Women in the Presence: Constructing Community and Seeking Spirituality in Mainline Protestantism*. Philadelphia: University of Pennsylvania Press, 1995.

Davis, Joseph E., ed. *Stories of Change: Narrative and Social Movements*. Albany, NY: State University of New York Press, 2002.

Dawkins, Richard. "God's Utility Function." *Scientific American 273*, no. 5 (November 1995): 80–85.

DeCerteau, Michel. *The Practice of Everyday Life*. Translated by S. Rendall. Berkeley, CA: University of California Press, 1984.

Department of Health and Human Services. "A Profile of Older Americans: 2010." Administration on Aging. Accessed August 4, 2010. http://www.aoa.gov/aoaroot/aging_statistics/Profile/2010/16.aspx.

Deweese, Charles W. *Prayer in Baptist Life*. Nashville, TN: Broadman Press, 1986.

Dillon, Michele. *Catholic Identity: Balancing Reason, Faith and Power*. New York: Cambridge University Press, 1999.

———. "Pierre Bourdieu, Religion, and Cultural Production." *Cultural Studies/Critical Methodologies 1*, no. 4 (2001): 411–29.

Dillon, Michele, and Paul Wink. *In the Course of a Lifetime: Tracing Religious Belief, Practice, and Change*. Berkeley, CA: University of California Press, 2007.

Dilworth-Anderson, Peggye, Ishan C. Williams, and Brent E. Gibson. "Issues of Race, Ethnicity, and Culture in Caregiving Research." *The Gerontologist 42*, no. 2 (2002): 237–72.

Dilworth-Anderson, Peggye, Gracie Boswell, and Monique D. Cohen. "Spiritual and Religious Coping Values and Beliefs among African American Caregivers: A Qualitative Study." *Journal of Applied Gerontology 26*, no. 4 (2007): 355–69.

Djupe, Paul A., and Patrick K. Hunt. "Beyond the Lynn White Thesis: Congregational Effects on Environmental Concern." *Journal for the Scientific Study of Religion 48*, no. 4 (2009): 670–86.

Dodson, Jualynne E., and Cheryl T. Gilkes. "There's Nothing Like Church Food." *Journal of the American Academy of Religion 63* (1995): 519–38.

Donovan, Rhonda, Allison Williams, Kelli Stajduhar, Kevin Brazil, and Denise Marshall. "The Influence of Culture on Home-Based Family Caregiving at End-of-Life: A Case Study of Dutch Reformed Family Care Givers in Ontario, Canada." *Social Science & Medicine 72*, no. 3 (2011): 338–46.

Douglas, Mary. "The Effects of Modernization on Religious Change." In *Religion and America*, edited by Mary Douglas and Steven M. Tipton, 25–43. Boston: Beacon, 1983.

Dox, Donnalee. "Spirit from the Body: Belly Dance as a Spiritual Practice." In *Belly Dance: Orientalism, Transnationalism, and Harem Fantasy*, edited by Anthony Shay and Barbara Sellers-Young, 303–40. Costa Mesa, CA: Mazda, 2005.

Durkheim, Emile. *The Elementary Forms of the Religious Life*. Translated by Joseph Ward Swain. New York: Free Press, 1964.

_____. "Individualism and the Intellectuals." In *Durkheim on Religion*, edited by W. S. F. Pickering, 59–73. London: Routledge & Kegan Paul, 1898 (1975).

Eade, John, and Michael J. Sallnow. *Contesting the Sacred: The Anthropology of Pilgrimage*. Urbana, IL: University of Illinois Press, 2000.

Ebaugh, Helen R., and Janet S. Chafetz. "Agents for Cultural Reproduction and Structural Change: The Ironic Role of Women in Immigrant Religious Institutions." *Social Forces 78*, no. 2 (1999): 585–613.

Ecklund, Elaine Howard. *Science vs. Religion: What Scientists Really Think*. New York: Oxford University Press, 2010.

Ecklund, Elaine H., and Elizabeth Long. "Scientists and Spirituality." *Sociology of Religion 72*, no. 3 (2011): 253–74.

Economist, The. "The Big Sort." Economist Newspaper Limited. June 19, 2008. Accessed April 22, 2013. http://www.economist.com/world/na/displaystory.cfm?story_id=11581447.

Edgell, Penny. *Religion and Family in a Changing Society*. Princeton, NJ: Princeton University Press, 2005.

Edgell, Penny, Joseph Gerteis, and Douglas Hartmann. "Atheists as 'Other': Moral Boundaries and Cultural Membership in American Society." *American Sociological Review 71*, no. 2 (2006): 211–34.

Edgell, Penny, and Samantha K. Ammons. "Religious Influences on Work-Family Trade-Offs." *Journal of Family Issues 28*, no. 6 (2007): 794–826.

Ehrenreich, Barbara. *Nickel and Dimed: On (Not) Getting by in America*. New York: Metropolitan Books, 2001.

Elias, Norbert. "On the Concept of Everyday Life." In *The Norbert Elias Reader: A Biographical Selection*, edited by Johan Goudsblom and Stephen Mennell, 166–74. Oxford, England: Blackwell, 1998 [1978].

Ellingson, Stephen. "The New Spirituality from a Social Science Perspective." *Dialog 40*, no. 4 (2001): 257–63.

Ellison, Christopher G., and Marc A. Musick. "Southern Intolerance: A Fundamentalist Effect?" *Social Forces 72*, no. 2 (1993): 379–98.

Ellison, Christopher G., and Darren E. Sherkat. "The 'Semi-Involuntary' Institution Revisited: Regional Variations in Church Participation among Black Americans." *Social Forces 73*, no. 4 (1995): 1415–37.

Ellison, Christopher G., and Robert A. Hummer, eds. *Religion, Families, and Health: Population-Based Research in the United States*. Piscataway, NJ: Rutgers University Press, 2010.

Emirbayer, Mustafa, and Ann Mische. "What Is Agency?" *American Journal of Sociology 103*, no. 4 (1998): 962–1023.

Erikson, Kai. "On Work and Alienation." *American Sociological Review 51*, no. 1 (1986): 1–8.

Espinoza, Gaston. "'God Made a Miracle in My Life': Latino Pentecostal Healing in the Borderlands." In *Religion and Healing in America*, edited by Linda Barnes and Susan Sered, 123–38. New York: Oxford University Press, 2004.

Farnsley, Arthur Emery, II. *Rising Expectations: Urban Congregations, Welfare Reform, and Civic Life*. Bloomington, IN: Indiana University Press, 2003.

_____. *Flea Market Jesus*. Eugene, OR: Cascade Books, 2012.

Feldman, Noah. "What Is It about Mormonism?" *New York Times Magazine*, January 6, 2008.

Fields, Karen E. *Revival and Rebellion in Colonial Central Africa*. Princeton, NJ: Princeton University Press, 1985.

Flanagan, Kieran, and Peter C. Jupp, eds. *A Sociology of Spirituality*. Hampshire, England: Ashgate, 2007.

Flory, Richard W., and Donald E. Miller, eds. *GenX Religion*. New York: Routledge, 2000.

Flory, Richard W., and Donald E. Miller. "The Embodied Spirituality of the Post-Boomer Generations." In *A Sociology of Spirituality*, edited by Kieran Flanagan and Peter C. Jupp, 201–18. Hampshire, England: Ashgate, 2007.

Forbes, Bruce David. "A Car Is Not Just a Car: Cultural and Spiritual Implications of the American Automobile." *Word and World 28*, no. 3 (2008): 282–90.

Forbes, Gordon, Linda Collinsworth, Rebecca Jobe, Kristen Braun, and Leslie Wise. "Sexism, Hostility toward Women, and Endorsement of Beauty Ideals and Practices: Are Beauty Ideals Associated with Oppressive Beliefs?" *Sex Roles 56*, no. 5 (2007): 265–73.

Forney, Craig A. *The Holy Trinity of American Sports: Civil Religion in Football, Baseball, and Basketball*. Macon, GA: Mercer University Press, 2007.

Foucault, Michel. "About the Beginning of the Hermeneutics of the Self." In *Religion and Culture: Michel Foucault*, edited by Jeremy R. Carrett, 158–81. New York: Routledge, 1999 [1980].

Franzosi, Roberto. *From Words to Numbers: Narrative, Data, and Social Science*. New York: Cambridge University Press, 2004.

Friedland, Roger. "Religious Nationalism and the Problem of Collective Representation." *Annual Review of Sociology 27* (2001): 125–52.

Frisk, Liselotte. "Religion, Spirituality, and Everyday Life in Sweden." Unpublished manuscript. 2010.

Froese, Paul, Christopher D. Bader, and Buster G. Smith. "Political Tolerance and God's Wrath in the United States." *Sociology of Religion 69*, no. 1 (2008): 29–44.

Ganz, Marshall. *Why David Sometimes Wins: Strategy, Leadership, and the California Agricultural Movement*. New York: Oxford University Press, 2009.

Gardner, Benjamin, and Charles Abraham. "What Drives Car Use? A Grounded Theory Analysis of Commuters' Reasons for Driving." *Transportation Research Part F: Traffic Psychology and Behaviour 10*, no. 3 (2007): 187–200.

Geertz, Clifford. "Religion as a Cultural System." In *The Interpretation of Cultures*, 87–125. New York: Basic Books, 1973.

Geppert, Cynthia, Michael P. Bogenschutz, and William R. Miller. "Development of a Bibliography on Religion, Spirituality and Addictions." *Drug and Alcohol Review 26*, no. 4 (2007): 389–95.

Gerber, Lynne. "My Body Is a Testimony: Appearance, Health, and Sin in an Evangelical Weight-Loss Program." *Social Compass 56*, no. 3 (2009): 405–18.

_____. *Seeking the Straight and Narrow: Weight Loss and Sexual Reorientation in Evangelical America*. Chicago: University of Chicago Press, 2011.

Giacalone, Robert A., and Carole L. Jurkiewicz. "Right from Wrong: The Influence of Spirituality on Perceptions of Unethical Business Activities." *Journal of Business Ethics 46*, no. 1 (2003): 85–97.

Gibson, Barbara E. "Co-Producing Video Diaries: The Presence of the 'Absent' Researcher." *International Journal of Qualitative Methods*, no. 4 (2005). Accessed April 22, 2013. http://ejournals.library.ualberta.ca/index.php/IJQM/article/view/4425/3534.

Glennon, Fred. "Blessed Be the Ties That Bind—the Challenge of Charitable Choice to Moral Obligation." *Journal of Church and State 42*, no. 4 (2000): 825–43.

Goffman, Erving. *Presentation of Self in Everyday Life*. New York: Doubleday, 1959.

Grant, Don, Kathleen O'Neil, and Laura Stephens. "Spirituality in the Workplace: New Empirical Directions in the Study of the Sacred." *Sociology of Religion 65*, no. 3 (2004): 265–83.

Graziano, Michael. "Why Is Music a Religious Experience?" *Huffington Post*. June 15, 2011. Accessed April 22, 2013. http://www.huffingtonpost.com/michael-graziano/why-is-mozart-a-religious_b_875352.html.

Green, John C., Mark J. Rozell, and Clyde Wilcox., eds. *The Christian Right in American Politics: Marching to the Millennium*. Washington, DC: Georgetown University Press, 2003.

Grider, Sylvia. "Spontaneous Shrines and Public Memorialization." In *Death and Religion in a Changing World*, edited by Kathleen Garces-Foley, 246–64. Armonk, NY: M.E. Sharpe, 2006.

Griffin, Wendy, ed. *Daughters of the Goddess: Studies of Identity, Healing, and Empowerment*. Lanham, MD: Rowman & Littlefield, 1999.

Griffith, R. Marie. *God's Daughters: Evangelical Women and the Power of Submission*. Berkeley, CA: University of California Press, 1997.

_____. "Body Salvation: New Thought, Father Divine, and the Feast of Material Pleasures." *Religion and American Culture 11*, no. 2 (2001): 119–53.

_____. *Born Again Bodies: Flesh and Spirit in American Christianity*. Berkeley, CA: University of California Press, 2004.

Griffiths, Paul J. *Religious Reading: The Place of Reading in the Practice of Religion*. New York: Oxford University Press, 1999.

Grim, Brian J., and Roger Finke. *The Price of Freedom Denied: Religious Persecution and Conflict in the 21st Century*. New York: Cambridge University Press, 2011.

Hadaway, C. Kirk, Penny Long Marler, and Mark Chaves. "What the Polls Don't Show: A Closer Look at U.S. Church Attendance." *American Sociological Review 58*, no. 6 (1993): 741–52.

Halford, Susan, and Tim Strangleman. "In Search of the Sociology of Work." *Sociology 43*, no. 5 (2009): 811–28.

Hall, Peter D. "Historical Perspectives on Religion, Government, and Social Welfare in America." In *Can Charitable Choice Work?* edited by Andrew Walsh, 78–120. Hartford, CT: Leonard E. Greenberg Center for the Study of Religion in Public Life, Trinity College, 2001.

Harpaz, Itzhak, and Xuanning Fu. "The Structure of the Meaning of Work: A Relative Stability Amidst Change." *Human Relations 55*, no. 6 (2002): 639–67.

Harper, Douglas. "Talking about Pictures: A Case for Photo Elicitation." *Visual Studies 17*, no. 1 (2002): 13–26.

Hartman, Harriet, and Moshe Hartman. "Jewish Attitudes toward Intermarriage." *Journal of Contemporary Religion 16*, no. 1 (2001): 45–69.

Heclo, Hugh. *On Thinking Institutionally*. Boulder, CO: Paradigm Publishers, 2008.

Heelas, Paul. "The Infirmity Debate: On the Viability of New Age Spiritualities of Life." *Journal of Contemporary Religion 21*, no. 2 (2006): 223–40.

Heelas, Paul, and Linda Woodhead. *The Spiritual Revolution: Why Religion Is Giving Way to Spirituality*. Malden, MA: Blackwell, 2004.

Heider, Anne, and R. Stephen Warner. "Bodies in Sync: Interaction Ritual Theory Applied to Sacred Harp Singing." *Sociology of Religion 71*, no. 1 (2010): 76–97.

Heisley, Deborah D., and Sidney J. Levy. "Autodriving: A Photo Elicitation Technique." *The Journal of Consumer Research 18*, no. 3 (1991): 257–72.

Hertel, Bradley. "Work, Family, and Faith: Recent Trends." In *Work, Family, and Religion in Contemporary Society*, edited by Nancy T. Ammerman and Wade C. Roof, 81–122. New York: Routledge, 1995.

Hervieu-Leger, Daniele. "Present-Day Emotional Renewals: The End of Secularization or the End of Religion?" In *A Future for Religion*, edited by William H. Swatos, Jr., 129–48. Newbury Park, CA: Sage, 1993.

———. *Religion as a Chain of Memory*. Translated by Simon Lee. New Brunswick, NJ: Rutgers University Press, 2000.

Hicks, Douglas A. *Religion and the Workplace: Pluralism, Spirituality, Leadership*. Cambridge, England: Cambridge University Press, 2003.

Hindu America Foundation. "Take Back Yoga." Accessed May 27, 2011. http://www.hafsite.org/media/pr/takeyogaback.

Hochschild, Arlie R. *The Second Shift: Working Parents and the Revolution at Home*. New York: Viking, 1989.

———. *The Time Bind: When Work Becomes Home and Home Becomes Work*. New York: Metropolitan Books, 1997.

Hodson, Randy. "A Meta-Analysis of Workplace Ethnographies: Race, Gender, and Employee Attitudes and Behaviors." *Journal of Contemporary Ethnography 33*, no. 1 (2004a): 4–38.

———. "Work Life and Social Fulfillment: Does Social Affiliation at Work Reflect a Carrot or a Stick." *Social Science Quarterly 85* (2004b): 221–39.

Hoge, Dean R., Benton Johnson, and Donald A. Luidens. *Vanishing Boundaries: The Religion of Mainline Protestant Baby Boomers*. Louisville, KY: Westminster/John Knox, 1994.

Hoover, Stewart M., and Lynn S. Clark. "Event and Publicity as Social Drama: A Case Study of the Re-Imagining Conference 1995." *Review of Religious Research* 39, no. 2 (1997): 153–71.

Hoover, Stewart M., Lynn S. Clark, and Diane F. Alters. *Media, Home, and Family.* New York: Routledge, 2004.

Hopewell, James F. *Congregation: Stories and Structures.* Philadelphia: Fortress Press, 1987.

Hout, Michael, and Claude Fischer. "Why More Americans Have No Religious Preference: Politics and Generations." *American Sociological Review* 67, no. 2 (2002): 165–90.

Iannaccone, Laurence R. "Religious Practice: A Human Capital Approach." *Journal for the Scientific Study of Religion* 29, no. 3 (1990): 297–314.

_____. "Why Strict Churches Are Strong." *American Journal of Sociology* 99, no. 5 (1994): 1180–211.

Idler, Ellen L., Marc Musick, Christopher G. Ellison, Linda K. George, Neal Krause, Marcia G. Ory, Kenneth I. Pargament, Lynn G. Underwood, and David R. Williams. "Measuring Multiple Dimensions of Religion and Spirituality for Health Research: Conceptual Background and Findings from the 1998 General Social Survey." *Research on Aging* 25, no. 4 (2003): 327–65.

International Religious Health Assets Programme (IRHAP). University of Cape Town School of Public Health and Family Medicine. Accessed August 2, 2010. http://www.arhap.uct.ac.za/index.php.

Jacobs, Janet. *Memorializing the Holocaust: Gender, Genocide and Collective Memory.* New York: I. B. Tauris, 2010.

John, Richard R. "Taking Sabbatarianism Seriously: The Postal System, the Sabbath, and the Transformation of American Political Culture." *Journal of the Early Republic* 10, no. 4 (1990): 517–67.

Johnson, Julie T. *Spiritual Journaling: Writing Your Way to Independence.* Rochester, VT: Bindu Books, 2006.

Jones, Alison D. *"A Modern Religion? The State, the People, and the Remaking of Buddhism in Urban China Today."* Dissertation, Harvard University, 2010.

Jones, L. Gregory. "Forgiveness." In *Practicing Our Faith: A Way of Life for Searching People*, edited by Dorothy C. Bass. 131–46. San Francisco: Jossey-Bass, 1997.

Josselson, Ruthellen, and Amia Lieblich, eds. *The Narrative Study of Lives.* Thousand Oaks, CA: Sage, 1993.

Jung, L. Shannon. *Food for Life: The Spirituality and Ethics of Eating.* Minneapolis, MN: Augsburg Press, 2004.

Juster, F. Thomas, and Frank P. Stafford. *Time, Goods, and Well-Being.* Ann Arbor, MI: Survey Research Center, Institute for Social Research, University of Michigan, 1985.

Kana'Iaupuni, Shawn Malia, Katharine M. Donato, Theresa Thompson-Colon, and Melissa Stainback. "Counting on Kin: Social Networks, Social Support, and Child Health Status." *Social Forces* 83, no. 3 (2005): 1137–64.

Kawachi, Ichiro, Nancy E. Adler, and William H. Dow. "Money, Schooling, and Health: Mechanisms and Causal Evidence." *Annals of the New York Academy of Sciences 1186*, no. 1 (2010): 56–68.

Kearns, Laurel. "Saving the Creation: Christian Environmentalism in the United States." *Sociology of Religion 57*, no. 1 (1996): 55–70.

Keillor, Garrison. "The News from Lake Wobegon, February 19, 2011." American Public Media. Accessed February 26, 2011. http://prairiehome.publicradio.org.

King, James E., Jr., Myrtle P. Bell, and Ericka Lawrence. "Religion as an Aspect of Workplace Diversity: An Examination of the U.S. Context and a Call for International Research." *Journal of Management, Spirituality and Religion 6*, no. 1 (2009): 43–57.

Klassen, Pamela E. "The Robes of Womanhood: Dress and Authenticity among African American Methodist Women in the Nineteenth Century." *Religion and American Culture 14*, no. 1 (2004): 39–82.

Koenig, Harold G., Michael E. McCullough, and David B. Larson, eds. *Handbook of Religion and Health*. New York: Oxford University Press, 2001.

Kohn, Melvin L. *Class and Conformity: A Study in Social Values*. Homewood, IL: Dorsey Press, 1969.

Kolodinsky, Robert, Robert Giacalone, and Carole Jurkiewicz. "Workplace Values and Outcomes: Exploring Personal, Organizational, and Interactive Workplace Spirituality." *Journal of Business Ethics 81*, no. 2 (2008): 465–80.

Kotler-Berkowitz, Laurence, Steven M. Cohen, Jonathon Ament, Vivian Klaff, Frank Mott, and Danyelle Peckerman-Neuman. "*National Jewish Population Survey (NJPS) 2000–01 Report*." New York: United Jewish Communities, 2003.

Kraus, Rachel. "They Danced in the Bible: Identity Integration among Christian Women Who Belly Dance." *Sociology of Religion 71*, no. 4 (2010): 457–82.

Kuru, Ahmet T. *Secularism and State Policies toward Religion, the United States, France, and Turkey*. New York: Cambridge University Press, 2009.

Laidlow, James, and Caroline Humphrey. "Action." In *Theorizing Rituals: Issues, Topics, Approaches, Concepts*, edited by Jens Kreinath, Jan Snoek, and Michael Stausberg, 265–83. Leiden, the Netherlands: Brill, 2006.

Lambert, Lake, III. *Spirituality, Inc: Religion in the American Workplace*. New York: New York University Press, 2009.

Lamont, Michele. *Money, Morals, and Manners*. Chicago: University of Chicago Press, 1992.

_____. *The Dignity of Working Men: Morality and the Boundaries of Race, Class, and Immigration*. Cambridge, MA: Harvard University Press, 2000.

Lapin, Rabbi Daniel. *Thou Shall Prosper: Ten Commandments for Making Money*. New York: Wiley, 2009.

Lim, Chaeyoon, and Robert D. Putnam. "Religion, Social Networks, and Life Satisfaction." *American Sociological Review 75*, no. 6 (2010): 914–33.

Linde, Charlotte. *Life Stories: The Creation of Coherence*. New York: Oxford University Press, 1993.

Lindsay, D. Michael. *Faith in the Halls of Power: How Evangelicals Joined the American Elite*. New York: Oxford University Press, 2007.

Lofland, John, and Lyn H. Lofland. *Analyzing Social Settings: A Guide to Qualitative Observation and Analysis*. Belmont, CA: Wadsworth Publishing, 1984.

Lovheim, Mia. "Intersecting Identities: Young People, Religion, and Interaction on the Internet." Dissertation, University of Uppsala, 2004.

Lu, Yunfeng, and Graeme Lang. "Impact of the State on the Evolution of a Sect." *Sociology of Religion 67*, no. 3 (2006): 249–70.

Luckmann, Thomas. *The Invisible Religion*. New York: Macmillan, 1967.

Luhrmann, Tanya M. *When God Talks Back: Understanding the American Evangelical Relationship with God*. New York: Alfred A. Knopf, 2012.

MacIntyre, Alasdair. *After Virtue: A Study in Moral Theory*. Notre Dame, IN: University of Notre Dame Press, 1984.

Maffesoli, Michel. *The Time of Tribes*. Beverly Hills, CA: Sage, 1995.

Mahoney, Annette. "Religion in Families, 1999–2009: A Relational Spirituality Framework." *Journal of Marriage and Family 72*, no. 4 (2010): 805–27.

Malinowski, Bronislaw. *Magic, Science, and Religion*. New York: Free Press, 1948.

Mancini, Jay A., and Rosemary Blieszner. "Aging Parents and Adult Children: Research Themes in Intergenerational Relations." *Journal of Marriage and Family 52*, no. 2 (1989): 275–90.

Manglos, Nicolette D. "Born Again in Balaka: Pentecostal Versus Catholic Narratives of Religious Transformation in Rural Malawi." *Sociology of Religion 71*, no. 4 (2010): 409–31.

Mark, Noah. "Birds of a Feather Sing Together." *Social Forces 77*, no. 2 (1998): 453–85.

Marler, Penny L. "Lost in the Fifties: The Changing Family and the Nostalgic Church." In *Work, Family, and Religion in Contemporary Society*, edited by Nancy T. Ammerman and Wade C. Roof, 23–60. New York: Routledge, 1995.

Marler, Penny L., and C. Kirk Hadaway. "Toward a Typology of Protestant 'Marginal Members.'" *Review of Religious Research 35*, no. 1 (1993): 34–54.

_____. "'Being Religious' or 'Being Spiritual' in America: A Zero-Sum Proposition?" *Journal for the Scientific Study of Religion 41*, no. 2 (2002): 289–300.

Marti, Gerardo. *Hollywood Faith: Holiness, Prosperity, and Ambition in a Los Angeles Church*. New Brunswick, NJ: Rutgers University Press, 2008.

Marx, Karl. "Contribution to a Critique of Hegel's Philosophy of Right." In *Karl Marx: Early Writings*, edited by T. B. Bottomore, 43–59. New York: McGraw-Hill, 1963.

Marx, Karl, and Frederich Engels. *Basic Writings on Politics and Philosophy*. Garden City, NY: Doubleday, 1959.

Maynes, Mary Jo, Jennifer L. Pierce, and Barbara Laslett. *Telling Stories: The Use of Personal Narratives in the Social Sciences and History*. Ithaca, NY: Cornell University Press, 2008.

McAdams, Daniel P. *The Stories We Live By: Personal Myths and the Making of the Self.* New York: William C. Morrow, 1993.

McCarthy, Kate. "Pluralist Family Values: Domestic Strategies for Living with Religious Difference." *The Annals of the American Academy of Political and Social Science 612,* no. 1 (2007): 187–208.

McDannell, Colleen. *Material Christianity.* New Haven, CT: Yale University Press, 1995.

McElmurry, Kevin. *"Alone/Together: The Production of Religious Culture in a Church for the Unchurched."* Dissertation, University of Missouri, 2009.

McGann, Mary. *A Precious Fountain: Music in the Worship of an African American Catholic Community.* Collegeville, MN: Liturgical Press, 2002.

McGuire, Meredith B. *Ritual Healing in Suburban America.* New Brunswick, NJ: Rutgers University Press, 1988.

_____. "Embodied Practices: Negotiation and Resistance." In *Everyday Religion: Observing Modern Religious Lives,* edited by Nancy T. Ammerman, 187–200. New York: Oxford University Press, 2007.

_____. *Lived Religion: Faith and Practice in Everyday Life.* New York: Oxford University Press, 2008.

McIntosh, William Alex, Dianne Sykes, and Karen S. Kubena. "Religion and Community among the Elderly: The Relationship between the Religious and Secular Characteristics of Their Social Networks." *Review of Religious Research 44,* no. 2 (2002): 109–25.

McRoberts, Omar M. *Streets of Glory: Church and Community in a Black Urban Neighborhood.* Chicago: University of Chicago Press, 2003.

Mead, George Herbert. *Mind, Self and Society.* Chicago: University of Chicago Press, 1934.

Merrill, Barbara, and Linden West. *Using Biographical Methods in Social Research.* London: Sage, 2009.

Meyer, John W., and Brian Rowan. "Institutionalized Organizations: Formal Structure as Myth and Ceremony." In *The New Institutionalism in Organizational Analysis,* edited by Walter W. Powell and Paul J. DiMaggio, 41–62. Chicago: University of Chicago Press, 1991.

Miles, Matthew B., and A. Michael Huberman. *Qualitative Data Analysis.* Thousand Oaks, CA: Sage, 1994.

Miller, David W. *God at Work.* New York: Oxford University Press, 2007.

Mills, C. Wright. "Situated Actions and Vocabularies of Motive." *American Sociological Review 5,* no. 6 (1940): 904–13.

Mirowsky, John, and Catherine E. Ross. *Education, Social Status, and Health.* New York: Aldine DeGruyter, 2003.

Mishler, Elliot G. *Research Interviewing: Context and Narrative.* Cambridge, MA: Harvard University Press, 1986.

Moaddel, Mansoor. *Jordanian Exceptionalism: A Comparative Analysis of State-Religion Relationships in Egypt, Iran, Jordan, and Syria*. New York: Palgrave, 2002.

Moberg, David O. "Expanding Horizons for Spirituality Research." 2011. Accessed September 7, 2012. http://hirr.hartsem.edu/sociology/Expanding%20 Horizons%20for%20Spirituality%20Research%202011.pdf.

Moff Hudec, Amy. "Courting Eternity: LDS Dating, Courtship, and Celestial Marriage in and out of Utah." Dissertation, Boston University, 2013.

Mohler, R. Albert. "The Subtle Body—Should Christians Practice Yoga?" In *AlbertMohler.com*. Louisville, Kentucky, 2010. Accessed April 22, 2013. http://www. albertmohler.com/2010/09/20/the-subtle-body-should-christians-practice-yoga.

Moody, Michael. "Caring for Creation: Environmental Advocacy by Mainline Protestant Organizations." In *The Quiet Hand of God*, edited by Robert Wuthnow and John Evans, 237–64. Berkeley, CA: University of California Press, 2002.

Morgan, David. *Visual Piety: A History and Theory of Popular Religious Images*. Berkeley, CA: University of California Press, 1998.

Munson, Ziad W. *The Making of Pro-Life Activists: How Social Movement Mobilization Works*. Chicago: University of Chicago Press, 2008.

Musick, Marc, and John Wilson. "Religious Switching for Marriage Reasons." *Sociology of Religion 56* (1995): 257–70.

Nash, Dennison. "'A Little Child Shall Lead Them': A Statistical Test of an Hypothesis That Children Were the Sources of the American 'Religious Revival.'" *Journal for the Scientific Study of Religion 7* (1968): 238–40.

Nason-Clark, Nancy. "When Terror Strikes at Home: The Interface between Religion and Domestic Violence." *Journal for the Scientific Study of Religion 43*, no. 3 (2004): 303–10.

National Alliance for Caregiving. "Caregiving in the U.S. 2009." In collaboration with AARP. Accessed August 4, 2009. http://www.caregiving.org/data/Caregiving_in_ the_US_2009_full_report.pdf.

National Opinion Research Center (NORC). "GSSDIRS General Social Survey: 1972– 2006 Cumulative Codebook." National Opinion Research Center at the University of Chicago. Accessed July 18, 2008. http://sda.berkeley.edu/archive.htm.

———. "GSS Cumulative Datafile, 1972–2008." National Opinion Research Center at the University of Chicago. Accessed June 2, 2009. http://sda.berkeley.edu/ cgi-bin/hsda?harcsda+gss08.

———. "GSSDIRS General Social Survey: 1972–2010 Cumulative Codebook." National Opinion Research Center at the University of Chicago. Accessed May 27, 2010. http://sda.berkeley.edu/cgi-bin/hsda?harcsda+gss10.

Neal, Lynn S. *Romancing God: Evangelical Women and Inspirational Fiction*. Chapel Hill, NC: University of North Carolina Press, 2006.

Neal, Lynn S. "Intolerance and American Religious History." *Religion Compass 4*, no. 2 (2010): 114–23.

Neitz, Mary Jo. "Queering the Dragonfest: Changing Sexualities in a Post-Patriarchal Religion." *Sociology of Religion 61*, no. 4 (2000): 369–92.

Nelson, Timothy J. *Every Time I Feel the Spirit: Religious Experience and Ritual in an African American Church.* New York: New York University Press, 2005.

Nippert-Eng, Christena. "Calendars and Keys: The Classification of 'Home' and 'Work.'" *Sociological Forum 11*, no. 3 (1996): 563–82.

Nonnemaker, James M., Clea A. McNeely, and Robert W. Blum. "Public and Private Domains of Religiosity and Adolescent Health Risk Behaviors: Evidence from the National Longitudinal Study of Adolescent Health." *Social Science & Medicine 57*, no. 11 (2003): 2049–54.

Norris, Pippa, and Ronald Inglehart. *Sacred and Secular: Religion and Politics Worldwide.* New York: Cambridge University Press, 2004.

Olupona, Jacob K., and Regina Gemignani, eds. *African Immigrant Religions in America.* New York: New York University Press, 2007.

Orsi, Robert A. *The Madonna of 115th Street: Faith and Community in Italian Harlem, 1880–1950.* New Haven, CT: Yale University Press, 1985.

———. *Thank You, St. Jude.* New Haven, CT: Yale University Press, 1996.

———. "Introduction: Crossing the City Line." In *Gods of the City*, edited by Robert A. Orsi, 1–78. Bloomington, IN: Indiana University Press, 1999.

———. *Between Heaven and Earth: The Religious Worlds People Make and the Scholars Who Study Them.* Princeton, NJ: Princeton University Press, 2005.

Palmisano, Stefania. "Spirituality and Catholicism in Italy." *Journal of Contemporary Religion 25*, no. 2 (2010): 221–41.

Pargament, Kenneth I. *The Psychology of Religion and Coping.* New York: Guilford, 1997.

———. *Spiritually Integrated Psychotherapy: Understanding and Addressing the Sacred.* New York: Guilford Press, 2011.

Parsons, Talcott. *The Social System.* New York: Free Press, 1951.

———. "Religion and Modern Industrial Society." In *Religion, Culture, and Society*, edited by Louis Schneider, 273–98. New York: Wiley, 1964.

Peek, Lori. "Becoming Muslim: The Development of a Religious Identity." *Sociology of Religion 66*, no. 3 (2005): 215–42.

Pellow, David N., and Robert J. Brulle. "Poisoning the Planet: The Struggle for Environmental Justice." *Contexts 6*, no. 1 (2007): 37–41.

Peterson, Anna L. "Religious Narratives and Political Protest." *Journal of the American Academy of Religion 64*, no. 1 (1996): 27–44.

Pettinger, Lynne. "Friends, Relations and Colleagues: The Blurred Boundaries of the Workplace." In *A New Sociology of Work?*, edited by Lynne Pettinger, Jane Parry, Rebecca Taylor, and Miriam Glucksmann, 39–55. Maldin, MA: Blackwell Publishing, 2005.

Pew Forum on Religion and Public Life. "U.S. Religious Landscape Survey." Accessed July 19, 2008. http://religions.pewforum.org/reports#.

_____. "Faith in Flux: Changes in Religious Affiliation in the U.S." Accessed May 2, 2009. http://pewforum.org/newassets/images/reports/flux/fullreport.pdf.

_____. "Religion and the Issues: Results from the 2010 Annual Religion and Public Life Survey." Accessed April 19, 2010. http://pewforum.org/Politics-and-Elections/Few-Say-Religion-Shapes-Immigration-Environment-Views.aspx#3.

Pink, Sarah. *Situating Everyday Life: Practices and Places*. Los Angeles: Sage, 2012.

Pipes, Paula F., and Helen R. Ebaugh. "Faith-Based Coalitions, Social Services, and Government Funding." *Sociology of Religion 63*, no. 1 (2002): 49–68.

Placher, William C. *Callings: Twenty Centuries of Christian Wisdom on Vocation*. Grand Rapids, MI: W. B. Eerdmans, 2005.

Polletta, Francesca. *It Was Like a Fever: Storytelling in Protest and Politics*. Chicago: University of Chicago Press, 2006.

Post, Paul. "Profiles of Pilgrimage: On Identities of Religion and Ritual in the European Public Domain." *Studia Liturgica 41*, no. 2 (2011): 129–55.

Powell, L. H., L. Shahabi, and C. E. Thoresen. "Religion and Spirituality: Linkages to Physical Health." *American Psychologist 58*, no. 1 (2003): 36–52.

Power, Emma. "Furry Families: Making a Human-Dog Family through Home." *Social & Cultural Geography 9*, no. 5 (2008): 535–55.

Pratt, Michael W., and Barbara H. Fiese, eds. *Family Stories and the Life Course: Across Time and Generations*. Mahwah, NJ: Lawrence Erlbaum Associates, 2004.

Putnam, Robert D. "Bowling Alone: America's Declining Social Capital." *Journal of Democracy 6*, no. 1 (1995): 65–78.

_____. *Bowling Alone: The Collapse and Revival of American Community*. New York: Simon & Schuster, 2000.

Putnam, Robert D., and David E. Campbell. *American Grace: How Religion Divides and Unites Us*. New York: Simon & Schuster, 2010.

Read, Jen'nan G., and John Bartkowski. "To Veil or Not to Veil? A Case Study of Identity Negotiation among Muslim Women in Austin, Texas." *Gender and Society 14*, no. 3 (2000): 395–417.

Regnerus, Mark D., and Christian Smith. "Selective Deprivatization among American Religious Traditions: The Reversal of the Great Reversal." *Social Forces 76*, no. 4 (1998): 1347–72.

Religionandnature.com. Accessed May 28, 2009. http://www.religionandnature.com/about.htm.

Rich, Michael, Steven Lamola, Jason Gordon, and Richard Chalfen. "Video Intervention/Prevention Assessment: A Patient-Centered Methodology for Understanding the Adolescent Illness Experience." *Journal of Adolescent Health 27* (2000): 155–65.

Rich, Michael, and Jennifer Patashnick. "Narrative Research with Audiovisual Data: Video Intervention/Prevention Assessment (VIA) and NVivo." *International Journal of Social Research Methodology 5*, no. 3 (2002): 245–61.

Richards, Jay W. *Money, Greed, and God: Why Capitalism Is the Solution and Not the Problem*. New York: HarperOne, 2010.

Rieger, Gerulf, Joan Linsenmeier, Lorenz Gygax, Steven Garcia, and J. Bailey. "Dissecting 'Gaydar': Accuracy and the Role of Masculinity–Femininity." *Archives of Sexual Behavior 39*, no. 1 (2010): 124–40.

Riesebrodt, Martin. *The Promise of Salvation*. Chicago: University of Chicago Press, 2010.

Riessman, Catherine. *Narrative Analysis*. Thousand Oaks, CA: Sage, 1993.

Ritchie, Kathy. "The Family Room Project (Frip): An Initial Qualitative Exploration of Family Rooms as Representations of Religiosity and Family Cohesion." Paper presented to the Society for the Scientific Study of Religion, Baltimore, October, 2010.

Ronald, Emily K. "More Than 'Alone with the Bible': Reconceptualizing Religious Reading." *Sociology of Religion 73*, no. 3 (2012).

Roof, Wade C. "Religion and Narrative." *Review of Religious Research 34*, no. 4 (1993a): 297–310.

_____. *A Generation of Seekers*. San Francisco: Harper San Francisco, 1993b.

_____. *Spiritual Marketplace: Baby Boomers and the Remaking of American Religion*. Princeton, NJ: Princeton University Press, 1999.

_____. "Religion and Spirituality: Toward an Integrated Analysis." In *Handbook of the Sociology of Religion*, edited by Michele Dillon, 137–48. New York: Cambridge University Press, 2003.

Rosenwald, George C., and Richard Ochberg. *Storied Lives: The Cultural Politics of Self-Understanding*. New Haven, CT: Yale University Press, 1992.

Rotolo, Thomas. "A Time to Join, a Time to Quit: The Influence of Life Cycle Transitions on Voluntary Association Membership." *Social Forces 78*, no. 3 (2000): 1133–61.

Rountree, Kathryn. "Goddess Pilgrims as Tourists: Inscribing the Body through Sacred Travel." *Sociology of Religion 63*, no. 4 (2002): 475–96.

Rubin, Roger H., Andrew Billingsley, and Cleopatra Howard Caldwell. "The Role of the Black Church in Working with Black Adolescents." *Adolescence 29*, no. 114 (1994): 251–66.

Rybczynski, Witold. "Waiting for the Weekend." *The Atlantic 268*, no. 2 (1991): 35–52.

Sack, Daniel. *Whitebread Protestants: Food and Religion in American Culture*. New York: St. Martin's Press, 2000.

Sample, Tex. *White Soul: Country Music, the Church and Working Americans*. Nashville, TN: Abingdon, 1996.

Sayer, Liana C. "Gender, Time and Inequality: Trends in Women's and Men's Paid Work, Unpaid Work and Free Time." *Social Forces 84*, no. 1 (2005): 285–303.

Schieman, Scott, and Paul Glavin. "Trouble at the Border?: Gender, Flexibility at Work, and the Work–Home Interface." *Social Problems 55*, no. 4 (2008): 590–611.

Schmidt, Leigh E. *Consumer Rites: The Buying and Selling of American Holidays*. Princeton, NJ: Princeton University Press, 1995.

_____. *Restless Souls: The Making of American Spirituality*. San Francisco: HarperSanFrancisco, 2005.

Schor, Juliet. *The Overworked American: The Unexpected Decline of Leisure.* New York: Basic Books, 1991.

Schwadel, Philip. "The Effects of Education on Americans' Religious Practices, Beliefs, and Affiliations." *Review of Religious Research 53*, no. 2 (2011): 161–82.

Scott, Marvin B., and Stanford Lyman. "Accounts." *American Sociological Review 33*, no. 1 (1968): 46–62.

Seeman, Teresa E., Linda F. Dubin, and Melvin Seeman. "Religiosity/Spirituality and Health: A Critical Review of the Evidence for Biological Pathways." *American Psychologist 58*, no. 1 (2003): 53–63.

Seligman, Adam. *Modernity's Wager: Authority, the Self, and Transcendence.* Princeton, NJ: Princeton University Press, 2000.

Serpell, James A., and Elizabeth S. Paul. "Pets in the Family: An Evolutionary Perspective." In *The Oxford Handbook of Evolutionary Family Psychology*, edited by Catherine Salmon and Todd K. Shackelford, 297–309. New York: Oxford University Press, 2011.

Sewell, William H., Jr. "A Theory of Structure: Duality, Agency, and Transformation." *American Journal of Sociology 98* (1992): 1–29.

Sharma, Ursula, and Paula Black. "Look Good, Feel Better: Beauty Therapy as Emotional Labour." *Sociology 35*, no. 4 (2001): 913–31.

Sherkat, Darren E. "Leaving the Faith: Testing Theories of Religious Switching Using Survival Models." *Social Science Research 20*, no. 2 (1991): 171–87.

_____. "Religious Intermarriage in the United States: Trends, Patterns, and Predictors." *Social Science Research 33*, no. 4 (2004): 606–25.

Sherkat, Darren E., and Christopher G. Ellison. "Structuring the Religion–Environment Connection: Identifying Religious Influences on Environmental Concern and Activism." *Journal for the Scientific Study of Religion 46*, no. 1 (2007): 71–85.

Shortell, Timothy, and Jerry Krase. "Seeing Islam in Global Cities: A Spatial Semiotic Analysis." Paper presented to the Meeting of the Society for the Scientific Study of Religion, Baltimore, October, 2010.

Simmel, Georg. "The Sociology of Sociability." *American Journal of Sociology 55*, no. 3 (1949): 254–61.

Singleton, Andrew. "'Your Faith Has Made You Well': The Role of Storytelling in the Experience of Miraculous Healing." *Review of Religious Research 43*, no. 2 (2001): 121–38.

Siren, Anu, and Liisa Hakamies-Blomqvist. "Sense and Sensibility. A Narrative Study of Older Women's Car Driving." *Transportation Research Part F: Traffic Psychology and Behaviour 8*, no. 3 (2005): 213–28.

Smilde, David A. "Skirting the Instrumental Paradox: Intentional Belief through Narrative in Latin American Pentecostalism." *Qualitative Sociology 26*, no. 3 (2003): 313–29.

_____. "A Qualitative Comparative Analysis of Conversion to Venezuelan Evangelicalism: How Networks Matter." *American Journal of Sociology 111*, no. 3 (2005): 757–96.

_____. *Reason to Believe: Cultural Agency in Latin American Evangelicalism.* Berkeley, CA: University of California Press, 2007.

Smith, Christian, ed. *Disruptive Religion: The Force of Faith in Social Movement Activism.* New York: Routledge, 1996.

_____. *American Evangelicalism: Embattled and Thriving.* Chicago: University of Chicago Press, 1998.

_____. *Moral, Believing Animals.* New York: Oxford University Press, 2003.

Smith, Christian, and David Sikkink. "Social Predictors of Retention in and Switching from the Religious Faith of Family of Origin: Another Look Using Religious Tradition Self-Identification." *Review of Religious Research* 45, no. 2 (2003): 188–206.

Smith, Christian, and Melinda L. Denton. *Soul Searching: The Religious and Spiritual Lives of American Teenagers.* Oxford, England: Oxford University Press, 2005.

Smith, Elta, and Courtney Bender. "The Creation of Urban Niche Religion: South Asian Taxi Drivers in New York City." In *Asian American Religions: The Making and Remaking of Borders and Boundaries,* edited by Tony Carnes and Fenggang Yang, 76–97. New York: New York University Press, 2004.

Sointu, Eeva. *Theorizing Complementary and Alternative Medicines: Wellbeing, Self, Gender, Class.* New York: Palgrave Macmillan, 2012.

Solberg, Winton U. *Redeem the Time: The Puritan Sabbath in Early America.* Cambridge, MA: Harvard University Press, 1977.

Somers, Margaret R. "The Narrative Constitution of Identity: A Relational and Network Approach." *Theory and Society* 23 (1994): 605–49.

Spiritual Directors International. "About Spiritual Directors International." Accessed May 27, 2011. http://sdiworld.org/about_us.html.

Stark, Rodney. *A Theory of Religion.* New Brunswick, NJ: Rutgers University Press, 1996.

Stark, Rodney, and Roger Finke. *Acts of Faith: Explaining the Human Side of Religion.* Berkeley, CA: University of California Press, 2000.

Starks, Brian, and Robert V. Robinson. "Moral Cosmology, Religion, and Adult Values for Children." *Journal for the Scientific Study of Religion* 46, no. 1 (2007): 17–35.

Stolzenberg, Ross M., Mary Blair-Loy, and Linda J. Waite. "Religious Participation in Early Adulthood: Age and Family Life Cycle Effects on Church Membership." *American Sociological Review* 60, no. 1 (1995): 84–103.

Storm, Ingrid. "Beyond the Lynn White Thesis: Congregational Effects on Environmental Concern." *Journal for the Scientific Study of Religion* 48, no. 4 (2009): 702–18.

Sullivan, Susan Crawford. *Living Faith: Everyday Religion and Mothers in Poverty.* Chicago, IL: University of Chicago Press, 2011.

Suzuki, Renata. "Diaries as Introspective Research Tools: From Ashton-Warner to Blogs." *Teaching English as a Second or Foreign Language* 8, no. 1 (2004). Accessed April 22, 2013. http://www.tesl-ej.org/wordpress/issues/volume8/ej29/ej29int/ .

Swartz, David. *Culture and Power: The Sociology of Pierre Bourdieu.* Chicago: University of Chicago Press, 1998.

Swidler, Ann. "Culture in Action: Symbols and Strategies." *American Sociological Review 51*, no. 2 (1986): 273–86.

Syvertsen, Amy K., Laura Wray-Lake, Constance A. Flanagan, D. Wayne Osgood, and Laine Briddell. "Thirty-Year Trends in U.S. Adolescents' Civic Engagement: A Story of Changing Participation and Educational Differences." *Journal of Research on Adolescence 21*, no. 3 (2011): 586–94.

Taves, Ann, and Courtney Bender. "Introduction: Things of Value." In *What Matters? Ethnographies of Value in a Not So Secular Age*, edited by Courtney Bender and Ann Taves, 1–33. New York: Columbia University Press, 2012.

Taylor, Charles. *A Secular Age*. Cambridge, MA: Belknap Press, 2007.

Taylor, Kevin M. *"Habits of the Hearth: Parenting, Religion, and the Good Life in Modern America."* Dissertation, Boston University, forthcoming.

Terkel, Studs. *Working: People Talk about What They Do All Day and How They Feel about What They Do*. New York: The New Press, 1972.

Thomas-Lepore, Caitlin E., Jennifer Bohanek, Robyn Fivush, and Marshall Duke. " 'Today I …': Ritual and Spontaneous Narratives During Family Dinners." Emory Center for Myth and Ritual in American Life. Accessed April 22, 2013. http://www.marial.emory.edu/pdfs/Thomas__31_04.pdf.

Tilly, Charles. *Stories, Identities, and Political Change*. Lanham, MD: Rowman Littlefield, 2002.

Tolle, Eckhart. "Creating a New Earth Together." Eckhart Teachings, Inc. Accessed July 7, 2012. http://www.eckharttolle.com/.

Tomassini, Cecilia, Stamatis Kalogirou, Emily Grundy, Tineke Fokkema, Pekka Martikainen, Marjolein Broese van Groenou, and Antti Karisto. "Contacts between Elderly Parents and Their Children in Four European Countries: Current Patterns and Future Prospects." *European Journal of Ageing 1*, no. 1 (2004): 54–63.

Treas, Judith, and Philip Cohen. "Maternal Coresidence and Contact: Evidence from Cross-National Surveys." In *Allocating Public and Private Resources across Generations*, edited by Anne H. Gauthier, C. Y. Cyrus Chu and Shripad Tuljapurkar, 117–37. Dordrecht, The Netherlands: Springer, 2006.

Turner, Victor. *The Ritual Process*. Ithaca, NY: Cornell University Press, 1977.

Tweed, Thomas A. "Asian Religions in America: Reflections on an Emerging Subfield." In *Religious Diversity and American Religious History: Studies in Traditions and Cultures*, edited by Walter Conser and Sumner Twiss, 189–217. Athens, GA: University of Georgia Press, 1998.

Twenge, Jean M., W. Keith Campbell, and Elise C. Freeman. "Generational Differences in Young Adults' Life Goals, Concern for Others, and Civic Orientation, 1966–2009." *Journal of Personality and Social Psychology 102*, no. 5 (2012): 1045–62.

van der Veer, Peter, and Hartmut Lehmann, eds. *Nations and Religion: Perspectives on Europe and Asia*. Princeton, NJ: Princeton University Press, 1999.

Vassenden, Anders, and Mette Andersson. "When an Image Becomes Sacred: Photo-Elicitation with Images of Holy Books." *Visual Studies 25*, no. 2 (2010): 149–61.

Verba, Sidney, Kay L. Schlozman, and Henry E. Brady. *Voice and Equality: Civic Voluntarism in American Politics*. Cambridge, MA: Harvard University Press, 1995.

Vergara, Camilo J. *How the Other Half Worships*. New Brunswick, NJ: Rutgers University Press, 2005.

Voas, David, and Steve Bruce. "The Spiritual Revolution: Another False Dawn for the Sacred." In *A Sociology of Spirituality*, edited by Kieran Flanagan and Peter C. Jupp, 43–61. Hampshire, England: Ashgate, 2007.

Volf, Miroslav, and Dorothy Bass, eds. *Practicing Theology: Beliefs and Practices in Christian Life*. Grand Rapids, MI: Eerdmans, 2001.

Wald, Kenneth D. "Religion and the Workplace: A Social Science Perspective." *Comparative Labour Law and Policy Journal 30*, no. 3 (2009): 471–84.

Warner, R. Stephen. "Religion, Boundaries, and Bridges." *Sociology of Religion 58*, no. 3 (1997): 217–38.

Washington, James Melvin. *Conversations with God: Two Centuries of Prayers by African Americans*. New York: HarperCollins, 1994.

Watson, Katie. "Gallows Humor in Medicine." *Hastings Center Report 41*, no. 5 (2012): 37–45.

Watson, Tony J. "Work and the Sociological Imagination." *Sociology 43*, no. 5 (2009): 861–77.

Wattles, Jeffrey H. *The Golden Rule*. New York: Oxford University Press, 1996.

Weber, Max. *The Protestant Ethic and the Spirit of Capitalism*. Translated by Talcott Parsons. New York: Scribner, 1958.

——. *The Sociology of Religion*. Boston: Beacon, 1963 [1922].

Wertheimer, Jack. "The American Synagogue: Recent Issues and Trends." In *American Jewish Yearbook 2005*, edited by David Singer and Lawrence Grossman, 3–83: American Jewish Committee, 2005.

Whyte, William F. *Street Corner Society: The Social Structure of an Italian Slum*. Chicago: University of Chicago, 1955.

Wilcox, W. Bradford. "For the Sake of the Children?: Mainline Protestant Family-Related Discourse and Practice." In *The Quiet Hand of God: Faith-Based Activism and the Public Role of Mainline Protestantism*, edited by Robert Wuthnow and John Evans, 287–316. Berkeley, CA: University of California Press, 2002.

Williams, Roman R. "Space for God: Lived Religion at Work, Home, and Play." *Sociology of Religion 71*, no. 3 (2010): 257–79.

Wilson, John, and Darren E. Sherkat. "Returning to the Fold." *Journal for the Scientific Study of Religion 33*, no. 2 (1994): 148–61.

Wirzba, Norman. "Attention and Responsibility: The Work of Prayer." In *The Phenomenology of Prayer*, edited by Bruce Ellis Benson and Norman Wirzba, 88–102. New York: Fordham University Press, 2005.

Wolfe, Alan. *The Transformation of American Religion*. New York: Free Press, 2003.

Wolfteich, Claire E. *American Catholics through the Twentieth Century: Spirituality, Lay Experience, and Public Life*. New York: Crossroad Publishing, 2001.

_____. *Lord, Have Mercy: Praying for Justice with Conviction and Humility*. San Francisco: Jossey-Bass, 2006.

Wood, Richard L. "Religious Culture and Political Action." *Sociological Theory 17*, no. 3 (1999): 307–32.

Wortham, Stanton. *Narratives in Action: A Strategy for Research and Analysis*. New York: Teachers College Press, 2001.

Wray-Lake, Laura, Amy K. Syvertsen, Laine Briddell, Wayne Osgood, and Constance A. Flanagan. "Exploring the Changing Meaning of Work for American High School Seniors from 1976 to 2005." *Youth & Society 43* no. 3 (2011): 1110–35.

Wulf, Christoph. "Praxis." In *Theorizing Rituals: Issues, Topics, Approaches, Concepts*, edited by Jens Kreinath, Jan Snoek, and Michael Stausberg, 395–411. Leiden, the Netherlands: Brill, 2006.

Wuthnow, Robert. *The Consciousness Reformation*. Berkeley, CA: University of California, 1976.

_____. *Meaning and Moral Order*. Berkeley, CA: University of California Press, 1987.

_____. *God and Mammon in America*. New York: Free Press, 1994.

_____. *Learning to Care*. New York: Oxford University Press, 1995.

_____. *After Heaven: Spirituality in America since the 1950s*. Berkeley, CA: University of California Press, 1998.

_____. *Creative Spirituality: The Way of the Artist*. Berkeley, CA: University of California Press, 2001.

_____. "Beyond Quiet Influence? Possibilities for the Protestant Mainline." In *The Quiet Hand of God: Faith-Based Activism and the Public Role of Mainline Protestantism*, edited by Robert Wuthnow and John Evans, 381–403. Berkeley, CA: University of California Press, 2002.

_____. *All in Sync: How Music and Art Are Revitalizing American Religion*. Berkeley, CA: University of California Press, 2003.

_____. *Saving America? Faith-Based Services and the Future of Civil Society*. Princeton, NJ: Princeton University Press, 2004.

_____. *After the Baby Boomers: How Twenty- and Thirty-Somethings Are Shaping the Future of American Religion*. Princeton, NJ: Princeton University Press, 2007.

Xanthopoulou, Despoina, Arnold B. Bakker, Evangelia Demerouti, and Wilmar B. Schaufeli. "Reciprocal Relationships between Job Resources, Personal Resources, and Work Engagement." *Journal of Vocational Behavior 74*, no. 3 (2009): 235–44.

Yang, Fenggang, and Helen R. Ebaugh. "Religion and Ethnicity among the New Immigrants: The Impact of Majority/Minority Status in Home and Host Countries." *Journal for the Scientific Study of Religion 40*, no. 3 (2001): 367–78.

Yang, Fenggang. *Religion in China: Survival and Revival under Communist Rule*. New York: Oxford University Press, 2012.

Zaleski, Philip, and Carol Zaleski. *Prayer: A History*. New York: Houghton Mifflin Harcourt, 2005.

Zinnbauer, Brian J., Kenneth I. Pargament, Brenda Cole, Mark S. Rye, Eric M. Butter, Timothy G. Belavich, Kathleen M. Hipp, Allie B. Scott, and Jill L. Kadar. "Religion and Spirituality: Unfuzzying the Fuzzy." *Journal for the Scientific Study of Religion* 36, no. 4 (1997): 549–64.

INDEX OF PARTICIPANTS
(BY PSEUDONYM)

Armstrong, Bethany, 94, 270–72

Bailey, Samantha, 48, 72, 83, 136, 180–81
Baker, Jane, 163
Baxter, Polly, 166, 176, 244
Bradley, Greg, 123
Buckley, Marjorie, 25, 29, 59, 101, 180, 267

Carrigan, Phyllis, 81, 215
Carter, Silvia, 39, 74, 136
Childs, Jim, 180–81
Cole, Nora, 140, 186
Collins, Greg, 39, 48, 193, 231, 263, 283
Collins, Theresa, 24, 28, 94, 100, 152–53, 165, 215, 227
Connors, Bessie, 132
Cook, Anna, 25, 38
Cooper, Emma, 37, 78, 85, 86, 96, 191–92, 268, 273
Crosby, Harris, 145–46, 209, 236
Curlew, Charles, 29, 59, 110, 164, 187–88, 205, 221

Dupree, James, 74, 114, 115, 144, 149, 190, 208, 215

Edwards, Victoria, 105, 157
Evans, Elizabeth, 195, 198, 227, 234, 241, 253

Fernandez, Carlos, 82, 179, 188, 197, 200, 218, 221, 276
Fletcher, Jessica, 50, 76, 113, 176, 230, 255–56
Frederick, Jocelyn, 124, 158, 182, 187, 254
Fuller, Mark, 114, 137, 144, 201, 209

Gardner, Cynthia, 37, 87–88, 102–04, 106, 142, 147, 177–78, 240, 273
Glazer, Shirley, 164, 244, 282–83
Green, Walter, 133, 155–56, 161, 230, 258, 278

Hage, Mary, 69, 102, 115, 133, 180, 198, 239–40
Halpern, Rachel, 86, 108, 130, 166–67, 206
Hamilton, Bill, 151, 176, 258
Hammond, Jennifer, 83, 112, 115, 137, 141, 148, 157, 201, 208–9, 236
Hart, Camilla, 59, 214
Henderson, Laura, 46, 86, 96, 102, 132, 151, 202–3, 217, 238
Horton, Carolyn, 37, 78, 133, 189–90, 227
Howell, Olivia, 45, 50, 61, 142, 163, 216, 233
Hsu, Andrew, 25, 37, 97–98, 108, 199, 204, 238, 246

Jackson, Jen, 94, 98–99, 102, 143, 158, 161, 165, 207, 209, 274–75

James, Amelia, 85, 115, 138–39, 154, 163

James, Stephen, MD, 30, 61, 69, 86, 99, 102, 137, 177–79, 188–89

Jameson, Sylvia, 98, 105, 284–85

Johnson, Gordon, 121, 123, 177

Johnson, Vicki, 30, 114, 162–63, 258, 266

Jones, Meredith, 130

Jones, Pam, 1, 25, 73, 106, 140, 142, 155, 159, 177, 231

Kahn, Steven, 132, 188, 201

Kingman, Jessica, 30, 59, 85, 86, 95, 104–5, 131, 152, 200, 208

Klein, Rebecca, 36, 77, 79, 116, 137, 163, 191, 257

Knight, Shirley, 26, 64, 131, 256, 281

LeCompte, Daphne, 77, 79, 124, 163, 166, 185–86, 204, 234

Lehman, John, 39, 49, 121, 123, 244

Levitt, Sam, 26, 59–60, 68, 85, 99, 106, 150, 153, 194, 219, 220

Lombardi, Ericka, 71, 116–117, 133, 137–38, 182, 195, 281

Marini, Phil, 179, 224

Matthews, Hank, 26, 114, 195, 245, 285

Mattison, Lily, 47, 78, 88–89, 118, 121, 148

McKenna, Charlotte, 62, 140, 257, 261, 273

Miller, Thomas, 35, 123, 200, 237

Mitchell, Robin, 26, 36, 49, 81, 141–43, 157, 165, 183, 214, 241, 246–48, 265–66

Mothersbaugh, Gwen, 114, 165

Nouvian, Alexis, 31, 74, 193, 231

Oliva, Julia, 66, 161

Parker, Francis, 83, 130, 159, 162, 267–70

Parker, Melissa, 76, 146–47, 158, 182, 199, 255

Parker, Miles, 108

Patterson, Eric, 46

Perkins, Mary Margaret (Margi), 26, 96, 106–7, 136, 154–55, 206, 236

Picket, Leonard, 202, 204, 230

Polani, Alex, 38, 50, 75, 83, 89, 217, 254

Poulsen, Mary, 123, 180, 252

Pullinger, William, 74, 112, 150, 273

Roberts, Joshua, 45, 73, 98, 256

Robinson, Barbara, 148–49, 194, 218, 282

Rosa, Ann, 29, 201, 232

Shoemaker, Grace, 51, 61, 73, 118, 131, 268–70, 280

Silverman, Joe, 45, 96–97, 105, 275

Simmons, Wendy, 62, 228, 262, 267

Sims, Steve, 72, 75, 88–89, 151, 183, 233

Sironi, Mary Margaret, 65, 269

Smith, Matthew, 123, 157, 187, 197, 255

Snow, Jonathan, 35, 79, 124

Thompson, Liz, 193

Travisano, John, 81, 84, 113, 180, 245–46, 284

Urban, Lawrence, 105, 186, 236

Valencia, Andrea, 140, 260

Waters, Alicia, 27, 77, 122, 133, 186, 253, 262–63

Waugh, Larry, 77, 117, 151, 206, 216–17, 262, 267, 269

Wilson, Jessica, 84, 109, 176–77, 244, 264

Winter, Michelle, 116, 132, 143, 162, 206–7, 208, 229, 295

Worthington, Francine, 74, 112–113, 235

Young, Catherine, 29, 65, 95, 101, 107, 138, 140, 150, 161, 223

Zelinsky, Patrick, 116

GENERAL INDEX

1960s, 23, 123
abortion, 239–40
activism, political, 81–82, 235, 241, 247
addiction, 262–64, 339n8
aesthetics, 75–76
African American Protestants, 42, 73,
  98–99, 245
African American religiosity, 125
African Americans, 33, 44, 158, 163
African traditions, 76, 329n22
age, effects of, 44 (*see also* lifecycle)
agency, 219, 222, 225, 234–36, 242–44,
  286–87, 297, 317
aging, 339n16 (*see also* parents, aging)
AIDS, 82, 117, 221, 269, 280, 283–84
Albanese, Catherine, 40
Alcoholics Anonymous, 263–64
American culture, 216
angels, 31
anxiety, 253
art, 97
artists, 190–192
atheists, 204
Atlanta, 11, 44, 176, 201, 204
attendance. *See* religious service
  attendance

autonomy, 170, 184
awe, 27, 35

baby boomers, 44, 127
Baptists, 124
beauty, 36
belief, 26, 118–20, 284–85, 289, 316–17
  (*see also* doctrine)
  and belonging, 19, 47–48
  rejection of, 47–48, 120
Bellah, Robert, 9, 40, 46, 323n8
Bender, Courtney, 39–40, 75, 327n18,
  330n26
Berger, Peter, 31, 36, 38, 300–01
Bible, 98–99, 118, 139, 158
  reading of, 29, 58, 66–68, 140, 261–62
  study groups, 93, 101, 105
birth control, 139
Black churches, 45, 112, 255, 307,
  338n5 (*see also* African American
  Protestants)
blue collar work, 193
bodies, 253–259, 287
  pampering, 257
Book of Common Prayer, 62, 285, 288
Book of Mormon, 65–66

Boston, 10–11, 44, 117
Boston University, xiv, xvi
boundaries, moral, 51–52
Bourdieu, Pierre, 8, 56, 324n13
Bozentko, Kyle, 336n1
Bruner, Jerome, 9, 13
Buddhism, 68, 88
business, 175, 179–80, 185–87 (*see also*
    occupations)

Cadge, Wendy, 51, 335n11
calendars, 145–168
careers, 177, 183 (*see also* occupations,
    vocation)
caregiving, 339n14
caring (*see also* circles of care)
    practice of, 21, 208, 214–16, 220
cars, as sacred space, 62, 73–74, 77, 83
Catholics, 42, 48, 54, 62, 67–69, 71, 73,
    80–81, 85–86, 93–94, 102, 116–18,
    124–25, 162–63, 228–29, 233–34,
    239–42, 307
chaplains, 336n19
charity, 81, 220–25, 237, 296
Chaves, Mark, 324n9
Chick-Fil-A, 187
children. *See* parenting
China, religion in, 298
Christians, 34, 65
Christmas, 165–66, 231 (*see also*
    holidays)
circles of care, 21, 134, 220, 236, 251,
    272–75, 277–81, 287, 297
civic skills, 222
clothing, as religious practice, 69, 328n14
college education, 34, 47, 169, 254,
    286–87, 338n4
Collins, Randall, 329n20
comfort, 115–116
Communion, 26 (*see also* Eucharist)
community service, 221–225 (*see also*
    volunteering)

Congregational Studies Project
    Team, xv
congregations, 19, 93, 110, 155, 163–64,
    220, 222–25, 245, 248, 296 (*see also*
    religious communities)
conflict in, 109–110
estrangement from, 120, 122, 284
fellowship in, 106, 115, 223
friendships in, 106–10, 118
leadership in, 115
connection, sense of 36
Conservative Protestants, 42, 50,
    124–26, 165, 178, 241–42, 285,
    290, 306–7 (*see also* Evangelicals)
conversation, 102–106, 108–10, 115, 117,
    125–27, 207, 278, 293, 295, 300–02
cooking, 148–49 (*see also* dietary rules,
    food, meals)
courtship, 135–37
crises, 137–38, 62–63, 107, 114, 118–20,
    121–22, 143, 252–53, 259–66,
    274–75, 280–81, 315
culture wars, 296
culture, production of, 300–302
CURA (Institute on Culture, Relgion,
    and World Affairs), xiv

Dalai Lama, 79
Dawkins, Richard, 38–39
death, 297
    experience of, 283–85
    stories about, 282
De Certeau, Michel, 56
Dia de los Muertos, 329n25
dietary rules. *See* food
Dillon, Michelle, 118, 327n2
disaffiliation, 122–23
diversity, religious, 138–39, 200–04,
    303–304 (*see also* tolerance)
divine actors, 9, 28, 63–64, 128, 301
doctors, 188–89, 209–10, 252
doctrine, 99, 114 (*see also* belief)

domestic violence, 333n10
doubt, 120, 283–84
dreadlocks, 76
Durkheim, Emile, 36, 291, 299, 323n5

Easter, 167 (*see also* holidays)
Ecklund, Elaine Howard, 327n22
education, 12, 313 (*see also* college
    education)
    religious, 101–02, 113–14, 123–24
Education for Ministry, 102
embodiment, 84–85 (*see also* bodies)
Emory University, xiv
emotions, 35, 98–100, 111, 135, 154,
    165, 275
enchantment, 298
Enlightenment, 323n5 (*see also*
    modernity)
environmentalism, 237–38
    religious, 337n10
Episcopal Church, 88, 94, 240
Ethical spirituality, 21, 49, 52, 183, 193,
    209, 292
    spiritual practices of, 80–82
ethnicity, 313
Eucharist, 112 (*see also* communion)
European religion, 3–4, 23, 52, 91,
    298–99
Evangelicals, 65, 80, 93–94, 98–99,
    203–205, 238, 239, 327n21 (*see also*
    Conservative Protestants)
exercise, 77, 84–85, 257–59
Extra-theistic spirituality, 34, 40–44,
    46, 54, 64, 75–80, 127, 141, 151–52,
    189–91, 206, 216–17, 227, 254,
    258, 292

family (*see also* households)
    extended, 134, 143–44, 159, 165,
        333n3, 333n9, 339n15
    formation, 332n21
Family Home Night (LDS), 140

food, 329n16
    religious practices, 69, 149–50, 253–54
Foucault, Michel, 57
friendship, 198, 205–207, 210, 232–33,
    278, 314–15, 336n15
fundamentalists, 70
funerals, 282–84

gardening, 133
Gay and Lesbian Advocates and
    Defenders, 81, 241
gay rights, 239–41, 246–48
gaydar, 303
Geertz, Clifford, 286, 326n8, 336n22
gender, 34, 181, 255, 257, 313, 330n33,
    339n12
General Social Survey, 324n21, 328n.6,
    328n12, 331n9, 332n20
God, 7, 25, 28–31, 42, 45–46, 49, 96,
    104, 120, 147, 157, 177, 199, 214, 260
    (*see also* divine actors)
    beliefs about, 26, 63–65, 78, 167, 178,
        240, 265, 269–72, 284
    conversations with, 18, 61–62, 83, 142,
        188, 263, 272
Goddesses, 25, 152, 192, 268
Golden Rule, 25, 207–18, 220, 249, 297
Golden Rule Christians, 2–3, 45, 323n2
grandparenting, 144, 165 (*see also* family,
    extended)
Griffith, Marie, 329n16
groups, spiritual growth, 100–105, 114

habitual activities, 16–18
havurah, 108
healing, 267–68, 316, 338n2
    rituals for, 76
health, 21, 250–51, 297
helping professions, 175, 179, 194–96
High Holidays, Jewish, 167
Hinduism, 70
Hitchens, Christopher, 79

holidays, 165–68, 227–28, 316
home altars, 329n25 (*see also* households, sacred spaces in)
homogamy, 136, 161, 169
    religious, 303, 333n4
homosexuality, 117–18, 239, 263
households, 20, 294
    composition of, 128–29, 313
    conflict in, 135, 139
    relationships in, 154, 158–59, 161–63, 166
    routines in, 145–156
    sacred spaces in, 66, 76, 132
houses, purchases and moves, 130–31
    photos of, 128
Hudec, Amy Moff, xiv-xv, 13
human finitude, 30
humor, 209, 336n20
Hurricane Katrina, 98

illness, chronic, 262
    families and, 273–77
    routine, 260
imagination, 100
immanent frame, 9
individualism, 39–40, 217–19, 227–28, 290
inner self, 27, 39, 52, 54
institutions, boundaries of, 6
    religious, 293
internet, 11–12, 80, 89, 330n30
Iraq war, 235–36
Islam, 299
Italy, 52–54

James, William, 40
Jesus, 29, 49, 50, 95, 100, 152, 208, 214, 280
Jewish identity, 130, 307
Jews, 12, 32, 62, 64, 67–69, 73–74, 85, 93–94, 116, 126–27, 150, 166–67, 220, 228, 245, 329n15

John Templeton Foundation, xiii
journaling, as spiritual practice, 76
justice, Catholic teaching, 233–34, 245–46

Keillor, Garrison, 105
kinship. *See* family
Kornfield, Jack, 88
kosher, 150 (*see also* food)
Kripalu Center, 71
Kushner, Harold, 79

Lama Surya Das, 79
Lambert, Lake, 187
language, shared, 37 (*see also* conversation)
Latinos, 12
Latter-day Saints. *See* Mormons
leisure, 156–60 (*see also* sports, vacations)
Lent, 67, 69, 81, 167, 215
life satisfaction, 109
life stories, xiv, 5, 8, 14–18, 104, 314
lifecycle, 175–177, 315, 332n18
    stages in, 164
liminality, 159
lived religion, xiii, 5, 16, 327n18, 328n4, 338n2
Louisville Institute, xii-xiv
Lourdes, 30
Luckmann, Thomas, 299–300

MacIntyre, Alasdair, 57
Maffesoli, Michel, 10, 303
mainline Protestants, 42, 67–68, 73–74, 93–94, 126, 238, 240–42, 285, 305, 326n16
managers, 199–200 (*see also* occupations)
marginal members, 116–121, 126–27, 221, 243, 262–64, 331n13, 332n15
marriage, 163–64, 198–99 (*see also* family, households)
    interfaith, 123, 136
    relationships in, 137

Marx, Karl, 171, 212, 323n5, 327n1
materialism, 230–232
materiality, 82–83, 85, 133–34
MaxQDA, 309
McDannell, Colleen, 324n11, 328n14
Mead, George Herbert, 300
meals, 107–08, 114, 147–50, 167–68,
    232–33, 254, 333n12 (*see also* food)
meaning-making, 26, 38–39, 53, 77–80,
    100, 120
media, 317
    religion in, 80, 121
medicine (*see also* healing)
    alternative, 256, 267, 269
    God and, 265, 272, 275–76, 286
    scientific, 251, 261, 297, 338n1
meditation, 70–73
mental health, 264–66, 273
methods of the study, 13–18 (*see also*
    MaxQDA, stories)
    congregational observation, 15
    gaining trust, 14–18
    interviewing, 13–16, 313–19
    oral diaries, 17–18, 172, 250, 270–72,
        319–21
    photo elicitation interviewing,
        15–16, 319
    qualitative analysis, 309–11
    sampling strategy, 10–13, 305–08
    congregations in, 11
    statistical tests, 311, 328n5
miracles, 29–30, 33, 122, 266–72
mission work, 237
mitzvot, 45
Moberg, David, 325n3
modernity, 288, 292, 299, 323n5 (*see also*
    secularization, Enlightenment)
    empiricism in, 29–30
money, 230
    scarcity of, 181–82, 190
Moore, Beth, 105
moral therapeutic deism, 323n3

morality, 44–46, 99–100, 213–19,
    281–82, 317
    community role, 292–93
Mormons, 42, 61, 65–66, 69, 85, 93–95,
    101, 107, 126, 137–38, 149–50, 161,
    202, 204, 290, 308, 328n9
mortality, 284 (*see also* human
    finitude)
music, 73–76, 112, 190–91, 256, 331n10,
    331n6
    in worship, 112–13
    singing together, 98–99
Muslims, 85 (*see also* Islam)
mystery, 26, 35

narratives, 7–10, 14–18 (*see also* stories)
    analysis of, 340n1
    theories of, 324n17
National Congregations Study, 331n9
nature, 27–28, 36, 83–85, 190, 258–59,
    316, 330n32
neighborhoods, 96, 133, 143, 224,
    226–29
neighbors, care for, 279–80
Neopagans, 33, 37, 45, 48, 65, 72, 83, 86,
    96, 102, 131, 151–52, 202–03, 217,
    238, 241, 308
neuroscience, 35
New Age, 40
news, 244–45 (*see also* media, NPR)
nonaffiliated participants, 72–73, 77–79,
    91, 204, 217–18, 225, 237, 249
nonaffiliated population (nones), 3–4,
    12, 32, 49, 75, 88–89, 91, 118
nonordinary reality, 9, 46
NPR, 255
nursing, 177

occupations, 20, 75, 104, 171–75, 210–11,
    294–95, 313, 317
    initial, 176–77
organizational behavior, 334n2, 335n9

Palmisano, Stefania, xv, 52
parenting, 139–45, 155, 163–64, 228, 230, 316, 334n15
parents, aging, 143, 260, 275–77, 297
Pargament, Kenneth, 325n2
parish (geographic), 228–29
Parsons, Talcott, 323n5
Passover, 167–68
pastoral care, 105–6, 114
Pessi, Anna Brigitte, xv
pets, 95, 150–53, 227, 334n13
Pettinger, Lynne, 197
Pew Religious Landscape survey, 305, 324n21, 332n14
pilgrimage, 76
place, importance of, 15–16, 337n8
political action, 296 (*see also* activism, political)
political identity, 304
politics, 239–48, 317, 337n14
    negative views of, 242
    disengagement from, 243–244
power, of states, 340n4
    relations of, 56–57
practices, 19–20, 25, 289–90, 316
    (*see also* specific practices)
    definition of, 56–59, 327n1, 328n4
    embodied, 330n35, 331n5
    portable, 63
    spiritual, 29, 57, 169
    with children, 140
prayer, 1, 19, 59–65, 85, 104, 146–47, 188, 199, 205, 208, 235, 253, 256, 261, 271–72, 274–75, 278–80, 289–90, 328n7, 328nn10–11, 339n10
    concerns expressed in, 64–65
    saying grace, 61, 149, 328n8
    U.S. patterns, 61
preaching, 99–100, 113
privatization, 168–69, 201, 294, 323n8
proselytizing, 201–204
Protestants (sense of place), 229

public life, 6, 8, 21, 81–82, 212–13, 218, 222–25, 235–49
Putnam, Robert, 46, 114, 202, 217, 223, 304, 337n14

quietness, 74, 97, 112, 115

race, 117
rational choice theory, xiii, 5, 291, 323n4
reading, 78–80
Reiki, 256, 268
Relief Society (LDS), 101, 107
religion, definitions of, 289–293
    effects of, 298
    in the United States, 10, 91–92, 124
    measures of, 2–5, 24, 58, 65, 68, 288, 290
    otherworldly, 9
    regulation of, 298–299
    rejection of, 51
religiosity, individual, 299
religious communities, 19, 33, 60, 86, 96, 138, 159–60, 179–80, 209–10, 216, 221–25, 230, 233, 237, 256, 273–75, 277, 279–80, 290, 297, 301–02
religious identity, 300, 304
religious service attendance, 32, 41, 51, 60, 86–87, 91–92, 111, 116–17, 140, 160–68, 165, 219, 234, 264, 275, 314, 318, 334n14
    demographic patterns, 125
    typical members, 111–15, 126
religious tradition, 19, 25, 44, 47–48, 60, 87, 147, 213–14, 245, 289
Republican party, 239
restaurants, 232–33
retirement, 180
Riesbrodt, Martin, 57–58, 290–91
ritual, 26, 36, 94–96, 286, 331n8
    spaces for, 96–98
Ronald, Emily, 327n1
Roof, Wade Clark, 40, 323n6
rosaries, 85

Sabbath, 160, 186
sacred, 9, 291
    consciousness of, 293
    spaces, 228, 296
sacred stories, definition, 18
saints, 152
salience (of spirituality), 59
Samhain, 86, 96
Scardaville, Melissa, 13
Schmidt, Leigh Eric, 40, 334n19
schools, 130, 142
science, authority of, 259
scientists, 187–90
Scott, Tracy, 13
scripture, 65–68 (*see also* Bible)
secularization, 2, 5, 52, 121, 127, 169,
    294, 299 (*see also* modernity,
    Enlightenment)
seekers, 40, 42, 50–51, 78, 89, 217, 254
self. *See* inner self
Seligman, Adam, 292
sexuality, 122
Sheilaism, 40, 326n15
shopping, 165–66, 231–32
shrines, 76 (*see also* sacred spaces)
silence. *See* quietness
singleness, 109, 134
smoking, 255
social capital, 114, 223, 228
social change, 225 (*see also* activism)
social class, 12, 141, 156, 171, 173–75,
    226, 248, 313, 331n11, 332n16,
    333n1, 335n4
social issues, 235–42 (*see also* politics)
social movements, 293
Social Science Research Council, 327n18
Somers, Margaret, 7
sorting, religious, 205–06 (*see also*
    homogamy)
Southern culture, 125
spiritual but not religious, 3–4, 49,
    52, 289

spiritual counselors, 76
spiritual tribes, 3, 10, 22, 65, 87, 106, 121,
    128, 169, 206–07, 249, 293–297,
    300–303, 329n20
    signaling and recognition, 206, 303
spiritualities
    alternative, 33, 89
    mixed, 42, 73, 76, 87–88, 147, 152,
        159–60, 268
    source of, 76–77
spirituality, 3–4, 9, 23 (*see also* Extra-
    theistic spirituality, Theistic
    spirituality, Ethical spirituality)
    and health, 251, 338n3
    definitions of, 23–27
    discourse about, 19, 288, 301
    generic, 51–52
    history of, 40
    in religious institutions, 127, 289
    individual, 23–24
    measures of, 24, 44, 310
    media images, 23, 31
    religious traditions of, 31
spiritually disengaged participants,
    88–89, 121–25, 151, 165–66,
    262–63
spiritually engaged participants, 87–88,
    93–110, 125–26, 156, 164, 169–70,
    177–80, 186, 195–96, 221–22, 294
sports, 157
SPSS, 311
St. Francis Day, 152
St. Vincent de Paul Society, 81
Stephen Ministries, 101
stewardship, 70
stories, 100 (*see also* life stories,
    narratives)
    coding of, 24–25, 58–59, 93, 129–30,
        172, 213, 250–51, 309–11
storytelling, 18
supernatural forces, 58
synagogue, 97

tattoo, 76, 109, 330n28
Taylor, Charles, 9, 35, 292, 324n8
television, 157–58
Terkel, Studs, 183–84
testimony, 8, 14
Thanksgiving, 166 (*see also* holidays)
Theistic spirituality, 28–34, 46, 206, 266–267, 290
theodicy, 269–70, 276, 286
theology, 238, 241 (*see also* belief)
Theosophical Society, 89
Thoreau, Henry David, 40
tithing, 70
tolerance, 217–219, 337n4 (*see also* diversity)
Tolle, Eckhart, 74
transcendence, 9, 29–31, 34–38, 46, 75, 291–92, 340n1
Turner, Victor, 159
Tweed, Tom, 328n13

Unitarian Universalism, 124

vacations, 158–59
Veggie Tales, 158
vocation, 171, 177–79, 195, 280, 335n5
volunteering, 224–25 (*see also* community service)

Weber, Max, 20, 171, 184, 211, 295, 323n5
weekend, 160
weight control, 254–256 (*see also* bodies)
Wicca, 38, 136, 217
Williams, Dar, 334n18
Williams, Roman, xiv-xv, 13, 325n23
Wolfe, Alan, 337n4
work (*see also* occupations)
    and family, 153–56
    decisions about, 154–55
    meaning of, 183–185, 194, 196, 335n8 (*see also* vocation)
    stresses of, 154, 195–96, 209
workplace, 294
    diversity in, 336n17
    power in, 171, 199–200, 202–03
    relationships in, 1, 196–99, 295, 336n14
    spiritual groups, 205
World Values Survey, 324n14
worship, 94–100, 112, 278, 318 (*see also* ritual, Eucharist, preaching)
    music in, 74
Wuthnow, Robert, 38, 57, 178, 190–91, 323n6

yoga, 70–71, 329nn17–18